*Software Engineering
on Sun Workstations®*

Bill Cureton
Editor

Software Engineering on Sun Workstations®

Springer-Verlag
New York Berlin Heidelberg London Paris
Tokyo Hong Kong Barcelona Budapest

Bill Cureton
INFO Enterprises
Gateway 1
426 North 44th St., Suite 250
Phoenix, AZ 85008-7689 USA

Library of Congress Cataloging-in-Publication Data
Software engineering on Sun workstations / Bill Cureton, editor.
      p. cm.
    Includes index.
     ISBN-13: 978-1-4613-9120-3   e-ISBN-13: 978-1-4613-9118-0
     DOI: 10.1007/978-1-4613-9118-0
    1. Software engineering. 2. Sun computers–Programming.
I. Cureton, Bill.
QA76.758.S646455 1993
005.1–dc20   93-17488

Printed on acid-free paper

Production managed by Karen Phillips; manufacturing supervised by Vincent Scelta.
Photocomposed pages prepared from the editor's Framemaker files.

9 8 7 6 5 4 3 2 1

Dedication

This humble edited tome is dedicated to the four most important people in my life. They are, my parents, who bought me the books and sent me to school, and my wife, who made me finish school and this book as well, and to my son Nicky who is just now learning to read and is starting school!

Acknowledgments

I wish to acknowledge the major contribution of many, many individuals in the creation and final preparation of this book. In fact, like many Academy Award acceptance speeches, there were, in reality, so many people involved with this project that some individuals are bound to be overlooked. I apologise.

First, I want to thank everyone directly involved from Sun Microsystems®. Many of the chapters in this book had their genesis as technical publications written and polished by engineers and technical writers. The list is simply too long to mention, and in some cases, while doing my research, I had discovered that the identity of many of the original authors had become obscured by time and revisions. Perhaps in a Second Edition I may be fortunate enough to identify key contributors by name. A few include Steve Muchnick, Vida Ghodssi, Keith Bierman in SunPro, and Pierre Bedard, Steven Uhlir and the ToolTalk team in SunSoft.

I also want to thank Bill Joy, John Gage, and George Symons for their continued encouragement with this project.

Finally, a deep debt of gratitude is due to the fine people at Springer-Verlag and TELOS in Santa Clara, CA, without whom this book would have never come together. I wish to thank my publisher at TELOS, Allan Wylde, Telos Publishing Associate Cindy Peterson, and the book production staff at Springer-Verlag New York.

Editor's Note

Between the time this project was begun back in 1992 and the Summer of 1993 several important events that will directly affect the use of Sun Workstations® in application development, and the entire computing landscape, have transpired.

First, and perhaps most importantly, in early 1993 the Common Operating System Environment or COSE consortium was announced. This group, led by Novell, USL, ATT, NCR, Sun, HP and others, is attempting to create a common operating environment based on Unix SVR4, from the remaining fragmented elements of the Unix camp. They are motivated, no doubt, by the threat, real or perceived, from that other OS juggernaut, Windows-NT from Microsoft. One important factor that will affect the reader of this edition of this book is that the sections discussing OpenLook and its associated DevGuide G.U.I. builder will need to be reassessed in light of Sun Microsystems apparent intent to support Motif in conjunction with the COSE architecture and strategy. This evolving situation will need to be "actively" monitored by anyone interested in developing applications on and for Sun Workstations in the future. The inevitability of Motif-on-Sun will elicit a sigh-of-relief from certain quarters.

Second, the Solaris® OS has gone through a profound metamorphosis in the period during which this book was compiled. The key elements of this change reflect the "switch" to the SVR4 base, the addition of support for symmetric multi-processing, and multi-threading. The latter two features are powerful enhancements. They will need to be supported by a new generation of development tools. Perhaps a future edition of this book will include chapters on these new developments.

Third, the movement towards the object-oriented paradigm is one of Sun Microsystems most compelling strengths in the next generation of software development. Sun Microsystems has played a seminal role in the creation and evolution of the C++ programming language, and Sun is one of the original co-founders of the Object Managment Group OMG (Cambridge, MA). Anyone interested in advanced object-oriented development is encouraged to track the startling progress of the OMG since 1989.

Finally, a few of the programming languages that began in 1992 as "Sun Core Programming Language" have been "returned" to their roots, as it were, for ongoing maintenance and enhancement. These are most notably "SunCommon Lisp™" which is now offered and maintained by Lucid (Menlo Park, CA) and "SunCobol™" which is now offered and maintained by MicroFocus (Palo Alto, CA).

I sincerely hope you find this book useful. The publisher and I would like to hear from you. If, indeed, you are developing client-server applications on and for the Sun platform you have chosen one of the best all-around development and runtime environments in the technical and business computing world today.

Bill Cureton
Phoenix, AZ
August 1993

Contents

ToolTalk® Overview

1.1 Introduction

The ToolTalk® service is used by independent applications to communicate with each other without having direct knowledge of each other. Applications communicate by creating and sending ToolTalk messages. The ToolTalk service receives these messages, determines the recipients, and then delivers the messages to the appropriate applications. See Figure 1.1.1. Before modifying your application to use the ToolTalk service, you must define (or locate) a message protocol: a set of ToolTalk messages describing operations that applications agree to perform. The message protocol specification includes the set of messages and how applications should behave when they receive the messages.

1.1.1 ToolTalk Scenarios

Software Engineering

To illustrate the use of the ToolTalk service, here are two scenarios of applications working together to help users solve their work problems. The message protocols used in these scenarios are hypothetical.

In computer-aided software engineering (CASE), the Tool-Talk service provides a way to connect and coordinate individual programs in a programming environment. For this scenario, a tool manager, graphical debugger, call grapher, editor, and source browser are all tools used in this ToolTalk-based developer's environment. These tools have been mod.

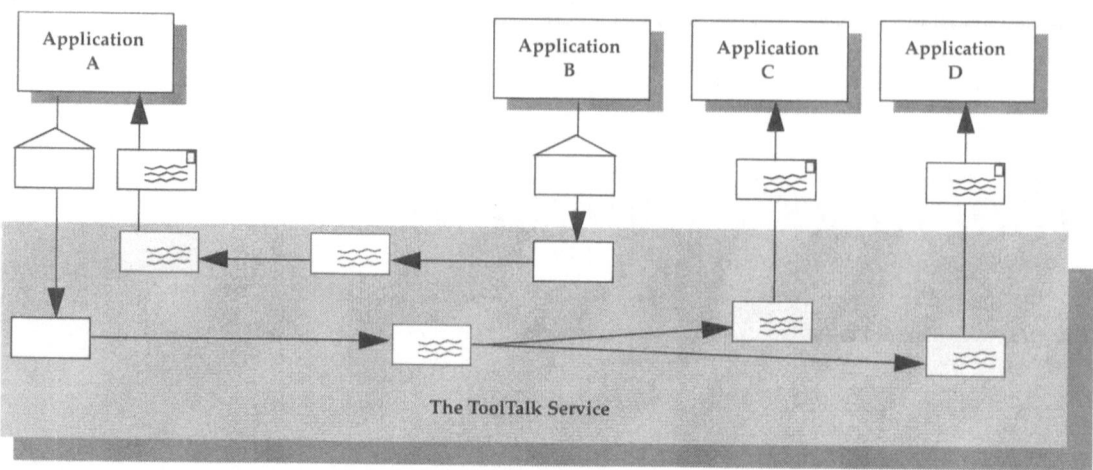

Figure 1.1.1. Applications using the ToolTalk service to communicate.

Table 1.1.1. CASE message protocol.

Message	Description
Started	Informs tool manager that this tool is started.
Stopped	Informs tool manager that this tool is stopped.
Launch	Requests a certain tool to start.
Quit	Requests a certain tool to stop.
Display	Requests that a tool that can edit a file load the file and scroll the file to a particular line number.
CallGraphFunction	Requests that a tool that can graph calls display the graph for this function in this file that is part of this program.
GetSelection	Requests that the tool with the current selection return the file name and line number.

ified to use the ToolTalk service and implement the messages shown in Table 1.1.1.

To determine what's causing a particular error message, a programmer starts the tool manager, a program used to co-ordinate the development tools in the environment. From the tool manager, the programmer double-clicks on the source browser and graphical debugger icons to start them. The tool manager sends a Launch message to each tool and as they start, they send a Started message to the tool manager with initialization information.

The programmer loads a source code file in the source browser and finds out where the error message is located in the source code. After selecting the text of the error message, the programmer moves to the graphical debugger and selects a "Set BreakPoint" menu item. The debugger sends a GetSelection message to the tools currently running in the environment (in this case, just the source browser.) The source browser returns the file name and line number and the debugger loads the file, moves to the line number, and sets the breakpoint.

The programmer then runs the program and locates the call that results in the error message. A feature of the debugger is the menu item, "Show Call Graph". After this menu item is selected, the debugger sends a CallGraphFunction message. The ToolTalk service starts up the installed call grapher if one isn't already running and delivers the message.

The call grapher loads the call graph for the specified file and scrolls to the specified function. The programmer sees another function that looks suspicious that's called just before the function producing the error. The programmer double-clicks on the suspicious function and the call grapher sends a Display message.

The ToolTalk service starts an editor and delivers the Display message. The editor loads the file and scrolls to the specified line number where the engineer discovers an error. After fixing the error, the programmer stops work by asking the tool manager to shut down all the tools. The tool manager sends Quit messages to all tools that are currently running. The tools clean up, send a reply to the Quit message, and exit.

Computer-Aided Design

In the computer-aided design (CAD) of hardware components, tools that are able to communicate with each other help automate the design process for the hardware engineer. In this scenario, there is a tool control program that orchestrates tool sequences and CAD tools that have been modified to use the ToolTalk service. All use a CAD message protocol that includes the messages shown in Table 1.1.2

The design engineer begins work by starting the tool control program. As a new tool is needed in the design sequence, the engineer starts the tool from the control program. Each tool initializes with the ToolTalk service and sends out a Tool-

Started message to notify the control program that it is now running.

Table 1.1.2. CAD message protocol.

Message	Description
ToolStarted	Informs interested tools that this tool started running.
ToolFinished	Informs interested tools that this tool has stopped running.
DesignOpened	Informs interested tools that a particular design data set was opened for access.
DesignWrite	Requests a certain tool to begin writing to a particular design data set.
DesignWriteDone	Informs interested tools that a particular design-write operation has been completed.
DesignRead	Requests a certain tool to begin reading a particular design data set.
DesignReadDone	Informs interested tools that a particular design-read operation has been completed.

The engineer begins work by loading a design into a PC layout tool for editing purposes. When the tool has loaded the design, it sends out a DesignOpen message, which notifies other tools in the environment that it has opened the file and begun to write design data. When the engineer has finished editing the data, the layout tool sends a DesignWriteDone message, which signals the control program. (In this protocol, only the control program registers interest in the DesignWriteDone message.)

The control program then sends a DesignRead message to the next tool required in the design sequence. After the next tool reads the design, it sends a DesignReadDone message to notify others that it as finished.

1.1.2
How
Applications Use
ToolTalk

As mentioned earlier applications create, send, and receive ToolTalk messages in order to communicate with each other. Sending applications create, fill in, and send a message; the ToolTalk service determines the recipients and delivers the message to the receiving applications. Receiving applications retrieve messages and after examining the information in the message, either discard the message or perform an operation and reply with the results.

An important ToolTalk feature is that sending applications need to know little about the receiving application. This is because applications that want to receive messages register their interest in specific types of messages with the ToolTalk service.

Registering Interest in ToolTalk Messages

The reason that sending applications need to know little about the receiving application is because applications that want to receive messages explicitly state what these messages should look like. This information is registered with ToolTalk in the form of *message patterns*. These message patterns usually match the message protocols that applications have agreed to use. Applications can add more patterns for individual use.

Message patterns are created much like a message is created; the same type of information is used in both. For each type of message an application wants to receive, it obtains an empty message pattern, fills in the attributes, and registers the pattern with the ToolTalk service.

When the ToolTalk service receives a message from a sender, it compares the information in the message to the patterns that are registered. Once matches have been found, the ToolTalk service delivers copies of the message to all recipients.

For each pattern describing a message it wants to receive, an application declares whether it can *handle* the message or just wants to *observe* it. Although many applications can observe a message, only one application can handle it to ensure that a requested operation is performed at most once. If the ToolTalk service cannot find a handler for a message, it returns the message to its sender indicating that delivery failed.

Applications provide message patterns to the ToolTalk service at installation time and/or while the application is running.

Sending ToolTalk Messages

To send a ToolTalk message, an application obtains an empty message, fills in the message attributes, and sends the message. ToolTalk messages are simple structures containing fields for address, subject, and delivery information. To send a ToolTalk message, an application need only provide this information:

- Should the recipient respond to the message; is this a notice or a request?

- What operation should be performed/has been performed? Are there arguments needed to perform the operation?
- What interest does the recipient share with the sender; is the recipient running in a specific user session or interested in a specific file?

To help narrow the focus of the message delivery, an application can provide more information in the message. See Section 4, "Sending Messages," for a complete listing and description of ToolTalk message attributes.

Receiving ToolTalk Messages

When the ToolTalk service determines that a message needs to be delivered to a specific process, it creates a copy of the message and notifies the process that a message is waiting. If a receiver is not running, the ToolTalk service looks for instructions (provided by the application at installation time) on how to start the application.

The process retrieves the message and examines its contents. The message may contain a notice that some operation has been performed. In this case, the process discards the message after reading the information. If the message contains a request to perform an operation, the process performs the operation and returns the result of the operation in a reply to the original message. Once the reply has been sent, the process can discard the original message.

1.1.3 ToolTalk Messaging Methods

The ToolTalk service provides two methods of addressing messages: process-oriented and object-oriented messaging. *Process-oriented messages* are messages addressed to processes. Applications that create a message address it to either a specific process or a particular type of process. Process-oriented messaging is a good way for existing applications to begin communicating with others. Modifications for supporting process-oriented messaging are straightforward and usually take a short time to implement.

Object-oriented messages are messages addressed to objects managed by applications. Applications that create a message address it to either a specific object or a particular type of object. Object-oriented messaging is particularly useful for applications that currently use objects or are being designed around objects. Even if an existing application is not object-oriented, the ToolTalk service provides a way for you to identify portions of application data as objects so that applications can begin communicating about these objects.

Process-Oriented Messaging

Process-oriented messaging provides a communication path between applications to deliver information or request that an operation be performed by the process receiving the message. To use process-oriented messaging, you need to be familiar with these ToolTalk concepts:

- Processes
- Sessions
- Files

Processes

One execution of an application, tool, or program that uses the ToolTalk service is called a *process* in this book. A process is a SunOS process that has initialized and registered with the ToolTalk service.

Procid. When a process opens communication with the ToolTalk service, it receives a process identifier (procid). Applications who want to send a message to a specific process must know the receiving application's procid. To find out this information, the sender can look at a previous message sent by the target application. The ToolTalk service automatically fills in a message's sender attribute with the sender's procid.

Ptype. You can instruct the ToolTalk service to consider your application as a potential message receiver when no process is running the application. This is done by providing message patterns and instructions for starting the application in a *process type* (*ptype*). The ptype file is compiled with the ToolTalk type compiler, *tt_type_comp*, at application installation time to make the information available to the ToolTalk service.

When an application has a ptype, part of the registration and initialization activities include registering the ptype with the ToolTalk service. Registering a ptype will automatically register the message patterns listed in it.

Sessions

A group of processes running in the same X session or process tree session is called a *session* in this book. A session also contains an instance of the ToolTalk communication program, *ttsession*.

When a process opens communication with the ToolTalk service, the process that actually provides the procid is ttsession. A side effect of opening ToolTalk communication is that the session in which the action takes place becomes the default session for the process.

The concept of a session is important in the delivery of messages. Senders can "scope" a message to a session and the ToolTalk service will deliver it to all processes that have message patterns that refer to the current session. To update message patterns with the current *session identifier* (*sessid*), applications "join" the session.

Files

A container for data that is of interest to applications is called a *file* in this book. The concept of a file is important in the delivery of messages. Senders can scope a message to a file and the ToolTalk service will deliver it to all processes that have message patterns that refer to the file without regard to the process's default session. To update message patterns with the current file pathname, applications "join" the file.

It is also possible to scope a message to a file within a session. The ToolTalk service will deliver the message to all processes that refer to both the file and session in their message patterns.

Object-Oriented Messaging

To use object-oriented messaging you need to be familiar with the process-oriented messaging concepts plus the ToolTalk concept of "object".

ToolTalk Objects

A ToolTalk *object* is a piece of application data for which a ToolTalk object specification has been created. Object data is stored in two parts as shown in Figure 1.1.2. One part is called the *object contents*, and is managed by the application that creates it. An object's contents is typically a piece, or pieces, of an ordinary file: a paragraph, a source code function, or a range of spreadsheet cells, for example.

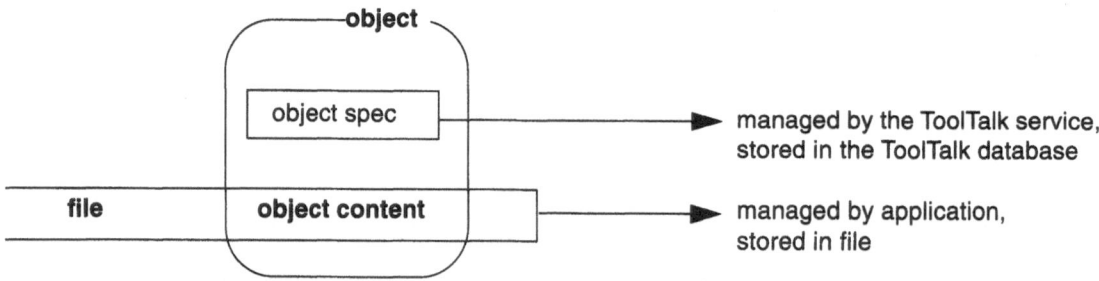

Figure 1.1.2. ToolTalk object data.

The second part of an object's data is the *object specification* (*spec*). Applications create and write specs to the ToolTalk database managed by the ToolTalk database program, *rpc.ttdb-serverd*.

A spec contains standard properties, such as the type of object, the name of the file in which the object's contents are located, and the object's owner. Applications can also add their own properties to a spec, such as the location of the object within a file. Because applications can store additional information in specs, you can identify data in existing files as objects without changing the formats of the files. You can also create objects of pieces of read-only files.[1]

Object Types.   When a message is addressed to a specific object or a type of object, the ToolTalk service must be able to determine to which application to deliver the message. Applications provide this information in *object types* (*otypes*). An otype file contains the ptype of the application that manages the object and message patterns that pertain to the object. These message patterns also contain instructions on what the ToolTalk service should do when a message is available but the application isn't running. ToolTalk can start the application to deliver a message, queue the message, or discard it.

The otype file is compiled with `tt_type_comp` at application installation time to make the information available to the ToolTalk service. When an application that manages objects registers with the ToolTalk service, it declares its ptype. When a ptype is registered, the ToolTalk service checks for otypes that mention the ptype and registers the patterns found in these otypes.

Object Files.   When object-oriented messaging is used, the ToolTalk definition of "file" is expanded to include the statement "container storing ToolTalk objects." Applications can query for objects in a file and perform operations on batches of objects.

1.1.4 ToolTalk Architecture

The following ToolTalk service components work together to provide interapplication communication and object information management:

- `ttsession`
  The ToolTalk communication process. One `ttsession` runs on a machine and communicates with other `tt-`

---

1. You cannot create object in files that are in a read-only file system. The ToolTalk service must be able to create a database in the same file system as the object.

`sessions` when a message needs to be delivered to an application in another session.

- `rpc.ttdbserverd`

  The ToolTalk database server process. One `rpc.ttdb-serverd` is installed on a disk partition that stores files of interest to ToolTalk clients or files containing ToolTalk objects.

- `libtt`

  The ToolTalk application programming interface (API) library. Applications include the API library in their program and call the ToolTalk functions found in the library.

The ToolTalk service uses SunSoft's ONC RPC to communicate between these ToolTalk components. It encodes messages according to the external data representation (XDR) standard.

The process and object type information that an application provides to the ToolTalk service is stored in the Classing Engine, an OpenWindows™ desktop type database. File and ToolTalk object information is stored in a NetISAM™ database managed by `rpc.dbserverd`.

The Classing Engine is automatically installed with Open-Windows V3. RPC and NetISAM are provided by SunOS.

See Figure 1.1.3 for an illustration of the ToolTalk service architecture.

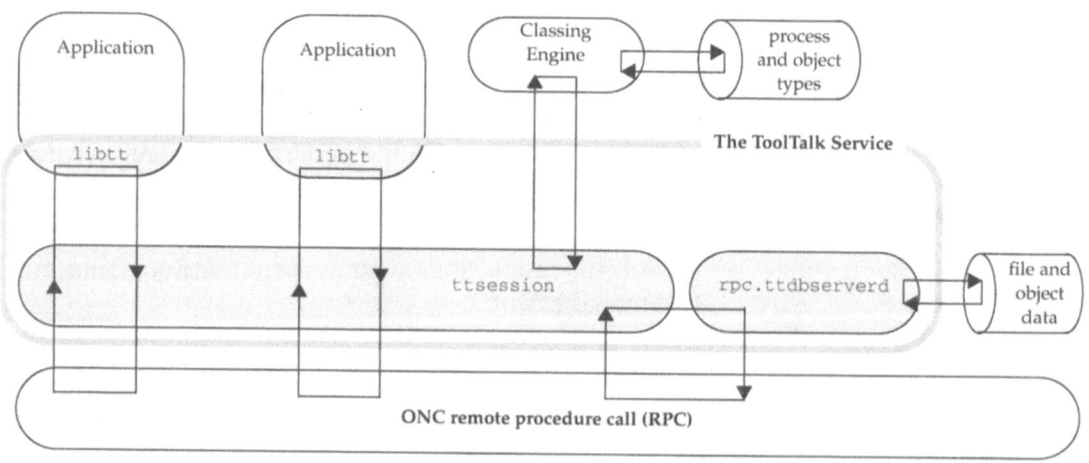

Figure 1.1.3. ToolTalk service architecture.

1.1.5
Modifying Your
Application

To use the ToolTalk service, an application calls ToolTalk functions from the ToolTalk application programming interface (API). The ToolTalk API provides functions for registering with the ToolTalk service, creating message patterns, sending messages, receiving messages, examining message information, and so forth. The first step in actually modifying your application is to include the ToolTalk API header file in your program.

The detailed instructions for modifying your application are found in Sections 2 through 6.

1.1.6
What You Need
to Integrate

To integrate with the ToolTalk service, you must install the OpenWindows V3 Programmer Set.

Note – OpenWindows V3 requires SunOS 4.1.x.

The instructions and software you'll need to integrate your application with the ToolTalk service are listed below.

Instructions

The information you will need to design or modify your application is found in this book. Step-by-step instructions show you how to modify your application to use the ToolTalk service.

For a tutorial on process-oriented messaging, see the *OpenWindows Version 3 Desktop Integration Guide*. The tutorial describes the concepts necessary for process-oriented messaging and provides step-by-step instructions for modifying your application to send and receive messages. In this tutorial, message patterns are created and registered while the application is running.

Sample Programs

To illustrate the step-by-step instructions in this book, the following sample programs are used.

- `ttsample1`
  A simple Xview broadcast slider/thermometer demonstration program. Start two or more copies to see the effect of broadcast messages.

- `Sun_EditDemo`
  An object-oriented Xview program that creates objects out of lines of code. Includes an object control window and simple editor. Objects are wrapped in text with C-style comments.

Another sample program not used in this book but interesting to look at is the `ttmon` program, a message monitoring Xview program that watches all ToolTalk message traffic in the local session.

These sample programs and a makefile are located in the following directory:

```
$OPENWINHOME/share/src/tooltalk/
```

ToolTalk Software

The ToolTalk service is available with the OpenWindows V3 release and is automatically installed with the OpenWindows system. Be sure to install the Programmer's Subset. Here are the ToolTalk service directories and files:

```
$OPENWINHOME/bin/
```

`install_tt`
ToolTalk installation script. Used by OpenWindows V3 installation script.

`rpc.ttdbserverd`
ToolTalk database management program. Must be installed on all filesystems that contain files referred to by applications in file scoped messages and files containing ToolTalk objects.

`ttdbck`
Utility to check and repair ToolTalk databases.

`ttcp`
`ttmv`
`ttrm`
`ttrmdir`
`tttar`
Unix shell commands enhanced to inform the ToolTalk service of the movement of files and objects.

`ttsession`
ToolTalk communication program that runs in each session.

`tt_type_comp`
ToolTalk type compiler for ptype and otype files.

```
$OPENWINHOME/lib/
    libtt.so.1.1
    libttstub.so.1.1
    libtt.a
```

```
$OPENWINHOME/include/desktop/
   tt_c.h
```
ToolTalk API header file. Include this file in your program.

```
$OPENWINHOME/lib/locale/C/LC_MESSAGES/
   Sun_ToolTalk.mo
```
ToolTalk catalog of error and event messages.

```
$OPENWINHOME/man/man1/
   install_tt.1
   tt_type_comp.1
   ttcp.1
   ttmv.1
   ttrm.1
   ttrmdir.1
   ttsession.1
   tttar.1
```

```
$OPENWINHOME/man/man3/
   ttapi.3
```

```
$OPENWINHOME/man/man8/
   rpc.ttdbserverd.8
   ttdbck.8
   ttdbserverd.8
```
Man pages for ToolTalk binaries, type compiler, enhanced shell commands, API, and database check utility.

Publish Your Ptypes and Otypes

Ptypes and otypes make it possible to send messages to types of processes, types of objects, and specific objects. This information is compiled at application installation time and stored in the Classing Engine database.

To communicate with other vendor's applications, you must know their ptypes and possibly their otypes (depending on what method of messaging you choose). SunSoft helps facilitate this by providing a Vendor Data Type Registration program. As type information is gathered, it will be publicly available through the SUCCESS™ database, SunSoft's on-line electronic support service for SunSoft's software developers. See the *OpenWindows Version 3 Desktop Integration Guide* for more information.

1.1.7
Setting Up the ToolTalk Service

Installing the ToolTalk Service

Starting a ToolTalk Session

Install the OpenWindows V3 Programmer's Subset.

ttsession is the ToolTalk message server. This background process must be running before any messages can be sent or received. Each message server defines a "session".

ttsession is automatically started by the first "open" call made by a ToolTalk client. Use the ttsession command to manually start a ttsession.

ttsession responds to two signals. If it receives the USR1 signal, it toggles the trace mode on or off. If it receives the USR2 signal, it rereads the types file.

```
ttsession    [-A max_active_msgs] [-a level] [-d
             display] [-s] [-t] [-v] [-{E|X}] [-h]
             [-c command]
```

-A   Specifies the maximum number of messages in-progress before a TT_ERR_OVERFLOW condition is returned. Default is 2000.

-a   Set the server authentication level. The level must be *unix, xauth*or *des.*

-d   Directs ttsession to start an X session for the given display. Normally, ttsession uses the $DIS-PLAY environment variable.

-s   Silent – don't print any warning messages.

-t   Turn on trace mode. Tracing is very helpful for seeing how messages are dispatched and delivered. The output is very voluminous. To toggle the trace mode on or off use the USR1 signal. If trace mode is turned on while ttsession is running, messages appear on the console.

Tracing displays the state of a message when it is first seen by ttsession. The lifetime of the message is then shown by showing the result of matching the message against type signatures (dispatch stage) and then showing the result of matching the message against any registered message patterns (delivery stage). Any attempt to send the message to a given process is also shown together with the success of that attempt.

-v	Print the version number and exit.
-E	Read in the types from the Classing Engine database. This option is the default.
-X	Read in the types from the alternate XDR format database in $HOME/.tt/types.xdr and /etc/tt/types.xdr.
-h	Print help on invoking ttsession and exit.
-c	Starts a process tree session and runs the given command. The special environment variable _SUN_TT_SESSION will be set to the name of this session. Any process started with this variable in the environment will default to being in this session. If command is omitted the value of $SHELL is used instead. Everything after -c on the command line is taken as the command to be executed, so -c should be the last option.

If neither -c or -d is specified, an X session is started using the server specified in the $DISPLAY environment variable.

X Window System (Including X11/NeWS)

Under the X Window System, a session is established by executing ttsession, either without arguments (taking the display from the $DISPLAY environment variable) or specifying the display with the -d switch.

    ttsession
or
    ttsession -d :0

When ttsession is invoked, it immediately forks and the parent copy exits, so that the process managing the session executes in the background. The session is registered as a property, named by the atom _SUN_TT_SESSION on the root of screen 0, giving the host and port number for communication with the process managing the session.

Background and Batch Sessions

If your application runs as a background job, in a batch session, or in a session bound to a character terminal, it should do so as its own session. This can be done by using the -c switch on ttsession:

    ttsession -c command-to-run-in-batch

Be sure to use the -c option last. Everything after -c is read as part of the command.

1.1.8 Managing ToolTalk Object and File

To keep specs up to date with the objects they describe, the ToolTalk service stores this information on the same file system as the object. This means that if the object moves, its spec must move too.

⚠ Caution – Despite the efforts of the ToolTalk service and integrated applications, it's possible for object references to be broken by removing, moving, or renaming files with shell commands like mv or rm. Broken references like this will show up as undeliverable messages.

Tell users of your application to use the ToolTalk-wrapped shell commands listed in Table 1.1.3 for copying, moving, and removing files referred to in messages and files containing objects.

Table 1.1.3. ToolTalk-wrapped shell commands.

Command	Description
ttcp	Copies file to new location. Updates file and object location information in ToolTalk database.
ttmv	Moves directory and/or files to new location. Updates file and object location information in ToolTalk database. Removes old version of file or directory.
ttrm	Removes specified file. Removes file and object information from the ToolTalk database.
ttrmdir	Removes empty directories (directories that contain no files) that have ToolTalk object specs associated with them. It's possible to create an object spec for a directory. When an object spec is created, the pathname of a file or directory is supplied. Removes object information from the ToolTalk database.
tttar	Archives or extracts multiple files and object information into (or from) a single archive, called a tarfile. Can also be used to just archive or extract ToolTalk file and object information into (or from) a tarfile.

1.1.9
For More Information

These documents contain further information on the Tool-Talk service:

Table 1.1.4. ToolTalk document roadmap.

Documents	*Topics*	*Audience*
OpenWindows Version 3 Installation and StartUp Guide	How to install the ToolTalk service	Advanced user, system administrator
ToolTalk 1.0 Setup and Administration Guide	How to setup the ToolTalk service and manage its files	System administrator
OpenWindows Version 3 Desktop Integration Guide	Process-oriented messaging tutorial, How to register your ptype and otype with SunSoft	Software developer
Designing and Writing A ToolTalk Procedural Protocol	How to write ToolTalk messages: A "Quickstart" guide	Software developer, advanced user
Tool Inter-Operability: A Hands On Demonstration	Tool and applications inter-operability examples	Software developer, advanced user

1.2
General
Application

To use the ToolTalk service, your application calls ToolTalk functions from the ToolTalk API library. You begin modifying your application to use the ToolTalk service by including the ToolTalk API header file. After initializing and starting a session with the ToolTalk service, you can provide additional information to the ToolTalk service by joining files and user sessions. When your process is ready to quit, you unregister these patterns and close your ToolTalk session.

In addition to providing instructions on how to participate in a ToolTalk session, this section tells you how to manage storage of values passed in from the ToolTalk service and how to handle errors that the ToolTalk service returns.

Modify your application to satisfy general application requirements for the ToolTalk service by:

- Including the ToolTalk API FIle
- Registering With the ToolTalk Service
- Setting Up to Receive Messages
- Managing Storage
- Handling Errors
- Unregistering from the ToolTalk Service.

Note – The code samples that illustrate the calls used to perform the operations are mostly fragments from the sample programs, `ttsample1` and `Sun_EditDemo`. These sample programs are in this directory:`$OPENWINHOME/share/src/tooltalk/`

1.2.1
Including the ToolTalk API File

The first step in modify your application to use the ToolTalk service is to include the ToolTalk API header file in your program. This file, `tt_c.h`, lives in this directory:

```
$OPENWINHOME/include/desktop/
```

Here's how `ttsample1` includes this file.

```
/*
 * ttsample1 -- dynamic pattern,
 * procedural notification
 */

#include <stdio.h>
#include <sys/param.h>
#include <sys/types.h>
#include <xview/xview.h>
#include <xview/panel.h>
#include <strings.h>

#include <desktop/tt_c.h>
```

1.2.2
Registering with the ToolTalk Service

When you register with the ToolTalk service, you have the choice of registering in the ToolTalk session the application was started in (the *initial session*) or locating another session and registering there.

The ToolTalk functions you need to register with the ToolTalk service are shown in Table 1.2.1.

Table 1.2.1. Initializing and registering with the ToolTalk service.

Return Type	ToolTalk Function
char *	tt_open(void)
int	tt_fd(void)
char *	tt_X_session(const char *xdisplay)
Tt_status	tt_default_session_set(const char *sessid)

Registering in the Initial Session

To initialize and register your process with the initial ToolTalk session, obtain a process identifier (procid) and a matching file descriptor.

`tt_open()` returns the procid for your process, and sets it as the default procid.

`tt_fd()` returns a file descriptor for your current procid that will become active when a message arrives for your application. See "When a message has arrived for your application, the file descriptor becomes active. Your code for being alerted that the file descriptor is active will vary depending on how your application is structured." for instructions on being notified when the file descriptor is active.

When `tt_open()` is the first call made to the ToolTalk service, it sets the initial session as the default session. The default session identifier (*sessid*) is important to the delivery of ToolTalk messages. The ToolTalk service will automatically fill in the default sessid if an application does not explicitly set the session message attribute. If the message is scoped to `TT_SESSION`, the message will be delivered to all applications in the default session who have registered interest in this type of message.

Here's sample code to initialize and register with the ToolTalk service.

```
int ttfd;

/*
 * Initialize ToolTalk, using the initial
 * default session, and obtain the file
 * descriptor that will become active whenever
 * ToolTalk has a message for this process.
 */

my_procid = tt_open();
ttfd = tt_fd();
```

Registering in a Specified Session

To register in a session other than the initial session, your program must find the name of the other session, set the new session as the default, and register with the ToolTalk service. The calls required must be in this order:

1. Get the name of the session, e.g. use `tt_X_session()`. This call retrieves the name of the session associated with an X11 display server. `tt_X_session()` takes the argument `char *xdisplay_name` where the `xdisplay_name` is the name of an X11 display server (e.g. `somehost:0`, `:0`, etc.)

2. `tt_default_session_set();`

3. `tt_open();`

4. `tt_fd();`

Here's an example of how you would join an X session called `somehost:0` which is not your initial session.

```
char    *my_session;
char    *my_procid;

my_session = tt_X_session("somehost:0");
tt_default_session_set(my_session);
my_procid = tt_open();
ttfd = tt_fd();
```

1.2.3 Setting Up to Receive Messages

When a message has arrived for your application, the file descriptor becomes active. Your code for being alerted that the file descriptor is active will vary depending on how your application is structured.

XView Programs

A program that uses the XView notifier, through `xv_main_loop()` or `notify_start()`, can have a callback function invoked when the file descriptor becomes active. Invoke `notify_set_input_func()` with the handle for the message object as a parameter.

Here's an example of an XView program setting up to receive messages.

```
/*
 * Arrange for XView to call receive_tt_message when the ToolTalk file
 * descriptor becomes active.
 */
notify_set_input_func(base_frame,
(Notify_func)receive_tt_message,
ttfd);
```

X Window System Xt (Intrinsics) Programs	An Xt-based program uses `XtAddInput()` to watch for arriving messages.
TNT Programs	An TNT-based program uses `wire_AddFileHandler()` to watch for arriving messages.
Other Xlib Programs	Programs structured around a `select(2)` or `poll(2)` system call use the file descriptor returned by `tt_fd()`.

Programs structured around a `select(2)` or `poll(2)` system call use the file descriptor returned by `tt_fd()`.

After the `select` call exits with this file descriptor active, use `tt_message_receive()` to obtain a handle for the incoming message.

1.2.4 Managing Storage

The ToolTalk service simplifies your application storage management by providing you a copy of the information it returns to you and by copying all information your application provides to the ToolTalk service.

Information You Provide to the ToolTalk Service

When you provide a pointer to the ToolTalk service, it copies the information referenced by the pointer. You can then dispose of the information you provided; the ToolTalk service won't use the pointer again to retrieve the information.

Information Provided by the ToolTalk Service

The ToolTalk service provides an allocation stack in the ToolTalk API library that it uses to store information persistently that it gives to you. For example, if you asked for the sessid of the default session with `tt_default_session()`, the ToolTalk service returns the address of the character string in the allocation stack (a `char *` pointer) that contains the sessid. When you have retrieved the sessid, dispose of the character string to clean up the allocation stack.

Note – The API allocation stack should not be confused with your program's run-time stack. The API stack will not discard information until you tell it to.

The ToolTalk service provides the calls listed in Table 2.2 to manage the storage of information in the ToolTalk API allocation stack:

Table 1.2.2. Using ToolTalk storage.

Return Type	ToolTalk Function
int	tt_mark(void)
void	tt_release(int mark)

Return Type	ToolTalk Function
void	tt_free(caddr_t p)
caddr_t	tt_malloc(size_t s)

The `tt_mark()` and `tt_release()` functions, used to mark and free information returned by a series of functions, are a general mechanism to help you easily manage storage. The `tt_mark()` and `tt_release()` functions are typically used at the beginning and end of a routine where the information returned by the ToolTalk service is no longer interesting after the routine has ended.

To ask the ToolTalk service to mark the beginning of your storage space, use `tt_mark()`. The ToolTalk service returns a mark, an integer that represents a location on the API stack. All the information that the ToolTalk service subsequently returns to you will be stored in locations that come after the mark. When you no longer need the information, call `tt_release()` and specify the mark that signifies the beginning of the information you no longer need.

In the following example, `ttsample1` calls `tt_mark()` at the beginning of the routine that examines the information in a message. When the information examined in the routine is no longer needed and the message has been destroyed, `tt_release()` is called with the mark to free storage on the stack.

```
/*
 * Get a storage mark so we can easily free all the data
 * ToolTalk returns to us.
 */

mark = tt_mark();

if (0==strcmp("ttsample1_value", tt_message_op(msg_in))) {
tt_message_arg_ival(msg_in, 0, &val_in);
xv_set(gauge, PANEL_VALUE, val_in, NULL);
}

tt_message_destroy(msg_in);
tt_release(mark);
return;
```

`tt_malloc()` reserves a specified amount of storage in the allocation stack for your use. You could use `tt_malloc()` within a filter routine used by the ToolTalk file query function, `tt_file_objects_query()`. This function returns all the objects in a file and runs it through a filter routine that you provide. Your filter routine may be looking for a specific object. Once your filter routine finds the object you were looking for, use `tt_malloc()` to create a storage location and copy the object into the location. When your filter function returns, the ToolTalk service will free all storage used by the objects in the file, but the object you stored via `tt_malloc()` will be available for further use. The way that the ToolTalk service behaves toward information passed into filter functions (and callbacks) is a special case. In all other instances, the ToolTalk service stores the information in the API allocation stack until you free it. See "One of the features of the ToolTalk service is callback support for messages, patterns, and filters. Callbacks are routines in your program that ToolTalk calls when a particular message arrives (message callback) or when a message matches a particular pattern you registered (pattern callback), When you call file query functions such as tt_file_objects_ query(), you point to a filter routine that the ToolTalk service calls as it returns items from the query. You tell the ToolTalk service about these callbacks by adding the callback to a message or pattern before sending the message or registering the pattern. When you call tt_file_objects_ query(), you provide the filter routine as an argument." for more information.To free storage set aside by `tt_malloc()`, use `tt_free()`.

To free storage of individual objects that the ToolTalk service provides you pointers to, use `tt_free()`. For example, if you asked for the sessid of the default session with `tt_default_session()`, you could free up the space in the API allocation stack that stores the sessid with `tt_free()` after you have examined the sessid. `tt_free()` takes an address in the allocation stack (a `char *` pointer or an address returned from `tt_malloc()`) as an argument.

Special Case: Callback and Filter Routines

One of the features of the ToolTalk service is callback support for messages, patterns, and filters. Callbacks are routines in your program that ToolTalk calls when a particular message arrives (*message callback*) or when a message matches a particular pattern you registered (*pattern callback*), When you call file query functions such as `tt_file_objects_` query(), you point to a filter routine that the ToolTalk service calls as it returns items from the query. You tell the ToolTalk service about these callbacks by adding the callback to a message or pattern before sending the message or registering the pattern. When you call `tt_file_objects_query`(), you provide the filter routine as an argument.

Callback and filter routines called by the ToolTalk service are called with two kinds of arguments:

- context arguments
  The arguments you passed in to the API call that triggered the callback. These arguments point to items your application owns.

- pointers to API objects
  The address of message or pattern attributes in storage.

The context arguments are passed through from the ToolTalk service to your application. The API objects referenced by pointers are freed by the ToolTalk service as soon as your callback or filter function returns. If you want to keep any of these objects, be sure to copy the objects before your function returns.

1.2.5
Handling Errors

Rather than have ToolTalk functions return error status in a global variable, the ToolTalk service returns error status in the function's return value. For example, the return value for `tt_default_session_set`() is a `Tt_status` code. If the ToolTalk service sets the default session to the sessid you specified without a problem, the `Tt_status` code is `TT_OK`. If a problem was encountered, the ToolTalk service would return another `Tt_status` code, `TT_ERR_SESSION`, to let you know the sessid you passed was not valid.

If a ToolTalk function has a natural return value such as a pointer or an integer, a special *error value* is returned instead of the real value. For example, the return value for `tt_open`() is a pointer to a procid. If the ToolTalk service could not respond to your application's `tt_open`() call, it returns a pointer to a `Tt_status` code instead of a valid procid. With the ToolTalk error handling functions, you check the pointer to see if it's pointing to a valid procid or a `Tt_status` code. If the pointer is to a valid procid, the checking function returns `TT_OK`.

Use the ToolTalk functions listed in Table 1.2.3 and the ToolTalk macros listed in Table 1.2.4 to check for and retrieve error values

Checking Returned Tt_status

ToolTalk functions with no natural return value just return an element of the Tt_status enum. Use the ToolTalk macro tt_is_err(), which returns an integer, to see if there was a warning or an error. If you receive 1, the Tt_status enum is an error. If you receive 0, the Tt_status enum is a warning. If there is an error, you can obtain the character string explaining the Tt_status code with tt_status_message() as shown in the following example.

Table 1.2.3. Retrieving ToolTalk error status.

Return Type	ToolTalk Function
char *	tt_status_message(Tt_status ttrc)
Tt_status	tt_int_error(int return_val)

Table 1.2.4. ToolTalk error macros.

Return Type	ToolTalk Macro	Expands to
Tt_status	tt_ptr_error(pointer)	tt_pointer_error((void *)(p))
Tt_status	tt_is_err(pointer)	(TT_WRN_LAST < (p))

```
char *spec_id, my_application_name;
Tt_status tterr;

tterr = tt_spec_write(spec_id);
if (tt_is_error(tterr)) {
fprintf(stderr, "%s: %s\n", my_application_name,
tt_status_message(tterr));
}
```

Checking Returned Pointers

When an error occurs during a ToolTalk function that returns a pointer, the ToolTalk service provide an address within the ToolTalk API library containing the appropriate Tt_status code. Use the ToolTalk macro tt_ptr_error() to find out if the pointer is valid. If the pointer is an error value, use tt_status_message() to get the Tt_status code string. The following sample code checks a pointer to see if it's an error value. If it is, the character string describing the Tt_status code is retrieved and printed.

```
char *old_spec_id, new_file, new_specid, my_application_name;
Tt_status tterr;

new_spec_id = tt_spec_move(old_spec_id, new_file);
tterr = tt_ptr_error(new_spec_id);
switch (tterr) {
    case TT_OK:
/*
 * Replace old_spec_id with new_spec_id in my internal
 * data structures.
 */
update_my_spec_ids(old_spec_id, new_spec_id);
break;
    case TT_WRN_SAME_OBJID:
/*
 * The spec must have stayed in the same filesystem,
 * since ToolTalk is reusing the spec id. Do nothing.
 */
break;
    case TT_ERR_FILE:
    case TT_ERR_ACCESS:
    default:
fprintf(stderr, "%s: %s\n", my_application_name,
tt_status_message(tterr));
break;
}
```

Checking Returned Integers

ToolTalk functions that return integers return wildly out-of-bounds values for errors. tt_int_error() will return TT_OK if the value is not wildly out of bounds. If a value is out of bounds, use tt_is_error() to determine if an error or a warning occurred. To retrieve the catalog string for a Tt_status code, use tt_status_message(). Here's sample code that checks a returned integer.

```
Tt_message msg;
int num_args;
Tt_status tterr;
char *my_application_name;

num_args = tt_message_args_count(msg);
tterr = tt_int_error(num_args);
if (tt_is_error(tterr)) {
fprintf(stderr, "%s: %s\n", my_application_name,
tt_status_message(tterr));
}
```

Error Propagation

Any ToolTalk functions that accept pointers always check the pointer passed in and return `TT_ERR_POINTER` if the pointer is an error value. This allows you to combine calls in reasonable ways without having to check after every single call.

In the following example, a message is created, filled in, and sent. If `tt_message_create()` fails, an error object is assigned to *m*, and all the `tt_message_xxx_set()` and `tt_message_send()` calls fail. Check the return code from `tt_message_send()` to detect the error without having to check between each call.

```
Tt_message m;

m=tt_message_create();
tt_message_op_set(m,"OP");
tt_message_address_set(m,TT_PROCEDURE);
tt_message_scope_set(m,TT_SESSION);
tt_message_class_set(m,TT_NOTICE);
tt_rc=tt_message_send(m);
if (tt_rc!=TT_OK)...
```

1.2.6 Unregistering from the ToolTalk Service

Use `tt_close()` when you want to stop interacting with the ToolTalk service and other ToolTalk session participants. `tt_close()` returns Tt_status and closes the current default procid.

```
/*
 * Before leaving, allow ToolTalk to clean up.
 */
tt_close();

exit(0);
}
```

1.3
Message
Patterns

This section describes how to provide message pattern information to the ToolTalk service. The ToolTalk service uses message patterns to determine message recipients. After receiving a message, the ToolTalk service compares the message to all current message patterns to find a matching pattern. Once a match is made, the message is delivered to the application listed in the message pattern. See Section 3.1 for a description of the information you can put into a message pattern.

You can provide message pattern information to the ToolTalk service using static and/or dynamic methods. To use the static method, define your ptype and otypes (if you create ToolTalk objects) and compile them with the ToolTalk type compiler, `tt_type_comp`. `tt_type_comp` stores your type information in the Classing Engine, a OpenWindows desktop type database. When you declare your ptype, the ToolTalk service creates message patterns based on your type information. These static message patterns will remain in effect until you close communication with the ToolTalk service.

To inform other applications of your ptype and otypes, use SunSoft's Vendor Data Type Registration program. See the *OpenWindows Version 3 Desktop Integration Guide* for more information.

To provide message pattern information while your application is running (dynamic method), create a message pattern and register it with the ToolTalk service. You can add callback routines to dynamic message patterns that the ToolTalk service will call when it matches a message to this pattern. You can register and unregister dynamic message patterns as needed.

You choose the static and/or dynamic method depending on the type of messages you want to receive. If you want to receive a defined set of messages, the static method provides an easy way to specify the message pattern information. Since type information is only specified once (when your application is installed), your application just needs to declare its ptype each time it starts.

Use the static method of providing message pattern information by:

- Defining Your Process Type
- Defining Your Object Types (if creating objects)
- Installing Your Type Information
- Declaring Your Process Type

If the types of messages you want to receive will vary while your application is running, the dynamic method provides the means to add, change, or remove message pattern information after your application is started.

Use the dynamic method of providing message pattern information by:

- Creating Message Patterns
- Filling Message Patterns
- Attaching Pattern Callbacks
- Registering Message Patterns
- Deleting Message Patterns

Regardless of the method you choose to provide message patterns to the ToolTalk service, you will want to update these patterns with your current session and file information so that you receive all messages that refer to the session or file in which you are interested. "Updating Message Patterns With THe Current Session Or File," Section 3.4, describes how to join sessions and files to update your message patterns.

1.3.1 Message Pattern Attributes

The attributes in your message pattern specify the type of messages you want to receive and, to some extant, the number of messages you receive. Here's how the ToolTalk service behaves when comparing message attributes to pattern attributes.

- If no pattern attribute is specified, the ToolTalk service counts the message attribute as matched. The fewer pattern attributes you specify, the more messages you become eligible to receive.
- If there are multiple values specified for a pattern attribute, one of the values must match the message attribute value. If no value matches, the ToolTalk service will not consider your application as a receiver.

In all of your message patterns, you must specify these attributes at the minimum:

- scope
- category

See Table 1.3.1 for a complete list of attributes you can put in your message patterns.

Table 1.3.1. ToolTalk message pattern attributes.

Pattern Attribute	Value	Description
category	`TT_OBSERVE, TT_HANDLE,`	Do you want to perform the operation listed in a message or just view a message?
scope	`TT_SESSION, TT_FILE,` `TT_BOTH,` `TT_FILE_IN_SESSION`	Are you interested in messages about a session and/or a file? (Join a session and/or file after the message pattern is registered to update the sessid and filename.)
arguments	*arguments or results*	What arguments are used for the operation in which you are interested?
class	`TT_NOTICE, TT_REQUEST`	Do you want to receive notices and/or requests?
file	`char *pathname`	What file should be mentioned in a message?
object	`char *objid`	What object should be mentioned in a message?
operation	`char *opname`	What operation should be mentioned in a message?
otype	`char *otype`	What type of object interests you?

Pattern Attribute	Value	Description
address	TT_PROCEDURE, TT_OBJECT, TT_HANDLER, TT_OTYPE	What type of address should a message contain?
disposition	TT_DISCARD, TT_QUEUE, TT_START	What should the ToolTalk service do when it can't deliver a message to your application?
sender	char *procid	What sender interests you?
sender_ptype	char *ptype	What type of sending process interest you?
session	char *sessid	What session should be mentioned in a message?
state	TT_CREATED, TT_SENT, TT_HANDLED, TT_FAILED, TT_QUEUED, TT_STARTED, TT_REJECTED	In what state should the message be?

1.3.2
Static Message Patterns

Note – The code samples that illustrate the calls used to perform the operations are mostly fragments from the sample program, Sun_EditDemo. This sample program can be found in this directory:

$OPENWINHOME/share/src/tooltalk/

Defining Your Process Type

The *process type* (ptype) provides application information that the ToolTalk service can use when the application isn't running. This information is used to start your process if necessary to receive a message, queue messages until it starts, or deliver ptype scoped messages to your process.

A ptype begins with an identifier known as a ptid. The optional start string following the ptid is a command that the ToolTalk service will execute to start a process running the program.

Following the start string are signatures describing the procedure and process messages that the program wishes to receive. Messages to be observed are described separately from those to be handled. A signature is divided into two parts by an arrow (=>). The first part specifies matching attribute values. The more attribute values specified in a signature, the fewer messages the signature will match.

The second part of a signature (after the arrow) specifies receiver values that the ToolTalk service will copy into messages that match the first part of the signature. A ptype signature can contain values for disposition and opnum. The ToolTalk service uses the disposition value (start, queue, or the default discard) to determine what to do with a message that matches the signature when no process is running the program. The opnum value is provided as a convenience to message receivers. When two signatures have the same operation name but different arguments, giving them different opnums makes incoming messages easy to identify.

Syntax

Here's the syntax for a ptype:

```
ptype          ::= 'ptype' ptid '{'
                   property*
                   ['observe:' psignature*]
                   ['handle:' psignature* ]
                   '}' [';']
property       ::= property_id value ';'
property_id    ::= 'per_file'
               |   'per_session'
               |   'start'
value          ::= string
               |   number
ptid           ::= identifier
psignature     ::= [scope] op args
                   ['=>'
                   ['start']['queue']
                   ['opnum='number]]
                   ';'
scope          :=  'file'
               |   'session'
               |   'file_in_session'
args           ::= '(' argspec {, argspec}* ')'
               |   '(void)'
               |   '()'
argspec        ::= mode type name
mode           ::= 'in' | 'out' | 'inout'
type           ::= identifier
name           :=  identifier
```

Property_id Information

ptid

process type identifier (ptid). A ptid must be unique for every installation. This identifier cannot be changed after installation time, so it is important that a unique name be chosen. Use a name that includes the trade-marked name of your product or company, such as Sun_EditDemo. Also use a few upper-case letters to help make your ptid unique. The ptid cannot exceed 32 characters, and should not be one of the reserved identifiers ptype, otype, per_file, per_session, start, opnum, queue, file, session, observe, or handle.

per_file

The maximum number of processes of this type that can concurrently observe a particular file. If this many processes of this type are already observing a document, the ToolTalk service will not start another process of this type.

Tools that cannot handle multiple processes updating the same file should set this limit to 1.

per_session

The maximum number of processes of this type that can concurrently run in a single session. If this many processes of this type are already running in a session, the ToolTalk service will not start another process of this type.

Tools that manage multiple documents in one process should set this limit to 1 so that all documents will be handled by a single process in each user session.

start

Start string for the process. If the ToolTalk service needs to start a process, it executes this command; /bin/sh is used as the shell. Before executing the command, the ToolTalk service defines TT_FILE as an environment variable with the value of the file attribute of the message that caused the application to be started. The started command runs in the environment of ttsession, not in the environment of the sender of the message that caused the start, so any context information must be carried by message arguments.

Psignature *Matching Information*

op

Operation name. This is matched against the op attribute in messages.

args

Arguments for the operation. If the args list is (void), the signature matches only messages with no arguments. If the args list is empty (just "()"), the signature matches without regard to the arguments.

scope

This pattern attribute is matched against the scope attribute in messages.

Psignature *Actions Information*

start

If the psignature matches a message, and no running process of this ptype has a pattern that matches the message, start a process of this ptype.

queue

If the psignature matches a message, and no running process of this ptype has a pattern that matches the message, queue the message until a process of this ptype registers a pattern that matches it.

opnum

Fill in the message's opnum attribute with the specified number. The opnum allows you to specify an operation more than once and list unique arguments with each instance of the operation.

Here's the ptype from the Sun_EditDemo program::

```
#include "Sun_EditDemo_opnums.h"

ptype Sun_EditDemo {
          /* setenv SUN_EDITDEMO_HOME to install dir for the demo */
        start "${SUN_EDITDEMO_HOME}/edit";
        handle:
        /* edit file named in message, start editor if necessary */
        session Sun_EditDemo_edit(void)
                                => start opnum=SUN_EDITDEMO_EDIT;

        /* tell editor viewing file in message to save file */
        session Sun_EditDemo_save(void)
                                => opnum=SUN_EDITDEMO_SAVE;
```

```
          /* save file named in message to new filename */
          session Sun_EditDemo_save_as(in string new_filename)
                              => opnum=SUN_EDITDEMO_SAVE_AS;

          /* bring down editor viewing file in message */
          session Sun_EditDemo_close(void)
                              => opnum=SUN_EDITDEMO_CLOSE;
};
```

The `Sun_EditDemo_opnums.h` file defines symbolic definitions for all the opnums used by `edit.c`. This allows both the `edit.types` file and `edit.c` file to share the same definitions.

Defining Your Object Types

The otypes for your application provide addressing information that the ToolTalk service uses when delivering object-oriented messages.

The number of otypes you have, and what they represent, depends on the nature of your application. A word processing application might have otypes for characters, words, paragraphs, and documents. A diagram editing application might have otypes for nodes, arcs, annotation boxes, and diagrams.

An otype is very similar to a ptype, consisting of a type identifier and a list of signatures. The signatures define the messages that can be addressed to objects of the type (that is, the operations that can be invoked on objects of the type).

Each signature is divided into two parts separated by an arrow (=>). The values preceding the arrow define matching criteria for incoming messages. The values listed after the arrow are receiver values which the ToolTalk service adds to each message that matches the first part of the signature. An otype writer uses these values to specify the ptid of the program that implements the operation, as well as the message's scope and disposition.

Syntax

Here's the syntax for an otype:

```
otype         ::= obj_header'{' objbody* '}'
['; ']
obj_header    ::= 'otype' otid [':' otid⁺]
objbody       ::= 'observe:' osignature*
              |   'handle:' osignature*
```

```
osignature    ::= op args [rhs][inherit] ';'
rhs           ::= ['=>' ptid [scope]]
                  ['start']['queue']
                  ['opnum='number]
inherit       ::= 'from' otid
args          ::= '(' argspec {, argspec}* ')'
              |   '(void)'
              |   '()'
argspec       ::= mode type name
mode          ::= 'in' | 'out' | 'inout'
type          ::= identifier
name          ::= identifier
otid          ::= identifier
ptid          ::= identifier
```

Semantics

Obj_Header Information

otid

Identifies the object type. An *object type identifier* (otid) must be unique for every installation. This identifier cannot be changed after installation time, so it is important that a unique name be chosen. It is recommended that the name begin with the ptid of the tool that implements the otype. The otid is limited to 64 characters, and should not be one of the reserved identifiers `ptype`, `otype`, `per_file`, `per_session`, `start`, `opnum`, `start`, `queue`, `file`, `session`, `observe`, or `handle`.

Osignature Information. The object body portion of the otype definition is a list of osignatures for messages about the object that your application wants to observe and handle. The osignatures contain many of the same fields as a psignature found in a ptype.

op

Operation name. This is matched against the op attribute in messages.

args

Arguments for the operation. If the args list is `(void)`, the signature matches only messages with no arguments. If the args list is empty (just "()"), the signature matches without regard to the arguments.

ptid

Process type identifier for the application that manages this type of object.

opnum

Fill in the message's opnum attribute with the specified number. The opnum allows you to specify an operation more than once and list unique arguments with each instance of the operation.

inherit

otypes form an inheritance hierarchy where operations can be inherited from base types. The ToolTalk service requires the otype definer to name explicitly all inherited operations and the otype to inherit from. This prevents later changes (like adding a new level to the hierarchy, or adding new operations to base types) from unexpectedly affecting the behavior of an otype.

The other elements of the otype definition (scope, queue, and start) have the same meaning as in ptype definitions, except that scope and message class appear on the right hand side of the arrow and are filled in by the ToolTalk service during message dispatch. This allows the definer of the otype to specify the attributes instead of requiring the message sender to know how the message should be delivered.

Here's the otype definition from the Sun_EditDemo edit.types file:

```
#include "Sun_EditDemo_opnums.h"
otype Sun_EditDemo_object {
        handle:
        /* hilite object given by objid, starts an editor if necessary */
        hilite_obj(in string objid)
                => Sun_EditDemo session start opnum=SUN_EDITDEMO_HILITE_OBJ;
};
```

The Sun_EditDemo_opnums.h file defines symbolic definitions for all the opnums used by edit.c. This allows both the edit.types file and edit.c file to share the same definitions.

Installing Your Type Information

In order for applications to be started and to have messages queued, the ptype definition must be put into the Classing Engine. To receive messages addressed to objects your application creates and manages, the otype definitions must also be installed in the Classing Engine. The Classing Engine makes ptype and otype information available on the host executing the sending process, the host executing the receiving process, and the hosts running the sessions to which the processes are joined.

To get your type information into the Classing Engine and available to the ToolTalk service, run the ToolTalk type compiler on your type file(s). This compiler creates Classing Engine definitions for your type information and stores them in the Classing Engine database.

Here are the steps:

1. **Run** `tt_type_comp` **on your ptype file.**

   ```
   % tt_type_comp <your-file>
   ```

`tt_type_comp` runs *your-file* through `cpp`, compiles the type definitions, and merges the information into the Classing Engine tables. By default, `tt_type_comp` will use the user's Classing Engine tables. To specify otherwise, use the `-d` option

```
% tt_type_comp -d user|system|network
```

and specify one of the following:

user	uses	`~/.cetables/cetables`
system	uses	`/etc/cetables/cetables`
network	uses	`$OPENWINHOME/lib/ce-tables/cetables`

For more information on `tt_type_comp`, see `tt_-type_comp(1)`.

After running `tt_type_comp`, tell the ToolTalk service to read the type information in the Classing Engine database. This will make your type information available to the ToolTalk service. To do this, follow these steps:

2. **Find out the process identifier of the** `ttsession` **process.**
   % ps -aux | grep ttsession

3. **Send** `ttsession` **a SIGUSR2 signal.**

   ```
   % kill -USR2 <ttsession pid>
   ```

Declaring Your Process Type

To register your ptype with the ToolTalk service, use `tt_p-type_declare()` during your application's ToolTalk initialization routine. The ToolTalk service will read the type information and create the message patterns listed in your ptype and any of your otypes that reference the specified ptype.

Here, Sun_EditDemo registers its ptype during its `ed-it.c` program initialization..

```
/*
 * Initialize our ToolTalk environment.
 */
int
edit_init_tt()
{
        int     mark;
        char    *procid = tt_open();
        int     ttfd;
        void    edit_receive_tt_message();

        mark = tt_mark();

        if (tt_pointer_error(procid) != TT_OK) {
                return 0;
        }
        if (tt_ptype_declare("Sun_EditDemo") != TT_OK) {
                fprintf(stderr,"Sun_EditDemo is not an installed ptype.\n");
                return 0;
        }
        ttfd = tt_fd();
        notify_set_input_func(edit_ui_base_window,
                              (Notify_func)edit_receive_tt_message,
                              ttfd);

}

        tt_session_join(tt_default_session());

        /*
         * Note that without tt_mark() and tt_release(), the above
         * combination would leak storage -- tt_default_session() returns
         * a copy owned by the application, but since we don't assign the
         * pointer to a variable we cannot not free it explicitly.
         */

        tt_release(mark);
        return 1;
}
```

1.3.3
Dynamic Message Patterns

To create and register a pattern, allocate a new pattern object, fill in the proper information, and register it. When you are done with the pattern (when you are no longer interested in messages that match it), either unregister or destroy the pattern.

Note – The code samples that illustrate the calls used to perform the operations are mostly fragments from the sample program, ttsample1. This sample program lives in this directory:
$OPENWINHOME/share/src/tooltalk/

The ToolTalk functions used to create, register, and unregister dynamic message patterns are listed in Table 1.3.2

Table 1.3.2. Creating, updating, and deleting message patterns.

Return Type	ToolTalk Function
Tt_pattern	tt_pattern_create(void)
Tt_status	tt_pattern_arg_add(Tt_pattern p, Tt_mode n, const char *vtype, const char *value)
Tt_status	tt_pattern_barg_add(Tt_pattern m, Tt_mode n, const char *vtype, const unsigned char *value, int len)
Tt_status	tt_pattern_iarg_add(Tt_pattern m, Tt_mode n, const char *vtype, int value)
Tt_status	tt_pattern_address_add(Tt_pattern p, Tt_address d)
Tt_status	tt_pattern_callback_add(Tt_pattern m, Tt_message_callback f)
Tt_status	tt_pattern_category_set(Tt_pattern p, Tt_category c)
Tt_status	tt_pattern_class_add(Tt_pattern p, Tt_class c)
Tt_status	tt_pattern_disposition_add(Tt_pattern p, Tt_disposition r)
Tt_status	tt_pattern_file_add(Tt_pattern p, const char *file)
Tt_status	tt_pattern_object_add(Tt_pattern p, const char *objid)
Tt_status	tt_pattern_op_add(Tt_pattern p, const char *opname)
Tt_status	tt_pattern_opnum_add(Tt_pattern p, int opnum)
Tt_status	tt_pattern_otype_add(Tt_pattern p, const char *otype)

Return Type	ToolTalk Function
Tt_status	tt_pattern_scope_add(Tt_pattern p, Tt_scope s)
Tt_status	tt_pattern_sender_add(Tt_pattern p, const char *procid)
Tt_status	tt_pattern_sender_ptype_add(Tt_pattern p, const char *ptid)
Tt_status	tt_pattern_session_add(Tt_pattern p, const char *sessid)
Tt_status	tt_pattern_state_add(Tt_pattern p, Tt_state s)
Tt_status	tt_pattern_user_set(Tt_pattern p, int key, void *v)
Tt_status	tt_pattern_register(Tt_pattern p)
Tt_status	tt_pattern_unregister(Tt_pattern p)
Tt_status	tt_pattern_destroy(Tt_pattern p)

Creating a Message Pattern

To get a "handle" or "opaque pointer" to a new pattern object, use `tt_pattern_create()`. Use this handle on succeeding calls to reference the pattern.

To fill in pattern information, use the `tt_pattern_<attribute>_add()` and `tt_pattern_<attribute>_set()` calls. See Table 1.3.1 for a complete list of pattern attributes.

Note – You can supply multiple values for each attribute you *add* to a pattern (some attributes are *set* and only have one value). The pattern attribute matches a message attribute if any of the values in the pattern match the value in the message. If no value is specified for an attribute, the ToolTalk service assumes that you want any value to match.

The following pattern attributes must always be supplied:

- Category
  Use `TT_OBSERVE` if you just want to look at messages.
  Use `TT_HANDLE` if you want to handle the message.

- Scope
  Use `TT_SESSION` to receive messages from other processes in your session. Use `TT_FILE` to receive messages about the file you've joined. Use `TT_FILE_IN_SESSION` to receive messages for the file you've joined while in this session.

Adding a Message Pattern Callback

You can add callbacks to message patterns so when the ToolTalk service matches a message, it automatically calls your callback routine to examine the message and take appropriate actions. Use `tt_pattern_callback_add()` to add a callback routine to your pattern.

When a message that matches a pattern with a callback is delivered to you, it is processed via the callback routine and when the routine is finished, it should return `TT_CALL-BACK_PROCESSED`. Be sure to destroy the message when you return `TT_CALLBACK_PROCESSED` to free the storage used by the message. Use `tt_message_destroy()` to destroy the message.

Here's a code fragment to illustrate this requirement:

```
Tt_callback action
sample_msg_callback(Tt_message m, Tt_pattern p)
{
    ... process the msg ...

    tt_message_destroy(m);
    return TT_CALLBACK_PROCESSED;
}
```

Registering a Message Pattern

When the pattern is complete, register it with `tt_pattern_register()`, and join the sessions or files you specified.

Here's how `ttsample1` creates and registers a pattern:

```
/*
 * Create and register a pattern so ToolTalk knows we are interested
 * in "ttsample1_value" messages within the session we join.
 */

pat = tt_pattern_create();
tt_pattern_category_set(pat, TT_OBSERVE);
tt_pattern_scope_add(pat, TT_SESSION);
tt_pattern_op_add(pat, "ttsample1_value");
tt_pattern_register(pat);
```

Deleting Message Patterns

To stop receiving messages that match a message pattern, use `tt_pattern_unregister()` to unregister the pattern or `tt_pattern_destroy()` to unregister and then destroy the pattern object.

> **Note** – If delivered messages that matched the pattern just removed have not been retrieved by your application (for example, the messages might be queued), the ToolTalk service does not destroy these messages.

The ToolTalk service will automatically unregister and destroy all message pattern objects when `tt_close()` is called.

1.3.4 Updating Message Patterns with the Current Session or File

To update your message patterns with the session and/or file you are currently interested in, join the session and/or file.

Join the Default Session

If you have declared a ptype or registered a message pattern that specifies `TT_SESSION` or `TT_FILE_IN_SESSION`, you will want to join the default session using `tt_session_-join()` so the ToolTalk service can update your message pattern with the default sessid. When your patterns are updated, you will begin to receive messages scoped to the session you joined.

> **Note** – If you had previously joined a session and then registered a ptype or a new message pattern, you must join the same session or a new session before you will receive messages that match your new patterns.

Use the ToolTalk functions listed in Table 1.3.3 to join the session in which you are interested.

Table 1.3.3. Joining sessions.

Return Type	ToolTalk Function
char *	tt_default_session(void)
Tt_status	tt_default_session_set(const char *sessid)
char *	tt_initial_session(void)

Return Type	ToolTalk Function
Tt_status	tt_session_join(const char *sessid)
Tt_status	tt_session_quit(const char *sessid)

Here's how `ttsample1` joins the default session.

```
/*
 * Join the default session
 */

tt_session_join(tt_default_session());
```

When you no longer want to receive messages that refer to the default session, inform the ToolTalk service with `tt_-session_quit()`. The sessid will be removed from your session-scoped message patterns.

Join Files Of Interest

If you have declared a ptype or registered a message pattern that specifies `TT_FILE` or `TT_FILE_IN_SESSION`, you will want to join files you are interested in by calling `tt_file_-join()`. Joining a file automatically adds the name of the file to all of your file-scoped message patterns. Use the ToolTalk functions listed in Table 1.3.4 to express your interest in specific files.

When you are no longer interested in receiving messages that refer to the file, call `tt_file_quit()`. The file name will be removed from your file-scoped message patterns.

Table 1.3.4. Joining files.

Return Type	ToolTalk Function
char *	tt_default_file(void)
Tt_status	tt_default_file_set(const char *docid)
Tt_status	tt_file_join(const char *filepath)
Tt_status	tt_file_quit(const char *filepath)

1.4
Sending
Messages

This section provides the ToolTalk message attributes, explains how messages are routed, and describes how to create messages, fill in message contents, attach callbacks to requests, and send messages.

To send ToolTalk messages, modify your application to support these operations:

- Creating and Filling In Messages
- Attaching Message Callback to Requests
- Sending Messages

1.4.1
ToolTalk
Messages
Message Attributes

ToolTalk messages contain attributes that store message information and provide delivery information to the ToolTalk service. ToolTalk uses this delivery information to route the messages to the appropriate receivers.

ToolTalk messages are simple structures containing attributes for address, subject (*operation* and *arguments*), and delivery information (*class and scope*.) Each message contains attributes from Table 1.4.1.

Addressing

Messages addressed to other applications can be addressed to a particular process (*process* address) or any process that has registered a pattern that matches your message (*procedure* address). When addressing a message to a process, you need to know the process identifier (procid) of the other application. Applications receive a procid when they open communication with ToolTalk. The procid is unique within the user's session in which the application was started.

Table 1.4.1. ToolTalk message attributes.

Message Attribute	Value	Description	Who Can Fill In
arguments	arguments or results	Arguments used in the operation. If the message is a reply, this field contains the results of the operation.	sender, replier
class	TT_NOTICE, TT_REQUEST	Specifies whether the recipient needs to perform an operation.	sender
file	char *pathname	The file involved in the operation.	sender, ToolTalk
object	char *objid	The object involved in this operation.	sender, ToolTalk
operation	char *opname	Name of operation to be performed.	sender
otype	char *otype	The type of object involved in this operation.	sender, ToolTalk
address	TT_PROCEDURE, TT_OBJECT, TT_HANDLER, TT_OTYPE	Where the message should be sent.	sender
handler	char *procid	The receiving process.	sender, ToolTalk
handler_ptype	char *ptype	The type of receiving process.	sender, ToolTalk
disposition	TT_DISCARD, TT_QUEUE, TT_START	Specifies what to do if the message can't be received by any running process.	sender, ToolTalk
scope	TT_SESSION, TT_FILE, TT_BOTH, TT_FILE_IN_SESSION	Who will be considered as possible recipients based on their registered interest in a session and/or a file.	sender, ToolTalk
sender_ptype	char *ptype	The type of the sending process.	sender, ToolTalk
session	char *sessid	The sending process's session.	sender, ToolTalk

Message Attribute	Value	Description	Who Can Fill In
status	int status, char *status_str	Additional information about the state of the message.	replier, ToolTalk

However, it is unusual for one process to know another's procid; more often a sender doesn't care which process performs an operation (request message) or learns of an event (notice message).

Notices and Requests

Applications can send two classes of ToolTalk messages, *notices* and *requests*. A notice is informational, a way for an application to announce an event. Applications that receive a notice absorb the message without returning results to the sender. A request is a call for an action, with the results of the action recorded in the message, and the message returned to the sender as a reply.

Scope

Applications using the ToolTalk service to communicate usually have something in common – the applications are running in the same session or they're interested in the same file or data. Applications register this interest by joining sessions or files (or both) with the ToolTalk service. This file and session information is used by the ToolTalk service in conjunction with the message patterns to determine which applications should receive a message.

File Scope. When a message is "scoped" to a file, only those applications that have joined the file (and match the remaining attributes) will receive the message. Applications that share interest in a file do not have to be running in the same session.

Session Scope. When a message is scoped to a session, only those applications that have joined the session will be considered as potential recipients.

File In Session Scope. Applications can be very specific about the distribution of a message by specifying file-in-session for the message scope. Only those applications that have joined both the file and the session indicated will be considered as potential recipients.

How the ToolTalk Service Routes Messages

A notice takes a one-way trip, as shown in Figure 1.4.1. The sender creates a message, fills in attribute values, and sends it. The ToolTalk service matches message and pattern attribute values, and gives a copy of the message to one handler and to all matching observers. File-scoped messages are automatically transferred across session boundaries to processes that have declared interest in the file.

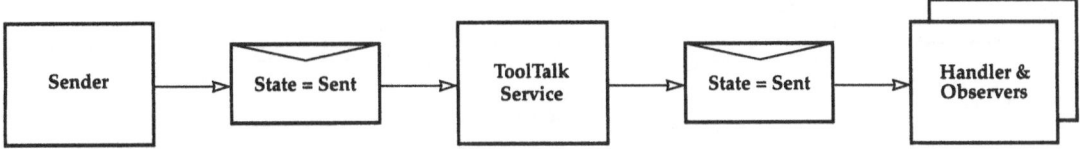

Figure 1.4.1. Notice routing.

A request, as shown in Figure 1.4.2, takes a round-trip from sender to handler and back; copies of the message take one-way side trips to observers. The ToolTalk service delivers a request to, at most, one handler. The handler adds results to the message and sends it back. Other processes can observe a request before it is handled, after, or both; observers absorb a request without sending it back.

1.4.2. ToolTalk Message Delivery Algorithm
Process-Oriented Message Delivery

To help you further understand how the ToolTalk service determines message recipients, this section walks through the creation and delivery of both process-oriented messages and object-oriented messages.

For many process-oriented messages, the sender knows the ptype or the procid of the process that should handle it. For other messages, the ToolTalk service can determine the handler from the operation and arguments of the message.

1. Initialize
   The sender obtains a message handle and fills in the address, scope, and class attributes.

   If the address is TT_PROCEDURE, the sender fills in the operation and arguments.
   If the sender has declared only one ptype, the ToolTalk service will fill sender_ptype in by default. Otherwise the sender must fill it in.
   If the scope is TT_FILE, file must be filled in or defaulted. If the scope is TT_SESSION, session must be filled in or de

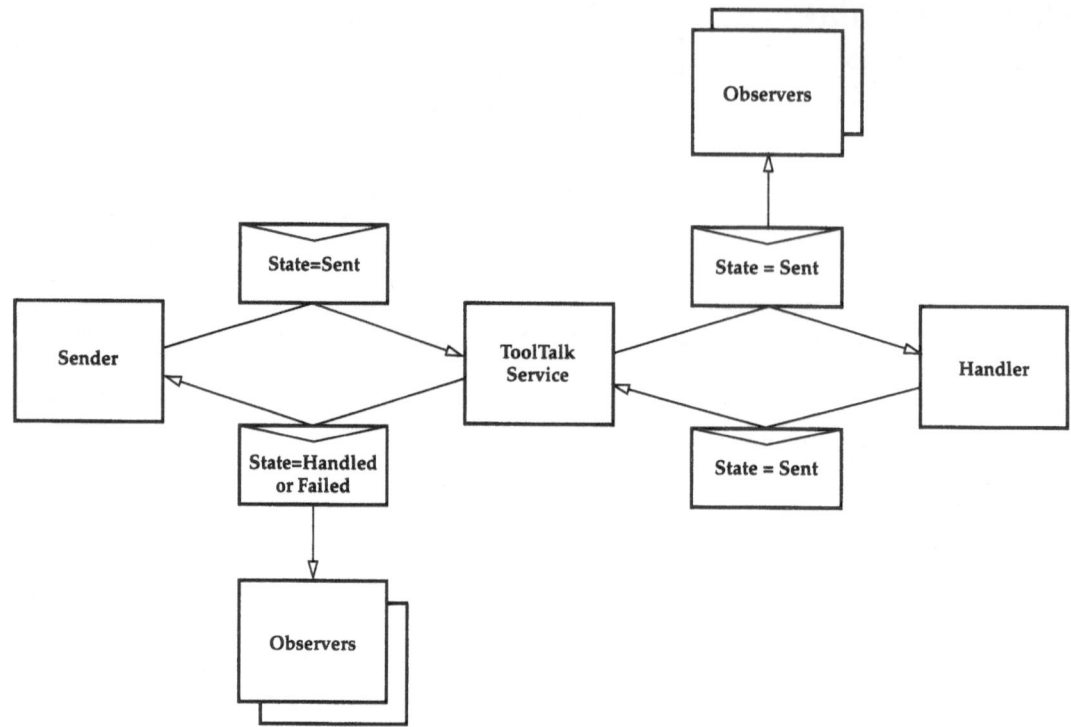

Figure 1.4.2. Request routing.

faulted. If the scope is TT_BOTH, both must be filled in or defaulted.

To speed up dispatch, the sender may fill in the handler_p-type if known. While this may speed operations somewhat, it reduces flexibility by not allowing processes of one ptype to substitute for another. Also, the disposition attribute must be specified by the sender in this case.

2. Dispatch to Handler
   The ToolTalk service compares the address, scope, message class, operation, and argument modes and types to all signatures in the Handle section of each ptype.

   Only one ptype will usually contain a message pattern that matches the operation and arguments and specifies Handle. If a handler ptype is found, then the ToolTalk service fills in opnum, handler_ptype, and disposition from the ptype message pattern.

   If the address is TT_HANDLER, the ToolTalk service looks for the specified procid and adds the message to the handler's message queue. TT_HANDLER messages cannot be observed because no pattern matching is done.

3. Dispatch to Observers
   The ToolTalk service compares the scope, class, operation, and argument types to all message patterns in the Observe section of each ptype.

   For all message patterns that match the message and specify TT_QUEUE or TT_START, the ToolTalk service attaches an "observe promise" record to the message that specifies the ptype and the queue/start options. The ToolTalk service then adds the ptype to its internal ObserverPtypeList.

4. Deliver to Handler
   If a running process has a handler message pattern registered that matches the message, the ToolTalk service delivers the message to it. Otherwise, the ToolTalk service honors the disposition (start or queue) options.

   If more than one process has registered a dynamic pattern that matches the handler information, the more specific pattern is given preference (by counting the number of non-wildcard matches). If two patterns are equally specific, the choice of handler is arbitrary.

5. Deliver to Observers
   The ToolTalk service delivers the message to all running processes that have Observer patterns registered which match the message. As each delivery is made, the ToolTalk service checks off any "observe promise" for the ptype of the observer. After this process, if there are any "observe promises" left unfulfilled, the ToolTalk service honors the start and queue options in the promises.

   The set of patterns matched against for delivery depends on the scope of the message. If the scope is TT_SESSION, only patterns for processes in the same session are checked. If the scope is TT_FILE, patterns for all processes observing the file are checked. If the scope is TT_BOTH, both sets of processes are checked.

Example

In this example, a debugger and a editor interact via ToolTalk messages so the debugger can use the editor to display the source around a breakpoint.

The editor has the following Handle pattern in its ptype:

```
(HandlerPtype: TextEditor;
 Op: ShowLine;
 Scope: TT_SESSION;
 Session: my_session_id;
 File: /home/gondor/joe/src/ebe.c)
```

When the debugger reaches a breakpoint, it sends a message with op (ShowLine), argument (the line number), file (the file name), session (the current session id), and scope (TT_SESSION).

The ToolTalk service matches this message against all registered patterns, finds the pattern registered by the editor, and delivers the message to the editor. The editor then scrolls to the line indicated in the argument.

Object-Oriented Messages Delivery

Many messages handled by the ToolTalk service are directed at objects but are actually delivered to the process that manages the object. The message signatures in an otype, which include the ptype of the process that can handle each specific message, help the ToolTalk service determine to which process to deliver an object-oriented message. Here are the steps in the creation and delivery of an object-oriented message.

1. Initialize
   The sender fills in the class, operation, arguments, and the target objid attributes.

   The sender attribute is automatically filled in by the ToolTalk service. The sender can either fill in the sender_ptype and session attributes or allow the ToolTalk service to fill in the default values for these.

2. Resolve
   The ToolTalk service looks up the objid in the ToolTalk database and fills in the otype and file attributes.

3. Dispatch to Handler
   The ToolTalk service searches through the otype definitions looking for Handler message patterns matching the message's operation and arguments.

   When a match is found, the ToolTalk service fills in scope, opnum, handler_ptype, and disposition from the otype message pattern.

4. Dispatch to Object-Oriented Observers
   The ToolTalk service compares the message's class, operation, and argument attributes against all Ob-

serve message patterns of the otype. When a match is found, if the message pattern specifies TT_QUEUE or TT_START, the ToolTalk service attaches an "observe promise" record to the message that specifies the ptype and the queue and start options.

5. Dispatch to Procedural Observers
The ToolTalk service continues to match the message's class, operation, and argument attributes against all Observe message patterns of all ptypes as in "". When a match is found, if the signature specifies TT_QUEUE or TT_START, the ToolTalk service attaches an "observe promise" record to the message, specifying the ptype and the queue/start options.

6. Deliver to Handler
If a running process has a Handler pattern registered which matches the message, the ToolTalk service delivers the message to it. Otherwise, the ToolTalk service honors the disposition (queue/start) options.

If more than one process has registered a dynamic pattern that matches the handler information, the more specific pattern is given preference (by counting the number of non-wildcard matches). If two patterns are equally specific, the choice of handler is arbitrary.

7. Deliver to Observers
The ToolTalk service delivers the message to all running processes that have Observer patterns registered which match the message. As each delivery is made, the ToolTalk service checks off any "observe promises" for the ptype of the observer. After this process, if there are any "observe promises" left unfulfilled, the ToolTalk service honors the disposition (queue/start) options in the promises.

The set of patterns matched against for delivery depends on the scope of the message. If the scope is TT_SESSION, only patterns for processes in the same session are checked. If the scope is TT_FILE, patterns for all processes observing the file are checked. If the scope is TT_BOTH, both sets of processes are checked.

Otype addressing

There are times when it is necessary to send an object-oriented message without knowing the objid. To handle these cases, the ToolTalk service provides otype addressing. This addressing mode requires the sender to specify the operation, arguments, scope, and otype. The ToolTalk service looks in the specified otype definition for a message pattern matching the message's operation and arguments to locate the handling and observing process. The dispatch and delivery then proceed as in messages to specific objects.

Example

In this example, a spreadsheet application, "FinnogaCalc", is integrated with the ToolTalk service. When it starts, it registers with the ToolTalk service by declaring its ptype, FinnogaCalc. and joining its default session. When it loads a worksheet, hatsize.wks, FinnogaCalc also tells the ToolTalk service it is observing the worksheet by joining the worksheet file. A second instance of FinnogaCalc (called FinnogaCalc$_2$) starts, loads a worksheet, wardrobe.wks, and registers with the ToolTalk service in the same way. The user tells FinnogaCalc and FinnogaCalc$_2$ that the value of cell B2 in hatsize.wks should appear in cell C14 of wardrobe.wks.

In order for FinnogaCalc to be able to send values to cell C14, FinnogaCalc$_2$ creates an object spec for the cell by calling a ToolTalk function. This object is identified by an objid. FinnogaCalc$_2$ then gives this objid to FinnogaCalc, perhaps by passing it via the clipboard. FinnogaCalc then remembers that its cell B2 gets its data from the object identified by this objid. When FinnogaCalc changes the value of cell B2, it sends a message to the object identified by this objid. The message contains an operation that FinnogaCalc$_2$ will recognize as meaning "here are new contents for a cell" and an argument containing the new data.

To deliver the message, the ToolTalk service:

1. Examines the spec associated with the objid and finds that the type of the objid is FinnogaCalc_cell and that the corresponding object is in the file wardrobe.wks

2. Consults the otype definition for Finnoga-Calc_cell. From the otype, the ToolTalk service determines that this message is observed by processes of ptype FinnogaCalc and that the scope of the message should be TT_FILE.

3. Matches the message against registered patterns and locates all processes of this ptype that are observing

the proper file. FinnogaCalc$_2$ matches, but Finnoga-Calc doesn't as it is looking at the wrong file.

4. Delivers the message to FinnogaCalc$_2$.

FinnogaCalc$_2$ can then update the value in `wardrobe.wks` and display the new value.

1.4.3 Creating and Filling in Messages

The ToolTalk functions used to create and fill in messages are listed in Table 1.4.2.

he ToolTalk service provides two methods of creating messages: these process- and object-oriented notice and request functions

- tt_pnotice_create()
- tt_prequest_create()

- tt_onotice_create()
- tt_orequest_create()

and the general-purpose function, `tt_message_create()`.

Table 1.4.2. Creating and filling in messages.

Return Type	ToolTalk Function
Tt_message	tt_onotice_create(const char *objid, const char *op)
Tt_message	tt_orequest_create(const char *objid, const char *op)
Tt_message	tt_pnotice_create(Tt_scope scope, const char *op)
Tt_message	tt_prequest_create(Tt_scope scope, const char *op)
Tt_message	tt_message_create(void)
Tt_status	tt_message_address_set(Tt_message m, Tt_address p)
Tt_status	tt_message_arg_add(Tt_message m, Tt_mode n, const char *vtype, const char *value)
Tt_status	tt_message_arg_bval_set(Tt_message m, int n, const unsigned char *value, int len)
Tt_status	tt_message_arg_ival_set(Tt_message m, int n, int value)
Tt_status	tt_message_arg_val_set(Tt_message m, int n, const char *value)

Return Type	ToolTalk Function
Tt_status	tt_message_barg_add(Tt_message m, Tt_mode n, const char *vtype, const unsigned char *value, int len)
Tt_status	tt_message_iarg_add(Tt_message m, Tt_mode n, const char *vtype, int value)
Tt_status	tt_message_class_set(Tt_message m, Tt_class c)
Tt_status	tt_message_file_set(Tt_message m, const char *file)
Tt_status	tt_message_handler_ptype_set(Tt_message m, const char *ptid)
Tt_status	tt_message_handler_set(Tt_message m, const char *procid)
Tt_status	tt_message_object_set(Tt_message m, const char *objid)
Tt_status	tt_message_op_set(Tt_message m, const char *opname)
Tt_status	tt_message_otype_set(Tt_message m, const char *otype)
Tt_status	tt_message_scope_set(Tt_message m, Tt_scope s)
Tt_status	tt_message_sender_ptype_set(Tt_message m, const char *ptid)
Tt_status	tt_message_session_set(Tt_message m, const char *sessid)
Tt_status	tt_message_status_set(Tt_message m, int status)
Tt_status	tt_message_status_string_set(Tt_message m, const char *status_str)
Tt_status	tt_message_user_set(Tt_message m, int key, void *v)

The ToolTalk service provides the process- and object-oriented notice and request functions to make message creation simpler for the common cases. They are functionally identical to strings of other `tt_message_create()` and `tt_message_<attribute>_set()` calls, but are easier to write and read.

Note – The code samples that illustrate the calls used to perform the operations in this section are mostly fragments from the sample programs, `ttsample1` and `Sun_Edit-Demo`. These sample programs can be found in this directory: `$OPENWINHOME/share/src/tooltalk/`

Creating and Filling In Procedural Messages

The ToolTalk service provides two methods for creating procedural messages: `tt_pnotice_create()` or `tt_prequest_create()`; and, `tt_message_create()`.

Using pnotice and prequest Functions

To get a "handle" or "opaque pointer" to a new message object for a procedural notice or request, use `tt_pnotice_create()` or `tt_prequest_create()`. Use this handle on succeeding calls to refer to the message.

When you use `tt_pnotice_create()` or `tt_prequest_create()`, you supply the following two attributes as arguments:

- scope

    Fill in the scope of the message delivery. Potential recipients could be joined to:

    ° TT_SESSION

    ° TT_FILE

    ° TT_BOTH

    ° TT_FILE_IN_SESSION

    Depending on the scope, the ToolTalk service will fill in the default session and/or file.

- op

    Fill in the operation that describes the notice or request you are making. To determine the operation name, consult the ptype definition for the target process or other protocol definition.

You can fill in more message attributes, such as operation arguments, with `tt_message_<attribute>_set` calls.

Here's sample code for creating a pnotice from `ttsample1`..

```
/*
 * Create and send a ToolTalk notice message
 * ttsample1_value(in int <new value)
 */

msg_out = tt_pnotice_create(TT_SESSION, "ttsample1_value");
tt_message_arg_add(msg_out, TT_IN, "integer", NULL);
tt_message_arg_ival_set(msg_out, 0, (int)xv_get(slider,
PANEL_VALUE));
tt_message_send(msg_out);
```

```
    /*
     * Since this message is a notice, we don't expect a reply, so
     * there's no reason to keep a handle for the message.
     */

    tt_message_destroy(msg_out);
```

Using tt_message_create

For a procedural message created with `tt_message_create()`, set these attributes using the `tt_message_<attribute>_set()` calls:

- class
  Use `TT_REQUEST` for messages that return values or status. You will be informed when the message is handled or queued, or when a process is started to handle the request.

  Use `TT_NOTICE` for messages that just notify other processes of events.

- address
  Use `TT_PROCEDURE` to send the message to any process that can perform this operation with these arguments. Fill in op and args attributes of this message.

  Use `TT_HANDLER` to send this to a particular process. Specify the handler attribute value.

  If you know the exact procid of the handler, you can address messages to it directly and the ToolTalk service will deliver the message directly – no pattern matching is done and no other applications can observe the message. The usual way this happens is for one process to make a general request and then pick the handler attribute out of the reply, directing further messages to the same handler. This allows two processes to rendezvous through broadcast message passing and then go into a dialogue.

- scope
  Fill in the scope of the message delivery. Potential recipients could be joined to:
  - TT_SESSION
  - TT_FILE
  - TT_BOTH
  - TT_FILE_IN_SESSION

Chapter 1. ToolTalk® Overview

Depending on the scope, the ToolTalk service will fill in the default session and/or file.

- op
  Fill in the operation that describes the notification or request you're making. To determine the operation name, consult the ptype definition for the target process or other protocol definition.

- args
  Fill in any arguments specific to the operation. Use `tt_message_arg_add()` to add each argument in turn. For each argument, specify:

  ° Tt_mode
  Specify `TT_IN`, `TT_OUT`, or `TT_INOUT`. If Tt_mode is `TT_IN` or `TT_INOUT`, specify the value.

  ° value type (vtype)

Creating and Filling In Object-Oriented Messages

The ToolTalk service provides two methods to create object-oriented messages: `tt_onotice_create()` or `tt_orequest_create()`; and `tt_message_create()`. The ToolTalk service provides the onotice (object-oriented notice) and orequest (object-oriented request) functions to make message creation simpler for the common cases. They are functionally identical to strings of other `tt_message_create()` and `tt_message_<attribute>_set()` calls, but are easier to write and read.

Using onotice and orequest Functions

To get a "handle" or "opaque pointer" to a new message object for a object-oriented notice or request, use `tt_onotice_create()` or `tt_orequest_create()`. Use this handle on succeeding calls to refer to the message.

When you use `tt_onotice_create()` or `tt_orequest_create()`, you supply the following two attributes as arguments:

- objid
  Fill in the unique object identifier.

- op
  Fill in the operation that describes the notice or request you are making. To determine the operation name, consult the ptype definition for the target process or other protocol definition.

You can fill in more message attributes, such as operation arguments, with `tt_message_<attribute>_set` calls.

Here's how `Sun_EditDemo` creates and sends an ore-quest during its notify callback function for `cntl_ui_hil-ite_button`.

```
/*
 * Notify callback function for 'cntl_ui_hilite_button'.
 */
void
cntl_ui_hilite_button_handler(item, event)
        Panel_item     item;
        Event          *event;
{

        Tt_message     msg;

        if (cntl_objid == (char *)0) {
                xv_set(cntl_ui_base_window, FRAME_LEFT_FOOTER,
                  "No object id selected", NULL);
                return;
        }
        msg = tt_orequest_create(cntl_objid, "hilite_obj");
        tt_message_arg_add(msg, TT_IN, "string", cntl_objid);
        tt_message_callback_add(msg, cntl_msg_callback);
        tt_message_send(msg);
}
```

Using tt_message_create

For an object-oriented message created with `tt_mes-sage_create()`, set these attributes using the `tt_mes-sage_<attribute>_set()` calls:

- class
  Use `TT_REQUEST` for messages that return values or status. You will be informed when the message is handled or queued, or when a process is started to handle the request.

  Use `TT_NOTICE` for messages that just notify other processes ofevents.

- address
  Use `TT_OBJECT` to send the message to a specific object that performs this operation with these arguments. Fill in object, op, and args attributes of this message.

  Use `TT_OTYPE` to send this message to this type of object that can perform this operation with these arguments. Fill in otype, op, and args attributes of the message.

- op

  Fill in the operation that describes the notification or request you're making. To determine the operation name, consult the ptype definition for the target process or other protocol definition.

- args

  Fill in any arguments specific to the operation. Use `tt_message_arg_add` to add each argument in turn. For each argument, specify:

  ◦ Tt_mode

  Specify `TT_IN`, `TT_OUT`, or `TT_INOUT`. If `Tt_-mode` is `TT_IN` or `TT_INOUT`, specify the value.

  ◦ value type (vtype)

1.4.4 Adding Message Callbacks

You can add callbacks to requests so when the reply is received, the callback routine is automatically called to examine the results of the reply and take appropriate actions. Use `tt_message_callback_add()` to add the callback routine to your request.

When the reply comes back and the message has been processed via the callback routine, be sure to destroy the message after the callback function returns `TT_CALLBACK_PROCESSED`. Use `tt_message_destroy()` to destroy the message.

Here's a code fragment to illustrate this requirement:

```
Tt_callback action
sample_msg_callback(Tt_message m, Tt_pattern p)
{
    ... process the msg ...

    tt_message_destroy(m);
    return TT_CALLBACK_PROCESSED;
}
```

In `Sun_EditDemo`'s `cntl_ui_hilite_button` function shown in "The ToolTalk service provides two methods to create object-oriented messages: tt_onotice_create() or tt_orequest_create(); and tt_message_create(). The ToolTalk service provides the onotice (object-oriented notice) and orequest (object-oriented request) functions to make message creation simpler for the common cases. They are functionally identical to strings of other tt_message_create() and tt_message_<attribute>_set() calls, but are easier to write and read."

on page 59, a callback is added to the request to highlight an object in the edit window. This callback, `cntl_msg_call-back`, examines the state field of the reply and takes action if the state is started, handled, or failed.

Here's the `cntl_msg_callback`:

```
 * Default callback for all the ToolTalk messages we send.
 */
Tt_callback_action
cntl_msg_callback(m, p)
     Tt_message m;
     Tt_pattern p;
{
     int        mark;
     char       msg[255];
     char       *errstr;
     mark = tt_mark();
     switch (tt_message_state(m)) {
          case TT_STARTED:
               xv_set(cntl_ui_base_window, FRAME_LEFT_FOOTER,
                   "Starting editor...", NULL);
               break;
          case TT_HANDLED:
               xv_set(cntl_ui_base_window, FRAME_LEFT_FOOTER, "", NULL);
               break;

          case TT_FAILED:
               errstr = tt_message_status_string(m);
               if (tt_pointer_error(errstr) == TT_OK && errstr) {
                   sprintf(msg,"%s failed: %s", tt_message_op(m), errstr);
               } else if (tt_message_status(m) == TT_ERR_NO_MATCH) {
                   sprintf(msg,"%s failed: Couldn't contact editor",
                           tt_message_op(m),
                           tt_status_message(tt_message_status(m)));
               } else {
                   sprintf(msg,"%s failed: %s",
                           tt_message_op(m),
                           tt_status_message(tt_message_status(m)));
               }
               xv_set(cntl_ui_base_window, FRAME_LEFT_FOOTER, msg, NULL);
               break;
          default:
               break;
     }
```

```
      /*
       * no further action required for this message. Destroy it
       * and return TT_CALLBACK_PROCESSED so no other callbacks will
       * be run for the message.
       */
      tt_message_destroy(m);
      tt_release(mark);
      return TT_CALLBACK_PROCESSED;
}
```

1.4.5
Sending a Message

Send the message with tt_message_send().

If the ToolTalk service returns TT_WRN_STALE_OBJID, the ToolTalk service has found a forwarding pointer in the ToolTalk database indicating that the object mentioned in the message has been moved. The ToolTalk service will go ahead and send the message with the fresh objid. Use tt_message_object() to retrieve the fresh objid from the message and put the new objid into your internal data structure.

If you will not need the message in the future (perhaps if the message was a notice), free up the storage space by deleting the message with tt_message_destroy(). If you're expecting a reply and want to compare it against your request, do not destroy the message until you've handled the reply.

1.5
Receiving
Messages

This section describes how to retrieve messages delivered to your application and how to handle the message once you've examined it. It also shows how to send replies to requests that you receive. As mentioned earlier, when you're through with a message, destroy the message to free up storage.

To retrieve a message from the ToolTalk service and handle it, modify your application to support these operations.

- Retrieving Messages
- Handling Messages
- Replying to Messages
- Destroying Messages

Note – The code samples that illustrate the calls used to perform the operations are mostly fragments from the sample programs, `ttsample1` and `Sun_EditDemo`. These sample programs are in this directory: `$OPENWINHOME/share/src/tooltalk/`

1.5.1
Retrieving
Messages

When a message arrives for your process, the ToolTalk-supplied file descriptor becomes active. When notified of the active state of the file descriptor, call `tt_message_receive()` to get a handle for the incoming message.

Note – Handles for messages remain constant. For example, when a process sends a message, both the message and any replies to the message have the same handle.

To easily identify and process messages you receive, you can:

- Add a callback to a dynamic pattern with `tt_pattern_callback_add()`. When you retrieve the message, the ToolTalk service will invoke any message or pattern callbacks. See Section 3, "Message Patterns," for more information on placing callbacks on patterns.
- Retrieve the message's opnum if you are receiving messages that match your ptype message patterns.

You can recognize and handle replies to messages you sent by:

- Placing specific callbacks on requests before you send them with `tt_message_callback_add()`. See Section 4, "Sending Messages," for more information on placing callbacks on messages.
- Comparing the handle of the message you sent with the message you just received. The handles will be the same if the message is a reply.
- Placing information meaningful to your application in a request with the `tt_message_user_set()` call.

Here's a code from `ttsample1` for receiving a message

How The ToolTalk Service Invokes Callbacks

The following flow diagram, Figure 5.1, illustrates how the ToolTalk service invokes message and pattern callbacks when `tt_message_receive()` is called to retrieve a new message.

1.5.2 Handling Messages

When handling a message, you examine the message and take appropriate action. To examine the attributes of a message you have received, use the ToolTalk functions listed in Table 1.5.1.

Before you start retrieving values, it's a good idea to obtain a mark on the ToolTalk API stack so you can release all at once the information the ToolTalk service returns to you. Here's how `ttsample1` allocates storage, examines a message's contents, and releases the storage.

```
/*
 * Get a storage mark so we can easily free all the data
 * ToolTalk returns to us.
 */

mark = tt_mark();

if (0==strcmp("ttsample1_value", tt_message_op(msg_in))) {
        tt_message_arg_ival(msg_in, 0, &val_in);
        xv_set(gauge, PANEL_VALUE, val_in, NULL);
}

tt_message_destroy(msg_in);
tt_release(mark);
return;
```

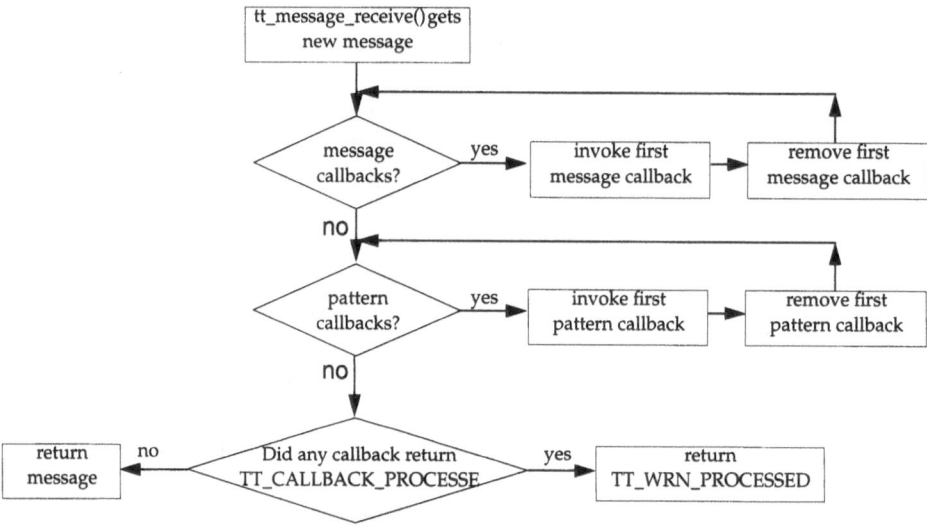

Figure 1.5.1. How callbacks are invoked.

Table 1.5.1. Examining message attributes.

Return Type	ToolTalk Function
Tt_address	tt_message_address(Tt_message m)
Tt_status	tt_message_arg_bval(Tt_message m, int n, unsigned char **value, int *len)
Tt_status	tt_message_arg_ival(Tt_message m, int n, int *value)
Tt_mode	tt_message_arg_mode(Tt_message m, int n)

Return Type	ToolTalk Function
char *	tt_message_arg_type(Tt_message m, int n)
char *	tt_message_arg_val(Tt_message m, int n)
int	tt_message_args_count(Tt_message m)
Tt_class	tt_message_class(Tt_message m)
Tt_disposition	tt_message_disposition(Tt_message m)
char *	tt_message_file(Tt_message m)
gid_t	tt_message_gid(Tt_message m)
char *	tt_message_handler(Tt_message m)
char *	tt_message_handler_ptype(Tt_message m)
char *	tt_message_object(Tt_message m)
char *	tt_message_op(Tt_message m)
int	tt_message_opnum(Tt_message m)
char *	tt_message_otype(Tt_message m)
Tt_pattern	tt_message_pattern(Tt_message m)
Tt_scope	tt_message_scope(Tt_message m)
char *	tt_message_sender(Tt_message m)
char *	tt_message_sender_ptype(Tt_message m)
char *	tt_message_session(Tt_message m)
Tt_state	tt_message_state(Tt_message m)
int	tt_message_status(Tt_message m)
char *	tt_message_status_string(Tt_message m)
uid_t	tt_message_uid(Tt_message m)
void *	tt_message_user(Tt_message m, int key)

Handling Requests

If you have received a request (Tt_class = TT_REQUEST), you must do one of the following:

- Reply to the request
- Reject or fail the request

Replying to Requests

When you receive a request, you need to do the following steps:

1. Perform the desired operation.

2. **Fill in any argument values with modes of** TT_OUT **or** TT_INOUT.

3. Send the reply to the message.

The ToolTalk functions used to reply to messages are listed in Table 1.5.2.

Table 1.5.2. Replying to requests.

Return Type	ToolTalk Function
Tt_mode	tt_message_arg_mode(Tt_message m, int n)
Tt_status	tt_message_arg_bval_set(Tt_message m, int n, const unsigned char *value, int len)
Tt_status	tt_message_arg_ival_set(Tt_message m, int n, int value)
Tt_status	tt_message_arg_val_set(Tt_message m, int n, const char *value)
Tt_status	tt_message_reply(Tt_message m)

Rejecting or Failing a Request

The ToolTalk functions used to reject or fail a request are listed in Table 1.5.3.

Rejecting a Request

If you have examined the request and your application is not currently able to handle the request but another application might be able to handle the request, use tt_message_reject() to reject the message. The ToolTalk service will then attempt to find another receiver to handle the request. If the ToolTalk service cannot find a handler that is currently running, it will examine the disposition attribute and either queue the message or attempt to start applications with ptypes that contain the appropriate message pattern.

Failing a Request

If you have examined the request and the requested operation cannot be performed by you or any other process of the same ptype as yours, use tt_message_fail() to inform the ToolTalk service that the operation could not be performed. The ToolTalk service will inform the sender that the request failed.

Table 1.5.3. Rejecting or failing requests.

Return Type	*ToolTalk Function*
Tt_status	tt_message_reject(Tt_message m)
Tt_status	tt_message_fail(Tt_message m)
Tt_status	tt_message_status_set(Tt_message m, int status)
Tt_status	tt_message_status_string_set(Tt_message m, const char *status_str)

To aid the sender in understanding why the request failed, use `tt_message_status_set()` and/or `tt_message_status_string_set()` before calling `tt_message_fail()`. The status code that you specify with `tt_message_status_set()` must be greater than 2047 (which = `TT_ERR_LAST`).

1.5.3 Destroying Messages

After you have processed a message (and perhaps sent a reply), free up the storage space by deleting the message with `tt_message_destroy()`.

1.6
Objects

This section tells you how to create ToolTalk specs for objects your application creates and manages. Before identifying the type of object you create, you need to define otypes and store them in the Classing Engine. See Chapter 1.3, "Message Patterns," for information on otypes.

The ToolTalk service uses spec and otype information when determining object-oriented message recipients.

Create and manage ToolTalk specs for your application objects by:

- Creating Object Specs
- Updating Object Specs
- Maintaining Object Specs
- Destroyiny Object Specs

Note – The code samples that illustrate the calls used to perform the operations are mostly fragments from the sample program, `Sun_EditDemo`. This sample program is in this directory:

`$OPENWINHOME/share/src/tooltalk/`

1.6.1
Creating Object Specs

In order for the ToolTalk service to be able to deliver messages to your objects, create a spec that identifies the object and its otype. When you create a spec, you get a string name, the objid, for the object.

You can put *properties* on the `spec`. One use of spec properties is to store the location of the objid in the spec properties. You can use this location to identify where the object is in your tool's internal data structures. While the simplest solution would probably be for you to store the objid in your own internal data, the ToolTalk service recognizes that this is not always possible. For example, for objects in plain ASCII text files, there's no place for you to store the objid.

Another use of spec properties is for the convenience of the end user. A user may want to associate properties with the object such as a comment or object name that they can view later. Your application or another ToolTalk-based tool could search for and display these properties for the user.

The ToolTalk functions used to create and write object specs are listed in Table 1.6.1.

Table 1.6.1. Creating objects.

Return Type	*ToolTalk Function*
char *	tt_spec_create(const char *filepath)
Tt_status	tt_spec_prop_set(const char *objid, const char *propname, const char *value)
Tt_status	tt_spec_prop_add(const char *objid, const char *propname, const char *value)
Tt_status	tt_spec_bprop_add(const char *objid, const char *propname, const unsigned char *value, int length)
Tt_status	tt_spec_bprop_set(const char *objid, const char *propname, const unsigned char *value, int length)
Tt_status	tt_spec_type_set(const char *objid, const char *otid)
Tt_status	tt_spec_write(const char *objid)

To create an object spec in memory and obtain an objid for the object, use `tt_spec_create()`. Use `tt_spec_type_set()` to assign an otype for the object spec. The type must be set before the spec is written for the first time, and cannot be changed thereafter.

To store properties in a `spec`, use `tt_spec_prop_set()`. You can add to the list of values associated with the property with `tt_spec_prop_add()`.

After setting the type and adding properties to a spec, make the object spec a permanent ToolTalk item and visible to other users with `tt_spec_write()`. When you call `tt_spec_write()`, the ToolTalk service writes the spec into the ToolTalk database.

When Sun_EditDemo creates an object for its user, it creates the object spec, sets the otype, writes the spec to the ToolTalk database, and wraps the user's selection with C-style comments. Here's how Sun_EditDemo does this:

```
/*
 * Make a ToolTalk spec out of the selected text in this textpane. Once
 * the spec is successfully created and written to a database, wrap the
 * text with C-style comments in order to delimit the object and send out
 * a notification that an object has been created in this file.
 */
Menu_item
edit_ui_make_object(item, event)
 Panel_item   item;
 Event        *event;
{
        int             mark = tt_mark();
        char            *objid;
        char            *file;
        char            *sel;
        Textsw_index    first, last;
        char            obj_start_text[100];
        char            obj_end_text[100];
        Tt_message      msg;

        if (! get_selection(edit_ui_xserver, edit_ui_textpane,
                        &sel, &first, &last)) {
            xv_set(edit_ui_base_window, FRAME_LEFT_FOOTER,
                    "First select some text", NULL);
             tt_release(mark);
            return item;
        }
        file = tt_default_file();

        if (file == (char *)0) {
            xv_set(edit_ui_base_window, FRAME_LEFT_FOOTER,
                    "Not editing any file", NULL);
             tt_release(mark);
            return item;
        }
```

```
        /* create a new spec */

        objid = tt_spec_create(tt_default_file());
        if (tt_pointer_error(objid) != TT_OK) {
                xv_set(edit_ui_base_window, FRAME_LEFT_FOOTER,
                        "Couldn't create object", NULL);
                tt_release(mark);
                return item;
        }

        /* set its otype */

        tt_spec_type_set(objid, "Sun_EditDemo_object");
        if (tt_spec_write(objid) != TT_OK) {
                xv_set(edit_ui_base_window, FRAME_LEFT_FOOTER,
                        "Couldn't write out object", NULL);
                tt_release(mark);
                return item;
        }

        /* wrap spec's contents (the selected text) with C-style */
        /* comments. */

        sprintf(obj_start_text," /* begin_object(%s) */", objid);
        sprintf(obj_end_text,"/* end_object(%s) */", objid);
        (void)wrap_selection(edit_ui_xserver, edit_ui_textpane,
                        obj_start_text, obj_end_text);

        /* now send out a notification that we've added a new object */

        msg =
tt_pnotice_create(TT_FILE_IN_SESSION,"Sun_EditDemo_new_object");
        tt_message_file_set(msg, file);
        tt_message_send(msg);

        tt_release(mark);
        return item;
}
```

Sun_EditDemo also sends out a procedure-addressed notice after it creates the new object to update other applications who observe messages with the Sun_EditDemo_new_object operation. If other applications are displaying a list of objects in a file managed by Sun_EditDemo, they update their list after receiving this notice.

1.6.2
Updating Object Specs

To update spec properties, use `tt_spec_prop_set()` and `tt_spec_prop_add()`, specifying the objid of the existing object spec. After you have updated the spec properties, call `tt_spec_write()` to write the changes into the ToolTalk database.

When you are updating an existing spec and the ToolTalk service returns `TT_WRN_STALE_OBJID` when you call `tt_spec_write()`, it has found a forwarding pointer to the object in the ToolTalk database indicating that the object has been moved. To obtain the fresh objid, create an object message with the old objid and send it. The ToolTalk service will return the same status code, `TT_WRN_STALE_OBJID`, but will update the message objid attribute with the fresh objid. Use `tt_message_object()` to retrieve the fresh objid from the message and put the new objid into your internal data structure.

1.6.3
Maintaining Object Specs

The ToolTalk service provides the functions listed in Table 1.6.2 to examine, query, compare, and move object specs. The ToolTalk service also provides ToolTalk-aware shell commands for copying, moving, and removing files that contain object data.

Examining Spec Information

You can examine the following spec information with the specified ToolTalk functions:

Table 1.6.2. Maintaining objects.

Return Type	ToolTalk Function
char *	tt_spec_file(const char *objid)
char *	tt_spec_type(const char *objid)
char *	tt_spec_prop(const char *objid, const char *propname, int i)
int	tt_spec_prop_count(const char *objid, const char *propname)
Tt_status	tt_spec_bprop(const char *objid, const char *propname, int i, unsigned char **value, int *length)
char *	tt_spec_propname(const char *objid, int n)
int	tt_spec_propnames_count(const char *objid)
char *	tt_objid_objkey(const char *objid)

Return Type	ToolTalk Function
Tt_status	tt_file_objects_query(const char *filepath, Tt_filter_function filter, void *context, void *accumulator)
int	tt_objid_equal(const char *objid1, const char *objid2)
char *	tt_spec_move(const char *objid, const char *newfilepath)

- Pathname of the file containing the object
  tt_spec_file()

- Otype of this object
  tt_spec_type()

- Properties stored on the spec
  tt_spec_prop()
  tt_spec_bprop()

Querying for Specs In A File

To query for existing specs in a file and use a filter mechanism to obtain the specs you are interested in, first create your filter function. Use tt_file_objects_query() to find all the objects in the named file.

As the ToolTalk service finds each object, it calls your filter function, passing the objid of the object and the two application-supplied pointers. Your filter function does some computation, and returns a Tt_filter_action value (TT_FILTER_CONTINUE or TT_FILTER_STOP) to either continue the query or stop and return immediately.

Here are the steps Sun_EditDemo goes through when obtaining a list of specs::

```
/*
 * Called to update the scrolling list of objects for a file. Uses
 * tt_file_objects_query to find all the ToolTalk objects.
 */
int
cntl_update_obj_panel()
{
        static int list_item = 0;
        char *file;
        int i;

        cntl_objid = (char *)0;

        for (i = list_item; i >= 0; i--) {
                xv_set(cntl_ui_olist, PANEL_LIST_DELETE, i, NULL);
        }
```

```
        list_item = 0;
        file = (char *)xv_get(cntl_ui_file_field, PANEL_VALUE);
        if (tt_file_objects_query(file,
          if (tt_file_objects_query(file,
                            (Tt_filter_function)cntl_gather_specs,
                            &list_item, NULL) != TT_OK) {
            xv_set(cntl_ui_base_window, FRAME_LEFT_FOOTER,
                   "Couldn't query objects for file", NULL);
            return 0;
        }

        return 1;
}
```

Within the `tt_file_objects_query()` function, it calls `cntl_gather_specs`, a filter function that inserts objects into a scrolling list.

Here's the filter function used during the query:

```
/*
 * Function to insert the objid given into the scrolling lists of objects
 * for a file. Used inside tt_file_objects_query as it iterates through
 * all the ToolTalk objects in a file.
 */
Tt_filter_action
cntl_gather_specs(objid, list_count, acc)
    char *objid;
    void *list_count;
    void *acc;
{

    int *i = (int *)list_count;

    xv_set(cntl_ui_olist, PANEL_LIST_INSERT, *i,
           PANEL_LIST_STRING, *i, objid,
           NULL);

    *i = (*i + 1);

    /* continue processing */
    return TT_FILTER_CONTINUE;
}
```

Comparing Object Specs

Use `tt_objid_equal()` to see if two objids are the same. `tt_objid_equal()` is better than `strcmp` for this purpose since it returns "1" even in the case where one objid is a forwarding pointer for the other.

Moving Object Specs

The objid contains a pointer to a particular file system where the spec information is stored. To keep spec information as available as the object described by the spec, the ToolTalk service stores the spec information on the same file system as the object. This means that if the object moves, the spec must move too.

Use tt_spec_move() to notify the ToolTalk service when an object moves from one file to another (say, through cut and paste). If a new objid is not required (because the new and old files are in the same file system), the ToolTalk service returns TT_WRN_SAME_OBJID. If the object moved to another file system, the ToolTalk service returns a new objid for the object and leaves a forwarding pointer in the ToolTalk database from the old objid to the new one. Update any internal data structures with the new objid.

When your process sends a message to an "out of date" objid (one with a forwarding pointer), tt_message_-send() will return a special status code, TT_WRN_STALE_-OBJID, and replace the object attribute in the message with a new objid that points to the same object in the new location. Update any internal data structures that refer to the object with the new objid.

Copying, Moving, or Removing Files with Object Data

When you copy, move, or destroy a file with object data in it, use the ToolTalk functions listed in Table 1.6.3. These functions ensure that the ToolTalk database servicing the disk partition where the file is stored is kept up-to-date.

Table 1.6.3. Copying, moving, or removing files with object data.

Return Type	ToolTalk Function
Tt_status	tt_file_move(const char *oldfilepath, const char *newfilepath)
Tt_status	tt_file_copy(const char *oldfilepath, const char *newfilepath)
Tt_status	tt_file_destroy(const char *filepath)

Caution – Despite the efforts of the ToolTalk service and integrated applications, it's still possible for object references to be broken by removing, moving, or renaming files with UNIX commands like mv or rm. Broken references like this will show up as undeliverable messages.

Encourage users of your application to use the following ToolTalk-aware shell commands for copying, moving, and removing files with object data.

- ttcp
- ttmv
- ttrm
- ttrmdir
- tttar

The man pages for these commands are located in this directory:

$OPENWINHOME/man/man1/

Destroying Object Specs

Use `tt_spec_destroy()` to destroy an object's spec instantly.

1.7
ToolTalk API

1.7.1
ToolTalk
Enumerated Types

The ToolTalk enumerated types fall into nine categories:

- tt_status
- tt_mode
- tt_scope
- tt_class
- tt_category
- tt_address
- tt_disposition
- tt_state
- tt_filter
- tt_callback

Tt_status

A Tt_status code is returned by all functions, sometimes directly and sometimes encoded in a "error return value." See Section 2, "General Application Requirements," for instructions on determining whether the Tt_status code is a warning or an error and for retrieving the catalog string for a Tt_status code.

The Tt_status codes are listed in Appendix C, "ToolTalk Error Messages." This appendix lists the following for each status code:

- message id

- catalog string (from Sun_ToolTalk.mo in $OPENWIN-HOME/locale/C/LC_MESSAGES)
- meaning
- remedy

Tt_mode

Tt_mode values specify who (sender, handler, observers) writes a message argument. Possible values are:

TT_IN
The argument is written by the sender and read by the handler and any observers.

TT_OUT
The argument is written by the handler and read by the sender and any reply observers.

TT_INOUT
The argument is written by the sender and the handler and read by all.

Tt_scope

Tt_scope values for the Scope attribute of a message or pattern indicate the set of processes eligible to receive the message. Possible values and meanings are:

TT_SESSION
All processes joined to the indicated session are eligible.

TT_FILE
All processes joined to the indicated file are eligible.

TT_BOTH
All processes joined to *either* the indicated file *or* the indicated session are eligible.

TT_FILE_IN_SESSION
All processes joined to *both* the indicated session *and* the indicated file are eligible.

Tt_class

These values for the class attribute of a message or pattern indicate whether or not the sender wants an action to take place after the message has been received. Possible values and meanings are:

TT_NOTICE
Notice of an event. Sender does not want feedback on this message.

TT_REQUEST
Request for some action to be taken. Sender must be notified of progress, success or failure, and must receive any return values.

Tt_category

`Tt_category` values for the category attribute of a pattern indicate the receiver's intent. Possible values and meanings are:

`TT_OBSERVE`
Just looking at the message. No feedback will be given to the sender.

`TT_HANDLE`
Will process the message, including filling in return values if any.

Tt_address

`Tt_address` indicates which message attributes form the address where the message will be delivered. Possible values and meanings are:

`TT_HANDLER`
Addressed to a specific handler that can perform this operation with these arguments. Fill in handler, op, and arg attributes of the message or pattern.

`TT_OBJECT`
Addressed to a specific object that performs this operation with these arguments. Fill in object, op, and arg attributes of the message or pattern.

`TT_OTYPE`
Addressed to the type of object that can perform this operation with these arguments. Fill in otype, op, and arg attributes of the message or pattern.

`TT_PROCEDURE`
Addressed to any process that can perform this operation with these arguments. Fill in the op and arg attributes of the message or pattern.

Tt_disposition

`Tt_disposition` values indicate whether the receiver should be started to receive the message or if the message should be queued until the receiving process is started at a later time. The message can also be thrown away if the receiver is not started.

Note that `Tt_disposition` values can be added together, so that `TT_QUEUE+TT_START` means both to queue the message and to try to start a process. This can be useful if the start can fail (or be vetoed by the user), to ensure the message is processed as soon as an eligible process does start.

Possible values and their meanings are:

```
TT_DISCARD = 0
```
No receiver for this message. Message is returned to sender with the `Tt_status` field containing `TT_FAILED`.

```
TT_QUEUE = 1
```
Queue the message until a process of the proper ptype receives the message.

```
TT_START = 2
```
Attempt to start a process of the proper ptype if none is running.

Tt_state

`Tt_state` values indicate a message's delivery status. Possible values and their meanings are:

```
TT_CREATED
```
Message has been created but not yet sent.
Only the sender of a message will see a message in this state.

```
TT_SENT
```
Message has been sent but not yet handled.

```
TT_HANDLED
```
Message has been handled, return values are valid.

```
TT_FAILED
```
Message could not be delivered to a handler.

```
TT_QUEUED
```
Message has been queued for later delivery.

```
TT_STARTED
```
Attempting to start a process to handle the message.

```
TT_REJECTED
```
Message has been rejected by a possible handler. This state is seen only by the rejecting process. The ToolTalk service changes the state back to `TT_SENT` before delivering the message to another possible handler. If all possible handlers have rejected the message, the ToolTalk service changes the state to `TT_FAILED` before returning the message to the sender.

Tt_filter

`Tt_filter_action` is the return value from a query callback filter procedure. Possible values and meanings are:

```
TT_FILTER_CONTINUE
```
Continue the query, feed more values to the callback.

```
TT_FILTER_STOP
```
Stop the query, don't look for any more values.

Tt_callback

These values are used to specify the action taken by the callback attached to messages or patterns. If no callback returns `TT_CALLBACK_PROCESSED`, `tt_message_receive()` will return the message. Possible values and their meanings are:

`TT_CALLBACK_CONTINUE`
If the callback returns `TT_CALLBACK_CONTINUE`, other callbacks will be run.

`TT_CALLBACK_PROCESSED`
If the callback returns `TT_CALLBACK_PROCESSED`, no further callbacks will be invoked for this event, and the message will not be returned by `tt_message_receive()`.

1.7.2
ToolTalk
Functions

tt_close

Tt_status	tt_close(void)

Closes the current default process identifier (procid).

Note – `tt_close()` should be the last ToolTalk function your process calls.

Returned Value

`Tt_status`
The status of the operation. Possible values are:

- ° TT_OK
- ° TT_ERR_NOMP
- ° TT_ERR_PROCID

Related Functions

`tt_open()`

tt_default_file

char	*tt_default_file(void)

Returns the current default file. Joining a file makes it the default file.

Returned Value

`char *`
Pointer to a character string specifying the current default file. If the pointer is `NULL`, no default is set.

Use `tt_ptr_error()`, which returns `Tt_status`, to determine if the pointer is valid. Possible `Tt_status` values are:

° `TT_OK`

° `TT_ERR_NOMP`

° `TT_ERR_PROCID`

Related Functions   `tt_file_join()`

tt_default_file_set   `Tt_status        tt_default_file_set(const char *docid)`

Sets the default file to the specified file.

Arguments   `const char *docid`
Pointer to a character string specifying the file you want as the default file.

Returned Value   `Tt_status`
The status of the operation. Possible values are:

° `TT_OK`

° `TT_ERR_NOMP`

° `TT_ERR_PROCID`

° `TT_ERR_FILE`

tt_default_procid   `char            *tt_default_procid(void)`

Retrieves the current default process identifier (procid) for your process. The procid is used in the sender field of messages.

Returned Value   `char *`
Pointer to character string that uniquely identifies the current default process.
Use `tt_ptr_error()`, which returns `Tt_status`, to determine if the pointer is valid. Possible `Tt_status` values are:

° `TT_OK`

° `TT_ERR_NOMP`

° `TT_ERR_PROCID`

tt_default_procid_set	Tt_status	tt_default_procid_set(const char*procid)

Sets the current default procid. The default procid is set by tt_open(). Only processes that do multiple tt_open() calls and juggle multiple procids ever need to use this function.

Arguments
const char *procid
Name of process you want to set up as the default process.

Returned Value
Tt_status
The status of the operation. Possible values are:

- ° TT_OK
- ° TT_ERR_NOMP
- ° TT_ERR_PROCID

Related Functions
tt_open()

tt_default_ptype	char	*tt_default_ptype(void)

Retrieves the current default process type (ptype). Declaring a ptype makes it the default ptype. The default ptype is used in the sender ptype field of your message.

Returned Value
char *
Pointer to character string that uniquely identifies the current default process type. If the pointer is NULL, no default is set.

Use tt_ptr_error(), which returns Tt_status, to determine if the pointer is valid. Possible Tt_status values are:

- ° TT_OK
- ° TT_ERR_NOMP
- ° TT_ERR_PROCID

Related Functions
tt_ptype_declare()

tt_default_ptype_set	Tt_status	tt_default_ptype_set(const char *ptid)

Sets the default process type (ptype) to the provided string.

Arguments	`const char *ptid` Use the character string that uniquely identifies the process you wish to set up as the default process.
Returned Value	`Tt_status` The status of the operation. Possible values are: ° `TT_OK` ° `TT_ERR_NOMP` ° `TT_ERR_PROCID`

tt_default_session   `char            *tt_default_session(void)`

Retrieves the current default session identifier from the ToolTalk service for the current default procid.

Returned Value

`char *`
Pointer to the unique identifier for the current session. If the pointer is `NULL`, no default is set.

Use `tt_ptr_error()`, which returns `Tt_status`, to determine if the pointer is valid. Possible `Tt_status` values are:

° `TT_OK`

° `TT_ERR_NOMP`

° `TT_ERR_PROCID`

Related Functions   `tt_default_procid()`

tt_default_session_ set

`Tt_status        tt_default_session_set`
`                 (const char *sessid)`

Sets the current default session identifier for the current default procid.

Note – The ToolTalk service uses the initial user session as the default session and supports one session per procid. To join other sessions, your program must first set the new session as the default and then initialize and register. The calls required must be in this order: `tt_default_session_ set`, `tt_open`, `tt_fd`

Arguments	`const char *sessid` Pointer to the unique identifier for the session in which you are interested.
Returned Value	`Tt_status` The status of the operation. Possible values are:

  ° `TT_OK`

  ° `TT_ERR_NOMP`

  ° `TT_ERR_PROCID`

  ° `TT_ERR_SESSION`

Related Functions	`tt_open()` `tt_fd()`
tt_error_int	`int          tt_error_int(Tt_status ttrc)`

Given a `Tt_status` code, returns an integer error object encoding the code.

Note – The integer error objects are negative integers, so only use this when the valid integer values are non-negative.

Arguments	`Tt_status ttrc` `Tt_status` code you want to encode.
Returned Value	`int` Encoded `Tt_status` code.
tt_error_pointer	`void          *tt_error_pointer(Tt_status ttrc)`

Given a `Tt_status` code, returns a pointer to an error object encoding the code.

Arguments	`Tt_status ttrc` `Tt_status` code you want to encode.
Returned Value	`void *` Pointer to encoded `Tt_status` code.
tt_fd	`int          tt_fd(void)`

Returns a file descriptor (fd) which is used to alert your program that a message has arrived for the default procid in the default session. File descriptors are either active or inactive. When your file descriptor becomes active, you need to call `tt_message_receive`.

Note – You must have a separate file descriptor for each procid. Each time you call `tt_open`, use `tt_fd` to get an associated file descriptor.

Returned Value

`int`
File descriptor for your current procid.

Use `tt_int_error()`, which returns `Tt_status`, to determine if the integer is valid. Possible `Tt_status` values are:

- `TT_OK`
- `TT_ERR_NOMP`
- `TT_ERR_PROCID`
- `TT_ERR_SESSION`

Related Functions

`tt_open()`

`tt_message_receive()`

tt_file_copy

`Tt_status        tt_file_copy(const char *oldfilepath, const char *newfilepath)`

Copies all the objects on the specified file to the new file. Any objects already on the second file are not removed.

Arguments

`const char *oldfilepath`
Pointer to the name of the file whose objects are to be copied.

`const char *newfilepath`
Pointer to the name of the file on which to create the copied objects.

Returned Value

`Tt_status`
The status of the operation. Possible values are:

- `TT_OK`
- `TT_ERR_DBAVAIL`

° TT_ERR_DBEXIST

° TT_ERR_FILE

° TT_ERR_NOMP

° TT_ERR_PATH

° TT_ERR_POINTER

| *Related Functions* | tt_file_move() |
| | tt_file_destroy() |

| **tt_file_destroy** | Tt_status | tt_file_destroy(const char *filepath) |

Removes all the objects on the files and directories rooted at filepath from the appropriate ToolTalk database. Call this function when you unlink(2) a file or rmdir(2) a directory.

Arguments
const char *filepath
Pointer to the pathname of the file to be removed.

Returned Value
Tt_status
The status of the operation. Possible values are:

° TT_OK

° TT_ERR_ACCESS

° TT_ERR_DBAVAIL

° TT_ERR_DBEXIST

° TT_ERR_FILE

° TT_ERR_NOMP

° TT_ERR_PATH

° TT_ERR_POINTER

Related Functions	tt_file_copy()
	tt_file_move()
	rmdir(2)
	unlink(2)

| **tt_file_join** | Tt_status | tt_file_join(const char *filepath) |

Informs the ToolTalk service that your process is interested in messages involving the file named by the provided string. The ToolTalk service adds this file value to any currently registered patterns with scope `TT_FILE`. The named file becomes the default file.

Arguments
```
const char *filepath
```
Pointer to the pathname of the file to be joined.

Returned Value
```
Tt_status
```
The status of the operation. Possible values are:

- ° `TT_OK`

- ° `TT_ERR_DBAVAIL`

- ° `TT_ERR_DBEXIST`

- ° `TT_ERR_NOMP`

- ° `TT_ERR_PATH`

tt_file_move
```
Tt_status          tt_file_move(const char
                   *oldfilepath,
                   const char *newfilepath)
```

Destroys all the objects on the files and directories rooted at the new filepath, and then moves all the objects on the first file to the second file.

If oldfilepath and newfilepath are in the same filesystem, then `tt_file_move()` replaces oldfilepath with newfilepath in the path associated with every object in that filesystem. That is, it picks up all the objects in the directory tree rooted at oldfilepath, and overlays them onto newfilepath. In this mode, `tt_file_move()` is like the system call `rename(2)`.

If oldfilepath and newfilepath are on different file systems, neither may be a directory.

Arguments
```
const char *oldfilepath
```
The name of the file or directory whose objects are to be moved.

```
const char *newfilepath
```
The name of the file or directory to which the objects are to be moved.

Returned Value
```
Tt_status
```
The status of the operation. Possible values are:

- ° `TT_OK`

- ° TT_ERR_ACCESS
- ° TT_ERR_DBAVAIL
- ° TT_ERR_DBEXIST
- ° TT_ERR_FILE
- ° TT_ERR_NOMP
- ° TT_ERR_PATH
- ° TT_ERR_POINTER

Related Functions

tt_file_copy()

tt_file_destroy()

rename(2)

**tt_file_objects_
query**

Tt_status   tt_file_objects_query(const
char *filepath, Tt_filter_
function filter, void *context, void *accumulator)

Instructs the ToolTalk service to find all the objects in the
named file and pass back the objids to the filter function you
created. The context pointer and accumulator pointer you
initially specify will also be passed to your filter function.

As the ToolTalk service finds each object, it calls your filter
function, passing the objid of the object and the two application-supplied pointers. Your filter function performs its computation, and returns a Tt_filter_action value to tell
the query function whether to continue or to stop. Tt_fil-
ter action values are:

- TT_FILTER_CONTINUE
- TT_FILTER_STOP

Arguments

const char *filepath
File name.

Tt_filter_function filter
Your filter function. Tt_filter_function is a typedef
"Tt_filter_action (*) (char *objid, void
*context, void *accumulator)".

void *context
A pointer to any information your filter needs to execute. The
ToolTalk service does not interpret this argument. It passes it
straight through to your filter function.

```
void *accumulator
```
A pointer to a place for your filter to store the results of the query and filter operations. The ToolTalk service does not interpret this argument, but passes it straight through to your filter function.

Returned Value

```
Tt_status
```
The status of the operation. Possible values are:

- ° `TT_OK`

- ° `TT_ERR_DBAVAIL`

- ° `TT_ERR_DBEXIST`

- ° `TT_ERR_NOMP`

- ° `TT_ERR_PATH`

- ° `TT_WRN_STOPPED`

tt_file_quit

```
Tt_status          tt_file_quit(const char
                   *filepath)
```

Informs the ToolTalk service that your process is no longer interested in messages involving the file named by the provided string. The ToolTalk service removes this file value from any currently registered patterns with scope `TT_FILE`. The default file is nulled.

Arguments

```
const char *filepath
```
File name.

Returned Value

```
Tt_status
```
The status of the operation. Possible values are:

- ° `TT_OK`

- ° `TT_ERR_DBAVAIL`

- ° `TT_ERR_DBEXIST`

- ° `TT_ERR_PATH`

tt_free

```
void               tt_free(caddr_t p)
```

Frees this storage from the ToolTalk API allocation stack.

You may find `tt_free` more convenient than using `tt_mark` and `tt_release` if your application is in a loop obtaining strings from the ToolTalk service and processing each in turn.

Arguments	`caddr_t p` Storage in the ToolTalk API allocation stack that had been given to your application.
Related Functions	`tt_malloc()`
tt_initial_session	`char          *tt_initial_session(void)`

Returns the session in which the process was created. This is either a process tree session or the X session associated with the display named in the `DISPLAY` environment variable.

Returned Value	`char *` Identifier for the current ToolTalk session. Use `tt_ptr_error()`, which returns `Tt_status`, to determine if the pointer is valid. Possible `Tt_status` values are:

- `TT_OK`

- `TT_ERR_NOMP`

tt_int_error	`Tt_status     tt_int_error(int return_val)`

Given an integer, returns `TT_OK` if the integer is not an error object or the encoded `Tt_status` value if the integer is an error object.

Arguments	`int return_val` Integer returned by a ToolTalk function.
Returned Value	`Tt_status` The status of the operation. Possible values are:

- `TT_OK`

- `TT_xxx`

tt_is_err	`int           tt_is_err(Tt_status s)`

A macro that tells you if the `Tt_status` enum you provided is a warning or an error. `tt_is_err()` expands to (`TT_WRN_LAST < (p)`).

Arguments	`Tt_status s` The `Tt_status` code you want to check.
Returned Value	`int` If you receive 1, the `Tt_status` enum is an error. If you receive 0, the `Tt_status` enum is either a warning or `TT_OK`.

| **tt_malloc** | caddr_t | tt_malloc(size_t s) |

Allocates storage on the ToolTalk API allocation stack.

This capability is provided so that your application-provided callback routines can take advantage of the allocation stack. For example, a query filter function might allocate storage to hold a result.

Arguments
size_t s
The amount of storage you want in bytes.

Returned Value
caddr_t
Storage in the ToolTalk API allocation stack given to your application. If NULL is returned, no storage is available.

Related Functions
tt_free()

| **tt_mark** | int | tt_mark(void) |

Marks a storage position in the ToolTalk API allocation stack. Your application typically does this at the beginning of a procedure.

Returned Value
int
Integer that marks your application's storage position in the ToolTalk API allocation stack.

Related Functions
tt_release()

| **tt_message_address** | Tt_address | tt_message_address(Tt_message m) |

Retrieves the address attribute from the specified message.

Arguments
Tt_message m
Opaque handle for the message involved in this operation.

Returned Value
Tt_address
Specifies which message attributes form the address of this message. Possible values are:

- ° TT_PROCEDURE
- ° TT_OBJECT
- ° TT_HANDLER
- ° TT_OTYPE

Use `tt_int_error()`, which returns `Tt_status`, to determine if the `Tt_address` integer is valid. Possible `Tt_status` values are:

- `TT_OK`
- `TT_ERR_NOMP`
- `TT_ERR_POINTER`

tt_message_address_set

Tt_status	tt_message_address_set(Tt_message m, Tt_address a)

Sets the address attribute for the specified message.

Arguments

Tt_message m
Opaque handle for the message involved in this operation.

Tt_address a
Specifies which message attributes form the address to which the message will be delivered. Possible values are:

- `TT_PROCEDURE`
- `TT_OBJECT`
- `TT_HANDLER`
- `TT_OTYPE`

Returned Value

Tt_status
The status of the operation. Possible values are:

- `TT_OK`
- `TT_ERR_NOMP`
- `TT_ERR_POINTER`

tt_message_arg_add

Tt_status	tt_message_arg_add(Tt_message m, Tt_mode n, const char *vtype, const char *value)

Adds a new argument to a message object. Add all arguments before the message is sent.

Note – Do not add arguments to a reply. Only change existing argument values with modes of `TT_OUT` or `TT_INOUT`.

Arguments	`Tt_message m` Opaque handle for the message involved in this operation.

	`Tt_mode n`
	Specifies who (sender, handler, observers) writes and reads a message argument. Possible modes are:
	  ° `TT_IN`
	  ° `TT_OUT`
	  ° `TT_INOUT`

	`const char *vtype` Type of the value.
	`const char *value` Contents for the message argument attribute. Use NULL for values of mode TT_OUT, or if the value will be filled in later with `tt_message_arg_val_set`, `tt_message_barg_val_set`, or `tt_message_iarg_val_set`.

Returned Value	`Tt_status`
	The status of the operation. Possible values are:
	  ° `TT_OK`
	  ° `TT_ERR_MODE`
	  ° `TT_ERR_NOMP`
	  ° `TT_ERR_POINTER`

Related Functions	`tt_message_arg_val_set()`
	`tt_message_barg_add()`
	`tt_message_iarg_add()`

tt_message_arg_bval	`Tt_status`	`tt_message_arg_bval(Tt_message m, int n, unsigned char **value, int *len)`

Retrieves the value of the *n*-th message argument as a byte string.

Arguments	`Tt_message m` Opaque handle for the message involved in this operation.

```
int n
```
Number of the argument you want to retrieve. The first argument is 0.

```
unsigned char **value
```
Address of a character pointer that the ToolTalk service should aim toward a string containing the contents of the argument.

```
int *len
```
Address of an integer that the ToolTalk service should set to the length of the value in bytes.

Returned Value

Tt_status
The status of the operation. Possible values are:

- ° TT_OK

- ° TT_ERR_NOMP

- ° TT_ERR_NUM

- ° TT_ERR_POINTER

```
unsigned char **value
```
Address of a character pointer that the ToolTalk service aimed at a string containing the contents of the argument.

```
int *len
```
Address of an integer that the ToolTalk service set to the length of the value in bytes.

tt_message_arg_bval_set

Tt_status	tt_message_arg_bval_set(Tt_message m, int n, const unsigned char *value, int len)

Sets the value and the type of the *n*-th message argument as a byte string. You (the sender) can use `tt_message_arg_bval_set` to fill in opaque data.

Also, this changes the value of the *n*-th message argument to a byte string. Used by the handler before replying to the message.

Arguments

Tt_message m
Opaque handle for the message involved in this operation.

```
int n
```
Number of the argument you want to set. The first argument is 0.

```
const unsigned char *value
```
Byte string with the contents for the message argument.

```
int len
```
Length of the value in bytes.

Returned Value

```
Tt_status
```
The status of the operation. Possible values are:

- ° TT_OK

- ° TT_ERR_NOMP

- ° TT_ERR_NUM

- ° TT_ERR_POINTER

Related Functions

```
tt_message_barg_add()
```

```
tt_message_arg_val_set()
```

```
tt_message_iarg_val_set()
```

tt_message_arg_ival

Tt_status	tt_message_arg_ival(Tt_message m, int n, int *value)

Retrieves the value of the *n*-th message argument as an integer.

Arguments

```
Tt_message m
```
Opaque handle for the message involved in this operation.

```
int n
```
Number of the argument you want to retrieve. The first argument is 0.

```
int *value
```
Pointer to an integer where the ToolTalk service should store the contents of the argument.

Returned Value

```
Tt_status
```
The status of the operation. Possible values are:

- ° TT_OK

- ° TT_ERR_NOMP

- ° TT_ERR_NUM

- ° TT_ERR_POINTER

int value
Value of the *n*-th argument.

tt_message_arg_ ival_set	Tt_status	tt_message_arg_ival_set(Tt_ message m, int n, int value)

Fills in the *n*-th message argument with an integer value.
 Also, changes the value of the *n*-th message argument to an integer.

Arguments

Tt_message m
Opaque handle for the message involved in this operation.

int n
Number of the argument you want to set. The first argument is 0.

int value
Contents (in integer form) for the message argument.

Returned Value

Tt_status
The status of the operation. Possible values are:

 ° TT_OK

 ° TT_ERR_NOMP

 ° TT_ERR_NUM

 ° TT_ERR_POINTER

Related Functions

tt_message_arg_ival_add()

tt_message_arg_val_set()

tt_message_barg_val_set()

tt_message_arg_mode	Tt_mode	tt_message_arg_mode(Tt_mes- sage m, int n)

Returns the mode of the *n*-th message argument.

Arguments

Tt_message m
Opaque handle for the message involved in this operation.

int n
Number of the argument in which you are interested. The first argument is 0.

Returned Value

Tt_mode
Specifies who (sender, handler, observers) writes and reads a message argument. Possible modes are:

  ° TT_IN

  ° TT_OUT

  ° TT_INOUT

Use tt_int_error(), which returns Tt_status, to determine if the Tt_mode integer is valid. Possible Tt_status values are:

  ° TT_OK

  ° TT_ERR_NOMP

  ° TT_ERR_NUM

  ° TT_ERR_POINTER

tt_message_arg_type
char   *tt_message_arg_type(Tt_message m, int n)

Retrieves the type of the *n*-th message argument.

Arguments

Tt_message m
Opaque handle for the message involved in this operation.

int n
Number of the argument in which you are interested. The first argument is 0.

Returned Value

char *
Type of the *n*-th message argument.
Use tt_ptr_error(), which returns Tt_status, to determine if the pointer is valid. Possible Tt_status values are:

  ° TT_OK

  ° TT_ERR_NOMP

  ° TT_ERR_NUM

  ° TT_ERR_POINTER

tt_message_arg_val
char   *tt_message_arg_val(Tt_message m, int n)

Returns a pointer to the value (assuming it is a character string) of the *n*-th message argument.

Arguments

`Tt_message m`
Opaque handle for the message involved in this operation.

`int n`
Number of the argument in which you are interested. The first argument is 0.

Returned Value

`char *`
Contents for the message argument.
Use `tt_ptr_error()`, which returns `Tt_status`, to determine if the pointer is valid. Possible `Tt_status` values are:

- `TT_OK`
- `TT_ERR_NOMP`
- `TT_ERR_NUM`
- `TT_ERR_POINTER`

tt_message_arg_val_set

`Tt_status     tt_message_arg_val_set(Tt_`
`              message m, int n,`
`              const char *value)`

Changes the value of the *n*-th message argument. Generally used by the handler before replying to the message.

Arguments

`Tt_message m`
Opaque handle for the message involved in this operation.

`int n`
Number of the argument you want to change. The first argument is 0.

`const char *value`
Contents for the message argument.

Returned Value

`Tt_status`
The status of the operation. Possible values are:

- `TT_OK`
- `TT_ERR_NOMP`
- `TT_ERR_NUM`
- `TT_ERR_POINTER`

tt_message_args_count	int	tt_message_args_count(Tt_message m)

Returns the number of arguments in the message.

Arguments

Tt_message m
Opaque handle for the message involved in this operation.

Returned Value

int
Total number of arguments in the message.

Use tt_int_error(), which returns Tt_status, to determine if the integer is valid. Possible Tt_status values are:

- ° TT_OK
- ° TT_ERR_NOMP
- ° TT_ERR_POINTER

tt_message_barg_add	Tt_status	tt_message_barg_add(Tt_message m, Tt_mode n, const char *vtype, const unsigned char *value, int len)

Adds an argument to a pattern that may have a value containing imbedded nulls.

Note – Do not add arguments to a reply. Only change existing argument values with modes of TT_OUT or TT_INOUT.

Arguments

Tt_message m
Opaque handle for the message involved in this operation.

Tt_mode n
Specifies who (sender, handler, observers) writes and reads a message argument. Possible modes are:

- ° TT_IN
- ° TT_OUT
- ° TT_INOUT

const char *vtype
Type of the value.

The ToolTalk service treats the value as an opaque byte string. To pass structured data, your application and the receiving application must encode and decode these opaque byte strings. The most common way of doing this is to use XDR.

```
const unsigned char *value
```
Value that the ToolTalk service should fill in.

```
int len
```
Length of the value in bytes.

Returned Value   Tt_status
The status of the operation. Possible values are:

- ° TT_OK

- ° TT_ERR_NOMP

- ° TT_ERR_POINTER

Related Functions   tt_message_barg_val_set()

tt_message_arg_add()

tt_message_iarg_add()

tt_message_callback_   Tt_status   tt_message_callback_add(Tt_
add   message m, Tt_message_call-
                                                  back f)

Registers a callback function that will be automatically invoked by tt_message_receive whenever a reply or other state-change to this message is returned.

Tt_callback_action is an enum containing the values TT_CALLBACK_CONTINUE andTT_CALLBACK_PRO-CESSED. If the callback returns TT_CALLBACK_PROCESSED, no further callbacks will be invoked for this event, and the message will not be returned by tt_message_receive. If the callback returns TT_CALLBACK_CONTINUE, other callbacks will be run, and if no callback returns TT_CALLBACK_PROCESSED, tt_message_receive will return the message.

This behavior can be used to create wrappers for ToolTalk messages. A library routine can construct a request, attach a callback to the message, send the message, and process the reply in the callback. By having the callback return TT_CALLBACK_PROCESSED, the message reply will not be returned to the main program, so the message and reply are completely hidden. Note that these callbacks are invoked from `tt_message_receive`, so it's still necessary for programs to arrange for `tt_message_receive` to be called when the file descriptor returned by `tt_fd` becomes active.

Arguments

`Tt_message m`
Opaque handle for the message involved in this operation.

`Tt_message_callback f`
`Tt_message_callback` is a type definition for a pointer to a function declared like: `Tt_callback_action func(Tt_message m, Tt_pattern p)`. The callback is passed the message in question and the pattern that matched it. The pattern handle will be null if the message didn't match a dynamic pattern (this is usually the case for message callbacks).

Returned Value

`Tt_status`
The status of the operation. Possible values are:

° `TT_OK`

° `TT_ERR_NOMP`

° `TT_ERR_POINTER`

tt_message_class

`Tt_class`	`tt_message_class(Tt_message m)`

Retrieves the class attribute from the specified message.

Arguments

`Tt_message m`
Opaque handle for the message involved in this operation.

Returned Value

`Tt_class`
Indicates whether or not the sender wanted an action to take place after the message is received. Possible values are:

° `TT_NOTICE`

° `TT_REQUEST`
Use `tt_int_error()`, which returns `Tt_status`, to determine if the `Tt_class` integer is valid. Possible `Tt_status` values are:

° `TT_OK`

         ° `TT_ERR_NOMP`

         ° `TT_ERR_POINTER`

tt_message_class_set   `Tt_status`   `tt_message_class_set(Tt_message m, Tt_class c)`

Sets the class attribute for the specified message.

Arguments

`Tt_message m`
Opaque handle for the message involved in this operation.

`Tt_class c`
Indicates whether or not you want an action to take place after the message is received. Possible values are:

         ° `TT_NOTICE`

         ° `TT_REQUEST`

Returned Value

`Tt_status`
The status of the operation. Possible values are:

         ° `TT_OK`

         ° `TT_ERR_NOMP`

         ° `TT_ERR_POINTER`

tt_message_create   `Tt_message`   `tt_message_create(void)`

Creates a new message object. The ToolTalk service returns a message handle that's really an opaque pointer to a ToolTalk structure. You do not manipulate the structure directly.

Returned Value

`Tt_message`
The unique opaque handle that identifies your message object.

    If ToolTalk is unable to create a message when requested, an invalid handle will be returned to you. When you attempt to use this handle, the ToolTalk service will report an error. Use `tt_pointer_error` to determine why the ToolTalk service was not able to create the message.

    Use `tt_ptr_error()`, which returns `Tt_status`, to determine if the pointer is valid. Possible `Tt_status` values are:

         ° `TT_OK`

         ° `TT_ERR_NOMP`

° `TT_ERR_NUM`

° `TT_ERR_POINTER`

Related Functions   `tt_message_send()`

`tt_message_destroy()`

tt_message_create_
super

`Tt_message`	`tt_message_create_super(Tt_`
	`message m)`

Re-addresses the specified message to the parent otype of the otype or object listed in the message. Returns the re-addressed message so you can fill in additional message attributes and send the message.

Arguments

`Tt_message m`
Opaque handle for the message involved in this operation.

Returned Value

`Tt_message`
Opaque unique handle for the re-addressed message.

Use `tt_ptr_error()`, which returns `Tt_status`, to determine if the pointer is valid. Possible `Tt_status` values are:

° `TT_OK`

° `TT_ERR_ADDRESS`

° `TT_ERR_NOMP`

° `TT_ERR_OBJID`

° `TT_ERR_OTYPE`

° `TT_ERR_POINTER`

Related Functions   `tt_message_send()`

`tt_message_destroy()`

tt_message_destroy

`Tt_status`	`tt_message_destroy(Tt_mes-`
	`sage m)`

Destroys the message. Destroying a message has no effect on the delivery of a message you have already sent.

If you sent a request and are expecting a reply with return values, destroy a message after you have received the reply. If you sent a notice, you can destroy the message after you send it.

Arguments	`Tt_message m` Opaque handle for the message involved in this operation.
Returned Value	`Tt_status` The status of the operation. Possible values are: ° `TT_OK` ° `TT_ERR_NOMP` ° `TT_ERR_POINTER`

Related Functions	`tt_message_create()`
	
	`tt_message_create_super()`

tt_message_disposi- **tion**	`Tt_disposition   tt_message_disposition(Tt_` `                   message m)`

Retrieves the disposition attribute from the specified message.

Arguments	`Tt_message m` Opaque handle for the message involved in this operation.
Returned Value	`Tt_disposition` Indicates whether the receiver should be started to receive the message or if the message should be queued until the receiving process is started at a later time. Possible values are: ° `TT_QUEUE` ° `TT_START` ° `TT_QUEUE+TT_START` Use `tt_int_error()`, which returns `Tt_status`, to determine if the `Tt_disposition` integer is valid. Possible `Tt_status` values are: ° `TT_OK` ° `TT_ERR_NOMP` ° `TT_ERR_POINTER`

tt_message_disposi-tion_set	Tt_status	tt_message_disposition_set (Tt_message m, Tt_disposition r)

Sets the disposition attribute for the specified message.

Arguments

Tt_message m
Opaque handle for the message involved in this operation.

Tt_disposition r
Indicates whether the receiver should be started to receive the message or if the message should be queued until the receiving process is started at a later time. Possible values are:

- ○ TT_QUEUE

- ○ TT_START

- ○ TT_QUEUE+TT_START

Returned Value

Tt_status
The status of the operation. Possible values are:

- ○ TT_OK

- ○ TT_ERR_NOMP

- ○ TT_ERR_POINTER

tt_message_fail	Tt_status	tt_message_fail(Tt_message m)

Informs the ToolTalk service that your process can not handle the request you just received and that the message should not be offered to other processes of the same ptype as yours. The ToolTalk service will send the message back to the sender with state TT_FAILED.

To help the requestor distinguish this case from the case where a message failed because no matching handler could be found, place an explanatory message code in the status attribute of the message with tt_message_status_set and tt_message_status_string_set before calling tt_message_fail.

Note – The status value must be greater than 2047 (TT_ERR_LAST) to avoid confusion with the ToolTalk service status values.

Arguments	`Tt_message m` Opaque handle for the message involved in this operation.
Returned Value	`Tt_status` The status of the operation. Possible values are:

- ° `TT_OK`
- ° `TT_ERR_NOMP`
- ° `TT_ERR_NOTHANDLER`
- ° `TT_ERR_POINTER`

Related Functions	`tt_message_status_set()` `tt_message_status_string_set()`

tt_message_file	`char          *tt_message_file(Tt_message` `                m)`

Retrieves the file attribute from the specified message.

Arguments	`Tt_message m` Opaque handle for the message involved in this operation.
Returned Value	`char *` File attribute of the specified message. Use `tt_ptr_error()`, which returns `Tt_status`, to determine if the pointer is valid. Possible `Tt_status` values are:

- ° `TT_OK`
- ° `TT_ERR_NOMP`
- ° `TT_ERR_POINTER`

tt_message_file_set	`Tt_status        tt_message_file_set(Tt_mes-`
	`                 sage m,`
	`                 const char *file)`

Sets the file attribute for the specified message.

Arguments	`Tt_message m`
	Opaque handle for the message involved in this operation.
	
	`const char *file`
	File name involved in this operation.

Returned Value	`Tt_status` The status of the operation. Possible values are:

- ° `TT_OK`
- ° `TT_ERR_FILE`
- ° `TT_ERR_NOMP`
- ° `TT_ERR_POINTER`

tt_message_gid	`gid_t` `tt_message_gid(Tt_message m)`

Retrieves the group ID attribute from the specified message.

The ToolTalk service automatically sets the group ID of a message with the group ID of the process that created the message.

Arguments	`Tt_message m` Opaque handle for the message involved in this operation.

Returned Value	`gid_t` The group ID of the message. If the "nobody" group (65534) is returned, the message handle is not valid.

Related Functions	`tt_message_uid()`
tt_message_handler	`char` `*tt_message_handler(Tt_message m)`

Retrieves the handler attribute from the specified message.

Arguments	`Tt_message m` Opaque handle for the message involved in this operation.

Returned Value	`char *` Character value that uniquely identifies the process that should handle the message (Tt_state = `TT_CREATED` or `TT_SENT`) or the process that did handle the message (Tt_state = `TT_SENT` or `TT_HANDLED`).

Use `tt_ptr_error()`, which returns `Tt_status`, to determine if the pointer is valid. Possible `Tt_status` values are:

- ° `TT_OK`
- ° `TT_ERR_NOMP`
- ° `TT_ERR_POINTER`

tt_message_handler_ptype	char	*tt_message_handler_ptype (Tt_message m)

Retrieves the handler ptype attribute from the specified message.

Arguments

Tt_message m
Opaque handle for the message involved in this operation.

Returned Value

char *
Type of process that should handle this message.
   Use tt_ptr_error(), which returns Tt_status, to determine if the pointer is valid. Possible Tt_status values are:

   ° TT_OK

   ° TT_ERR_NOMP

   ° TT_ERR_POINTER

tt_message_handler_ptype_set	Tt_status	tt_message_handler_ptype_set(Tt_message m, const char *ptid)

Sets the handler process type (ptype) attribute for the specified message.

Arguments

Tt_message m
Opaque handle for the message involved in this operation.

const char *ptid
Type of process that should or did handle this message.

Returned Value

Tt_status
The status of the operation. Possible values are:

   ° TT_OK

   ° TT_ERR_NOMP

   ° TT_ERR_POINTER

tt_message_handler_set	Tt_status	tt_message_handler_set(Tt_message m, const char *procid)

Sets the handler attribute for the specified message.

Arguments	Tt_message m Opaque handle for the message involved in this operation.
	const char *procid Character value that uniquely identifies the process you want to handle the message.
Returned Value	Tt_status The status of the operation. Possible values are:
	° TT_OK
	° TT_ERR_NOMP
	° TT_ERR_POINTER

tt_message_iarg_add

Tt_status	tt_message_iarg_add(Tt_message m, Tt_mode n, constchar *vtype, int value)

Adds a new argument to a message object and sets the value to a given integer. Add all arguments before the message is sent.

Note – Do not add arguments to a reply. Only change existing argument values with modes of TT_OUT or TT_INOUT.

Arguments

Tt_message m
Opaque handle for the message involved in this operation.

Tt_mode n
Specifies who (sender, handler, observers) writes and reads a message argument. Possible modes are:

° TT_IN

° TT_OUT

° TT_INOUT

const char *vtype
Type of the value.

int value
Value to fill in.

Returned Value	`Tt_status` The status of the operation. Possible values are:

- ° `TT_OK`
- ° `TT_ERR_MODE`
- ° `TT_ERR_NOMP`
- ° `TT_ERR_POINTER`
- ° `TT_ERR_VTYPE`

Related Functions	`tt_message_arg_ival_set()`
	`tt_message_arg_add()`
	`tt_message_barg_add()`

tt_message_object	`char          *tt_message_object(Tt_mes-` `                sage m)`

Retrieves the object attribute from the specified message.

Arguments	`Tt_message m` Opaque handle for the message involved in this operation.

Returned Value	`char *` Object involved in this message. Use `tt_ptr_error()`, which returns `Tt_status`, to determine if the pointer is valid. Possible `Tt_status` values are:

- ° `TT_OK`
- ° `TT_ERR_NOMP`
- ° `TT_ERR_OBJID`
- ° `TT_ERR_POINTER`

tt_message_object_ set	`Tt_status        tt_message_object_set(Tt_` `                message m, const char *objid)`

Sets the object attribute for the specified message.

Arguments	`Tt_message m` Opaque handle for the message involved in this operation.

`const char *objid`
Object involved in this message.

Returned Value	`Tt_status` The status of the operation. Possible values are:
	° `TT_OK`
	° `TT_ERR_NOMP`
	° `TT_ERR_POINTER`

tt_message_op
```
char             *tt_message_op(Tt_message m)
```

Retrieves the operation (op) attribute from the specified message.

Arguments

`Tt_message m`
Opaque handle for the message involved in this operation.

Returned Value

`char *`
Operation the receiver should perform.
  Use `tt_ptr_error()`, which returns `Tt_status`, to determine if the pointer is valid. Possible `Tt_status` values are:

° `TT_OK`

° `TT_ERR_NOMP`

° `TT_ERR_POINTER`

tt_message_op_set
```
Tt_status         tt_message_op_set(Tt_mes-
                  sage m, const char *opname)
```

Sets the operation (op) attribute for the specified message.

Arguments

`Tt_message m`
Opaque handle for the message involved in this operation.

`const char *opname`
Operation the receiver should perform.

Returned Value

`Tt_status`
The status of the operation. Possible values are:

° `TT_OK`

° `TT_ERR_NOMP`

° `TT_ERR_POINTER`

tt_message_opnum	`int`	`tt_message_opnum(Tt_message m)`

Retrieves the operation number (opnum) attribute from the specified message.

Arguments

`Tt_message m`
Opaque handle for the message involved in this operation.

Returned Value

`int`
The number of the operation (opnum) involved in this message.

Use `tt_int_error()`, which returns `Tt_status`, to determine if the `Tt_disposition` integer is valid. Possible `Tt_status` values are:

- `TT_OK`
- `TT_ERR_NOMP`
- `TT_ERR_POINTER`

tt_message_otype	`char`	`*tt_message_otype(Tt_message m)`

Retrieves the object type (otype) attribute from the specified message.

Arguments

`Tt_message m`
Opaque handle for the message involved in this operation.

Returned Value

`char *`
Type of the object involved in this message.

Use `tt_ptr_error()`, which returns `Tt_status`, to determine if the pointer is valid. Possible `Tt_status` values are:

- `TT_OK`
- `TT_ERR_NOMP`
- `TT_ERR_POINTER`

tt_message_otype_ set	`Tt_status`	`tt_message_otype_set(Tt_message m, const char *otype)`

Sets the object type (otype) attribute for the specified message.

Arguments	`Tt_message m` Opaque handle for the message involved in this operation.
	`const char *otype` Type of the object involved in this message.
Returned Value	`Tt_status` The status of the operation. Possible values are:

- ° `TT_OK`
- ° `TT_ERR_NOMP`
- ° `TT_ERR_OTYPE`
- ° `TT_ERR_POINTER`

tt_message_pattern	`Tt_pattern`	`tt_message_pattern(Tt_message m)`

Retrieves the pattern attribute from the specified message.

Arguments	`Tt_message m` Opaque handle for the message involved in this operation.
Returned Value	`Tt_pattern` Opaque handle for a message pattern. Use `tt_ptr_error()`, which returns `Tt_status`, to determine if the handle is valid. Possible `Tt_status` values are:

- ° `TT_OK`
- ° `TT_ERR_NOMP`
- ° `TT_ERR_POINTER`

tt_message_receive	`Tt_message`	`tt_message_receive(void)`

Returns a handle for the next message waiting to be delivered to your process. `tt_message_receive()` also runs any message or pattern callbacks applicable to this message. Check Tt_status with `tt_message_status()` to see if the return value is `TT_WRN_STARTING`. If it is, the ToolTalk service started your application to deliver this message. You must reply to this message.

Note – If the returned handle is 0, no message is available. This can occur if a message or pattern callback processes the message. It can also happen if the time between the `tt_fd()` file descriptor becoming active and the `tt_message_receive()` call is too long. The ToolTalk service will time out and offer the message to another process.

Returned Value

`Tt_message`
Handle for the message object.
  Use `tt_ptr_error()`, which returns `Tt_status`, to determine if the handle is valid. Possible `Tt_status` values are:

- ° `TT_OK`
- ° `TT_ERR_NOMP`

tt_message_reject

`Tt_status      tt_message_reject(Tt_message m)`

Informs the ToolTalk service that your process can not handle this message. The ToolTalk service will try other handlers.

Arguments

`Tt_message m`
Opaque handle for the message involved in this operation.

Returned Value

`Tt_status`
The status of the operation. Possible values are:

- ° `TT_OK`
- ° `TT_ERR_NOMP`
- ° `TT_ERR_NOTHANDLER`
- ° `TT_ERR_POINTER`

tt_message_reply

`Tt_status      tt_message_reply(Tt_message m)`

Informs the ToolTalk service that your process has finished handling the message, and all return values (any arguments with the `TT_OUT` or `TT_OUTIN` mode) have been filled in. The ToolTalk service will send the message back to the sender and fill in the state attribute with `TT_HANDLED`.

Arguments	`Tt_message m` Opaque handle for the message involved in this operation.
Returned Value	`Tt_status` The status of the operation. Possible values are:

    ° `TT_OK`

    ° `TT_ERR_NOMP`

    ° `TT_ERR_NOTHANDLER`

    ° `TT_ERR_POINTER`

    ° `TT_ERR_PROCID`

tt_message_scope	`Tt_scope`	`tt_message_scope(Tt_message m)`

Retrieves the scope attribute from the specified message.

Arguments	`Tt_message m` Opaque handle for the message involved in this operation.
Returned Value	`Tt_scope` Identifies the set of processes eligible to receive the message. Possible values are:

    ° `TT_SESSION`

    ° `TT_FILE`

    ° `TT_BOTH`

    ° `TT_FILE_IN_SESSION`

Use `tt_int_error()`, which returns `Tt_status`, to determine if the `Tt_scope` integer is valid. Possible `Tt_status` values are:

    ° `TT_OK`

    ° `TT_ERR_NOMP`

    ° `TT_ERR_POINTER`

tt_message_scope_set	`Tt_status`	`tt_message_scope_set(Tt_message m, Tt_scope s)`

Sets the scope attribute for the specified message.

Arguments	`Tt_message m` Opaque handle for the message involved in this operation.
	`Tt_scope s` Identifies the set of processes eligible to receive the message. Possible values are:
	° `TT_SESSION`
	° `TT_FILE`
	° `TT_BOTH`
	° `TT_FILE_IN_SESSION`
Returned Value	`Tt_status` The status of the operation. Possible values are:
	° `TT_OK`
	° `TT_ERR_NOMP`
	° `TT_ERR_POINTER`

tt_message_send	`Tt_status` `tt_message_send(Tt_message` `m)`

Sends the specified message.

Arguments	`Tt_message m` Opaque handle for the message involved in this operation.
Returned Value	`Tt_status` The status of the operation. Possible values are:
	° `TT_OK`
	° `TT_ERR_ADDRESS`
	° `TT_ERR_CLASS`
	° `TT_ERR_FILE`
	° `TT_ERR_NOMP`
	° `TT_ERR_OBJID`
	° `TT_ERR_OTYPE`
	° `TT_ERR_OVERFLOW`
	° `TT_ERR_POINTER`

	° TT_ERR_PROCID
	° TT_ERR_SESSION
	° TT_WRN_STALE_OBJID

tt_message_sender
```
char            *tt_message_sender(Tt_mes-
                sage m)
```

Retrieves the sender attribute from the specified message.

Arguments

```
Tt_message m
```
Opaque handle for the message involved in this operation.

Returned Value

```
char *
```
Character value that uniquely identifies the process that sent the message.

Use `tt_ptr_error()`, which returns `Tt_status`, to determine if the pointer is valid. Possible `Tt_status` values are:

° TT_OK

° TT_ERR_NOMP

° TT_ERR_POINTER

tt_message_sender_ptype
```
char            *tt_message_sender_ptype(Tt_
                message m)
```

Retrieves the sender ptype attribute from the specified message.

Arguments

```
Tt_message m
```
Opaque handle for the message involved in this operation.

Returned Value

```
char *
```
Process that sent this message.

Use `tt_ptr_error()`, which returns `Tt_status`, to determine if the pointer is valid. Possible `Tt_status` values are:

° TT_OK

° TT_ERR_NOMP

° TT_ERR_POINTER

| `tt_message_sender_ptype_set` | Tt_status | `tt_message_sender_ptype_set(Tt_message m, const char *ptid)` |

Sets the sender ptype attribute for the specified message.

Arguments

`Tt_message m`
Opaque handle for the message involved in this operation.

`const char *ptid`
Type of process that is sending this message.

Returned Value

`Tt_status`
The status of the operation. Possible values are:

- `TT_OK`
- `TT_ERR_NOMP`
- `TT_ERR_POINTER`

| `tt_message_session` | char | `*tt_message_session(Tt_message m)` |

Retrieves the session attribute from the specified message.

Arguments

`Tt_message m`
Opaque handle for the message involved in this operation.

Returned Value

`char *`
Identifier of the session to which this message applies.
    Use `tt_ptr_error()`, which returns `Tt_status`, to determine if the pointer is valid. Possible `Tt_status` values are:

- `TT_OK`
- `TT_ERR_NOMP`
- `TT_ERR_POINTER`

| `tt_message_session_set` | Tt_status | `tt_message_session_set(Tt_message m, const char *sessid)` |

Sets the session attribute for the specified message.

Arguments	`Tt_message m` Opaque handle for the message involved in this operation.
	`const char *sessid` Identifier of the session in which you are interested.
Returned Value	`Tt_status` The status of the operation. Possible values are:

- ° `TT_OK`
- ° `TT_ERR_NOMP`
- ° `TT_ERR_POINTER`

tt_message_state

`Tt_state`	`tt_message_state(Tt_message m)`

Retrieves the state attribute from the specified message.

Arguments	`Tt_message m` Opaque handle for the message involved in this operation.
Returned Value	`Tt_state` Indicates a message's current delivery state. Possible values are:

- ° `TT_CREATED`
- ° `TT_SENT`
- ° `TT_HANDLED`
- ° `TT_FAILED`
- ° `TT_QUEUED`
- ° `TT_STARTED`
- ° `TT_REJECTED`

Use `tt_int_error()`, which returns `Tt_status`, to determine if the `Tt_state` integer is valid. Possible `Tt_status` values are:

- ° `TT_OK`
- ° `TT_ERR_NOMP`
- ° `TT_ERR_POINTER`

tt_message_status	int	tt_message_status(Tt_mes-sage m)

Retrieves the status attribute from the specified message.

Arguments

Tt_message m
Opaque handle for the message involved in this operation.

Returned Value

int
An integer that describes the status stored in the status attribute of this message.

Use tt_int_error(), which returns Tt_status, to determine if the integer is valid. Possible Tt_status values are:

- ° TT_OK
- ° TT_ERR_NOMP
- ° TT_ERR_POINTER

Related Functions

tt_message_status_string()

tt_message_status_ set	Tt_status	tt_message_status_set(Tt_ message m, int status)

Sets the status attribute for the specified message.

Note – The status value must be greater than 2047 (TT_ ERR_LAST) to avoid confusion with the ToolTalk service status values.

Arguments

Tt_message m
Opaque handle for the message involved in this operation.

int status
Status to be stored in this message.

Returned Value

Tt_status
The status of the operation. Possible values are:

- ° TT_OK
- ° TT_ERR_NOMP
- ° TT_ERR_POINTER

tt_message_status_ string	char *tt_message_status_ string(Tt_message m)

Retrieves the character string stored with the status attribute for the specified message.

Arguments
Tt_message m
Opaque handle for the message involved in this operation.

Returned Value
char *
Status string stored in this message.
    Use tt_ptr_error(), which returns Tt_status, to determine if the pointer is valid. Possible Tt_status values are:

  ° TT_OK

  ° TT_ERR_NOMP

  ° TT_ERR_POINTER

Related Functions
tt_message_status()

tt_message_status_ string_set	Tt_status tt_message_status_string_ set(Tt_message m, const char *status_str)

Sets a character string with the status attribute for the specified message.

Arguments
Tt_message m
Opaque handle for the message involved in this operation.

const char *status_str
Status string stored in this message.

Returned Value
Tt_status
The status of the operation. Possible values are:

  ° TT_OK

  ° TT_ERR_NOMP

  ° TT_ERR_POINTER

Related Functions
tt_message_status_set()

tt_message_uid	uid_t tt_message_uid(Tt_message m)

Retrieves the user ID attribute from the specified message.

The ToolTalk service automatically sets the user ID of a message with the user ID of the process that created the message.

Arguments

Tt_message m
Opaque handle for the message involved in this operation.

Returned Value

uid_t
The user ID of the message, or the "nobody" user (65534) if the message handle is not valid.

Related Functions

tt_message_gid()

tt_message_user

void   *tt_message_user(Tt_message
                m, int key)

Retrieves the user information stored in data cells associated with the specified message object you created. Since the user data is part of the message object (the storage buffer in your application), not the actual message, you can only retrieve user information that you placed on the message.

Arguments

Tt_message m
Opaque handle for the message involved in this operation.

int key
User data cell in which you are interested. It must be unique over all user data cells for this message.

Returned Value

void *
A piece of arbitrary user data that is one word in size.
    Use tt_ptr_error(), which returns Tt_status, to determine if the pointer is valid. Possible Tt_status values are:

° TT_OK

° TT_ERR_NOMP

° TT_ERR_POINTER

**tt_message_user_
set**

Tt_status   tt_message_user_set(Tt_mes-
                sage m, int key,
                void *v)

Stores user information in data cells associated with the specified message object.

Note that the user data is part of the message object (the storage buffer in your application), not the actual message. Data stored by the sender in user data cells is not seen by any handlers or observers. Use arguments for data that handlers or observers need to see.

Arguments

`Tt_message m`
Opaque handle for the message involved in this operation.

`int key`
User data cell in which you are interested.

`void *v`
A piece of arbitrary user data that is one word in size.

Returned Value

`Tt_status`
The status of the operation. Possible values are:

- `TT_OK`
- `TT_ERR_NOMP`
- `TT_ERR_POINTER`
- `TT_ERR_PROCID`

Related Functions

tt_objid_equal

`tt_message_arg_add()`

`int            tt_objid_equal(const char *objid1, const char *objid2)`

Tests to see if two objids are equal. `tt_objid_equal()` is better than `strcmp` for the purpose since it returns "1" even in the case where one objid is a forwarding pointer for the other.

Arguments

`const char *objid1`
Identifier of one of the objects involved in this operation.

const char *objid2
Identifier of the other object involved in this operation.

Returned Value

`int`
Integer indicating whether or not the objids are equal. Possible values are:

- `0 - no`
- `1 - yes`

Use `tt_int_error()`, which returns `Tt_status`, to determine if the integer is valid. Possible `Tt_status` values are:

- `TT_OK`
- `TT_ERR_NOMP`
- `TT_ERR_OBJID`

tt_objid_objkey

```
char           *tt_objid_objkey(const char
               *objid)
```

Returns the "unique key" portion of a objid.

Arguments

`const char *objid`
Identifier of the object involved in this operation.

Returned Value

`char *`
Unique key of the objid. No two objids have the same unique key.

Use `tt_ptr_error()`, which returns `Tt_status`, to determine if the pointer is valid. Possible `Tt_status` values are:

- `TT_OK`
- `TT_ERR_OBJID`

tt_onotice_create

```
Tt_message      tt_onotice_create(const char
               *objid, const char *op)
```

Creates a message with:

- Tt_address = TT_OBJECT
- Tt_class = TT_NOTICE

The handle for the created message is returned so you can add arguments, other attributes, and send the message.

Arguments

`const char *objid`
Identifier of the desired object.

`const char *op`
Operation to be performed by the receiver.

Returned Value

`Tt_message`
The unique handle that identifies your message.

Use `tt_ptr_error()`, which returns `Tt_status`, to determine if the handle is valid. Possible `Tt_status` values are:

° `TT_OK`

° `TT_ERR_NOMP`

° `TT_ERR_PROCID`

tt_open   `char        *tt_open(void)`

Returns the process identifier (procid) for the calling process, and sets this procid as the default procid for the process. `tt_open()` is typically the first ToolTalk function you call from your process.

A process may call `tt_open()` more than once to obtain more than one procid. Each procid has its own associated `tt_fd()` file descriptor, and can join another session. To switch to another procid use `tt_default_procid_set()`.

Returned Value   `char *`
Character value that uniquely identifies your process.

Use `tt_ptr_error()`, which returns `Tt_status`, to determine if the pointer is valid. Possible `Tt_status` values are:

° `TT_OK`

° `TT_ERR_NOMP`

Related Functions   `tt_fd()`

                          `tt_default_procid_set()`

tt_orequest_create   `Tt_message    tt_orequest_create(const char *objid, const char *op)`

Creates a message with:

• `tt_address = TT_OBJECT`
• `tt_class = TT_REQUEST`

The handle for the created message is returned so you can add arguments, other attributes, and send the message.

Arguments   `const char *objid`
Identifier of the desired object.

                          `const char *op`
The operation to be performed by the receiver.

Returned Value   `Tt_message`
The unique handle that identifies your message.

Use `tt_ptr_error()`, which returns `Tt_status`, to determine if the handle is valid. Possible `Tt_status` values are:

- ° TT_OK
- ° TT_ERR_NOMP
- ° TT_ERR_PROCID

tt_otype_base

```
char            *tt_otype_base(const char
                *otype)
```

Returns the base otype that the given otype is derived from, or NULL if the given otype is not derived.

Arguments

`char *otype`
Object type involved in this operation.

Returned Value

`char *`
Name of the base otype, or NULL if the given otype is not derived.

Use `tt_ptr_error()`, which returns `Tt_status`, to determine if the pointer is valid. Possible `Tt_status` values are:

- ° TT_OK
- ° TT_ERR_NOMP
- ° TT_ERR_OTYPE

Related Functions

```
tt_otype_is_derived()

tt_otype_derived()

tt_otype_deriveds_count()

tt_spec_type()

tt_message_otype()
```

tt_otype_derived

```
char            *tt_otype_derived(const char
                *otype, int i)
```

Returns the *i*-th otype derived from the given otype.

Arguments

`const char *otype`
Object type involved in this operation.

`int i`
Zero-based index into the otypes derived from the given otype.

Returned Value	`char *` Name of the *i*-th otype derived from the given otype.

Use `tt_ptr_error()`, which returns `Tt_status`, to determine if the pointer is valid. Possible `Tt_status` values are:

- ° `TT_OK`

- ° `TT_ERR_NOMP`

- ° `TT_ERR_OTYPE`

Related Functions	`tt_otype_is_derived()`

`tt_otype_base()`

`tt_otype_deriveds_count()`

`tt_spec_type()`

`tt_message_otype()`

tt_otype_deriveds_ count	`int` `tt_otype_deriveds_count` `(const char *otype)`

Returns the number of otypes derived from the given otype.

Arguments	`const char *otype` Object type involved in this operation.

Returned Value	`int` The number of otypes derived from the given otype.

Use `tt_int_error()`, which returns `Tt_status`, to determine if the integer is valid. Possible `Tt_status` values are:

- ° `TT_OK`

- ° `TT_ERR_NOMP`

- ° `TT_ERR_OTYPE`

Related Functions	`tt_otype_is_derived()`

`tt_otype_base()`

`tt_otype_derived()`

`tt_spec_type()`

`tt_message_otype()`

tt_otype_hsig_arg_mode	Tt_mode	tt_otype_hsig_arg_mode (const char *otype, int sig, int arg)

Returns the Tt_mode of the arg'th argument of the sig'th request signature of the given otype.

Arguments

const char *otype
Object type involved in this operation.

int sig
Zero-based index into the request signatures of the specified otype.

int arg
Zero-based index into the arguments of the specified signature.

Returned Value

Tt_mode
The Tt_mode of the specified argument, which determines who (sender or handler) writes and reads a message argument. Possible modes are:

° TT_IN

° TT_OUT

° TT_INOUT

Use tt_int_error(), which returns Tt_status, to determine if the integer is valid. Possible Tt_status values are:

° TT_OK

° TT_ERR_NOMP

° TT_ERR_NUM

° TT_ERR_OTYPE

Related Functions

tt_otype_hsig_arg_type()

tt_otype_hsig_count()

tt_otype_hsig_args_count()

tt_otype_hsig_op()

| **tt_otype_hsig_arg_ type** | char | *tt_otype_hsig_arg_type (const char *otype, int sig, int arg) |

Returns the data type of the arg'th argument of the sig'th request signature of the given otype.

Arguments

`const char *otype`
Object type involved in this operation.

`int sig`
Zero-based index into the request signatures of the specified `otype`.

`int arg`
Zero-based index into the arguments of the specified signature.

Returned Value

`char *`
Data type of the specified argument.
Use `tt_ptr_error()`, which returns `Tt_status`, to determine if the pointer is valid. Possible `Tt_status` values are:

- ° TT_OK

- ° TT_ERR_NOMP

- ° TT_ERR_NUM

- ° TT_ERR_OTYPE

Related Functions

`tt_otype_hsig_arg_mode()`

`tt_otype_hsig_count()`

`tt_otype_hsig_args_count()`

`tt_otype_hsig_op()`

| **tt_otype_hsig_args_ count** | int | tt_otype_hsig_args_count (const char *otype, int sig) |

Returns the number of arguments of the sig'th request signature of the given otype.

Arguments

`const char *otype`
Object type involved in this operation.

`int sig`
Zero-based index into the request signatures of the specified otype.

Returned Value	`int` The number of arguments of the sig'th request signature of the given otype. Use `tt_int_error()`, which returns `Tt_status`, to determine if the integer is valid. Possible `Tt_status` values are: ° `TT_OK` ° `TT_ERR_NOMP` ° `TT_ERR_NUM` ° `TT_ERR_OTYPE`

Related Functions	`tt_otype_hsig_arg_type()`
	
	`tt_otype_hsig_arg_mode()`
	
	`tt_otype_hsig_count()`
	
	`tt_otype_hsig_op()`

tt_otype_hsig_count

`int            tt_otype_hsig_count(const char *otype)`

Returns the number of request signatures for the given otype.

Arguments	`const char *otype` Object type involved in this operation.
Returned Value	`int` The number of request signatures for the given otype. Use `tt_int_error()`, which returns `Tt_status`, to determine if the integer is valid. Possible `Tt_status` values are: ° `TT_OK` ° `TT_ERR_NOMP` ° `TT_ERR_OTYPE`

Related Functions	`tt_otype_hsig_arg_type()`
	
	`tt_otype_hsig_arg_mode()`
	
	`tt_otype_hsig_args_count()`
	
	`tt_otype_hsig_op()`

tt_otype_hsig_op	char *tt_otype_hsig_op(const char *otype, int sig)

Returns the op name of the sig'th request signature of the give otype.

Arguments

```
const char *otype
```
Object type involved in this operation.

```
int sig
```
Zero-based index into the request signatures of the given otype.

Returned Value

```
char *
```
Operation attribute of the specified request signature.

Use tt_ptr_error(), which returns Tt_status, to determine if the pointer is valid. Possible Tt_status values are:

- ° TT_OK
- ° TT_ERR_NOMP
- ° TT_ERR_NUM
- ° TT_ERR_OTYPE

Related Functions

tt_otype_hsig_arg_type()

tt_otype_hsig_arg_mode()

tt_otype_hsig_args_count()

tt_otype_hsig_count()

tt_otype_is_derived	int tt_otype_is_derived(const char *derivedotype, const char *baseotype)

Returns 1 if and only if derivedotype is derived directly or indirectly from baseotype.

Arguments

```
const char *derivedotype
```
The purportedly derived otype.

```
const char *baseotype
```
Candidate base otype.

Returned Value

```
int
```
Returns 1 if and only if derivedotype is derived directly or indirectly from baseotype.

Use `tt_int_error()`, which returns `Tt_status`, to determine if the integer is valid. Possible `Tt_status` values are:

- ° `TT_OK`
- ° `TT_ERR_NOMP`
- ° `TT_ERR_OTYPE`

Related Functions

`tt_otype_deriveds_count()`

`tt_otype_base()`

`tt_otype_derived()`

`tt_spec_type()`

`tt_message_otype()`

tt_otype_osig_arg_mode

`Tt_mode`	`tt_otype_osig_arg_mode (const char *otype, int sig, int arg)`

Returns the Tt_mode of the arg'th argument of the sig'th notice signature of the given otype.

Arguments

`const char *otype`
Object type involved in this operation.

`int sig`
Zero-based index into the notice signatures of the specified otype.

`int arg`
Zero-based index into the arguments of the specified signature.

Returned Value

`Tt_mode`
The Tt_mode of the specified argument, which determines who (sender or handler) writes and reads a message argument. Possible modes are:

- ° `TT_IN`
- ° `TT_OUT`
- ° `TT_INOUT`

Use `tt_int_error()`, which returns Tt_status, to determine if the Tt_mode value is valid. Possible Tt_status values are:

    ◦ TT_OK

    ◦ TT_ERR_NOMP

    ◦ TT_ERR_NUM

    ◦ TT_ERR_OTYPE

Related Functions   `tt_otype_osig_arg_type()`

    `tt_otype_osig_count()`

    `tt_otype_osig_args_count()`

    `tt_otype_osig_op()`

tt_otype_osig_arg_ type

```
char                *tt_otype_osig_arg_type
                    (const char *otype, int sig,
                    int arg)
```

Returns the data type of the arg'th argument of the sig'th notice signature of the given otype.

Arguments   `const char *otype`
Object type involved in this operation.

    `int sig`
Zero-based index into the notice signatures of the specified otype.

    `int arg`
Zero-based index into the arguments of the specified signature.

Returned Value   `char *`
Data type of the specified argument.
    Use `tt_ptr_error()`, which returns `Tt_status`, to determine if the pointer is valid. Possible `Tt_status` values are:

    ◦ TT_OK

    ◦ TT_ERR_NOMP

    ◦ TT_ERR_NUM

    ◦ TT_ERR_OTYPE

Related Functions   `tt_otype_osig_arg_mode()`

    `tt_otype_osig_count()`

    `tt_otype_osig_args_count()`

    `tt_otype_osig_op()`

tt_otype_osig_args_count	int	tt_otype_osig_args_count (const char *otype, int sig)

Returns the number of arguments of the sig'th notice signature of the given otype.

Arguments

const char *otype
Object type involved in this operation.

int sig
Zero-based index into the notice signatures of the specified otype.

Returned Value

int
The number of arguments of the sig'th notice signature of the given otype.

Use tt_int_error(), which returns Tt_status, to determine if the integer is valid. Possible Tt_status values are:

° TT_OK

° TT_ERR_NOMP

° TT_ERR_NUM

° TT_ERR_OTYPE

Related Functions

tt_otype_osig_arg_type()

tt_otype_osig_arg_mode()

tt_otype_osig_count()

tt_otype_osig_op()

tt_otype_osig_count	int	tt_otype_osig_count(const char *otype)

Returns the number of notice signatures for the given otype.

Arguments

const char *otype
Object type involved in this operation.

Returned Value

int
The number of notice signatures for the given otype.

Use tt_int_error(), which returns Tt_status, to determine if the integer is valid. Possible Tt_status values are:

° TT_OK

Related Functions

`tt_otype_osig_arg_type()`

`tt_otype_osig_arg_mode()`

`tt_otype_osig_args_count()`

`tt_otype_osig_op()`

`tt_otype_osig_op`

`char`	`*tt_otype_osig_op(const char *otype, int sig)`

Returns the op name of the sig'th notice signature of the give otype.

Arguments

`const char *otype`
Object type involved in this operation.

`int sig`
Zero-based index into the notice signatures of the given otype.

Returned Value

`char *`
Operation attribute of the specified notice signature.

Use `tt_ptr_error()`, which returns `Tt_status`, to determine if the pointer is valid. Possible `Tt_status` values are:

° `TT_OK`

° `TT_ERR_NOMP`

° `TT_ERR_NUM`

° `TT_ERR_OTYPE`

Related Functions

`tt_otype_osig_arg_type()`

`tt_otype_osig_arg_mode()`

`tt_otype_osig_args_count()`

`tt_otype_osig_count()`

`tt_pattern_address_ add`

`Tt_status`	`tt_pattern_address_add(Tt_ pattern p, Tt_address d)`

Adds a value to the address field for the specified pattern.

| *Arguments* | Tt_pattern p |
| | A unique handle for a message pattern. You receive this handle after you issue tt_pattern_create(). |

Tt_address d
Specifies which pattern attributes form the address that messages will be matched against. Possible values are:

- TT_PROCEDURE
- TT_OBJECT
- TT_HANDLER
- TT_OTYPE

Returned Value

Tt_status
The status of the operation. Possible values are:

- TT_OK
- TT_ERR_NOMP
- TT_ERR_POINTER

tt_pattern_arg_add

Tt_status   tt_pattern_arg_add(Tt_pattern p, Tt_mode n, constchar *vtype, const char *value)

Adds an argument to a pattern. Add pattern arguments before registering your pattern with the ToolTalk service.

Arguments

Tt_pattern p
Opaque handle for the pattern involved in this operation.

Tt_mode n
Specifies who (sender, handler, observers) writes and reads a message argument. Possible modes are:

- TT_IN
- TT_OUT
- TT_INOUT

const char *vtype
Type of the value. Use 'ALL' to match without regard to argument value type.

const char *value
Value to fill in (must be an unsigned character string.) Use NULL to indicate that any value matches.

Returned Value Tt_status
The status of the operation. Possible values are:

° TT_OK

° TT_ERR_NOMP

° TT_ERR_POINTER

Related Functions tt_pattern_register()

tt_pattern_barg_add()

tt_pattern_iarg_add()

tt_pattern_barg_add Tt_status   tt_pattern_barg_add(Tt_pat-
tern m, Tt_mode n, constchar
*vtype, const unsigned char
*value, int len)

Adds an argument with a value containing imbedded nulls to a pattern.

Arguments Tt_pattern m
Opaque handle for the pattern involved in this operation.

Tt_mode n
Specifies who (sender, handler, observers) writes and reads a message argument. Possible modes are:

° TT_IN

° TT_OUT

° TT_INOUT

const char *vtype
Type of the value.
  The ToolTalk service treats the value as an opaque byte string. To pass structured data, your application and the receiving application must encode and decode these unique values. The most common way of doing this is to use XDR.

const unsigned char *value
Value to be filled in. Use NULL to specify that any value matches.

int len
Length of the value in bytes.

Returned Value Tt_status
The status of the operation. Possible values are:

° `TT_OK`

° `TT_ERR_NOMP`

° `TT_ERR_POINTER`

Related Functions

`tt_pattern_register()`

`tt_pattern_arg_add()`

`tt_pattern_iarg_add()`

tt_pattern_callback_add

`Tt_status`	`tt_pattern_callback_add(Tt_`
	`pattern m,`
	`Tt_message_callback f)`

Registers a callback function that will be automatically invoked by `tt_message_receive()` whenever a message matches the pattern.

`Tt_callback_action` is an enum containing the values `TT_CALLBACK_CONTINUE` and `TT_CALLBACK_PRO-CESSED`. If the callback returns `TT_CALLBACK_PRO-CESSED`, no further callbacks will be invoked for this event, and the message will not be returned by `tt_message_re-ceive()`; if the callback returns `TT_CALLBACK_CON-TINUE`, other callbacks will be run, and if no callback returns `TT_CALLBACK_PROCESSED`, `tt_message_receive()` will return the message.

Arguments

`Tt_pattern m`
Opaque handle for the pattern involved in this operation.

`Tt_message_callback f`
`Tt_message_callback` is a type definition for a pointer to a function declared like: `Tt_callback_action func(Tt_message m, Tt_pattern p)`. The callback is passed the message in question and the pattern that matched it.

Returned Value

`Tt_status`
The status of the operation. Possible values are:

° `TT_OK`

° `TT_ERR_NOMP`

° `TT_ERR_POINTER`

Related Functions	`tt_pattern_register()`
tt_pattern_category	`Tt_category` `tt_pattern_category(Tt_pattern p)`

Returns the category value of the specified pattern.

Arguments

`Tt_pattern p`
Opaque handle for a message pattern.

Returned Value

`Tt_category`
Indicates the receiver's intent. Possible values are:

- ° `TT_OBSERVE`

- ° `TT_HANDLE`

Use `tt_int_error()`, which returns `Tt_status`, to determine if the `Tt_category` integer is valid. Possible `Tt_status` values are:

- ° `TT_OK`

- ° `TT_ERR_NOMP`

- ° `TT_ERR_POINTER`

Related Functions	`tt_pattern_category_set()`
tt_pattern_category_set	`Tt_status` `tt_pattern_category_set(Tt_pattern p, Tt_category c)`

Fills in the category field for the specified pattern.

Arguments

`Tt_pattern p`
A unique handle for a message pattern. You receive this handle after you issue `tt_pattern_create()`.

`Tt_category c`
Indicates the receiver's intent. Possible values are:

- ° `TT_OBSERVE`

- ° `TT_HANDLE`

Returned Value

`Tt_status`
The status of the operation. Possible values are:

- ° `TT_OK`

- ° `TT_ERR_CATEGORY`

- ° `TT_ERR_NOMP`

- ° `TT_ERR_POINTER`

      Chapter 1. ToolTalk® Overview

Related Functions	tt_pattern_category()	
tt_pattern_class_ add	Tt_status	tt_pattern_class_add(Tt_pat- tern p, Tt_class c)

Adds a value to the class information for the specified pattern. If the class is TT_REQUEST, the sender expects a reply to the message. If the class is TT_NOTICE, the sender will not expect a reply.

Arguments

Tt_pattern p
A unique handle for a message pattern. You receive this handle after you issue tt_pattern_create().

Tt_class c
Indicates whether or not the sender wants the receiver to take action after the message is received. Possible values are:

- ° TT_NOTICE

- ° TT_REQUEST

Returned Value

Tt_status
The status of the operation. Possible values are:

- ° TT_OK

- ° TT_ERR_NOMP

- ° TT_ERR_POINTER

tt_pattern_create	Tt_pattern	tt_pattern_create(void)

Requests a new pattern object. After receiving the pattern object, fill in the message pattern fields to indicate what type of messages you want to receive and register this information with the ToolTalk service.

Note – You can supply multiple values for each attribute you *add* to a pattern (some attributes are *set* and only have one value). The pattern attribute matches a message attribute if any of the values in the pattern match the value in the message. If no value is specified for an attribute, the ToolTalk service assumes that you want any value to match.

Returned Value

Tt_pattern
Opaque handle for a message pattern. Use this handle in future calls to identify the pattern object.

Use `tt_ptr_error()`, which returns `Tt_status`, to determine if the pointer is valid. Possible `Tt_status` values are:

- TT_OK
- TT_ERR_NOMP

Related Functions
`tt_pattern_register()`

tt_pattern_destroy

`Tt_status`	`tt_pattern_destroy(Tt_pattern p)`

Destroys a pattern object. Destroying a pattern object automatically unregisters the pattern with the ToolTalk service.

Arguments
`Tt_pattern p`
A unique handle for a message pattern. You receive this handle after you issue `tt_pattern_create()`.

Returned Value
`Tt_status`
The status of the operation. Possible values are:

- TT_OK
- TT_ERR_NOMP
- TT_ERR_POINTER

Related Functions
`tt_pattern_register()`

tt_pattern_disposition_add

`Tt_status`	`tt_pattern_disposition_add(Tt_pattern p, Tt_disposition r)`

Adds a value to the disposition field for the specified pattern.

Arguments
`Tt_pattern p`
A unique handle for a message pattern. You receive this handle after you issue `tt_pattern_create()`.

`Tt_disposition r`
Indicates whether the receiver should be started to receive the message or if the message should be queued until the receiving process is started at a later time. The message can also be thrown away if the receiver is not started. Possible values are:

- TT_DISCARD
- TT_QUEUE

○ `TT_START`

○ `TT_QUEUE+TT_START`

Returned Value Tt_status
The status of the operation. Possible values are:

○ `TT_OK`

○ `TT_ERR_NOMP`

○ `TT_ERR_POINTER`

tt_pattern_file_add | Tt_status | `tt_pattern_file_add(Tt_pat-tern p,`
`const char *file)`

Adds a value to the file field of the specified pattern.

Note – When you join a file, the ToolTalk service updates the file field of your registered patterns.

Arguments `Tt_pattern p`
A unique handle for a message pattern. You receive this handle after you issue `tt_pattern_create()`.

`const char *file`
Name of the file in which you are interested.

Returned Value `Tt_status`
The status of the operation. Possible values are:

○ `TT_OK`

○ `TT_ERR_NOMP`

○ `TT_ERR_POINTER`

tt_pattern_iarg_add | Tt_status | `tt_pattern_iarg_add(Tt_pat-tern m, Tt_mode n,`
`const char *vtype, int value)`

Adds a new argument to a pattern and sets the value to a given integer. Add all arguments before the pattern is registered.

Arguments `Tt_pattern m`
Opaque handle for the pattern involved in this operation.

```
Tt_mode n
```
Specifies who (sender, handler, observers) writes and reads a message argument. Possible modes are:

- ° `TT_IN`
- ° `TT_OUT`
- ° `TT_INOUT`

```
const char *vtype
```
Type of the value.

```
int value
```
Value to fill in.

Returned Value `Tt_status`
The status of the operation. Possible values are:

- ° `TT_OK`
- ° `TT_ERR_MODE`
- ° `TT_ERR_NOMP`
- ° `TT_ERR_POINTER`
- ° `TT_ERR_VTYPE`

Related Functions `tt_pattern_register()`

tt_pattern_object_ add

`Tt_status`	`tt_pattern_object_add(Tt_ pattern p, const char *objid)`

Adds a value to the object field of the specified pattern.

Arguments `Tt_pattern p`
A unique handle for a message pattern. You receive this handle after you issue `tt_pattern_create()`.

```
const char *objid
```
Identifier for the specified object. Objid's are returned from `tt_spec_create()` or `tt_spec_move()`.

Returned Value `Tt_status`
The status of the operation. Possible values are:

- ° `TT_OK`
- ° `TT_ERR_NOMP`
- ° `TT_ERR_POINTER`

tt_pattern_op_add	Tt_status tt_pattern_op_add(Tt_pat- tern p, const char *opname)

Adds a value to the operation field of the specified pattern.

Arguments
Tt_pattern p
A unique handle for a message pattern. You receive this handle after you issue tt_pattern_create().

const char *opname
The name of the operation (op) your process can perform.

Returned Value
Tt_status
The status of the operation. Possible values are:

- ° TT_OK
- ° TT_ERR_NOMP
- ° TT_ERR_POINTER

tt_pattern_otype_ add	Tt_status tt_pattern_otype_add(Tt_pat- tern p, const char *otype)

Adds a value to the object type (otype) field for the specified pattern.

Arguments
Tt_pattern p
A unique handle for a message pattern. You receive this handle after you issue tt_pattern_create().

const char *otype
The name of the object type your application manages.

Returned Value
Tt_status
The status of the operation. Possible values are:

- ° TT_OK
- ° TT_ERR_NOMP
- ° TT_ERR_OTYPE
- ° TT_ERR_POINTER

tt_pattern_register	Tt_status tt_pattern_register(Tt_pat- tern p)

Registers your pattern with TT, so that your process will start receiving messages that match the pattern. Once a pattern is registered, no further changes can be made in the pattern.

> **Note –** When you join a session or file, the ToolTalk service updates the file and session field of your registered patterns.

Arguments

`Tt_pattern p`
A unique handle for a message pattern. You receive this handle after you issue `tt_pattern_create()`.

Returned Value

`Tt_status`
The status of the operation. Possible values are:

- ° `TT_OK`
- ° `TT_ERR_NOMP`
- ° `TT_ERR_POINTER`
- ° `TT_ERR_PROCID`

Related Functions

`tt_pattern_unregister()`

`tt_pattern_scope_add`

`Tt_status        tt_pattern_scope_add(Tt_pattern p,`
`                         Tt_scope s)`

Adds a value to the scope field for the specified pattern.

Arguments

`Tt_pattern p`
A unique handle for a message pattern. You receive this handle after you issue `tt_pattern_create()`.

`Tt_scope s`
Specifies which process are eligible to receive the message. Possible values are:

- ° `TT_SESSION`
- ° `TT_FILE`
- ° `TT_BOTH`
- ° `TT_FILE_IN_SESSION`

Returned Value

`Tt_status`
The status of the operation. Possible values are:

- ° `TT_OK`
- ° `TT_ERR_NOMP`
- ° `TT_ERR_POINTER`

tt_pattern_sender_ add	Tt_status	tt_pattern_sender_add(Tt_ pattern p, const char *pro- cid)

Adds a value to the sender field for the specified pattern.

Arguments

Tt_pattern p
A unique handle for a message pattern. You receive this handle after you issue tt_pattern_create().

const char *procid
Character value that uniquely identifies the process in which you are interested.

Returned Value

Tt_status
The status of the operation. Possible values are:

° TT_OK

° TT_ERR_NOMP

° TT_ERR_POINTER

tt_pattern_sender_ ptype_add	Tt_status	tt_pattern_sender_ptype_ad- d(Tt_pattern p, const char *ptid)

Adds a value to the sender's process type (ptype) field for the specified pattern.

Arguments

Tt_pattern p
A unique handle for a message pattern. You receive this handle after you issue tt_pattern_create().

const char *ptid
Use the character string that uniquely identifies the type of process in which you are interested.

Returned Value

Tt_status
The status of the operation. Possible values are:

° TT_OK

° TT_ERR_NOMP

° TT_ERR_POINTER

tt_pattern_session_ add	Tt_status	tt_pattern_session_add(Tt_ pattern p, const char *sessid)

Adds a value to the session field for the specified pattern.

> **Note –** When you join a session, the ToolTalk service updates the session field of your registered patterns.

Arguments

Tt_pattern p
A unique handle for a message pattern. You receive this handle after you issue tt_pattern_create().

const char *sessid
Session in which you are interested.

Returned Value

Tt_status
The status of the operation. Possible values are:

- ° TT_OK

- ° TT_ERR_NOMP

- ° TT_ERR_POINTER

tt_pattern_state_ add

Tt_status	tt_pattern_state_add(Tt_pattern p, Tt_state s)

Adds a value to the state field for the specified pattern.

Arguments

Tt_pattern p
A unique handle for a message pattern. You receive this handle after you issue tt_pattern_create().

Tt_state s
Indicates a message's current delivery state. Possible values are:

- ° TT_CREATED

- ° TT_SENT

- ° TT_HANDLED

- ° TT_FAILED

- ° TT_QUEUED

- ° TT_STARTED

- ° TT_REJECTED

Related Functions

Tt_status
The status of the operation. Possible values are:

- ° TT_OK

- ° TT_ERR_NOMP

- ° TT_ERR_POINTER

tt_pattern_unregister	Tt_status	tt_pattern_unregister(Tt_pattern p)

Unregisters the specified pattern from the ToolTalk service. Your process will stop receiving messages that match this pattern.

Arguments

Tt_pattern p
A unique handle for a message pattern. You receive this handle after you issue tt_pattern_create().

Returned Value

Tt_status
The status of the operation. Possible values are:

   ° TT_OK

   ° TT_ERR_NOMP

   ° TT_ERR_POINTER

Related Functions

tt_pattern_register()

tt_pattern_user	void	*tt_pattern_user(Tt_pattern p, int key)

Returns the value in the indicated user data cell for the specified pattern object.

Every pattern object allows an arbitrary number of user data cells, each one word (a void *) in size. The user data cells are identified by integer keys. Your tool can use these in any way you see fit, to associate arbitrary data with a pattern object. Note that the user data is part of the pattern object (the storage buffer in your application), not the actual pattern. The content of user cells has no effect on pattern matching.

Arguments

Tt_pattern p
A unique handle for a message pattern. You receive this handle after you issue tt_pattern_create().

int key
User data cell in which you are interested. Your application assigns the keys to the user data cells which are part of the pattern object with tt_pattern_user_set(). Values must be unique over all data cells for this pattern.

Returned Value

void *
String containing a piece of arbitrary user data that is one word in size.

Use `tt_ptr_error()`, which returns `Tt_status`, to determine if the pointer is valid. Possible `Tt_status` values are:

- ° `TT_OK`
- ° `TT_ERR_NOMP`
- ° `TT_ERR_POINTER`

Related Functions
tt_pattern_user_set

`tt_pattern_user_set()`

`Tt_status`	`tt_pattern_user_set(Tt_pattern p, int key, void *v)`

Stores information in the user data cells associated with the specified pattern object.

Arguments

`Tt_pattern p`
A unique handle for a message pattern. You receive this handle after you issue `tt_pattern_create()`.

`int key`
User data cell in which you are interested. Values must be unique over all data cells for this pattern.

`void *v`
String containing a piece of arbitrary user data that is one word in size.

Returned Value

`Tt_status`
The status of the operation. Possible values are:

- ° `TT_OK`
- ° `TT_ERR_NOMP`
- ° `TT_ERR_POINTER`

Related Functions
tt_pnotice_create

`tt_pattern_user()`

`Tt_message`	`tt_pnotice_create(Tt_scope scope, const char *op)`

Creates a message with:

- Tt_address = TT_PROCEDURE
- Tt_class = TT_NOTICE

The handle for the created message is returned so you can add arguments, other attributes, and send the message.

Arguments

Tt_scope scope
A portion of the message that helps determine which processes are eligible to receive the message. A potential recipient could be joined to:

° TT_SESSION

° TT_FILE

° TT_BOTH

° TT_FILE_IN_SESSION

If the scope is TT_SESSION, the Session is set to the current default session. If the scope is TT_FILE, the File is set to the current default file. If the scope is BOTH or FILE_IN_SESSION, both File and Session are set to the defaults.

const char *op
The operation to be performed by the receiver.

Returned Value

Tt_message
The unique handle that identifies your message.

If ToolTalk is unable to create a message when requested, an invalid handle will be returned to you. When you attempt to use this handle, the ToolTalk service will report an error.

Use tt_ptr_error(), which returns Tt_status, to determine if the pointer is valid. Possible Tt_status values are:

° TT_OK

° TT_ERR_NOMP

° TT_ERR_PROCID

tt_pointer_error

Tt_status	tt_pointer_error(void *pointer)

Given an opaque pointer (Tt_message or Tt_pattern), or character pointer (char *), returns TT_OK if the pointer is valid or the encoded Tt_status value if the pointer is an error object.

To avoid the annoyance of having to cast the opaque or character pointer to void * in every call, a macro tt_ptr_error(p) is provided that expands to tt_pointer_error((void *)(p)).

Arguments

void *pointer
Opaque pointer or character pointer to be checked.

Returned Value	`Tt_status`
	The status of the operation. Possible values are:
	  ° `TT_OK`
	  ° `TT_ERR_NOMP`
	  ° `TT_ERR_POINTER`

tt_prequest_create	`Tt_message` `tt_prequest_create(Tt_scope` `scope, const char *op)`

Creates a message with:

- Tt_address = TT_PROCEDURE
- Tt_class = TT_REQUEST

The handle for the created message is returned so you can add arguments, other attributes, and send the message.

Arguments

`Tt_scope scope`
A portion of the message that helps determine which processes are eligible to receive the message. A potential recipient could be joined to:

  ° `TT_SESSION`

  ° `TT_FILE`

  ° `TT_BOTH`

  ° `TT_FILE_IN_SESSION`

If the scope is `TT_SESSION`, the Session is set to the current default session. If the scope is `TT_FILE`, the File is set to the current default file. If the scope is `BOTH` or `FILE_IN_SESSION`, both File and Session are set to the defaults.

`const char *op`
The operation to be performed by the receiver.

Returned Value

`Tt_message`
The unique handle that identifies your message.

If ToolTalk is unable to create a message when requested, an invalid handle will be returned to you. When you attempt to use this handle, the ToolTalk service will report an error.

Use `tt_ptr_error()`, which returns `Tt_status`, to determine if the pointer is valid. Possible `Tt_status` values are:

  ° `TT_OK`

| | ° `TT_ERR_NOMP` |
| | ° `TT_ERR_PROCID` |

| **tt_ptr_error** | `Tt_status`   `tt_ptr_error(pointer)` |

A macro that expands to `tt_pointer_error((void *)(p))`. `tt_ptr_error()` helps you avoid the annoyance of having to cast the opaque or character pointer to `void *` in every call.

Arguments

`pointer`
Pointer to the `Tt_status` code.

Returned Value

`Tt_status`
The status of the operation. Possible values are:

° `TT_OK`

° `TT_ERR_NOMP`

° `TT_ERR_POINTER`

| **tt_ptype_declare** | `Tt_status`   `tt_ptype_declare(const char *ptid)` |

Registers your process type (ptype) with the ToolTalk service.

Arguments

`const char *ptid`
Use the character string specified in your ptype that uniquely identifies your process.

Returned Value

`Tt_status`
The status of the operation. Possible values are:

° `TT_OK`

° `TT_ERR_NOMP`

° `TT_ERR_PTYPE`

| **tt_release** | `void`   `tt_release(int mark)` |

Frees all storage allocated on the ToolTalk API allocation stack since your `tt_mark()` call.

Your application typically calls this at the end of a procedure to release all storage allocated within the procedure.

Arguments

`int mark`
Integer that marks your application's storage position in the ToolTalk API allocation stack.

Related Functions

tt_session_bprop

```
tt_mark()

Tt_status          tt_session_bprop(const char
                   *sessid, const char *prop-
                   name, int i, unsigned char
                   **value, int *length)
```

Obtains the *i*-th value (first value is number 0) of the named property of the session identified by sessid. If there are *i* values or fewer, both returned value and returned length are zeroed.

Arguments

```
const char *sessid
```
The session you have joined. Use the sessid value the ToolTalk service returns after you issue `tt_default_session()`.

```
const char *propname
```
The name of the property from which you want to obtain values.

```
int i
```
The number of the item in the property list for which you want to obtain the value. The list numbering begins with 0.

```
unsigned char **value
```
Address of a character pointer that the ToolTalk service should aim to a string containing the contents of the property.

```
int *len
```
Address of an integer that the ToolTalk service should set to the length of the value in bytes.

Returned Value

```
Tt_status
```
The status of the operation. Possible values are:

- ° TT_OK
- ° TT_ERR_DBAVAIL
- ° TT_ERR_DBEXIST
- ° TT_ERR_NOMP
- ° TT_ERR_NUM
- ° TT_ERR_PROPNAME
- ° TT_ERR_SESSION

unsigned char **value
Address of a character pointer that the ToolTalk service aimed at a string containing the contents of the property.

int *len
Address of an integer that the ToolTalk service set to the length of the value in bytes.

tt_session_bprop_ add	Tt_status tt_session_bprop_add(const char *sessid, const char *propname, const unsigned char *value, int length)

Adds a new byte-string value to the end of the list of values for the named property of the session identified by sessid.

Arguments

const char *sessid
Name of the session you have joined. Use the sessid value the ToolTalk service returns after you issue tt_default_session().

const char *propname
The name of the property to which you want to add values.

const unsigned char *value
The value to add to the session property.

int length
The size of the value in bytes.

Returned Value

Tt_status
The status of the operation. Possible values are:

- ° TT_OK
- ° TT_ERR_DBAVAIL
- ° TT_ERR_DBEXIST
- ° TT_ERR_NOMP
- ° TT_ERR_PROPLEN
- ° TT_ERR_PROPNAME
- ° TT_ERR_SESSION

tt_session_bprop_ set	Tt_status tt_session_bprop_set(const char *sessid, const char

```
                              *propname, const unsigned
                              char *value, int length)
```

Replaces any current values stored under the named property of the session identified by sessid with the given byte-string value.

Arguments

```
const char *sessid
```
Name of the session you have joined. Use the sessid value the ToolTalk service returns after you issue `tt_default_session()`.

```
const char *propname
```
The name of the property whose value you want to replace.

```
const unsigned char *value
```
The value to which the session property is set. If value is NULL, the property is removed entirely.

```
int length
```
The size of the value in bytes.

Returned Value

```
Tt_status
```
The status of the operation. Possible values are:

° TT_OK

° TT_ERR_DBAVAIL

° TT_ERR_DBEXIST

° TT_ERR_NOMP

° TT_ERR_PROPLEN

° TT_ERR_PROPNAME

° TT_ERR_SESSION

tt_session_join

```
Tt_status          tt_session_join(const char
                              *sessid)
```

Joins the session named by the provided string and makes it the default session for your process.

Arguments

```
const char *sessid
```
Name of the session you wish to join. Use the sessid value the ToolTalk service returns after you issue `tt_default_session()`, `tt_X_session()`, or `tt_initial_session()`.

Returned Value	`Tt_status` The status of the operation. Possible values are:

- `TT_OK`

- `TT_ERR_DBAVAIL`

- `TT_ERR_DBEXIST`

- `TT_ERR_NOMP`

- `TT_ERR_PATH`

Related Functions	`tt_default_session()`
`tt_session_prop`	`char        *tt_session_prop(const char *sessid, const char *prop-name, int i)`

Returns the *i*-th value (first value is number 0) of the specified session property.

Note – If this value has embedded nulls, you have no way to determine how long it is. Use `tt_session_bprop()` for values with embedded nulls.

Arguments	`const char *sessid` Name of the session you have joined. Use the sessid value the ToolTalk service returns after you issue `tt_default_session()`.

`const char *propname`
The name of the property from which you want to retrieve a value. The name must be less than 64 characters.

`int i`
The number of the item in the property name list for which you want to obtain the value. The list numbering begins with 0.

Returned Value	`char *` The value of the requested property. NULL is returned if there are *i* values or fewer.

Use `tt_ptr_error()`, which returns `Tt_status`, to determine if the pointer is valid. Possible `Tt_status` values are:

- `TT_OK`

- ° TT_ERR_DBAVAIL

- ° TT_ERR_DBEXIST

- ° TT_ERR_NOMP

- ° TT_ERR_NUM

- ° TT_ERR_PROPNAME

- ° TT_ERR_SESSION

tt_session_prop_add

Tt_status	tt_session_prop_add(const char *sessid, const char *propname, const char *value)

Adds a new character-string value to the end of the list of values for the property of the specified session.

Arguments

const char *sessid
Name of the session you have joined. Use the sessid value the ToolTalk service returns after you issue tt_default_session().

const char *propname
The name of the property to which you want to add a value. The name must be less than 64 characters.

const char *value
The character string you want to add to the property name list.

Returned Value

Tt_status
The status of the operation. Possible values are:

- ° TT_OK

- ° TT_ERR_DBAVAIL

- ° TT_ERR_DBEXIST

- ° TT_ERR_NOMP

- ° TT_ERR_PROPLEN

- ° TT_ERR_PROPNAME

- ° TT_ERR_SESSION

tt_session_prop_count

int	tt_session_prop_count(const char *sessid, const char *propname)

Returns the number of values stored under the named property of the session identified by sessid.

Arguments

`const char *sessid`
Name of the session you have joined. Use the sessid value the ToolTalk service returns after you issue `tt_default_session()`.

`const char *propname`
The name of the property you want to examine.

Returned Value

`int`
The number of values in the specified property list.
Use `tt_int_error()`, which returns `Tt_status`, to determine if the integer is valid. Possible `Tt_status` values are:

- `TT_OK`
- `TT_ERR_DBAVAIL`
- `TT_ERR_DBEXIST`
- `TT_ERR_NOMP`
- `TT_ERR_PROPNAME`
- `TT_ERR_SESSION`

tt_session_prop_set

`Tt_status    tt_session_prop_set(const char *sessid, const char *propname, const char *value)`

Replaces all current values stored under the named property of the session identified by sessid with the given character-string value.

Arguments

`const char *sessid`
Name of the session you have joined. Use the sessid value the ToolTalk service returns after you issue `tt_default_session()`.

`const char *propname`
The name of the property you want to examine.

`const char *value`
The new value you want to insert. If you want to remove a value from the property list, specify the value as NULL.

Returned Value

`Tt_status`
The status of the operation. Possible values are:

- ° TT_OK

- ° TT_ERR_DBAVAIL

- ° TT_ERR_DBEXIST

- ° TT_ERR_NOMP

- ° TT_ERR_PROPLEN

- ° TT_ERR_PROPNAME

- ° TT_ERR_SESSION

tt_session_propname

```
char          *tt_session_propname(const
              char *sessid, int n)
```

Returns the *n*-th element of the list of currently-defined property names for the session identified by sessid.

Arguments

`const char *sessid`
Name of the session you have joined. Use the sessid value the ToolTalk service returns after you issue `tt_default_session()`.

`int n`
The number of the item in the property name list for which you want to obtain the name. The list numbering begins with 0.

Returned Value

`char *`
The name of the desired property from the session property list. NULL is returned if there are *n* properties or fewer

Use `tt_ptr_error()`, which returns `Tt_status`, to determine if the pointer is valid. Possible `Tt_status` values are:

- ° TT_OK

- ° TT_ERR_DBAVAIL

- ° TT_ERR_DBEXIST

- ° TT_ERR_NOMP

- ° TT_ERR_NUM

- ° TT_ERR_SESSION

**tt_session_prop-
names_count**

```
int           tt_session_propnames_count
              (const char *sessid)
```

Returns the number of currently-defined property names for the session.

Arguments

```
const char *sessid
```
Name of the session you have joined. Use the sessid value the ToolTalk service returns after you issue `tt_default_session()`.

Returned Value

```
int
```
The number of property names for the session.

Use `tt_int_error()`, which returns `Tt_status`, to determine if the integer is valid. Possible `Tt_status` values are:

- ° TT_OK
- ° TT_ERR_DBAVAIL
- ° TT_ERR_DBEXIST
- ° TT_ERR_NOMP
- ° TT_ERR_SESSION

Tt_status

TT_ERR_SESSION

TT_ERR_DBEXIST

TT_ERR_DBAVAIL

tt_session_quit

Tt_status	tt_session_quit(const char *sessid)

Informs the ToolTalk service that your application is no longer interested in this ToolTalk session. The ToolTalk service will stop delivering messages scoped to this session.

Arguments

```
const char *sessid
```
Name of the session you want to quit.

Returned Value

```
Tt_status
```
The status of the operation. Possible values are:

- ° TT_OK
- ° TT_ERR_NOMP
- ° TT_ERR_SESSION
- ° TT_WRN_NOTFOUND

tt_spec_bprop	Tt_status tt_spec_bprop(const char *objid, const char *propname, int i, unsigned char **value, int *length)

Retrieves the *i*-th value (first value is number 0) of this property.

Arguments

const char *objid
Identifier of the object involved in this operation.

const char *propname
Name of the property in which you are interested. The name must be less than 64 characters.

int i
Item of the list in which you are interested. The list numbering begins with 0.

unsigned char **value
Address of a character pointer that the ToolTalk service should aim to a string containing the contents of the spec's property. If there are *i* values or fewer, the pointer will be set to 0.

int *len
Address of an integer that the ToolTalk service should set to the length of the value in bytes.

Returned Value

Tt_status
The status of the operation. Possible values are:

- ° TT_OK
- ° TT_ERR_DBAVAIL
- ° TT_ERR_DBEXIST
- ° TT_ERR_NOMP
- ° TT_ERR_NUM
- ° TT_ERR_OBJID
- ° TT_ERR_PROPNAME

unsigned char **value
Address of a character pointer that the ToolTalk service aimed at a string containing the contents of the property. If there are *i* values or fewer, the pointer will be set to 0.

`int *len`
Address of an integer that the ToolTalk service set to the length of the value in bytes. If there are i values or fewer, the length will be 0.

tt_spec_bprop_add

Tt_status	tt_spec_bprop_add(const char *objid, const char *propname, const unsigned char *value, int length)

Adds a new byte-string to the end of the list of values associated with this spec property.

Arguments

`const char *objid`
Identifier of the object involved in this operation.

`const char *propname`
Name of the property in which you are interested.

`const unsigned char *value`
Byte string you want to add to the property value list.

`int length`
Length of the value in bytes.

Returned Value

`Tt_status`
The status of the operation. Possible values are:

- `TT_OK`
- `TT_ERR_DBAVAIL`
- `TT_ERR_DBEXIST`
- `TT_ERR_NOMP`
- `TT_ERR_OBJID`
- `TT_ERR_PROPLEN`
- `TT_ERR_PROPNAME`

tt_spec_bprop_set

Tt_status	tt_spec_bprop_set(const char *objid, const char *propname, const unsigned char *value, int length)

Replaces any current values stored under this spec property with a new byte-string.

Arguments	`const char *objid` Identifier of the object involved in this operation.
	`const char *propname` Name of the property in which you are interested.
	`const unsigned char *value` Byte string you want to add to the property value list. Note: If the value is NULL, the property is removed entirely.
	`int length` Length of the value in bytes.
Returned Value	Tt_status The status of the operation. Possible values are:

- ° TT_OK

- ° TT_ERR_DBAVAIL

- ° TT_ERR_DBEXIST

- ° TT_ERR_NOMP

- ° TT_ERR_OBJID

- ° TT_ERR_PROPLEN

- ° TT_ERR_PROPNAME

tt_spec_create	char *tt_spec_create(const char *filepath)

Creates a spec (in memory) for an object. Use the objid that the ToolTalk service returns in future calls to manipulate the object.

Note – The object will not be a permanent ToolTalk item or visible to other processes until the creating process does a `tt_spec_write()`.

Arguments	`const char *filepath` File name.
Returned Value	`char *` Identifier for this object.

Use tt_ptr_error(), which returns Tt_status, to determine if the pointer is valid. Possible Tt_status values are:

- ° TT_OK
- ° TT_ERR_DBAVAIL
- ° TT_ERR_DBEXIST
- ° TT_ERR_NOMP
- ° TT_ERR_OTYPE
- ° TT_ERR_PATH

Related Functions   tt_spec_type_set()

tt_spec_write()

tt_spec_destroy   Tt_status   tt_spec_destroy(const char
                                    *objid)

Immediately destroys an object's spec.

Arguments   const char *objid
              Identifier of the object involved in this operation.

Returned Value   Tt_status
                   The status of the operation. Possible values are:

- ° TT_OK
- ° TT_ERR_DBAVAIL
- ° TT_ERR_DBEXIST
- ° TT_ERR_NOMP
- ° TT_ERR_OBJID

tt_spec_file   char   *tt_spec_file(const char
                                    *objid)

Retrieves the name of the file containing the object described by the spec.

Arguments   const char *objid
              Identifier of the object involved in this operation.

Returned Value   char *
                   The file's absolute pathname.

Use `tt_ptr_error()`, which returns `Tt_status`, to determine if the pointer is valid. Possible `Tt_status` values are:

- ° `TT_OK`
- ° `TT_ERR_DBAVAIL`
- ° `TT_ERR_DBEXIST`
- ° `TT_ERR_NOMP`
- ° `TT_ERR_OBJID`

tt_spec_move

```
char            *tt_spec_move(const char
                *objid, const char *newfile-
                path)
```

Notifies the ToolTalk service that this object has moved to a different file. The ToolTalk service returns a new objid for the object, and a forwarding pointer is left from the old objid to the new one.

Note – If a new objid is not required (because the new and old files are in the same file system), `TT_WRN_SAME_OBJID` is returned.

For efficiency and reliability, your application should replace any references it has to the old objid with references to the new one.

Arguments

`const char *objid`
Identifier of the object involved in this operation.

`const char *newfilepath`
New file name.

Returned Value

`char *`
New unique identifier of the object involved in this operation.

Use `tt_ptr_error()`, which returns `Tt_status`, to determine if the pointer is valid. Possible `Tt_status` values are:

- ° `TT_OK`
- ° `TT_ERR_DBAVAIL`
- ° `TT_ERR_DBEXIST`

- ° TT_ERR_NOMP
- ° TT_ERR_OBJID
- ° TT_ERR_PATH
- ° TT_WRN_SAME_OBJID

tt_spec_prop

```
char          *tt_spec_prop(const char
              *objid, const char *propname,
              int i)
```

Retrieves the *i*-th value (first value is number 0) of the property associated with this object spec.

Note – If this value has embedded nulls, you have no way to determine its length.

Arguments

```
const char *objid
```
Identifier of the object involved in this operation.

```
const char *propname
```
Name of the property in which you are interested.

```
int i
```
Item of the list in which you are interested. The list numbering begins with 0.

Returned Value

```
char *
```
Contents of the property value. A NULL value is returned if there are *i* values or less.

Use tt_ptr_error(), which returns Tt_status, to determine if the pointer is valid. Possible Tt_status values are:

- ° TT_OK
- ° TT_ERR_DBAVAIL
- ° TT_ERR_DBEXIST
- ° TT_ERR_NOMP
- ° TT_ERR_NUM
- ° TT_ERR_OBJID
- ° TT_ERR_PROPNAME

tt_spec_prop_add	Tt_status	tt_spec_prop_add(const char *objid, const char *propname, const char *value)

Adds a new item to the end of the list of values associated with this spec property.

Arguments

`const char *objid`
Identifier of the object involved in this operation.

`const char *propname`
Property in which you are interested.

`const char *value`
New character-string to be added to the property value list.

Returned Value

`Tt_status`
The status of the operation. Possible values are:

- ° `TT_OK`
- ° `TT_ERR_DBAVAIL`
- ° `TT_ERR_DBEXIST`
- ° `TT_ERR_NOMP`
- ° `TT_ERR_OBJID`
- ° `TT_ERR_PROPNAME`
- ° `TT_ERR_PROPLEN`

Related Functions

`tt_spec_prop_set()`

tt_spec_prop_count	int	tt_spec_prop_count(const char *objid, const char *propname)

Returns the number of values listed in this spec property.

Arguments

`const char *objid`
Identifier of the object involved in this operation.

const char *propname
Name of the property in which you are interested.

Returned Value

`int`
Number of values listed in the spec property.

Use tt_int_error(), which returns Tt_status, to determine if the integer is valid. Possible Tt_status values are:

- ° TT_OK
- ° TT_ERR_DBAVAIL
- ° TT_ERR_DBEXIST
- ° TT_ERR_NOMP
- ° TT_ERR_OBJID
- ° TT_ERR_PROPNAME

tt_spec_prop_set

Tt_status   tt_spec_prop_set(const char *objid, const char *propname, const char *value)

Replaces any values currently stored under this property of the object spec with a new value.

Arguments

const char *objid
Identifier of the object involved in this operation.

const char *propname
Name of the property in which you are interested.

const char *value
Value you want to put in the property value list. If value is NULL, the property is removed entirely.

Returned Value

Tt_status
The status of the operation. Possible values are:

- ° TT_OK
- ° TT_ERR_DBAVAIL
- ° TT_ERR_DBEXIST
- ° TT_ERR_NOMP
- ° TT_ERR_OBJID
- ° TT_ERR_PROPNAME
- ° TT_ERR_PROPLEN

Related Functions	tt_spec_prop_add()
tt_spec_propname	char *tt_spec_propname(const char *objid, int n)

Returns the *n*-th element of the property name list for this object spec.

Arguments

const char *objid
Identifier of the object involved in this operation.

int n
Item of the list in which you are interested. The list numbering begins with 0.

Returned Value

char *
Property name. NULL is returned if there are *n* properties or less.

Use tt_ptr_error(), which returns Tt_status, to determine if the pointer is valid. Possible Tt_status values are:

- ° TT_OK
- ° TT_ERR_DBAVAIL
- ° TT_ERR_DBEXIST
- ° TT_ERR_NOMP
- ° TT_ERR_NUM
- ° TT_ERR_OBJID

tt_spec_propnames_ count	int tt_spec_propnames_count (const char *objid)

Returns the number of property names for this object.

Arguments

const char *objid
Identifier of the object involved in this operation.

Returned Value

int
Number of values listed in the spec property.

Use tt_int_error(), which returns Tt_status, to determine if the integer is valid. Possible Tt_status values are:

- ° TT_OK
- ° TT_ERR_DBAVAIL

○ TT_ERR_DBEXIST

○ TT_ERR_NOMP

○ TT_ERR_OBJID

tt_spec_type	char *tt_spec_type(const char *objid)

Returns the name (otid) of the object type.

Arguments

`const char *objid`
Identifier of the object involved in this operation.

Returned Value

`char *`
Type of this object.
    Use `tt_ptr_error()`, which returns `Tt_status`, to determine if the pointer is valid. Possible `Tt_status` values are:

○ TT_OK

○ TT_ERR_DBAVAIL

○ TT_ERR_DBEXIST

○ TT_ERR_NOMP

○ TT_ERR_OBJID

tt_spec_type_set	Tt_status tt_spec_type_set(const char *objid, const char *otid)

Assigns an object type (otype) value to the object spec. The type must be set before the spec is written for the first time, and cannot be changed thereafter.

Arguments

`const char *objid`
Identifier of the object involved in this operation.

`const char *otid`
Otype you want to assign to the spec.

Returned Value

`Tt_status`
The status of the operation. Possible values are:

○ TT_OK

○ TT_ERR_DBAVAIL

○ TT_ERR_DBEXIST

	° TT_ERR_NOMP
	° TT_ERR_OBJID
	° TT_ERR_READONLY
Related Functions	tt_spec_create()
	tt_spec_write()

tt_spec_write

Tt_status	tt_spec_write(const char *objid)

Writes the spec and any associated properties to the ToolTalk database. It is not necessary to do a write after a destroy.

Note – Several changes can be "batched" between write calls; for example, you might create an object spec, set some properties, and then write all the changes at once with one write call.

Arguments

const char *objid
Identifier of the object involved in this operation.

Returned Value

Tt_status
The status of the operation. Possible values are:

° TT_OK

° TT_ERR_DBAVAIL

° TT_ERR_DBEXIST

° TT_ERR_NOMP

° TT_ERR_OBJID

Related Functions

tt_spec_create()

tt_spec_type_set()

tt_status_message

char	*tt_status_message(Tt_status ttrc)

Returns a pointer to a message describing the problem indicated by this Tt_status code.

Arguments

Tt_status ttrc
Tt_status code you received during an operation.

Returned Value

char *
Pointer to character string describing Tt_status code.

Use `tt_ptr_error()`, which returns `Tt_status`, to determine if the pointer is valid. Possible `Tt_status` values are:

° `TT_OK`

° `TT_`*xxx*

tt_X_session

```
char           *tt_X_session(const char
                *xdisplaystring)
```

Returns the session associated with the named X Window System display.

Arguments

`const char *xdisplaystring`
Name of an X11 display server, such as somehost:0, :0, and so forth.

Returned Value

`char *`
Identifier for the current ToolTalk session.

Use `tt_ptr_error()`, which returns `Tt_status`, to determine if the pointer is valid. Possible `Tt_status` values are:

° `TT_OK`

° `TT_NOMP`

SPARCompiler™ Compilation Technology

2.1 Introduction

The SPARCompiler family of robust, optimizing compilers and environments provides the cornerstone of Sun's software engineering portfolio. With seven powerful compilers—Ada, C, C++, COBOL, Common Lisp, FORTRAN, and Pascal—and the full range of SPARCsystem platforms, Sun offers you the advantage of a single source for the system and tools you need to make the most of your software development investment.

Designed in concert with SPARC technology, SPARCompiler products take full advantage of the SPARC architecture to provide optimization that delivers unprecedented performance. The code generation modules of the SPARCompiler products utilize state-of-the-art innovations in compiler technology, particularly in code optimization. Because compilers for SPARC and other Reduced Instruction Set Computer (RISC) architectures synthesize instruction sequences that correspond to Complex Instruction Set Computers' (CISC) more complicated instructions, RISC compilers often produce more instructions (up to 20% more) than comparable CISC machines. However, these are almost all single-cycle instructions. Therefore, good optimization technology plays a very important role in SPARC system performance.

An individual SPARC machine is an implementation of the SPARC Instruction Set Architecture (ISA). The performance of a SPARCsystem is a function of the architecture, the hardware implementation, and the code generated by the compiler. Because the SPARC ISA and SPARCompiler technology were developed in concert, the compilers take careful advantage of the architecture to improve performance. Among the architectural features SPARC includes are:

- Register windows
- Delayed branches and delayed loads
- Hardware interlocks
- Floating-point coprocessors

Optimized for the SPARC architecture and hardware implementations, SPARCompiler products can significantly increase application speed and therefore play an integral role in the performance of SPARCsystems.

2.2 SPARCompiler Family Overview

The seven members of the SPARCompiler family—Ada, C, C++, COBOL, Common Lisp, FORTRAN, and Pascal—all share key features that enhance each product, enable coordination between the products, and maximize your development dollar. The major features, and their benefits, are as shown in Table 2.1.

Table 2.1. Features/benefits.

Features	Benefits
Optimized for the SPARC architecture	Deliver unprecedented performance on SPARC platforms.
Interlanguage calling	Because they enable you to combine your existing code with modules written in other languages, SPARCompilers protect your current software investment.
Multiple levels of optimization	Provide flexibility to control compile-time versus execution-time and memory size versus space trade-offs in the compiled code.
International character set support	Meet the needs of global markets.
Industry and *de facto* standards	Ensure compatibility and portability while providing competitive advantages through language enhancements.

Features	Benefits
Access to graphics and OpenWindows™ XView™ libraries, UNIX system calls, and SunOS™ enhanced utilities.	Reduce time and resources required for sophisticated applications and shorten time to market.
Integration with SPARCworks programming tools and the OpenWindows window system.	Create an integrated development environment that enhances programmer productivity.

The Sun SPARCompiler products combine lexical, syntactic, and static semantic components (the language "front ends") with code generation and optimization modules (the language "back ends"). Four of the SPARCompiler products—C, C++, FORTRAN, and Pascal—share the same back end, while the other three back ends provide language specific optimizations and features. As Figure 2.1 shows, all seven languages are targeted to the SPARC architecture and are supported by powerful programming environments.

The next section describes the C, C++, FORTRAN, and Pascalcompilers, while the following three sections discuss the Ada, Common Lisp, and COBOL compilers.

2.3
C, C++,
FORTRAN, and
Pascal

As mentioned above, four of the SPARCompilers—C, C++, FORTRAN, and Pascal—share a single, very efficient back end. These particular languages share a common back end due to the characteristics of the languages themselves, historical engineering effort at Sun, and the needs of the development tool environments. The major benefit of focusing engineering efforts on a common back end is that any performance improvement or bug fix enhances all four of these compilers.

Compiler Structure

Figure 2.2 shows how a program flows through the compilation phases that transform it into an executable program. The solid arrows describe the path when optimization and inline code expansion are both enabled. When either is disabled, certain components are skipped.

Sun's optimization technology is designed to satisfy several goals, including:

- Support for multiple source languages
- Production of high-quality, high-performance code
- Reduction of compilation time to no more than necessary to do ambitious optimization

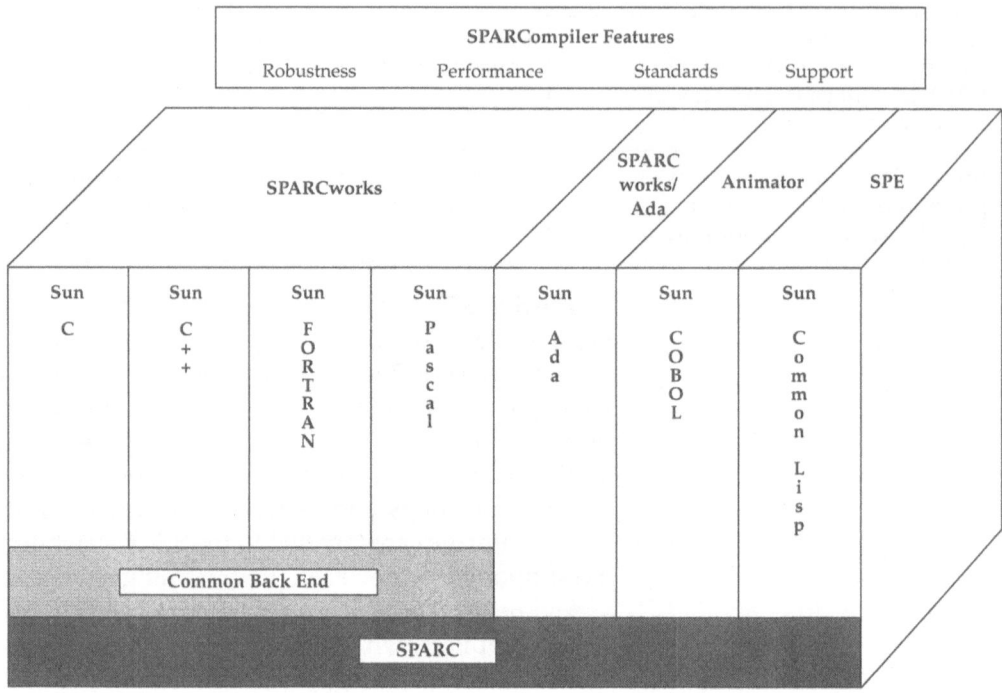

Figure 2.1. SPARCompiler features.

The rest of this section describes the various phases of the compilation process, with emphasis on optimization.

Preprocessors are programs that manipulate source text; they transform the code into a form acceptable by a compiler or assembler. cpp is the most widely used preprocessor. It is independent of any language (although it was designed to be used with C) and can be used to define symbolic constants, insert files into the source stream, expand macros, and conditionally compile segments of code.

The front end scans and parses the source-language statements that constitute a procedure and checks static semantics. The target of the front end is an intermediate language called Sun IR (Intermediate Representation). Sun IR is a language- and machine-independent representation that is suitable for global optimization and code generation. The following features of Sun IR facilitate global optimization:

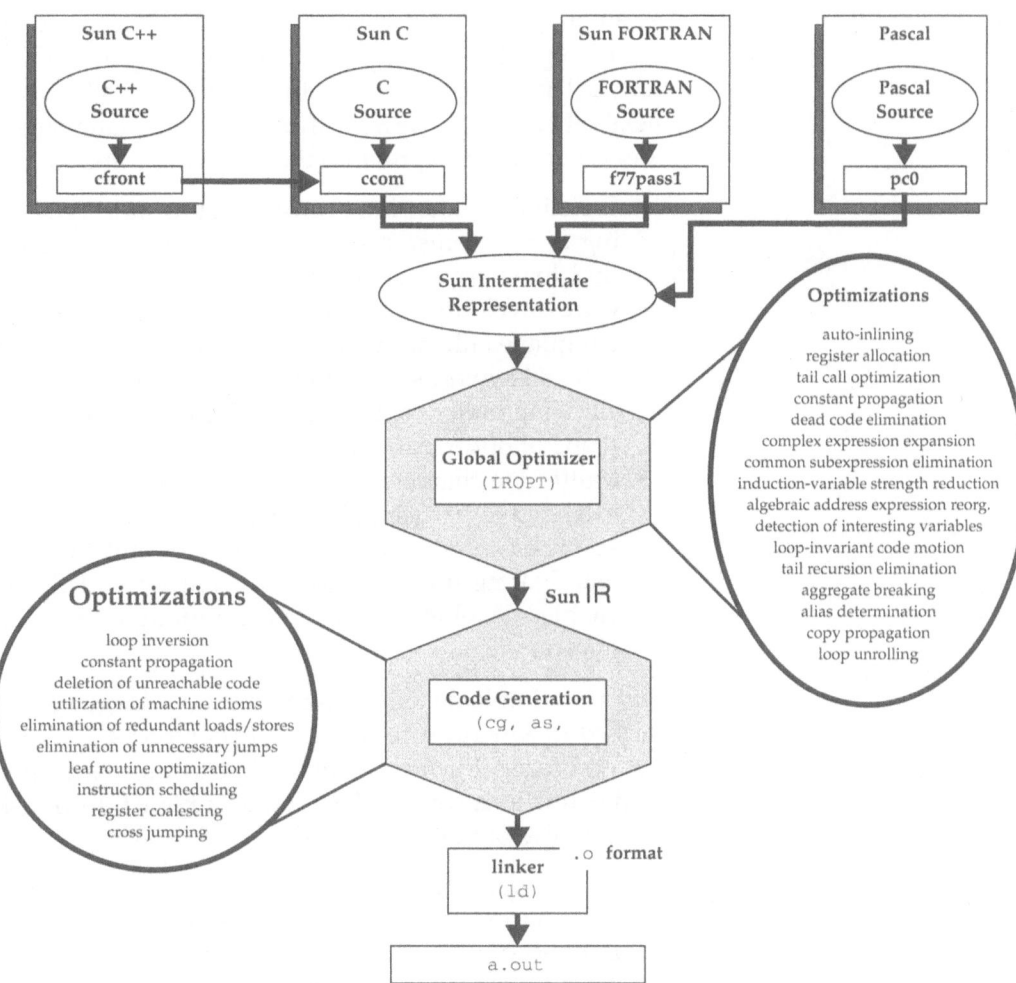

Figure 2.2. SPARCompiler structure and features.

- A language-independent symbol table structure that explicitly represents storage classes, constants and variables
- Facilities to represent static equivalencing and dynamic aliasing
- A general framework for control flow analysis, data flow analysis, and most advanced global optimization techniques.

The following short sections summarize the features of the four front ends that share the common back end.

| Sun C™ | Sun C offers an ANSI C language compliant compiler, as well as an advanced K&R version. With the ANSI C compiler, your programs are fully portable across all ANSI C platforms. The two compilers included in Sun C allow you the flexibility to choose between these different C languages. The Sun C package also provides the following features: |

- Function prototyping to ensure better static type checking of programs. Static type checking enables you to find logic errors at compile time, which reduces software development and maintenance time.
- Language enhancements, such as the `const` and `volatile` keywords, help improve program correctness by allowing better control of variables and improving the scope of optimization.
- Multi-byte characters support writing code that can be localized to particular countries.
- `-fsingle` command-line options permit FORTRAN-like floating-point expression evaluation. This option enables developers to write computation-intensive applications in C.

| Sun C++™ | Sun C++ implements the complete C++ language as described in American Telephone &Telegraph's *C++ Language System Product Reference Manual*. Sun C++ also incorporates all the functionality of AT&T's latest `cfront` C++ translator. The features of Sun C++ include: |

- ANSI C facilities
- Position-independent code generation
- Enhanced `cpp` preprocessor that handles C++ tokens
- A set of classes commonly used in the development of object-oriented programs.

| Sun FORTRAN™ | Sun FORTRAN provides an ANSI FORTRAN 77 development system with VAX/VMS™ FORTRAN 4.0 extensions. Sun FORTRAN conforms to the ANSI X3.9-1978 and ISO 1539-1980 FORTRAN standards. In addition, it has been validated by NIST and conforms to FIPS 69-1 BS6832 and MIL-STD 1753. The features of Sun FORTRAN include: |

- Extensive VMS compatibility
- Complex expression optimization
- Fast and accurate degree-based transcendental functions
- Support for C preprocessor directives

Chapter 2. SPARCompiler™ Compilation Technology

- DO/ENDDO and DO WHILE statements.

Sun has also added several other extensions to the FOR-TRAN compiler for supercomputer compatibility, including the POINTER datatype and quad- precision floating point.

Sun Pascal™

Sun Pascal is an optimizing, feature-rich compiler for Pascal, a widely used structured language originally designed as an aid for teaching programming. Sun Pascal fully conforms to ISO Level 0 Pascal (equivalent to ANSI/IEEE 770X3.97-1983). Sun Pascal also offers language extensions compatible with many Pascal compilers, specifically those of HP/Apollo DO-MAIN® Pascal. Sun Pascal's features include:

- Conformant arrays, as specified in the ISO Level 1 Pascal Standard
- Variable-length string type
- Single- and double-precision IEEE floating-point support
- PUBLIC and PRIVATE declarations
- External C and FORTRAN declarations

After lexical, syntactic and static semantic processing, the remainder of the compilation steps are performed by the back end shared by the C, C++, FORTRAN, and Pascal products.

The machine-independent ("global") optimizer is called iropt. It is applied to files and begins by performing automatic inlining, followed by alias analysis. Next a series of data flow analyses and transformations are applied to each procedure in the file. For example, data flow analysis could determine that a variable has the same constant value every time control reaches a particular point, and is therefore a candidate for replacement by a constant. The result of the transformations is a modified version of the Sun IR for the program.

Automatic inlining provides many benefits. Obviously modules that have been inlined have no "procedure call overhead." In addition, by moving the body of the module into the caller, many new opportunities for optimization are created. In effect, this provides interprocedural analysis.

The aliaser module deals with problems of aliases arising from the presence of multiple names that map to the same memory areas. It is essential to good optimization that the range of possible aliases be determined. Variables that are aliases do not readily lend themselves to optimization.

Therefore it is essential to minimize the range of aliases when doing ambitious optimization. In standard FORTRAN, the set of names that may refer to the same location may be determined exactly. This is known as "static aliasing." Languages such as C, C++, Sun's extended FORTRAN, and Pascal introduce an additional challenge called dynamic aliasing. For example, in C, aliases may arise from memory overlaps, array references, use of pointers, etc. Dynamic aliases are defined as aliases that cannot be determined exactly and are therefore given special attention by the aliaser module.

The following additional global optimizations are performed by `iropt`. Definitions of these optimizations can be found in "Appendix A—Optimization Definitions."

* Aggregate breaking
* Algebraic address expression reorganization
* Common subexpression elimination
* Complex expression expansion
* Copy and constant propagation
* Dead code elimination
* Induction-variable strength reduction
* Loop-invariant code motion
* Loop unrolling
* Global register allocation
* Tail call optimization

The *inliner* performs inline assembly language expansion. Inline expansion provides a way for the compiler writer or user to specify assembly language code sequences to replace source-language calls. To do this, the compiler writer and/or user provides a collection of "inline template files." The greatest service provided by the assembler inliner is that special code sequences (such as special supervisor instructions, and implementation dependent instructions) can be accessed without changes to the compilation system. In addition, Sun provides some templates to accelerate performance of some common library interfaces.

The postpass optimizer performs the following local optimizations. Definitions can be found in "Appendix A—Optimization Definitions."

* Constant propagation
* Cross jumping
* Dead code elimination

- Elimination of redundant loads/stores
- Elimination of unnecessary jumps
- Instruction scheduling
- Leaf routine optimization
- Loop inversion
- Register coalescing

The assembler then generates relocatable object code. The linker then:

- Combines separately compiled object files
- Resolves intermodule references
- Searches libraries to satisfy unresolved references.

In the case of static linking, the linker combines the relocatable object with other necessary relocatable objects (commonly from library files), and produces the executable file. Dynamic linking is a bit more complicated.

Levels of Optimization

The SPARCompilers support several levels of optimization that require various amounts of compilation time and produce correspondingly varying code quality. The default is to do no optimization at all. This is not recommended for any use except debugging, where it is important to minimize compilation time. Each level includes the optimizations of the previous levels. In addition to the "no optimization" level, these are:

O1
At this level, only postpass optimization is invoked. Using level O1 is recommended only if the higher levels of optimization result in excessive compilation time, or running out of swap space.

O2
This invokes all the global optimizations, except automatic inlining prior to code generation.

Note – This is the standard optimization level for most modules.

O3
This performs the same optimizations as O2, but on a wider class of expressions, including references and definitions of external and indirect variables.

O4

This level traces, as carefully as it can, what pointers may point to, and makes them candidates for optimization. It also invokes automatic inlining. This level of optimization is recommended for the most computation-intensive modules, and not recommended for modules that are not computation-intensive.

Multiple levels of optimization are provided because aggressive optimization involves trade-offs:

- Compile time vs. execution time
- Memory space vs. execution time

As a rule of thumb, higher levels of optimization increase compile time, decrease execution time and require more memory and disk space to compile programs. Figure 2.3 shows optimization trade-offs using the SPECmark benchmark test.

For some programs, levels O3 and O4 significantly increase compilation time with a small effect on run-time performance beyond that provided by level O2. In these cases the developer may choose to compile at level O2 to avoid the compile-time penalty. In fact, in some cases, by optimizing different procedures at different levels, you can produce overall faster executing code. Use of multiple optimization levels is usually the best way to enhance performance for a large application. Level options can easily be encoded in a Makefile.

Another feature of the back end is automatic back-off of the optimization level. If the compilation of a routine would fail due to lack of sufficient swap space, the optimizer automatically recompiles that routine (only) at the next lower optimization level. When this happens, the user is alerted by means of a warning message.

Selection of optimization flags has been simplified for the common case. Typically, users want a single option, and define their intent as "to generate the best code possible in a reasonable amount of time that runs well on my machines." The -fast compiler option is intended to provide this. It provides a convenient way to get near maximum performance with one switch by bundling together several independent options. Any subset of -fast attributes can be specified explicitly as indicated below.

The -fast option combines:

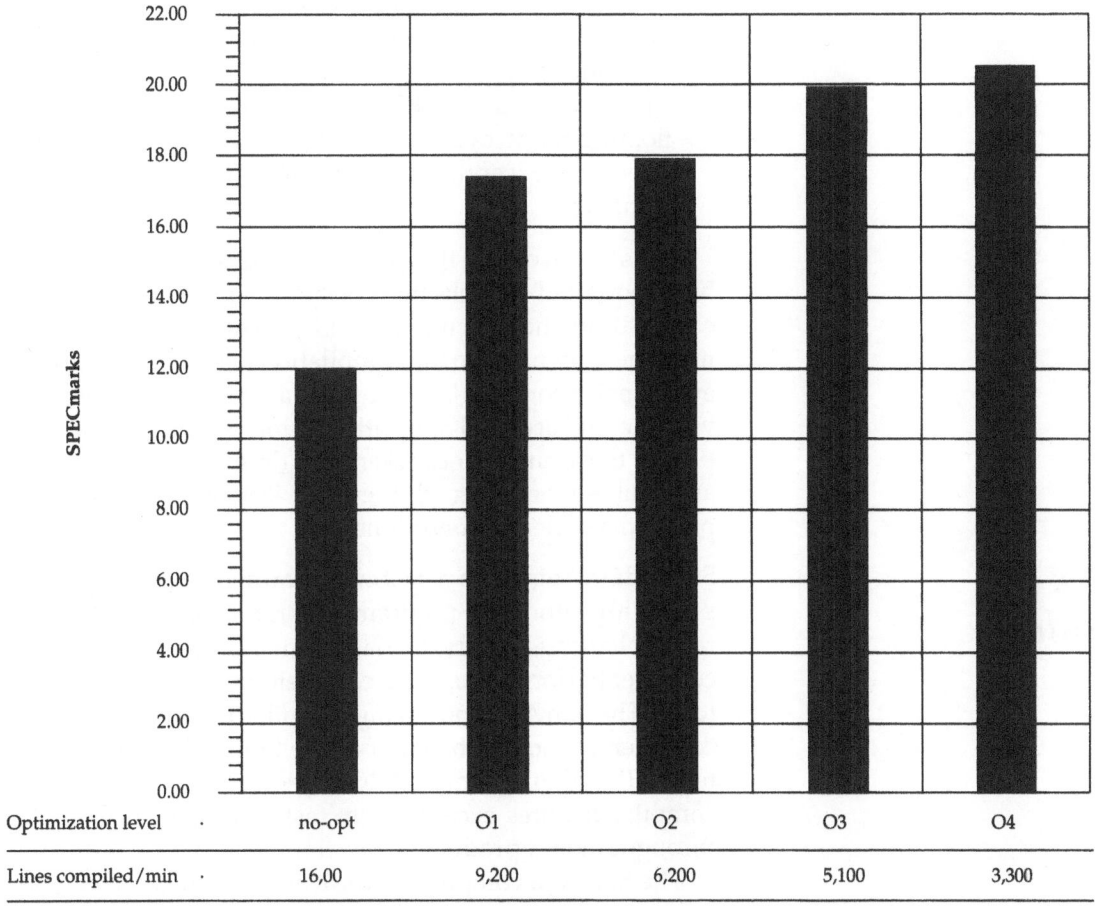

Optimization level ·	no-opt	O1	O2	O3	O4
Lines compiled/min ·	16,00	9,200	6,200	5,100	3,300

Figure 2.3. Effect of optimization level on execution time and compilation time. SPECmark tests run on a SPARCstation 2 with SunOS 4.1.4, using Sun Fortran 1.4 and Sun C 1.1.

- Default optimization level: in the absence of an explicit -O*n* option following -fast, uses -O2 to obtain the best trade-off between compile and execution time.
- Best choice for compile-time hardware: In the absence of an explicit -cg{87,89} on SPARC-based systems, -fast generates the fastest code for the hardware of the compile-time machine.
- -dalign: assumes double word alignment of double-precision floating-point variables in FORTRAN, unless -nodalign is explicitly specified after -fast.
- -fsingle: for C code, generates single-precision floating-point expression evaluation for single-precision operands.

- -libmil: uses the Sun-provided libm.il inline expansion templates automatically after any user-specified templates.
- -fnonstd: causes hardware traps to be enabled for floating-point overflow, division by zero, and invalid operation exceptions, rather than following the IEEE standard.

-fast is an option that provides a feature many Sun users have requested. It picks the most popular options, balancing compilation and execution speeds, assumes that the target machine is identical to the compilation machine and exploits every major compilation feature available. It does not provide the highest level of optitimization (-fast -O4 accomplishes that), and it does assert that double-precision values are double word aligned; therefore it is not suitable for all programs under all conditions.

2.4 Ada

Sun Ada™ combines a fast, full-featured optimizing compiler with automated program-generation tools for minimal recompilations, library management utilities that enhance compiler performance, and a complete suite of programming tools. The Sun Ada optimizing compiler, based on the Verdix compiler system, is the heart of the Sun Ada language system. Highly tuned for SPARC-based systems, the Sun Ada compiler features exceptionally fast complilation for quick throughput and productive development.

The Sun Ada compiler is constructed of three major components. The front end performs lexical, syntactic and semantic analysis on Ada source code and emits a target independent linear intermediate language (IL). The IL is processed by an optimizer (OPTIM) and then the code generator (CG) produces SPARC object code. The OPTIM optimizing module performs many modern code optimizations, several of which are specific to Ada. The front end also handles some optimizations, such as automatic inlining, that contribute to the speed of the code produced. In addition to optimizations in generated code, a passive task optimization has been introduced that can improve rendezvous times for some common uses of tasks by as much as a factor of eight. Also, the exception tables and look-up algorithms have been optimized to yield fast exception-handling performance.

Figure 2.4 shows the Sun Ada development environment.

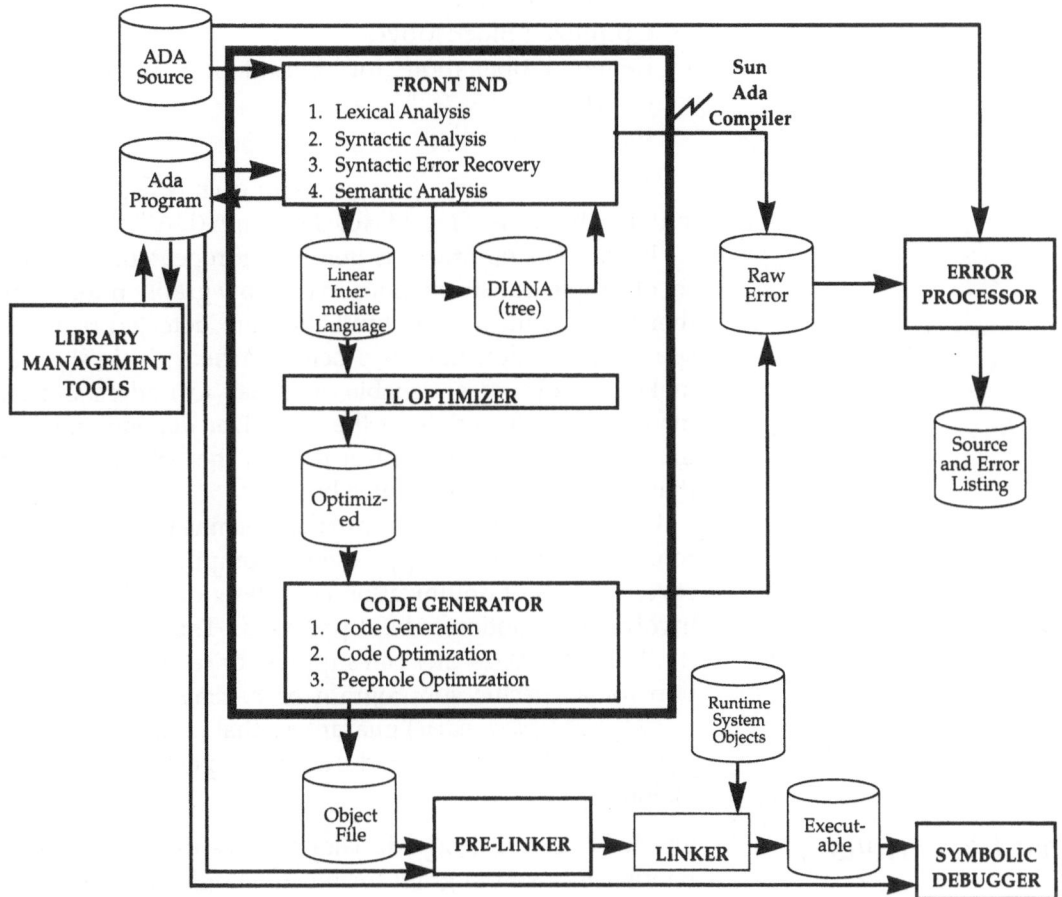

Figure 2.4. Sun Ada.

Optimizations

The following optimizations are performed automatically by the Sun Ada compiler. All three components of the compiler, the front end, the optimizer, and the code generator contribute optimizations. Definitions of these options can be found in "Appendix A—Optimization Definitions."

- Algebraic Address Expression Reorganization
- Common Subexpression Elimination
- Constant Folding
- Copy Propagation
- Dead Code Elimination
- Elimination of Redundant Loads/Stores
- Elimination of Unnecessary Jumps
- Induction-Variable Strength Reduction

- Loop-Invariant Code Motion
- Optimized Block Moves
- Range Propagation for Elimination of Constraint Checking
- Register Allocation

OPTIM constructs a flowgraph for each Ada subprogram and then builds a Directed Acyclic Graph (DAG) for each basic block. The optimizer is iterative; it repeatedly applies a set of simple transformations to the flow graph, until no further opportunities for optimization are detected or until a specified iteration limit has been reached. This structure makes the optimizer reliable and easy to understand and maintain. Performance of the optimizer depends more on the complexity of the control flow in the Ada source code than on the number of source lines.

When programming close to the machine level, certain optimizations must be suppressed. Compiler switches offer several levels of optimization and allow optimizations that involve code motion to be suppressed. The pragma OPTIMIZE_CODE (OFF|ON) can suppress or re-enable optimization for a specific subprogram or package. The pragma VOLATILE (*object_name*) guarantees that loads and stores to the named object will be performed as expected after optimization.

Fast Exceptions

One key Sun Ada design decision is that adding an exception handler to a subprogram (or block) should not slow down the normal execution of that subprogram. In particular, exception handlers do not incur *any* performance penalties unless an exception is raised. This is a highly desirable feature, but it has the drawback of complicating the handling of exceptions. For user code that raises exceptions frequently, this optimization improves performance by computing complex tables at link time that permit high-speed searches for the proper exception handler. As a result of this optimization, Sun Ada customers have the best of both worlds; there is no overhead for normal execution in subprograms that contain exception handlers, and when an exception is raised, exception handling is very fast.

Passive Tasks

The passive task optimization is a textbook example of: "Program semantics exposed by the programming language can be optimized by the compiler." It simply recognizes that a large percentage of all Ada tasks are used exclusively to serialize activities—for example, to serialize access to a data structure. Passive task optimization can be viewed as compiling each accept block into a subprogram and each task entry into a semaphore. The other half of the optimization occurs when compiling a call to the passive task. Instead of generating calls to the run-time system to do a rendezvous, calls are generated to lock the semaphore and do a procedure call. Semaphores and procedure calls are much faster than full-blown rendezvous, especially because they involve only one task (as opposed to two), since the passive task is never made known to the run-time system. On return from the rendezvous, a special resume handler activates one of the tasks suspended on the semaphore, if any.

Passive tasks are a general class of task that includes "monitors." Monitor tasks are extremely important to fast performance in typical Ada real-time situations, and both Sun Ada and the accompanying debugger support it completely.

Remote Compilation

The -L option to the compiler and many other Sun Ada tools permits the user to specify the name of the Ada library context in which the compilation is to take place. This means that only one copy of a source file need exist, even if it is shared by projects being developed for different target environments (for example, both the development host and an embedded target).

Large Program Support

Many of the Sun Ada tools have been enhanced to support very large programming projects. For example, the prelinker is designed to compute quickly the elaboration order of large numbers of units.

Interlanguage Calling

The Ada language defines the INTERFACE pragma for calling subprograms written in other languages. Sun Ada fully supports the INTERFACE pragma for C, C++, FORTRAN, and Pascal. Sun Ada also supports two additional pragmas, INTERFACE_NAME and EXTERNAL_NAME, which allow Ada to access global data declared in other languages and allow other languages to call Ada subprograms (callbacks). These and other aspects of this topic are covered in detail in the "Interface Programming" section of the Sun Ada Programmer's Guide.

Miscellaneous Optimizations and Pragmas

Ada elaboration order checks are eliminated for packages with static elaboration (for example, those with no dynamic initialization of library level or global variables).

Sun Ada also supports inline subprogram expansion for all types of procedures and functions, including generic and machine-code procedures. Not only does this eliminate call overhead, but it also allows optimizers to work across subprogram boundaries.

Sun Ada shares generic bodies, so multiple instantiations of a generic with similar parameters use the same object code. This saves code space at the expense of execution time. Sun Ada does support unshared instantiation, so actual parameters can be propagated throughout a generic body.

The following are some of the more important pragmas supported by Sun Ada:

pragma NOT_ELABORATED

Suppresses the generation of elaboration code for library packages and issues warnings for constructs that require elaboration.

pragma INLINE_ONLY

Suppresses generation of a callable version of the subprogram. Otherwise behaves the same as INLINE.

pragma NON_REENTRANT

Uses a statically allocated parameter block for parameter passing and reduces call overhead. Can only be applied to subprograms nested immediately within a library package.

pragma NO_IMAGE

Suppresses the generation of image tables for enumeration types. Use of the IMAGE attribute causes an error message. This does not affect the debugger's ability to display enumeration values symbolically.

2.5 Sun Common Lisp™

Sun Common Lisp is now available exclusively from Lucid Inc. of Menlo Park, California.

Sun Common Lisp is an implementation of Common Lisp with extensive enhancements to reflect the proposed ANSI Common Lisp standard. Sun Common Lisp is a general-purpose programming language with a rich set of built-in functions for processing both symbolic and numerical data and a wide variety of predefined data types. Sun Common Lisp provides the flexibility that comes from run-time binding of functions and from the fact that Lisp programs can be very naturally processed as Lisp data.

Beyond this, Sun Common Lisp is an interactive programming system that includes:

- An interpreter
- An incremental compiler
- A garbage collector
- Window interfaces
- An object-oriented programming system
- A debugger
- An error-handling facility.

Features like the LispView interface for the X Window system, the Multitasking Facility, and the Foreign Function Interface, among others, are major extensions beyond the proposed Common Lisp standard. Many of these development environment features and tools are described in the *SPARCworks Development Environment* white paper. The rest of this section provides an overview of CLOS, the Sun Common Lisp dual compilation system and SPARC support for Lisp.

The Common Lisp Object System (CLOS)

Sun Common Lisp supports the Common Lisp Object System, an object-oriented extension to Common Lisp, that is part of the forthcoming draft ANSI Common Lisp standard. CLOS has its origins in other Lisp-based object-oriented paradigms such as Flavors and CommonLoops. CLOS incorporates the years of experience gained from these models, and has been designed to run on a large array of hardware platforms and operating systems.

Among the fundamental notions of CLOS are classes, instances, generic functions, and methods. Important features of the system are inheritance (including multiple inheritance), method combination, and multi-methods.

For application delivery, Sun Common Lisp offers CLOS extensions that precompile the dispatch code used by generic functions. Although CLOS applications run correctly without a compiler or precompiled dispatch code, they run faster if the dispatch code is precompiled.

Dual Compiler System

Sun Common Lisp has two distinct compilation modes: one that emphasizes compilation speed and one that emphasizes run-time performance.

- The *development mode* compiles the code quickly with few optimizations. Frequent compilations during the development of a Lisp application make compilation speed an important factor in programmer productivity.
- The *production mode* fully optimizes the compiled code for the most efficient run-time performance available. Most users use the production mode of the compiler when they have completed development of a section of code and compile it for the final time.

The Lisp production mode compiler does constant folding and constant propagation, dead code elimination, and tail call optimization (tail recursion elimination and tail merging). Type declarations are not necessary in Lisp; however, when used they allow the compiler to do further optimizations. With appropriate declarations in the source code, the compiler will

- Eliminate run-time type checking for arithmetic operations

- Generate fast code for standard integer computation and for floating-point computation

- Provide fast array access

In many cases the compiler will automatically propagate type information to parts of the code that do not contain declarations.

Development mode is the default, but the user can change the compilation mode by changing the optimization setting of the compiler. In production mode, the user can also specify the amount of run-time error checking, or safety, retained in the compiled code. The development mode inherently retains a high degree of safety.

Users have typically found a three to five times improvement in compilation speed when they use development mode rather than the production mode. Run-time degradation is roughly 50%, depending on the nature of the program. Part of the performance advantage of the development compiler comes from its generating less garbage to be paged or collected.

Optimization Reporting Facility

The user can increase the efficiency of code compiled when using the production mode by providing type declarations that eliminate run-time type checking. In addition, the compiler helps the user optimize code by displaying reports about the optimization attempts that it makes while it compiles code. Optimization reports describe instances where the compiler optimized a section of code and when it did not, but could have, if it had more type information. This useful information allows users to add declarations that improve the performance of an application and reduce the amount of time spent optimizing code.

Foreign Function Interface

Sun Common Lisp provides a Foreign Function interface that allows users to link compiled C, C++, Pascal, and FORTRAN code with Lisp programs and to link Lisp programs into executing C, C++, Pascal, and FORTRAN code. The Foreign Function Interface automatically handles the data type coercions necessary to pass data between Lisp and the foreign code.

Correspondence between Lisp types and a set of low-level foreign data types is predefined, and Sun Common Lisp provides constructs for defining new foreign structure types. Foreign data structures can be accessed in Lisp and passed back and forth between the different languages.

Ephemeral Garbage Collection

The Ephemeral Garbage Collector (EGC) replaces long garbage collection intervals with several shorter intervals that are generally imperceptible to users. Most garbage collections last only a few milliseconds, so that productive development time or execution of critical applications is not interrupted.

When the EGC is on, new Lisp objects are created in a small consing area, which when full, can be collected quickly. Objects from this small ephemeral area that survive the garbage collection process migrate to more long-lived areas of memory where garbage is collected less frequently, resulting in more focused garbage collection of only highly volatile areas. When all ephemeral levels have been filled with objects, the entire system can be collected with the stop-and-copy collector. The EGC can be turned on or off as desired, so that garbage collection does not impact the system at any particular time.

Multitasking (Stack Groups)

Lisp 4.0 includes the capability to run lightweight processes, implemented in stack groups, for multitasking Lisp applications. The Multitasking Facility allows the user to schedule execution of multiple processes running concurrently in the same Lisp environment. The advantage of using the Multitasking Facility is that it allows users to split larger jobs into separate tasks that execute independently.

The Multitasking Facility has its own scheduler that uses state information to stop a process and restart it later without changing the results of its execution. Lisp also provides constructs for handling and scheduling processes that make the implementation of multiprocessing applications both easy and natural. In addition, within Sun Common Lisp the developer can set the priorities of processes to control execution.

SPARC Support for Lisp

In the past, Lisp programs have had a reputation for slow execution compared to other compiled languages. This slowness has been largely due to the high degree of flexibility and the sophisticated error detection and recovery facilities that are the hallmarks of Lisp. For example, each arithmetic operation is generally preceded by one or more instructions that examine the type of each operand and then branch to the appropriate type of operation. Any program that must perform these checks at runtime is at a performance disadvantage when compared to less flexible languages such as C and FORTRAN, which make those decisions during compilation.

One way to make Lisp run faster is to eliminate some of the run-time type checks. The programmer has the option to declare that a given variable will always hold values of a specific type. The compiler can then eliminate the type-checking instructions and produce object code with performance and safety comparable to other programming languages.

The disadvantage of such an approach is that it eliminates some of the flexibility designed into Lisp. The programmer can trade the advantage of flexibility and easier-to-debug programs for faster execution. On Sun workstations the optimization reports greatly facilitate this step, but it is still a necessary part of the development cycle.

Historically, Lisp machines have been noted for their handling of this problem. In such special-purpose computers, type checking of operands does not require additional instructions. Instead, the check is done as part of the machine instruction either in special hardware or in microcode. Developers could take advantage of all of Lisp's flexibility and still have programs run quickly. This efficiency comes at a price, though: compared to general-purpose workstations, Lisp machines are more expensive, have a less flexible and less open architecture, and are harder to integrate with other systems.

The SPARC architecture used in the Sun-4™ and SPARC-system product families offers Sun Common Lisp developers many of the more important advantages of the dedicated Lisp machine without the problems associated with a specialized combination of hardware and software. SPARC provides Lisp application programs the potent combination of excellent run-time performance and the ability to detect the most common errors very quickly.

Finally, since a typical Lisp program consists of a large number of small functions, Sun Common Lisp takes advantage of the SPARC register windows. The compiler uses register windows to achieve very fast function calling and argument processing. It is particularly effective in cases that involve a shallow stack of called functions that pass a small number of arguments and programs for which tail call optimization is effective. The speed of this function-calling mechanism can have a major impact on application performance.

Tagged Arithmetic

Lisp provides programmers with a number of interesting opportunities to trade execution time for ease of debugging. In general, for every increase in execution-time performance, there is a decrease in program flexibility and available information for error analysis. As an example, consider the following simple function:

```
(defun adder (first second)
  (+ first second))
```

The programmer has not provided any information as to the type of arguments to be passed to adder. Because of this, a test must be done at runtime to identify the kind of addition to be performed. This test adds a sizeable overhead to execution of the function.

If the programmer knows that only fixnum (single-precision integer) values will be passed to the function and that the result of the addition will also be a fixnum, then it is possible to inform the Lisp compiler of this through type declarations, as shown below:

```
(defun adder (first second)
  (declare (fixnum first second))
  (the fixnum (+ first second)))
```

If the optimization parameters for *speed* and *safety* of generated code are set to maximum and minimum values respectively, then the Lisp compiler is free to bypass the type checking and generate code for fixnum addition. However, if either value passed to this faster version of adder is not a fixnum, then it produces an erroneous result, rather than returning a correct (possibly non-fixnum) value or reporting an error. Normally, it is not possible to catch this sort of error without paying a run-time penalty.

SPARCsystem computers offer an elegant solution to this speed vs. safety problem with their tagged arithmetic instructions. These instructions divide the value to be processed into two fields, as shown below:

Special instructions in the SPARC architecture support addition and subtraction between tagged integers. The tag fields are checked at the same time the arithmetic is performed. If the tag fields of both arguments are zero, then they are fixnums and the result is returned. If either tag is nonzero or an arithmetic overflow occurs, then a condition code is set. Optionally, the instruction can cause a trap to occur on a nonzero tag or fixnum overflow.

In the fully declared adder function above, the tagged add and trap on overflow instruction permit fast execution and still provide excellent error detection. If the arguments and results are as declared, then the generated code wastes no time in error detection. A non-fixnum result causes a trap to a routine that allocates and returns an extended-precision integer (a bignum). An invalid argument causes a trap to the Lisp debugger.

If declarations are not used, the tagged add instruction uses a condition code to identify its outcome. If both arguments are fixnums, execution time increases over the fully declared function by one conditional branch instruction (in production mode of the compiler). If the tagged add fails, then a generic addition function is invoked that can handle all types of numeric data.

This means that Sun Common Lisp on SPARCsystems can be counted on to deal correctly with any error that results from fixnum addition or subtraction without any sacrifice in execution speed. While other computer systems require that programmers risk an incorrect result to get the fastest possible execution, SPARC's tagged arithmetic instructions offer Lisp developers high speed and error detection.

Tag Bits for List Processing

As the name of the language might imply, processing of linked lists is a common activity in Lisp programs. The `car` (find the value of the current list element) and `cdr` (find the next list element) operations are executed frequently. (A list element, in the sense used here, is also known as a cons cell[1].) It is not unusual for a malfunctioning program to attempt to take the `car` or `cdr` of something that is not a valid list element. This is an error that most Lisp systems detect at higher compiler safety settings.

On SPARC-based systems, the misuse of `car` and `cdr` is always detected, even with safety set to 0. Lisp takes advantage of the SPARC architecture's requirement that word-oriented loads and stores require word-aligned addresses, that is, ones that are divisible by four. An invalid address invokes a trap handler that in turn reports the precise cause of the error to the Lisp debugger.

As for `fixnums`, Sun Common Lisp divides pointers into data and tag fields. This time, the data field is the address of the target value without the two low-order bits. In a valid word pointer, these rightmost bits are always zero. In Sun Common Lisp, a list element has a tag value of 1. All other types of Lisp objects have tag values other than 1.

Lisp uses the combined word-address-and-tag value of a list element as its base address. This address, with its tag value of 1, actually points to the second byte of the first word of the list element, as shown:

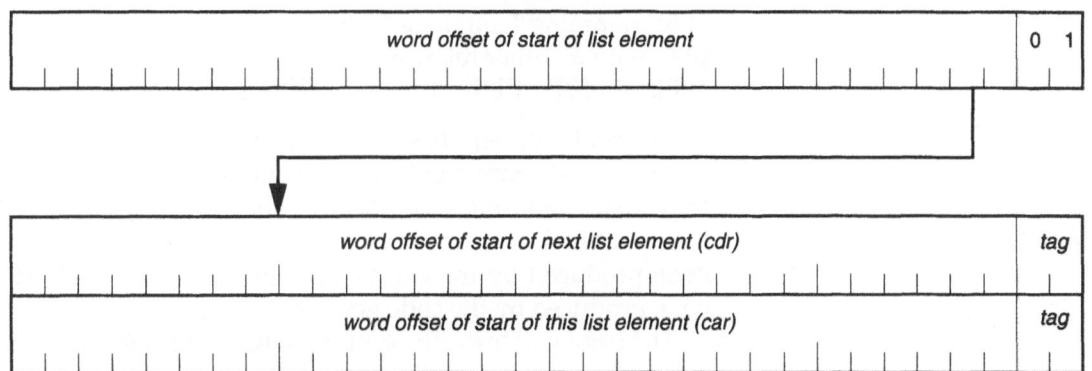

1. The object `nil` is also considered a list element for present purposes; the mechanism described here works correctly for `nil`.

The address of the `cdr` of a list element is this base value minus 1, and the address of the `car` is the base value plus 3. If the target of the operation is a valid list element, then `car` or `cdr` always produces an address on a word boundary. Taking the `car` or `cdr` of any other type of object always causes a trap, because the calculated address is not divisible by four. Because invalid address detection is an integral part of SPARC address processing, no additional time is necessary to detect this type of error.

This is another case where a compiler safety setting of 0 in Sun Common Lisp offers as high a degree of error detection as a much higher setting on other Lisp systems, without the overhead other systems experience.

2.6
Sun COBOL™

The Sun COBOL product is based on the MicroFocus™ compiler system. The basic MicroFocus product has been enhanced by Sun Microsystems to provide superior performance on networked file systems. This enhancement was accomplished by replacing the general C-ISAM file handler with the Sun NetISAM™ file handler. The NetISAM file handler gives better network performance for indexed-sequential files across a network. The COBOL section of the *SPARCompiler Benchmark* white paper highlights the dramatic performance improvements attained through the use of this optimized file handler.

Sun COBOL programs can call any procedure using the C parameter-passing mechanism.

The Sun COBOL compiler system was validated in 1990 by the National Institute of Standards and Technology (NIST) as compliant at the high level with ANSI X3.23-1985 "Programming Language COBOL." The system also complies with all other relevant standards, including ISO 1989-1985 and FIPS PUB 21-2, and is XPG3 compliant.

Sun COBOL Compiler and Interpreter

The compiler system has the classic division into front end and back end components that communicate through an intermediate code file. In addition, there is an interpreter/loader utility, `cobrun`, that can execute the intermediate code produced by the front end, and can load the SPARC code produced by the code generator.

The front end lexically, syntactically and semantically analyzes the source code; the back end is a code generator that outputs SPARC instructions in a form similar to that used in .o files, known as "generated code form." This generated code file can be loaded and run using the interpreter/loader

Chapter 2. SPARCompiler™ Compilation Technology

utility `cobrun`. The back end can also use `ld` to produce statically linked executable modules in system-standard `a.out` format.

The trade-offs of these different translation alternatives are examined in the next section.

Choosing Between Interpreted, Generated, and Compiled Code

Each of the three translated forms—interpreted, generated, and compiled—has different attributes. Thus, the compiler provides flexibility that allows users to tailor their code development and execution to suit the needs of each specific situation. The code translation alternatives are depicted in Figure 2.5.

A file that contains interpreted form code can be interpreted on any Micro Focus platform, not only SPARC systems. Interpreted form is particularly convenient for Independent Software Vendors (ISVs) who develop portable applications, or for programmers who want to port an application from a Micro Focus system on other hardware to a Sun workstation.

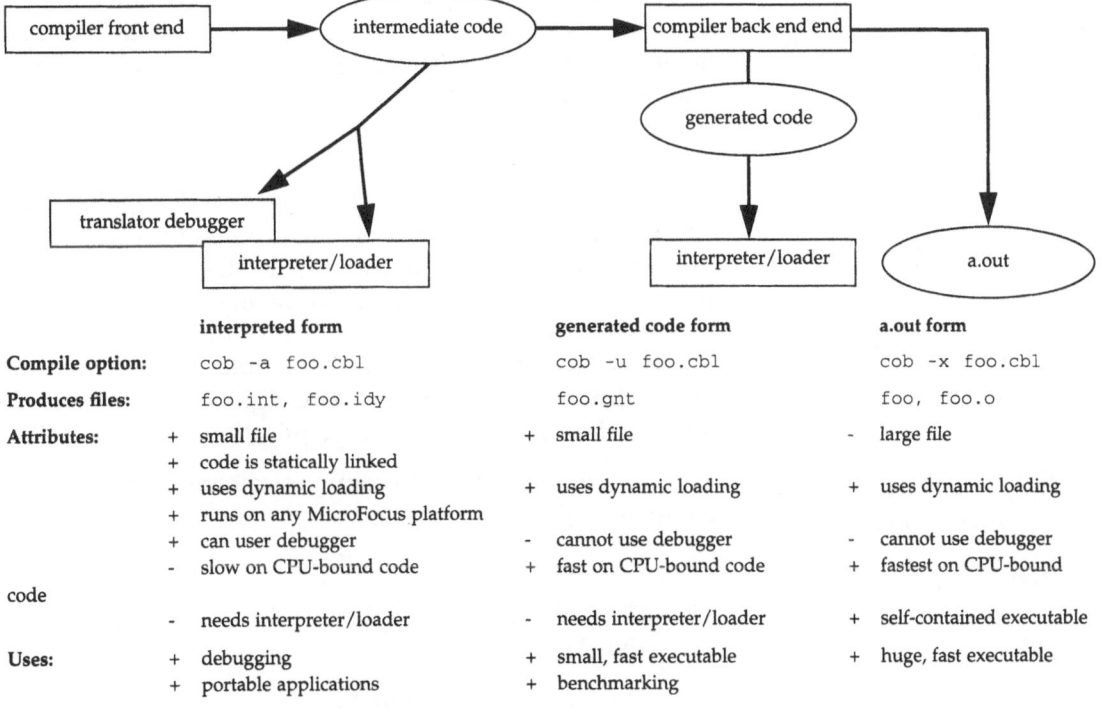

	interpreted form	generated code form	a.out form
Compile option:	`cob -a foo.cbl`	`cob -u foo.cbl`	`cob -x foo.cbl`
Produces files:	`foo.int, foo.idy`	`foo.gnt`	`foo, foo.o`
Attributes:	+ small file	+ small file	- large file
	+ code is statically linked		
	+ uses dynamic loading	+ uses dynamic loading	+ uses dynamic loading
	+ runs on any MicroFocus platform		
	+ can user debugger	- cannot use debugger	- cannot use debugger
	- slow on CPU-bound code	+ fast on CPU-bound code	+ fastest on CPU-bound code
	- needs interpreter/loader	- needs interpreter/loader	+ self-contained executable
Uses:	+ debugging	+ small, fast executable	+ huge, fast executable
	+ portable applications	+ benchmarking	

Figure 2.5. Code translation alternatives.

Dynamic Loading in Sun COBOL

The "dynamic loading" referred to in this document should be distinguished from the SunOS "dynamic linking" feature. Dynamic loading is a feature of the MicroFocus implementation that loads COBOL modules at runtime, rather than binding them together permanently into an executable at link time. When a UNIX file that contains COBOL source code is compiled to intermediate or generated code form, a .int or .gnt file is created for each COBOL program within that file. As the programs are called at runtime, the corresponding .int and .gnt files are dynamically brought into memory by the Sun COBOL Runtime System (RTS) for interpretation or execution. However, dynamic loading does convey an advantage similar to dynamic linking: executables are much smaller than statically linked a.out programs because common libraries are accessed at runtime.

There are two recommended uses of dynamic loading of COBOL modules. First, an ISV can construct an application so that its major parts are contained in separate .int or .gnt files. These parts are then invoked by the main program and dynamically loaded by the RTS as the features they implement are used. When an application is structured in this manner, the ISV can issue updates to customers by supplying only the .int or .gnt files that require replacement. This structure may significantly reduce maintenance costs of the application.

The second use of dynamic loading is for debugging large applications consisting of many modules. If the code is kept in separate dynamically loadable COBOL modules, individual ones can be recompiled for debugging by simply recompiling those files with the -a option of the cob command. This procedure debugs only those modules that were recompiled with the -a option; this saves significant maintenance and development costs for that application.

Flags, Directives, and Switches for Sun COBOL

There are three methods to communicate information to the compiler and run-time system:

1. Through command-line flags

2. Through compiler options (also known as "directives")

3. Through run-time switches.

There are approximately thirty command-line flags. These flags control aspects of the compilation process (such as the form of compilation, the name of the output file, and various linking attributes).

There are approximately one hundred compiler options. These options adjust the semantics of the language that the compiler accepts. For example, compiler options are available that recognize COBOL features specific to IBM Microsoft COBOL, to flag features outside a specified dialect, and to change record type defaults to variable length. In addition, there are an additional dozen compiler directives specifically for the code generator. System-wide default compiler directives are set for all programs in the file /usr/lib/cobol/cobopt. Directives can also be communicated via the environment variable *COBOPT*, on the command line with the -C flag, or embedded in a source file. Finally, there are approximately twenty switches that affect the run-time behavior of programs. These switches are communicated through the environment variable *COBSW*.

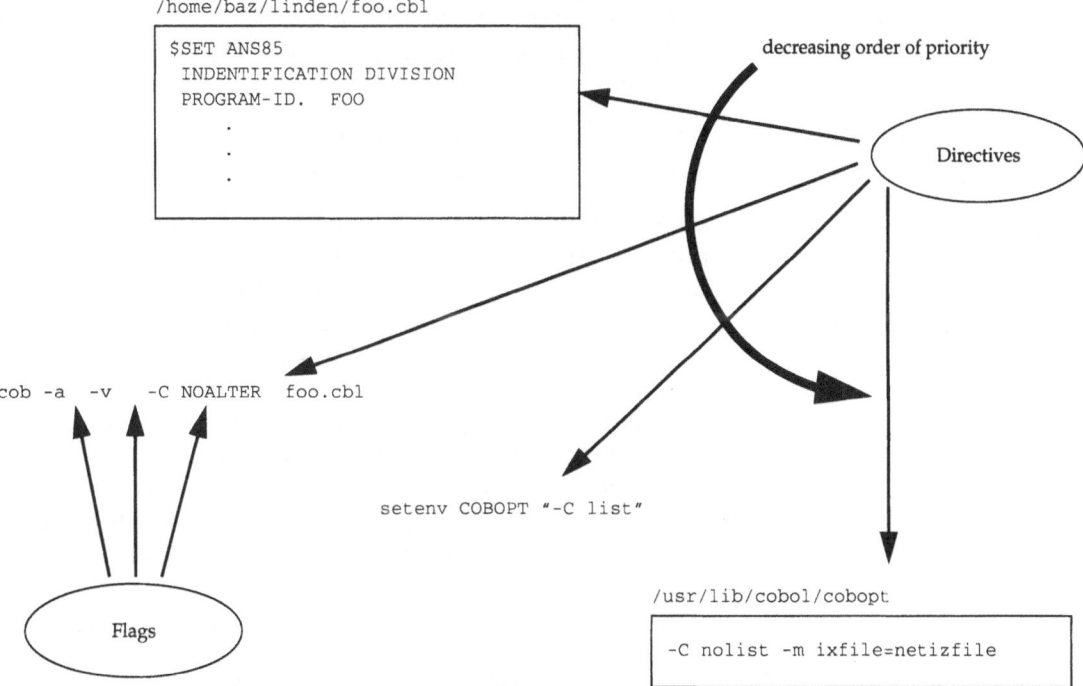

Figure 2.6. Differences Between Compiler Flags and Directives.

2.7
References

SPARCompiler Technology

Muchnick, Steven S. *Optimizing Compilers for the SPARC Architecture,* in Sun Technology, Vol. 1, No. 3, Summer 1988

Also in:

"The Sun Technology Papers", M. Hall and J. Barry (eds), Springer-Verlag, 1990

"Reduced Instruction Set Computers" (Second Ed.), Stallings (ed.), IEEE Computer Society Press, Los Alamitos, CA, 1990

Muchnick, Steven S. *Optimization in the SPARC Compilers,* in Procedures of the Sun Users Group Conference, Atlanta, June 1991

Also to appear in:

Procedures of SUN USER '91, Birmingham, England, September 1991

README (SUG publication), next issue

SPARC Technology

Garner, R. *SPARC: Scalable Processor Architecture,* in "The Sun Technology Papers", M. Hall and J. Barry (eds), Springer-Verlag, 1990

Compiler Technology

Aho, Alfred V., Sethi, R. and Ullman J.D. *Compilers: Principles, Techniques, and Tools,* Addison-Wesley, 1986

2.A
Appendix A—
Optimization
Definitions

As used in compilers, *optimization* refers to methods that improve the run-time performance of a compiled program, as compared to one translated by entirely straightforward methods. Optimization algorithms usually operate either on an intermediate code form or on object code.

Most optimizations concentrate on reducing execution time, but a few are specifically directed toward reducing the space a program occupies. Occasionally these goals conflict, so that, for example, a transformation that reduces execution time may increase the size of the object code. This size increase is rarely a problem because it is not usually very significant and, in almost all cases, reducing execution time is much more desirable than reducing the size of an object program.

One of the goals of the SPARCompiler product family is to produce the most highly optimized code possible. This is balanced by providing command-line switches that engage different levels of optimization to suit the needs of the phases of the development cycle. The remainder of this section provides definitions for the optimizations that are mentioned in the body of this report:

- *Aggregate Breaking*—an optimization that allows the individual components of composite objects to be treated as if they were scalars by other optimizations. This optimization is especially well-suited to work with copy propagation, register allocation and inlining. By viewing some structure components as scalars, the optimizer can avoid extraneous memory operations and can enable other optimizations that cannot be used effectively on entire structures.
- *Algebraic Address Expression Reorganization*—systematically transforms address expressions and collects region constants[1] to form simpler expressions from complex ones. A general-purpose transformation engine iteratively applies rules from a transformation grammar until no more simplification can be achieved.
- *Automatic Inlining*—A process whereby the code of a procedure body is placed directly into the body of the caller, in place of the call. This has several benefits:

  ° Call overhead is eliminated (this is usually a minor effect)

  ° Interprocedural optimizations are exposed (for example, common subexpression elimination, dead code elimination, and register allocation).

  ° In the current Sun implementation, the caller and the callee must reside in the same text file. A variety of sophisticated heuristics are employed to reduce the probability of adverse performance effects due to code size expansion. Entry points for the inline functions are preserved, so they can be called from functions residing in other files and from the debugger.

- *Common Subexpression Elimination*—saves expression values and reuses them, instead of recomputing them.
- *Complex Expression Expansion*—complex expression expansion works by separating complex expressions into subtrees for the real and imaginary parts of the complex expression. By splitting complex expressions in this manner, it is possible to increase the speed of complex arithmetic because the separate parts of the complex ex-

---

1. Region constants are expressions that have the same value throughout execution of some segment of a procedure, such as a loop.

pressions reside in registers during function calls, instead of in memory.

- *Constant Folding*—constant-valued expressions are evaluated by the compiler and the results are inserted into the generated code.
- *Constant Propagation*—a technique that replaces references to variables that are known to contain constant values with the constants themselves. The primary benefit of this optimization is that other optimizations such as constant folding and algebraic simplification can replace runtime computations with those done at compile time.
- *Copy Propagation*—copy operations that assign a simple value to a variable are of interest to copy propagation if, at runtime, the source of the assignment can be referenced faster than its target. For each such copy, all uses of the target that can be reached by this copy are replaced by the source, if the source is not redefined between the copy operation and its use.
- *Cross Jumping*—a technique that combines identical code found both immediately before a branch instruction and immediately before the branch target. This redundant code can be combined into one sequence.
- *Dead Code Elimination*—information is maintained by the optimizer to track what code is reachable. An expression computation is dead if there is no execution path along which the computation can reach any use of the value it computes. A variable definition is dead if it cannot reach any uses.
- *Detection of Interesting Variables*—a strategy to reduce compilation time by concentrating optimization effort on the parts of programs that are expected to yield the largest improvement for the smallest amount of work. By analyzing the types and patterns of variable references, the optimizer determines which variables are more likely to be candidates for optimization. These "interesting" variables are then targeted for optimization.
- *Elimination of Redundant Loads/Stores*—As an example, the load is redundant in the following case:

```
st  %fn, [eq]
ld  [eq], %fn
```

- *Elimination of Unnecessary Jumps*—For example:

```
jmp a                                jmp b
  . . .                                . . .
  . . .          becomes               . . .
  . . .                                . . .
a: jmp b                             a:jmp b
```

- *Induction-Variable Strength Reduction*—replaces slower operations (for example, multiplications) by faster ones (for example, additions or shifts).
- *Instruction Scheduling*—fine-grained execution parallelism allows several instructions to execute simultaneously, as long as they use distinct functional units. Since both SPARCsystems' Floating Point Units (FPUs) and the delay slots following branches and loads provide such parallelism, the postpass optimizers for these systems rearrange instructions in the generated code to take advantage of this parallelism.
- *Leaf Routine Optimization*—leaf routines (routines that call no others) are comparatively common. If a leaf routine uses few registers and needs no local stack, it can be entered and exited with the minimum possible overhead by omitting the `save` and `restore` instructions and correspondingly adjusting the register numbers used in it. This saves cycles and also reduces the number of register windows employed.
- *Loop-Invariant Code Motion*—finds those computations within a loop that yield the same results for each iteration of the loop and moves them out of the loop.
- *Loop Inversion*—used to convert pre-test loops into post-test loops. This optimization allows loops that have two branches per iteration to be turned into loops that have one branch per iteration.
- *Loop Unrolling*—replaces the body of a loop with several copies of the body, adjusting the loop control code accordingly. This optimization reduces the run-time looping overhead by reducing the number of loop iterations taken. More importantly, increasing the size of the loop body also increases the effectiveness of instruction scheduling.
- *Optimized Block Moves*—tight inline code is generated for block moves when it is known that the source and destination locations do not overlap.

- *Range Propagation for Elimination of Constraint Checking*—once a range check has been performed on an object, the object is tracked so that redundant range checks are eliminated. Related checks can also be eliminated, if, for example, the range of one object is within the range of another. Some null reference checks for pointer types are also eliminated by range propagation.
- *Register Allocation*—decides which objects are worth placing in registers, and which objects can share a register with others within a region of code. For each candidate, the benefit is determined by the number of machine cycles saved by allocating it to a register instead of memory.
- *Register Coalescing*—minimizes the number of registers required to compute a value. Using the fewest registers for one computation ensures that as many as possible are available for use in other computations.
- *Tail Call Optimization*—subroutine calls that are performed immediately before the caller returns are called *tail calls*. By placing a routine's `restore` instruction in the delay slot of the tail call, the called subroutine uses the same register window that its caller used.
- *Tail Recursion Elimination*—converts some self-recursive procedures into iterations. This typically saves register window overflows (on calls) and underflows (on returns) and it saves stack allocation, manipulation and deallocation.

The SPARCworks™ Programming Environment

3.1 Introduction

SPARCworks™ is a set of six programming tools for use with SPARCompilers. The SPARCworks programming environment speeds and simplifies the tasks software developers do most often — edit and merge source code, compile programs, debug programs, and tune program performance.

SPARCworks tools form part of an overall development environment that includes SunOS™ programming utilities, the DeskSet™ productivity tools (including File Manager and Mail Tool), and the OpenWindows™ Developer's Guide for interactively building OPEN LOOK® graphical interfaces.

The SPARCworks programming environment consists of the following six tools:

- **SPARCworks Manager** — for managing and coordinating other SPARCworks programming tools
- **SourceBrowser** — for statically analyzing source code and program structure
- **Debugger** — for dynamically analyzing programs, observing behavior while the program runs, and collecting information for performance profiling
- **Analyzer** — for tuning program performance, including memory allocation

- **FileMerge** — for merging source files and coordinating source code changes
- **MakeTool** — for building programs and browsing makefiles.

Most SPARCworks functions are available from the terminal-mode command line, a fact important to users without access to a Sun™ window environment. However, this section discusses only the OPEN LOOK window interface to SPARCworks tools.

Compatible Compilers

The following SPARCompilers can be used with SPARCworks tools:

- SPARCompiler C / ANSI C
- SPARCompiler C++
- SPARCompiler FORTRAN
- SPARCompiler Pascal.

Other Sun compilers, such as SPARCompiler Ada and SPARCompiler COBOL, provide their own programming environments.

3.2 SPARCworks Manager

SPARCworks Manager provides an easy-to-use, unified means to start SPARCworks tools and control the programming environment. Figure 3.1 shows the SPARCworks Manager window with SPARCworks tool icons displayed. Each tool can be started by double-clicking on its icon or by dragging the icon onto the screen workspace. A tool that is started from the SPARCworks Manager is thereafter associated with that instance of SPARCworks Manager, and can be controlled as part of a management *session*.

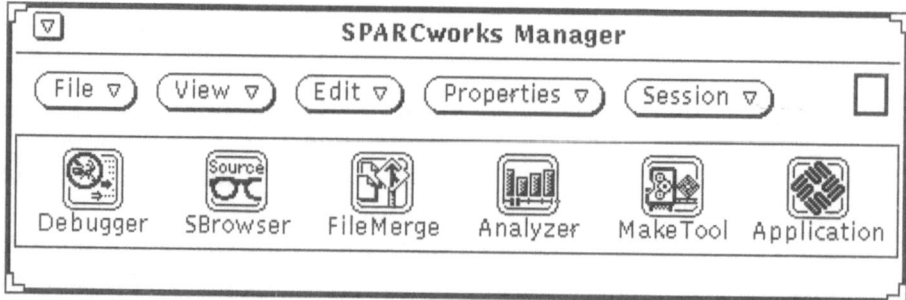

Figure 3.1. Sparcworks Manager window.

In addition to managing the other five standard SPARCworks tools, SPARCworks Manager can also control custom applications written by users or by third-party developers. When integrated with SPARCworks and executed under SPARCworks Manager, the standard SPARCworks tools and custom applications combine to provide you with the following advantages:

- **Drag-and-drop execution** — You can drag an on-screen deskset object (a file icon, for example) with the mouse pointer and drop it on a SPARCworks tool, which recognizes whether or not the object can be loaded or otherwise acted upon.
- **Session control** — You can group development activities into logical management *sessions*. Multiple sessions can proceed simultaneously, each controlled by its own Tool Manager.
- **Workspace organization** — Tool Manager helps you make the best use of on-screen workspace. SPARCworks tools associated with a management session can be closed to a single icon.
- **Central control** — The SPARCworks Manager can set environment variables and the working directory for all SPARCworks tools used in a session.

3.3 SourceBrowser

SourceBrowser is the SPARCworks tool for static program analysis. Static analysis of a compiled program involves examination of its code. The program does not need to be executing during static analysis. Searching through high-level source code with a text editor is a primitive form of static analysis.

SourceBrowser can perform "queries" on source code (analogous to searching in a text editor) that are constrained by the semantics of the source language it is browsing and by other, user-imposed constraints. In addition, SourceBrowser maintains a list of previous queries so that it can return to view earlier results, eliminating the performance penalty that would be required to repeat the query.

When SPARCompilers execute with the -sb command option, they create a database that SourceBrowser uses to speed searches, making it much faster at matching than simple text editors. SPARCompilers also inform SourceBrowser of exactly which source files were compiled to produce an executable or library so that they can be loaded and browsed automatically. By default, SourceBrowser queries all source files, but you can limit the query to focus on any subset of source files. SourceBrowser considers all header files to be source files during queries.

SourceBrowser relies on SPARCompilers to generate the list of symbols it uses. Unlike the SPARCworks Debugger, which uses symbols embedded in the compiled executable, SourceBrowser uses its own database of symbols that is independent of the executable. This arrangement has two benefits: it speeds SourceBrowser search activities and minimizes the amount of information that the compiler must include in executables to enable SourceBrowser to do its work.

SourceBrowser Window

SourceBrowser operates by responding to user *queries* that instruct it to find all occurrences of a specified identifier, string constant, or search pattern.

Figure 3.2 shows the SourceBrowser base window. In addition to the standard OPEN LOOK window header, the window contains a control area filled with buttons, button menus, and a field where you enter text before instructing SourceBrowser to search for matches. The control area also displays a message that reports on the number of matches that result from a query.

Below the control area is a scrollable match pane that displays all matches found by the current query. Below the match pane is the source pane, which displays the contents of the source file in which a match was made. Text above the source pane lists the current working directory, the name of the file being displayed, and the line numbers of the first and last lines being displayed.

Beneath the source pane is a message area that displays the type and value that is the subject of the current query.

SourceBrowser Capabilities
Finds Symbols and Strings in Source

This section highlights the features and capabilities of SourceBrowser.

In a SourceBrowser session, users issue queries that instruct SourceBrowser to find all occurrences of a specified symbol, string constant, identifier, or search pattern. In response, SourceBrowser displays *matches* (occurrences of the text that SourceBrowser was ordered to find) with their surrounding source code.

SourceBrowser maintains a list of all queries that were conducted during a session. This feature makes it easy to issue a query, view the resulting matches, conduct another

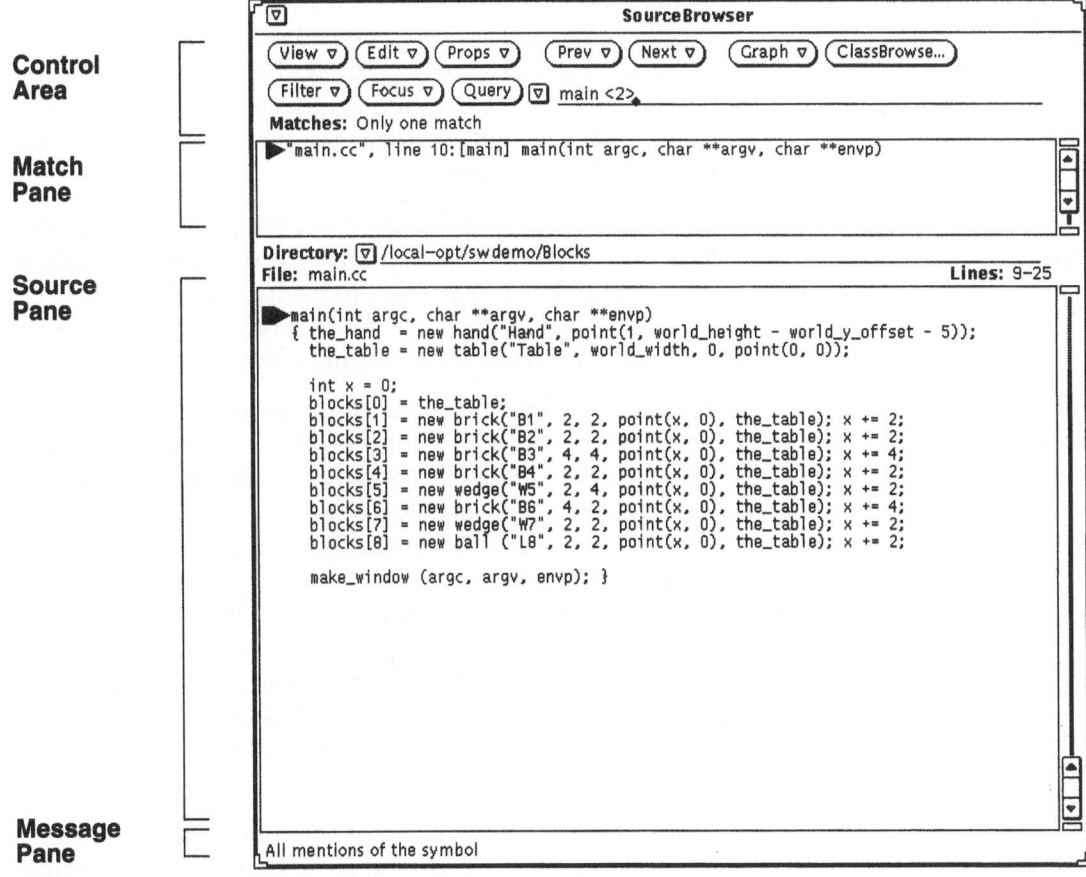

Control Area

Match Pane

Source Pane

Message Pane

```
┌─────────────────────────────────────────────────────────────────────┐
│ ▽                        SourceBrowser                                │
├─────────────────────────────────────────────────────────────────────┤
│ ( View ▽ ) ( Edit ▽ ) ( Props ▽ )   ( Prev ▽ ) ( Next ▽ )   ( Graph ▽ ) ( ClassBrowse… ) │
│ ( Filter ▽ ) ( Focus ▽ ) ( Query ) ▽  main <2>                        │
│ Matches: Only one match                                               │
├─────────────────────────────────────────────────────────────────────┤
│ ▶"main.cc", line 10:[main] main(int argc, char **argv, char **envp)   │
│                                                                       │
├─────────────────────────────────────────────────────────────────────┤
│ Directory: ▽ /local-opt/swdemo/Blocks                                 │
│ File: main.cc                                               Lines: 9-25│
│ ▶main(int argc, char **argv, char **envp)                             │
│   { the_hand  = new hand("Hand", point(1, world_height - world_y_offset - 5)); │
│     the_table = new table("Table", world_width, 0, point(0, 0));      │
│                                                                       │
│     int x = 0;                                                        │
│     blocks[0] = the_table;                                            │
│     blocks[1] = new brick("B1", 2, 2, point(x, 0), the_table); x += 2;│
│     blocks[2] = new brick("B2", 2, 2, point(x, 0), the_table); x += 2;│
│     blocks[3] = new brick("B3", 4, 4, point(x, 0), the_table); x += 4;│
│     blocks[4] = new brick("B4", 2, 2, point(x, 0), the_table); x += 2;│
│     blocks[5] = new wedge("W5", 2, 4, point(x, 0), the_table); x += 2;│
│     blocks[6] = new brick("B6", 4, 2, point(x, 0), the_table); x += 4;│
│     blocks[7] = new wedge("W7", 2, 2, point(x, 0), the_table); x += 2;│
│     blocks[8] = new ball ("L8", 2, 2, point(x, 0), the_table); x += 2;│
│                                                                       │
│     make_window (argc, argv, envp); }                                 │
│                                                                       │
├─────────────────────────────────────────────────────────────────────┤
│ All mentions of the symbol                                            │
└─────────────────────────────────────────────────────────────────────┘
```

Figure 3.2. SourceBrowser base window.

query, and then return to the original query with a minimum number of commands.

Matches Wildcards and Regular Expressions

In addition to literal text, query patterns can contain *wildcards*, as used in shell-style patterns, or *regular expressions*, as used in vi, grep, and other SunOS editors and utilities. The SourceBrowser Property Window lets you specify which convention to use.

Performs Semantic Queries

SourceBrowser can respond to queries that filter matches according to the semantics of the source language. For example, a developer using the C language could issue a very specific query such as "Show all occurrences of the variable *age* when *age* is used as a structure field name." The search can be further focused on specific items of certain classes of code, such as files or functions.

Adapts to Many Languages	SourceBrowser has no built-in, architectural affinity for any specific language. Instead, SourceBrowser obtains information about each supported language by reading a configuration file. The configuration file can be expanded to incorporate additional languages as new compilers are integrated with SourceBrowser.
Provides Text Editor for Source	Users can edit source directly in the text pane. The text pane uses Text Editor commands that are the same as those in other OPEN LOOK applications such as MailTool. Files under the control of Source Code Control System can be checked out directly from a menu in the text pane.
Handles Large Applications	The first time SourceBrowser runs a query it creates an index file for use in subsequent queries. The index file allows SourceBrowser to maintain a high level of efficiency regardless of the amount of code it is browsing.
	SourceBrowser also includes several features specially designed to improve performance while browsing large amounts of code. In one experiment, all of `/usr/src` for the SunOS was compiled for browsing with SourceBrowser. The resulting SourceBrowser database was between 40 and 50 Mbytes. Even with such a large database, SourceBrowser was able to respond to queries in one or two seconds after it had created its index file.
Produces Call and Class Graphs	SourceBrowser can produce function call graphs for procedural languages and class graphs for the C++ object-oriented language. Call and class graphs are valuable overviews of function and object relationships, especially for large programs.
	Simple call and class graphs are shown in Figure 3.3. The graphs show relationships among functions and classes for simple programs. Horizontal and vertical scroll bars are provided for viewing larger graphs.
Class Browser	In addition to the Class Grapher, SourceBrowser provides another tool to help understand how SPARCompiler C++ classes are defined and used. Class Browser, activated from SourceBrowser, helps you effectively browse through C++ source code and libraries. The Class Browser base window is shown in Figure 3.4.

The Class Browser provides the following capabilities:

- **List and select from available classes** — view an alphabetical list of available classes and select one from the list to display information.

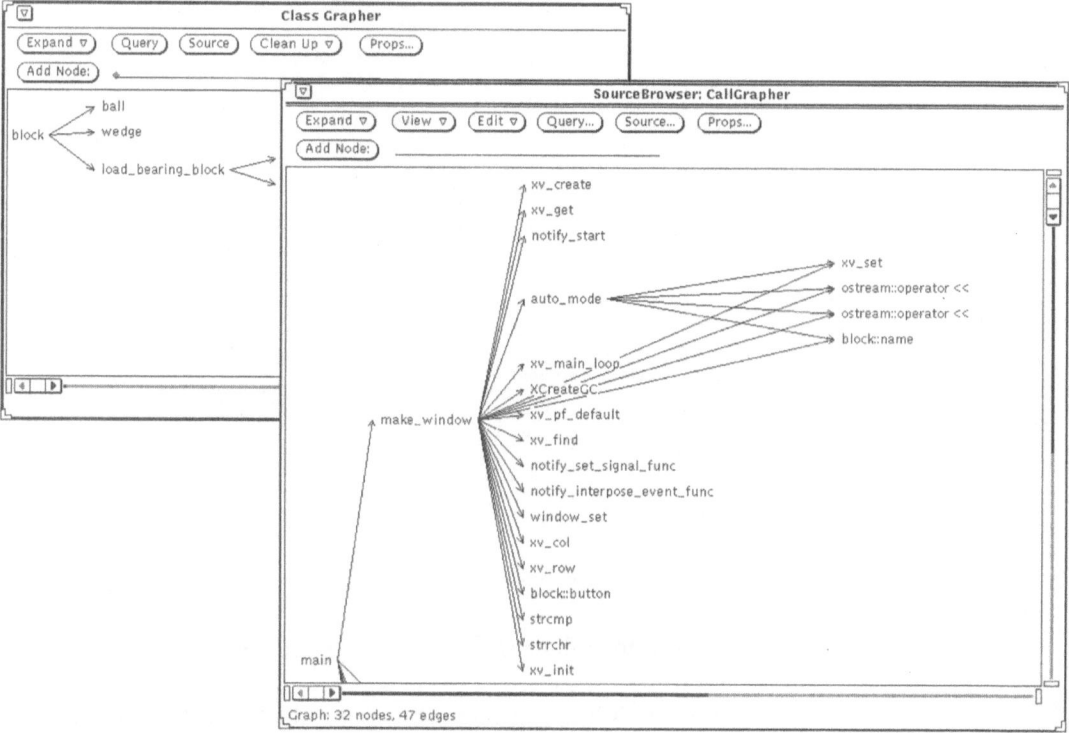

Figure 3.3. SourceBrowser call and class graphs.

- **Navigate from class to class** — easily follow inheritance links to browse information.
- **Display class data and member functions** — view the data members and member functions of a specified class.
- **Show access protection of class members** — display access restrictions along with data members and member functions to reveal valid class-defined interfaces.
- **Identify friend classes** — discover the friend classes and functions of a specified class.
- **Display the source of member classes** — select a class and display its source code.
- **Issue queries for class usage** — use the SourceBrowser query facility to find usages of a specified class.
- **Interact with Class Grapher** — select a node in Class Grapher and display class information in Class Browser.

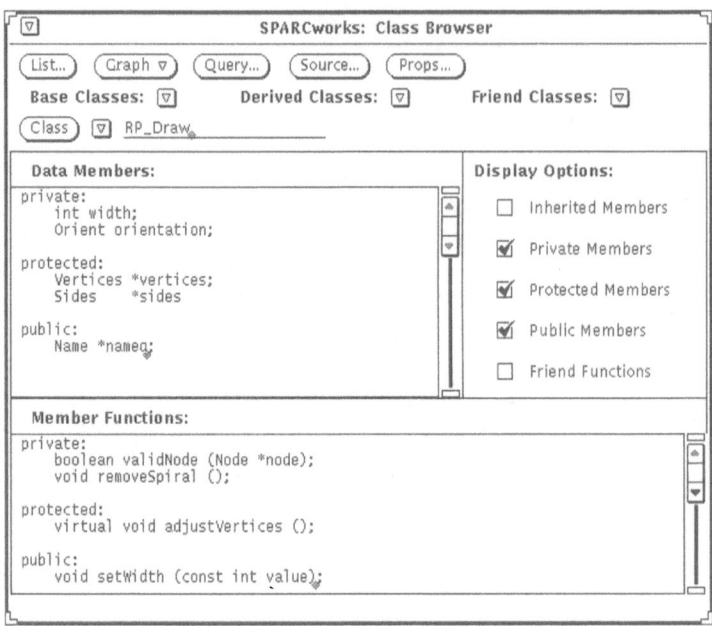

Figure 3.4. ClassBrowser base window.

Using SourceBrowser

You initiate a SourceBrowser query in one of two ways:

- Select a text string anywhere on the screen and click the Query button
- Type a string in the text entry field next to the Action button and press the Return key.

The first method makes use of the selection service and is especially useful when SourceBrowser is used with other OPEN LOOK programs such as the SPARCworks Debugger.

Filtering To Obtain Useful Matches

The number of matches the SourceBrowser can handle is limited only by the available swap space. For a symbol like NULL, a query might produce such a large number of matches that the information present is not useful. SourceBrowser filter capabilities can be used to reduce the number of matches.

You can instruct SourceBrowser to restrict its search on the basis of semantic information specific to a particular language. For example, choosing Filter from the View menu produces a pop-up window (Figure 3.5) in which you can specify that the SourceBrowser search only for C-language declarations of the symbol.

Figure 3.5. Setting a filter for C language declarations.

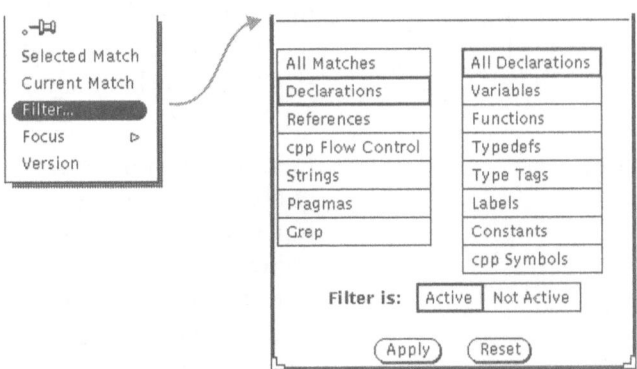

Language-Specific Filtering

The choices on the Filter pop-up window are language-specific and change automatically with the languages that have been compiled into the SourceBrowser database. The choices shown in Figure 3.6 are for FORTRAN.

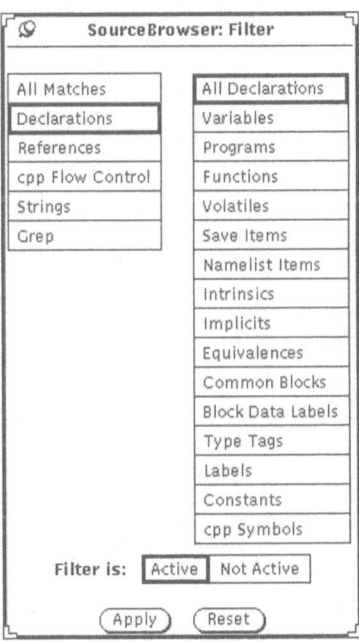

Figure 3.6. Filter choices for the FORTRAN language.

When a project requires that object files be compiled from sources written in different languages, the linker (ld) records this fact in the SourceBrowser database at link time. The Filter pop-up window shows the union of all semantic constructs for the languages that were used to produce the final executable.

Focusing

In addition to filtering, users can restrict SourceBrowser to query only certain sections of the source: a specific language, function, or set of source files, for example. This restriction is known as *focusing*.

In Figure 3.7, SourceBrowser is being instructed to focus its queries on the function hello and the source file hello.c.

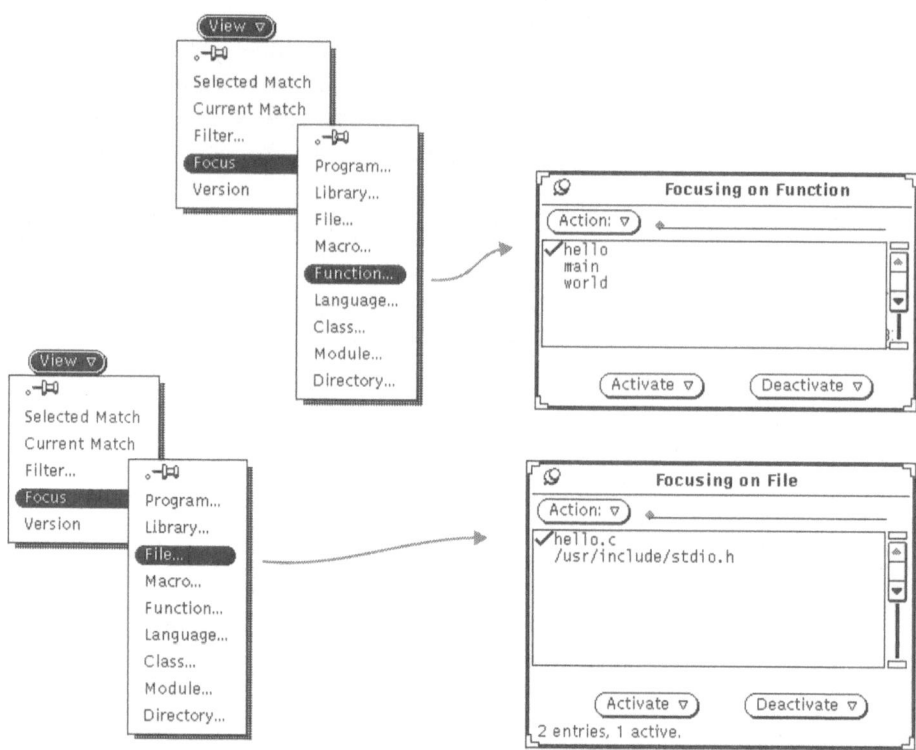

Figure 3.7. Focusing a Query.

Any number of items in the lists can be activated; SourceBrowser thereafter limits its queries to source that is the union of all active items from all Focus lists. With the settings shown in Figure 3.7, a search for the NULL symbol would match only text that is either in the function `hello` or the file `hello.c` (or both).

Matching Strings

The information stored in the SourceBrowser database is determined by the compiler that generates the database—SPARCompilers have been designed to store strings and symbols. Strings are stored along with the quotation marks that are used in the language, which identifies them as strings and enables SourceBrowser to perform queries on them (to limit a query to strings only, set a filter for Strings).

Queries for strings are very useful for debugging an application that has printed a message (typically an error message). A user can search for a string in the message and find the place in source where the message is printed. In conjunction with Debugger, the user can then determine the exact circumstance that caused the message to be printed and rapidly uncover the source of the error.

Checking Out Files from SCCS

The source pane in SourceBrowser can be enabled as an editing window, with features identical to OPEN LOOK Text Edit. A pop-up menu in the source pane enables editing (Figure 3.8). If the source is controlled by the Source Code Control System (SCCS), the same menu can check out the source file for editing. This feature is also found in the Debugger source window — source files can be checked out from SCCS and edited in either window.

3.4
Debugger

The SPARCworks Debugger dynamically analyzes a program, letting you observe its behavior while it is running. Debugger gives you complete control of program execution and simultaneously collects performance data for later use with SPARCworks Analyzer. From within Debugger you can identify a problem, edit source code, rebuild the program, and then continue dynamic analysis.

In addition to the mouse-selectable functions of the OPEN LOOK interface (which you can customize to suit your needs), Debugger provides a pane in which you can type commands directly to the command line. The algorithms underlying Debugger are those of `dbx`, a mature dynamic analyzer descended from Berkeley 4.2 BSD.

Debugger Features

The following list summarizes the activities you can perform with Debugger and gives an overview of its many features.

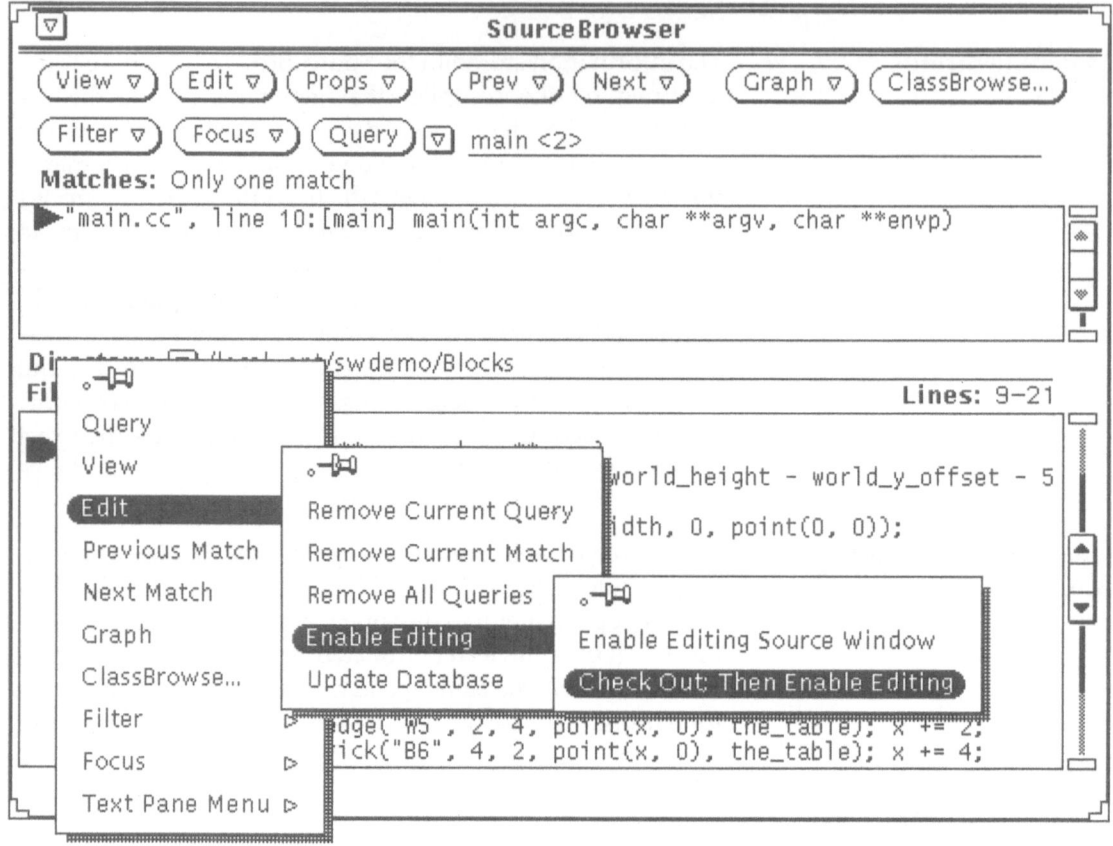

Figure 3.8. Checking out a file for editing in the source pane.

- **Display source code** — the debugger displays source code corresponding to the machine code being executed.
- **Single step** through the program by machine instructions or by source lines. You can decide to step into procedures or over them.
- **Set breakpoints** at source line, address, exception, instruction count, procedure, or function. You can also set conditional breakpoints.
- **Set watchpoints** for variables, functions, source lines, or expressions you enter at the command line. Execute a command or evaluate an expression when the value of the watchpoint changes. You can set conditional watchpoints and watchpoints that focus on a particular function or procedure.

- **Analyze low-level code** — the debugger analyzes assembly language code as well as code written in high-level languages.
- **Navigate the call stack** — move up and down the call stack.
- **Modify data** — edit code at source level; change the values of variables at a low level.
- **Handle overloaded names** — when variables from different functions or procedures have the same name, you can differentiate each name by fully qualifying it with the name of the function (and source file, if necessary) in which it occurs.
- **Run subprograms**.
- **Evaluate operators and native language expressions**.
- **Analyze live processes** — attach Debugger to an executing program such as a daemon, debug the process, and then detach Debugger. Programs do not need to run as children of Debugger in order for you to analyze them.
- **Handle signals** — intercept signals and act on them; ignore other signals that might halt execution.
- **Analyze dynamically linked shared libraries** — dynamically linked shared libraries that have been specified during linking can be analyzed with Debugger.
- **Analyze multiple languages** — Debugger works with the same SPARCompilers that as SourceBrowser: at this writing, they are C, C++, FORTRAN, and Pascal.
- **Load symbol-table information automatically** — load compiled symbol table information on demand. Makes starting Debugger with a large program much faster.
- **Analyze optimized code** — code compiled with the -Og option can be analyzed.
- **List command history** — a history command provides most of the same functionality as the C-shell `history` command.
- **Step out of functions with a single command** — after you have stepped into a function, a single command lets you quickly return to the calling function.
- **Monitor the value of expressions and variables** — a Data Display pop-up window monitors the values of expressions and variables, including the values of nested pointers.
- **Evaluate FORTRAN array slices** — print the values of portions of FORTRAN arrays.

- **Save, restore, and replay sequences of commands** — save analysis sessions in the form of command sequences. The sequence can then be replayed to restore the analysis session, or a subset of the sequence can be replayed for an "undo" effect (on programs that are determinate).
- **Check out source from SCCS** — like the source pane in SourceBrowser, the source pane in Debugger can be enabled as an OPEN LOOK editing window. If the source file is controlled by SCCS, Debugger can check out the file.

Debugger Interface

Figure 3.9 shows the Debugger base window. Beneath the standard OPEN LOOK window header are the following elements:

- **Button menu control panel** — contains button menus that provide access to the most important and commonly used debugging commands, as well as an assortment of debugging utility commands and property window controls.

Beneath the buttons, the window displays current program location (by file and function) and the full path name of the source code file being displayed.

- **Source pane** — usually displays the current locus of execution in the source code, indicated by a bold arrow to the left of the source line. An outlined arrow indicates an active call on the stack. Stop sign glyphs to the left of source lines indicate where breakpoints are set. When the program is executing in single steps, the source text view in the pane is updated to keep up with the changing locus of execution.
- **Command button control area** — buttons in this area provide easy access to the most commonly used items from the button menus at the top of the window. Users can customize this area by adding buttons to execute any dbx command.
- **Command pane** — you can enter dbx commands from the keyboard in this pane. The pane echoes the commands generated by control panel buttons. Messages returned by dbx also appear in this window.

Data Display Window

The Data Display window (Figure 3.10) monitors the values of expressions and variables whenever execution halts.

Chapter 3. The SPARCworks Programming Environment

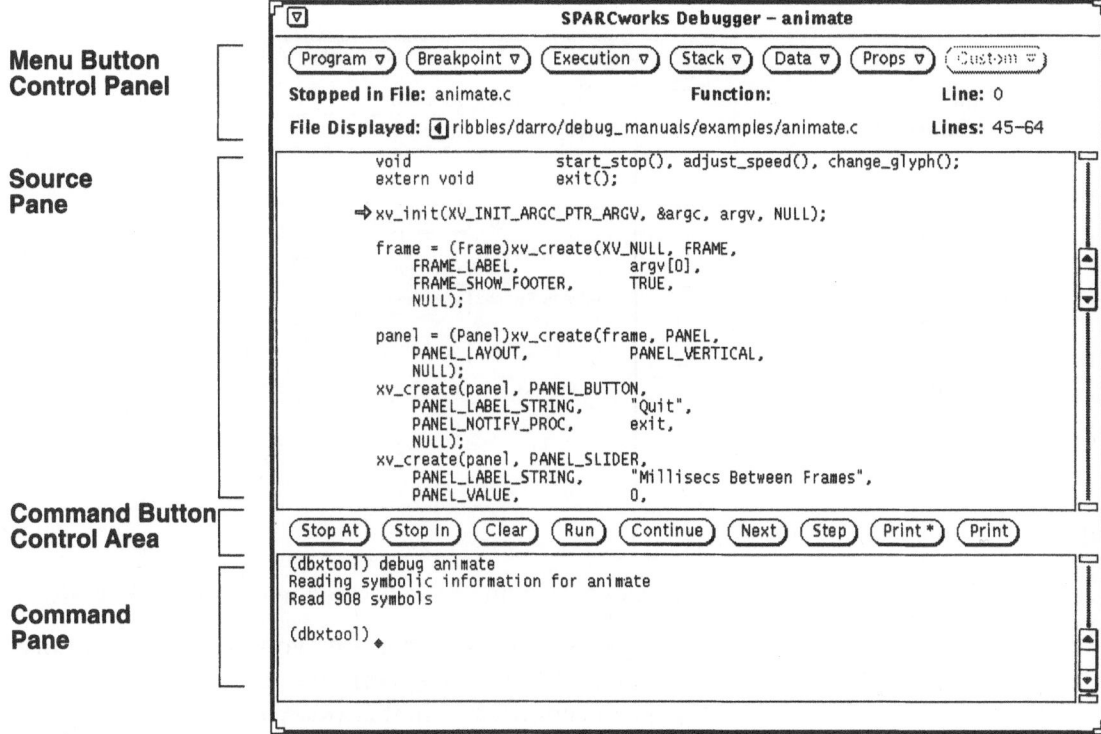

Figure 3.9. SPARCworks Debugger window.

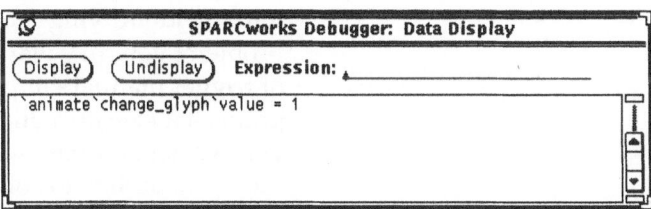

Figure 3.10. Data Display window.

Collector Window

In addition to its duties as a dynamic analyzer, the Debugger also collects data for use with the Analyzer performance-tuning tool.

The Debugger Collector window sets data collection parameters. Then, as the application executes under Debugger, the Collector gathers performance and test coverage data and writes the data to a file. The execution run is called an *experiment*; the file is referred to as an *experiment record*. Figure 3.11 shows the default settings of the Collector when it is first activated.

File Parameters

Type of Sampling

Data Collection Parameters

Profiling Timer

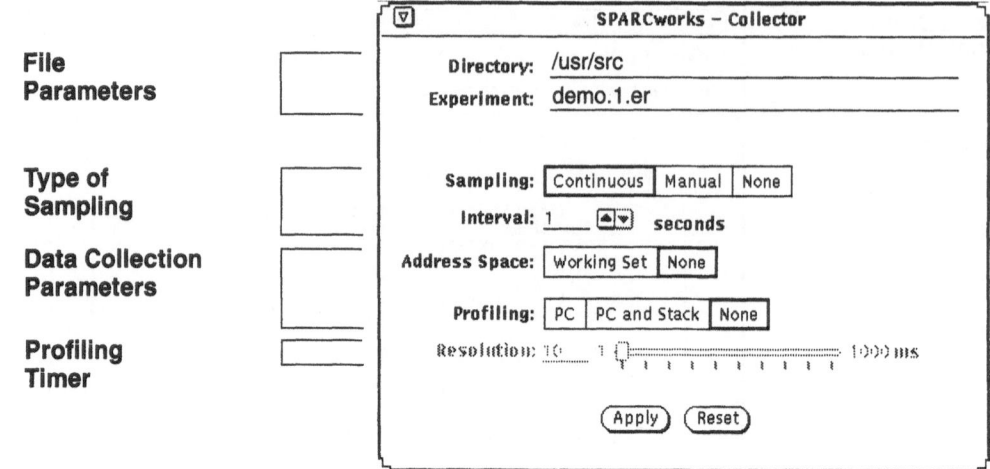

Figure 3.11. Collector Window.

The Collector window is divided into four main areas:

- **File parameters** — in this area you name the directory and file name for the experiment record.
- **Type of sampling** — in this area you choose the type of sampling for the experiment. Each sample contains information on the target program, collected over a specified period of time. Continuous sampling is useful for initially identifying problem areas. As you focus in on a problem, you may want to adjust the sampling interval or trigger manual sampling at a specific point in the program as it executes under control of the Debugger.
- **Data collection parameters** — In this area you specify the types of data to collect during the experiment.

The Collector always accumulates data for an overview display of the experiment. Additional data collection parameters are:

- **Working Set** — causes the Collector to accumulate memory use data.

- **PC** — causes the Collector to accumulate program counter profiling data. This data identifies the functions in which the program spends the most time.

- **PC and Stack** — causes the Collector to accumulate return addresses on the call stack. This data is useful for profiling applications that have a hierarchical, modular design and for complex applications that make heavy use of standard library files.

- **Profiling timer** — specifies how often data is to be collected.

Section 3.6 describes how the collected data is analyzed.

3.5 Using SourceBrowser with Debugger

Because SourceBrowser and Debugger use the selection service, they are integrated with each other and with other OPEN LOOK applications.

When you run SourceBrowser along with Debugger you combine the benefits of static and dynamic analysis. For example:

- When you stop at a function in Debugger, you can then go to the SourceBrowser to find how the function is defined. You can also find all the other places where it is used.
- You can use SourceBrowser to search for a variable. If the search finds the variable in an interesting line of source code, you can move to Debugger, set a breakpoint, and examine the values taken on by the variable in the statement during execution.

A Brief Example

To use SourceBrowser with Debugger, you must first compile your program with the appropriate options: -g to instrument the executable for Debugger (and, incidentally, for SPARCworks Analyzer), and -sb to create the SourceBrowser database. For this example, the user compiles the source file hello.c with the command

cc -g -sb hello.c

In this example, assume that debugging has started with Debugger. During dynamic analysis, the user has discovered a bug somewhere near line 33 in the file hello.c, and suspects that the bug involves the variable file. The user wants to know how file is defined and where else it is used—a job for SourceBrowser. Before moving to SourceBrowser, the user selects the variable file in Debugger, as shown in Figure 3.12.

The user now moves to SourceBrowser and issues a query that instructs it to find file. When the user clicks on the Query button, the selection service informs SourceBrowser that file is the object of the query (file has been selected in Debugger). The user steps through the resulting matches

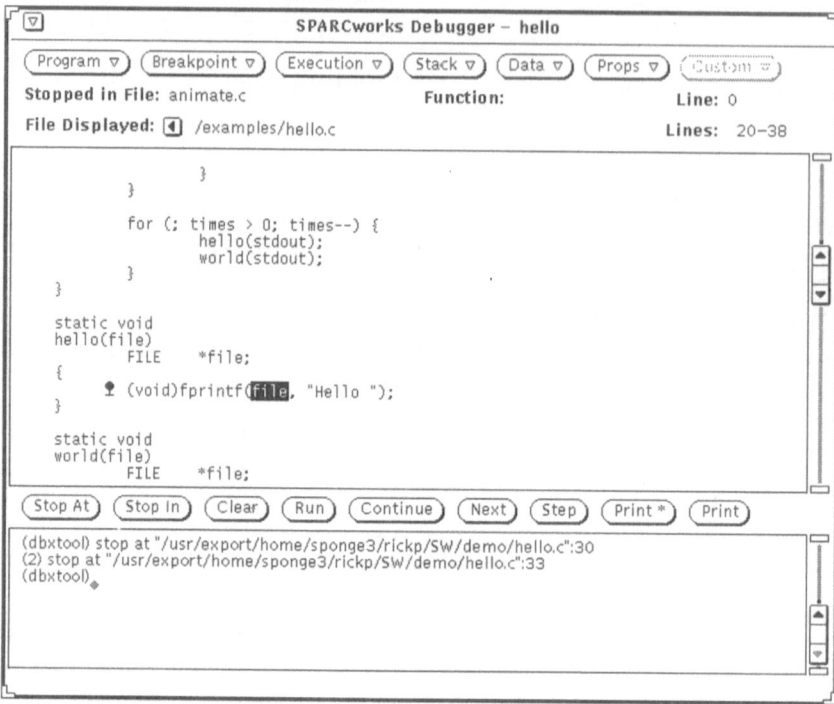

Figure 3.12. Selecting a variable in Debugger.

in SourceBrowser by repeatedly pushing the Next button, examining the places where `file` is used in the program (Figure 3.13).

To continue the debugging process, the user would move back and forth between SourceBrowser and Debugger, using SourceBrowser to find interesting instances of source text and Debugger to display the values of variables and pointers while the program executes.

3.6 Analyzer

After you have successfully compiled a program and eliminated its major bugs, you will want to evaluate its performance. The SPARCworks Analyzer measures and displays an application's performance profile, suggesting ways to improve performance.

Any program that has been compiled for debugging is capable of generating data for the Analyzer. The Debugger collects performance data while the program runs under Debugger control. The performance data is placed in a file that the Analyzer subsequently examines and presents in a variety of graphic and text displays.

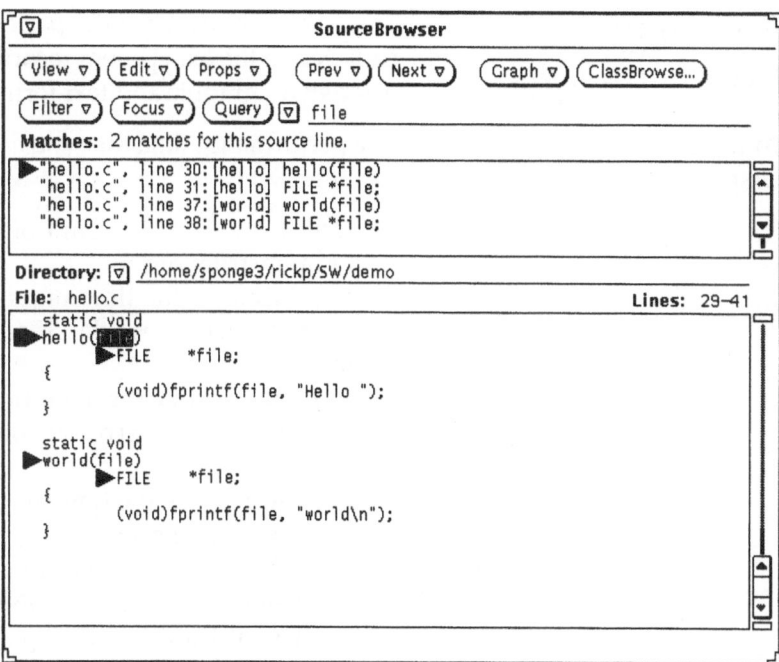

```
┌────────────────────────────────────────────────────────────────────┐
│ ▽                        SourceBrowser                               │
│ ┌─────┐ ┌──────┐ ┌───────┐  ┌───────┐ ┌───────┐  ┌───────┐ ┌──────────────┐ │
│ ( View ▽) (Edit ▽) (Props ▽)  (Prev ▽) (Next ▽)  (Graph ▽) (ClassBrowse...) │
│ (Filter ▽) (Focus ▽) (Query ▽) ▽ file                                │
│ Matches: 2 matches for this source line.                             │
│ ┌──────────────────────────────────────────────────────────────┐   │
│ │▶"hello.c", line 30:[hello] hello(file)                        ▲│   │
│ │ "hello.c", line 31:[hello] FILE *file;                        ▲│   │
│ │ "hello.c", line 37:[world] world(file)                        ▼│   │
│ │ "hello.c", line 38:[world] FILE *file;                        ▼│   │
│ └──────────────────────────────────────────────────────────────┘   │
│ Directory: ▽ /home/sponge3/rickp/SW/demo                             │
│ File:  hello.c                                      Lines:  29-41    │
│ ┌──────────────────────────────────────────────────────────────┐   │
│ │     static void                                                │   │
│ │ ▶hello(████)                                                   │   │
│ │         ▶FILE    *file;                                        │   │
│ │     {                                                          │   │
│ │         (void)fprintf(file, "Hello ");                         │   │
│ │     }                                                          │   │
│ │                                                                │   │
│ │     static void                                                │   │
│ │ ▶world(file)                                                   │   │
│ │         ▶FILE    *file;                                        │   │
│ │     {                                                          │   │
│ │         (void)fprintf(file, "world\n");                        │   │
│ │     }                                                        ▲ │   │
│ │                                                              ▼ │   │
│ └──────────────────────────────────────────────────────────────┘   │
└────────────────────────────────────────────────────────────────────┘
```

Figure 3.13. Querying for the selected variable in SourceBrowser.

Features

The Analyzer eliminates the need to compile and link an application with special data collection instrumentation — any program that has been instrumented for debugging can be analyzed. Moreover, the Analyzer simplifies and enhances the task of collecting data: you can collect a variety of performance data types, and you can control the data collection process while an application is running.

By letting you focus on the areas where performance problems occur, the Analyzer easily tests your hypotheses about a program's behavior.

After you have tuned your program, the Analyzer assists you in rebuilding it. As a further help in rebuilding your program with improved performance, the Analyzer identifies improved ordering for loading functions into the program's address space. The Analyzer then rebuilds the program by passing the new ordering to the SunOS linker and produces an executable with reduced working set size.

Collecting Experiment Data

Experiment data is collected by the Debugger, as described in Section 3.4 on the "collector window." Following collection, the data is written to a file called the *experiment record*.

Analyzing Experiment Data

Analyzer Features and Displays

The Analyzer examines the performance data that has been collected in the experiment record and displays its results in a variety of graphic and text formats.

The performance data that you can examine in the Analyzer includes:

- **User time** — the amount of time spent executing program instructions.
- **Fault time** — the time required to service fault-driven memory activities, classified into text and data page faults.
- **I/O Time** — time the operating system spent waiting on I/O (input/output) operations, such as writing to a disk or tape.
- **System Time** — the time the operating system spent executing system calls.
- **Trap time** — time spent in executing traps (automatic exceptions or memory faults).
- **Lock wait time** — time spent waiting for lightweight process locks.
- **Sleep time** — time the program spent sleeping.
- **Suspend time** — time spent suspended (includes time spent in debugger during breakpoints).
- **Idle time** — time spent waiting to run while system was busy.
- **Function Sizes** — the sizes of functions in the program.
- **Module Sizes** — the sizes of modules in the program.
- **Segment Sizes** — the sizes of segments in the program.
- **Memory Usage** — memory page reference and modification data. Memory pages are characterized in the following ways:

  ° **Modified** —a page that is written on is identified as a modified page. Modified pages show pages that are not only modified, but are also referenced.

  ° **Referenced** — a page that is executed from or read from a page.

  ° **Mapped** — a page that is not modified but for which the system has allocated a mapping. The mapping assigns a virtual page to a physical page.

  ° **Unmapped** — a page for which the system has not designated a mapping.

Chapter 3. The SPARCworks Programming Environment

- **Resource Usage** — information about the system resources that are used by the program, including major and minor page faults, process swaps, number of input and output blocks, number of messages sent and received, number of signals handled, number of voluntary and involuntary context switches, number of system calls, number of characters of I/O, and number of working set memory pages.

The Analyzer provides four displays in which to view and organize the performance data: Overview, Histogram, Pages, and Statistics.

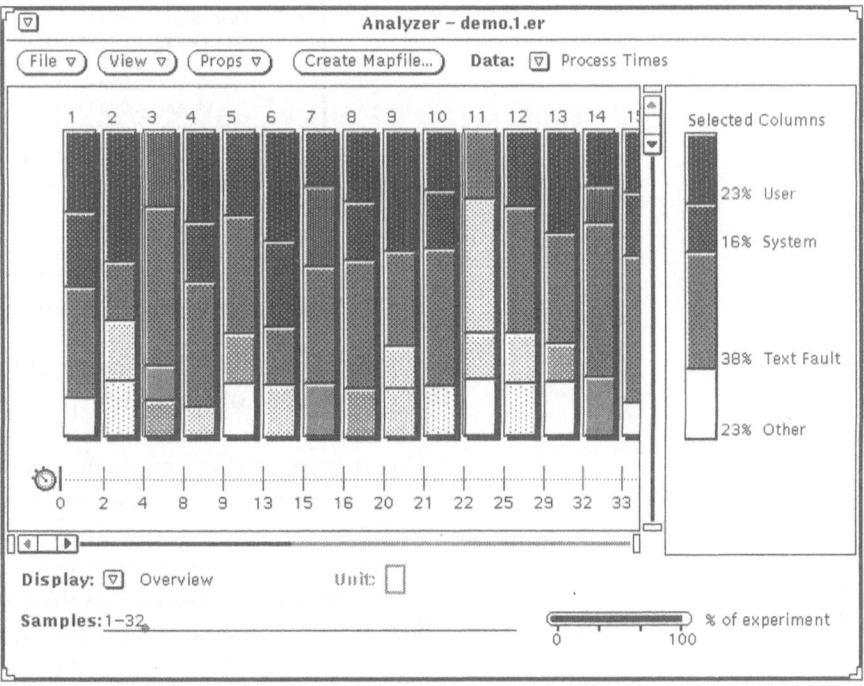

Figure 3.14. Oerview display.

Overview Display. Figure 3.14 shows the Overview display, which is automatically displayed after an experiment is loaded. Data for the Overview display is always accumulated when the Debugger Collector has been activated, so the Overview display is always available in the Analyzer. The Overview display is useful for conducting the initial examination of program performance. Each column in the display represents a single sample of experiment data. The columns can be displayed in uniform widths or in widths proportional to the duration of each sample. The Overview display can show, in a pop-up window, more detailed performance data specific to a sample you have selected (see Figure 3.15).

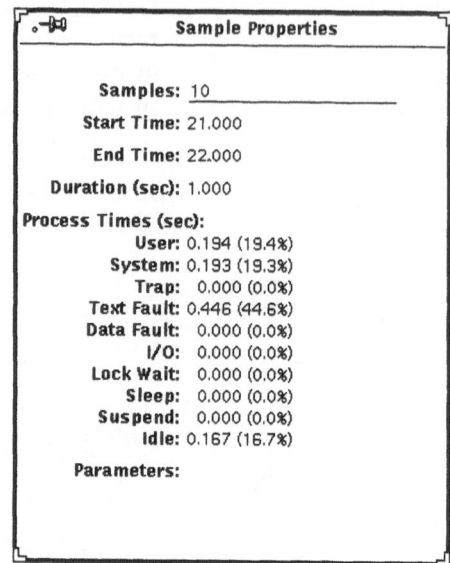

Figure 3.15. Selection properties pop-up window..

Histogram Display. The Histogram display provides another overall view of application performance, and is considered by many users to be the most useful Analyzer display. The histogram quickly reveals the functions in which the application is spending most user time. After viewing the data in the Analyzer, you may decide to tune the program so that it calls those functions less often, or you may want to rewrite the functions themselves so that they execute more quickly.

For display and analysis purposes, the Analyzer dissects the application in one of three ways: according to function, module, or segment:

- **Function** — Function is the default histogram display. This display identifies the functions in which the running program spent most of its time during the experiment. These functions are prime candidates for tuning performance.
- **Module** — The Module histogram display shows a higher level of data aggregation than the function histogram. The module histogram is useful when an application is made up of such a large number of functions that you

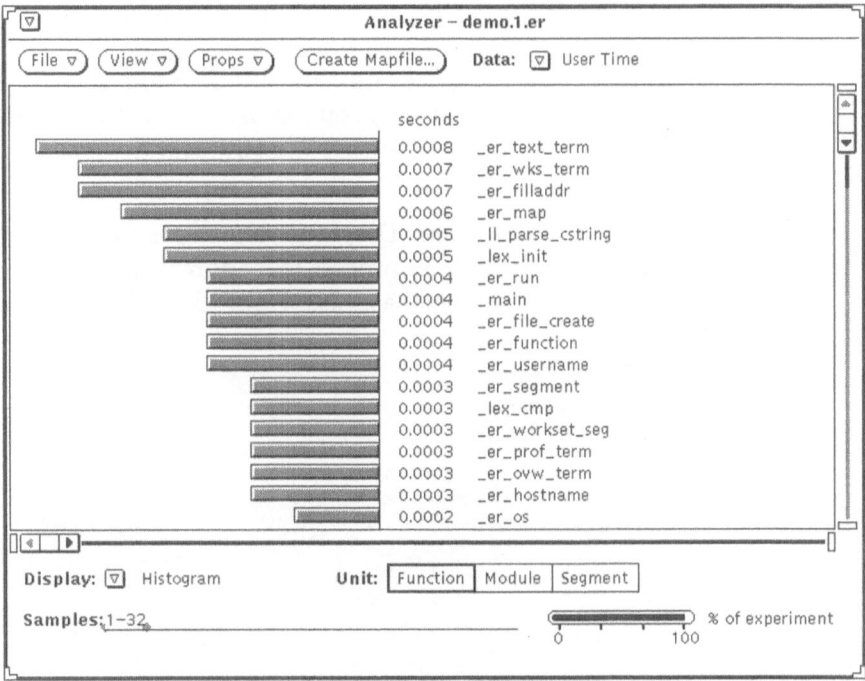

Figure 3.16. Histogram display.

cannot easily understand performance behavior from viewing a function histogram.

Modules are units of executable code that correspond to individual source files. This division of the program is sensible because programming practice usually groups related functions into separate source files.

- **Segment** — The Segment histogram display shows yet a higher level of data aggregation. Typical programs are divided into two to eight segments. The program itself is one segment; other segments result when the program dynamically links to shared libraries during an experiment.

The segment level of data aggregation results in a very coarse performance view. The view is useful, however, because you can easily see how much of your application's execution time is spent in the code of a shared library. If a great deal of time is spent in libraries, you may be forced to limit your performance tuning efforts to calling library functions less often; if little time is spent in libraries, consider improving the performance of your own functions.

You can display histogram data sorted either alphabetically or numerically. To find a specific function, module, or segment, you can use the scroll bars provided and search visually, or use the Find feature to search for text strings in a name.

Pages Display. The Pages display shows the memory usage of process text address space on a memory-page or segment basis (see Figure 3.17).

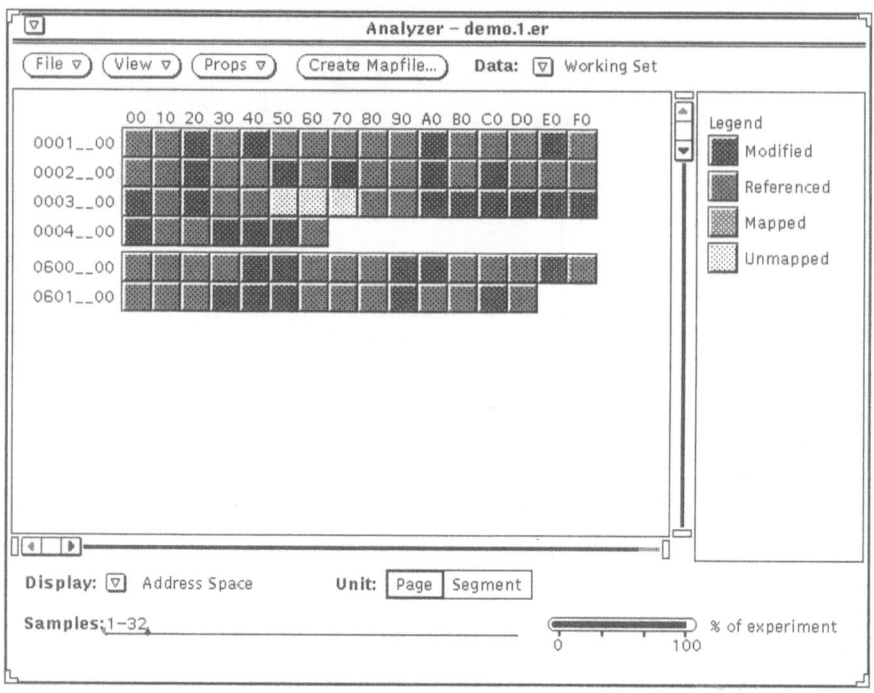

Figure 3.17. Pages display.

SPARC systems use pages that occupy either 4 or 8 Mbytes of memory. The Analyzer categorizes these pages into four classes:

- **Modified** — a *modified* page is written to in the course of program execution.
- **Referenced** — a *referenced* page is read from during execution, but not written to.

- **Mapped** — a *mapped* page is not modified during program execution, but the system has nontheless allocated a mapping for it. The mapping assigns a virtual page to a physical page of memory.
- **Unmapped** — an *unmapped* page has not been designated a mapping by the system.

The Pages display helps you identify memory that is most valuable to the application (modified and referenced pages) as well as memory that is unused because the experiment did not exercise all the program's functionality or because the program has dead code or memory allocation problems. The Pages display offers two viewing modes: pages and segments. The Pages mode shows you an individual page and the segment that contains that page; the Segment mode shows you individual segments and the pages that are contained in those segments.

Statistics. The Statistics display provides statistical information about an application's performance that is not obvious or visible in any of the other Analyzer displays.

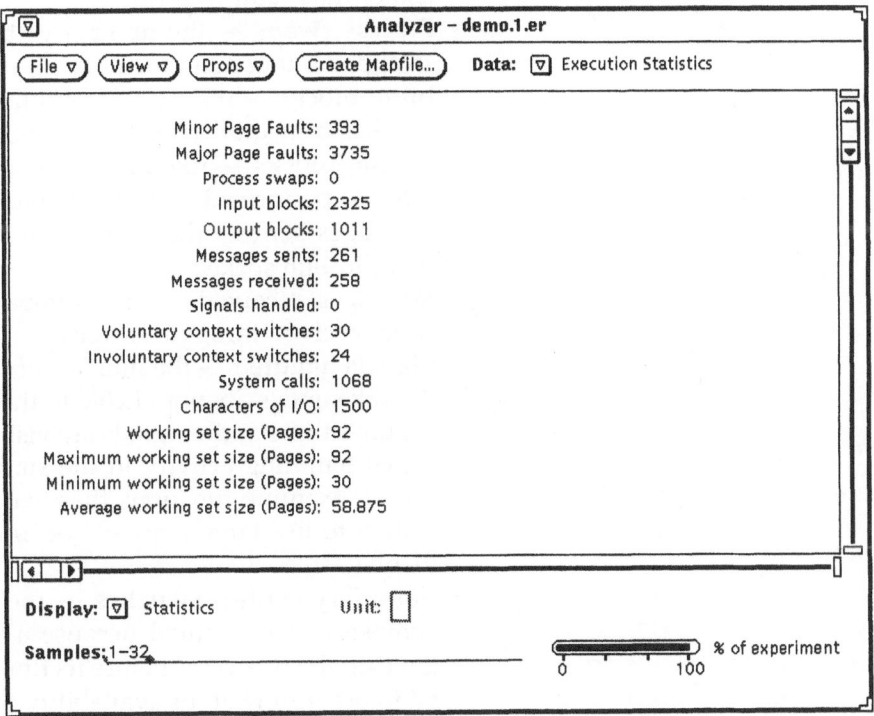

Figure 3.18. Statistics display.

The Statistics display often yields surprising information about system behavior that affects application performance. For example, the display shows the number of times a process is swapped out of main memory. A high number of process swaps may indicate that a large number of other processes were running at the time you collected experiment data or that the workstation was provided with too little memory. Although you cannot change these conditions directly by altering your application, they may affect the minimum system requirements you recommend for the application.

The following data is shown in the statistics display:

- **Minor page faults** — the number of page faults serviced that did not require any physical input/output (I/O) activity.
- **Major page faults** — the number of page faults serviced that did require physical I/O activity. Pages serviced include kernel-initiated page ahead operations. If this number is nonzero, then the overview display shows text or data fault wait time.
- **Process swaps** — the number of times a process was swapped out of main memory.
- **Input blocks** — the number of times a read system call was performed on a noncharacter or special file.
- **Output blocks** — the number of times a write system call was performed on a noncharacter or special file.
- **Messages sent** — the number of messages that were sent through sockets.
- **Messages received** — the number of messages that were received through sockets.
- **Signals handled** — the number of signals handled. Although signals are not visible in the other displays, the routines that handle signals are visible. Therefore, large signal handling activity in the statistics display alerts you to examine functions that handle signals and are shown to use large amounts of time in the histogram display.
- **Voluntary context switches** — the number of times a context switch resulted because a process voluntarily gave up the processor before its time slice was completed in order to wait for availability of a resource.

- **Involuntary context switches** — the number of times a context switch resulted because the process was preempted by a higher priority process or because the process exceeded its time slice.
- **System calls** — the total number of system calls produced by the process.
- **Characters of I/O** — the number of characters transferred in or out of a process by read and write calls to a character device or file.
- **Working set size** — total number of memory pages allocated to the working set.
- **Maximum working set size** — the maximum number of memory pages used by the working set in any one sample.
- **Minimum working set size** — the minimum number of memory pages used by the working set in any one sample.
- **Average working set size** — the number of memory pages used by the working set while the program was running, averaged over the total number of samples.

Reordering Program Text

The Analyzer can reorder text to help reduce the text working set size. The text is reordered automatically when you select Reorder Program on the base Analyzer window after having collected profiling data. The strategy used by the Analyzer for reordering the program text is to classify each function according to how often it is called. The Analyzer sorts the functions in descending order of function count and stores the reordering in a *mapfile*. The Analyzer then relinks the program, keeping often-called functions together. This strategy can produce significant reductions in the text working set size because infrequently used functions are grouped together on pages that are rarely part of the text working set.

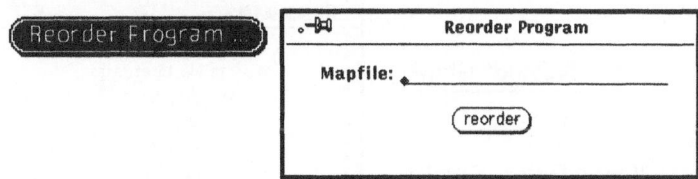

Figure 3.19. Reordering program text.

Exporting Experiments

You can export the data collected by the Debugger into files for use by other programs such as spreadsheets or custom-written applications. The format of the export data file is well documented in SPARCworks technical documentation.

3.7 FileMerge

SPARCworks FileMerge provides a convenient way to merge two text files or directories of files. Most FileMerge functionality is duplicated in the SunOS diff(1) utility, but the FileMerge window interface helps merge files more easily and quickly than any command-line based tool.

In addition to loading two files to be merged, a user can specify a third file, called the *ancestor* of the two files. The two files to be merged are called *descendants* of the ancestor. When an ancestor file has been specified, FileMerge marks lines in the descendants that are different from the ancestor and produces a merged file based on all three files.

FileMerge Window

The graphical interface for FileMerge consists of one main window, in which users do most of their work, and two pop-up windows for handling files and settings properties.

The FileMerge window is shown in Figure 3.20. The left and right text panes at the top show input files to be merged in read-only form; the text pane at the bottom is the output file — an editable, merged version of the two input files.

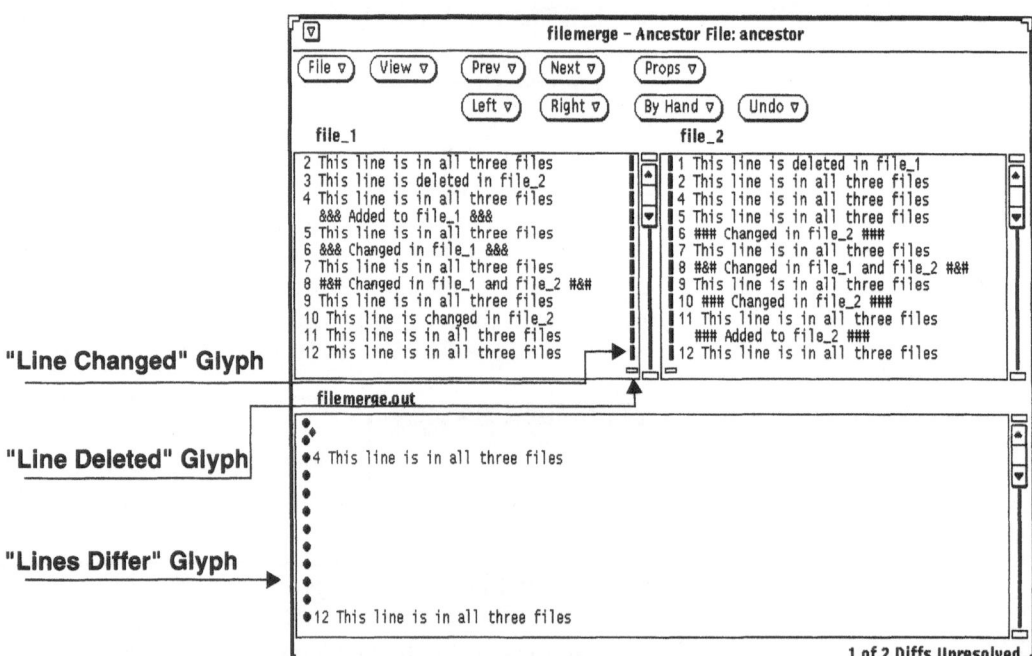

Figure 3.20. FileMerge window with loaded files and common ancestor.

When an ancestor file has been specified for the two files to be merged (as shown in Figure 3.20), lines in each descen-

Chapter 3. The SPARCworks Programming Environment

dant are marked according to their relationship to the corresponding lines in the common ancestor:

- If a line is identical in all three files, then no glyph is displayed.
- If a line is not in the ancestor but was added to one or both of the descendants, then a plus sign glyph (+) is displayed next to the line in the file where the line was added.
- If a line is present in the ancestor but was removed from one or both of the descendants, then a minus sign (-) is displayed as a placeholder in the file from which the line was removed.
- If a line is in the ancestor but has been changed in one or both of the descendants, then a vertical bar glyph (|) is displayed next to the line in the file where the line was changed.

When two files have been loaded without an ancestor file, FileMerge does not mark additions and deletions in the input files because it has no reference to determine whether a line has been added to one file or deleted from the other.

Merging Files

By default, FileMerge constructs the merged output file by placing in it all lines that are common between the two input files. When a line is different between the two files, the user accepts a line from one of the files and places it in the output file. The user indicates a preference for one file or the other by clicking on control-panel buttons. As each difference is resolved, FileMerge advances automatically to the next difference.

If neither input file contains a suitable line to use in the output file, the user can edit the output file directly. In some cases, the differences from one input file will always be preferred over the other. In these cases, the difference lines from one or the other input file can be placed in the output file with a single control-panel button click.

Viewing Differences Read-Only

In some cases you may want to display source files in read-only mode. In these cases, FileMerge does not display a merged version of the files but only the loaded source files in the left and right panes. The second row of control buttons, which ordinarily govern how differences are merged into an output file, are also hidden in read-only mode.

Loading Lists of Files

The command line interface to FileMerge lets users specify lists of files to load sequentially. This capability is very useful when two entire directories must be merged. A list of ancestor files can also be specified.

To load files from a list, the files to be merged must be pairs of files with identical local names. The files themselves must be stored in separate directories. You then create a list of file names in a *listfile* and start FileMerge from the command line, specifying the name of the listfile, the two directories to be merged, an output directory, and optionally a third directory of ancestor files. You can then automatically load files successively as you finish resolving differences in each file pair.

3.8 MakeTool

MakeTool is an OPEN LOOK interface to make(1), the SunOS utility that oversees program compilation and ensures that programs are compiled from the newest sources. In addition, MakeTool contains a browser that helps you interpret makefiles by expanding macros and rules.

MakeTool Icons

MakeTool in its closed form is represented by one of three icons, as shown in Figure 3.21. Each icon represents a different condition of a make build process. A glance at the icon tells you the status of a long make task.

- The first icon indicates that a make has successfully completed. This icon is also displayed before the first make of a session.
- The second icon shows that make has been started but is not yet completed. This icon is animated: it shows source files being fed into a "make machine" and rolling out on a conveyor belt as compiled objects.
- The third icon indicates that make has failed due to an error.

Successful Make   **Make In Progress**   **Failed Make**

Figure 3.21. MakeTool icons.

MakeTool Window

The MakeTool base window (Figure 3.22) opens when Make-Tool starts. MakeTool loads a makefile automatically using the same search algorithm as make. If MakeTool finds a makefile, it is loaded and displayed in the main MakeTool window. The name of the working directory is displayed on the first text entry line; the name of the makefile that was found in the working directory is shown on the second line.

Control Area

Transcript Pane

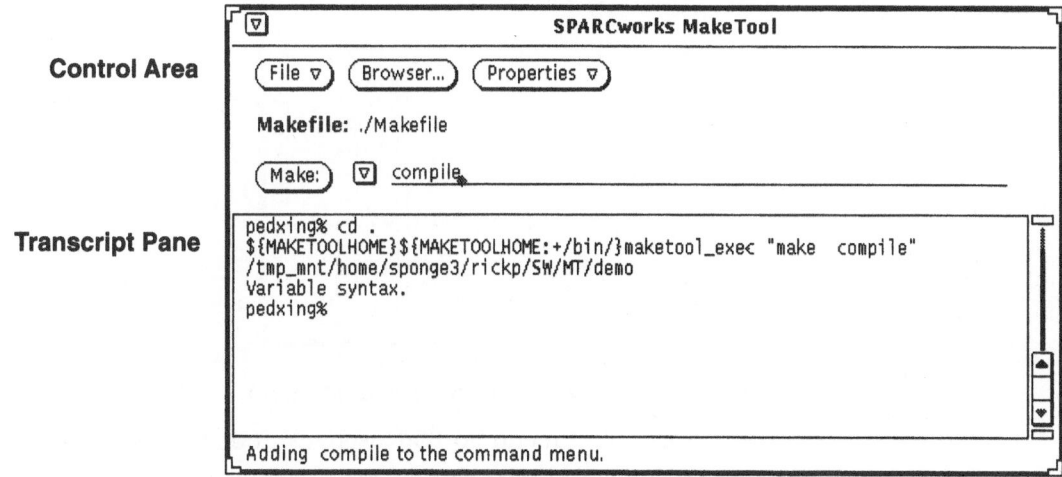

Figure 3.22. MakeTool base window.

To build a `make` target, the user clicks on the Make button. MakeTool responds by changing directories to the working directory (if necessary), setting shell environment variables as required, and issuing a `make` command.

All commands MakeTool issues are echoed in the Transcript pane in the MakeTool window. The Transcript pane is a standard OPEN LOOK terminal pane, so all standard Command Tool features can be used in it — including typing of commands directly into the window at the command prompt.

Building the Make Menu

The abbreviated button next to the Make button reveals a menu that is filled with arguments and options to the Make command. As MakeTool loads a makefile, it examines the makefile to find high-level `make` targets and places them in the menu. Subsequently, the user can initiate a build of one of these targets simply by selecting from the menu. Because the targets are displayed in a menu, users do not need to list the text of a makefile in order to identify the targets they want to build, as is often the case when they use `make` directly from the command line.

MakeTool maintains a history of recently used `make` options and arguments and keeps them in the Make Target ab-

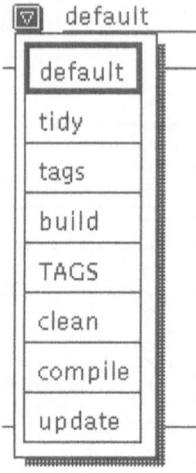

Figure 3.23. Make abbreviated menu.

breviated menu so that users can quickly rebuild a target using those same arguments.

Makefile Browser

As developers have learned to exploit the power of make and apply it to larger and larger projects, makefiles have grown more complex and difficult to maintain. Macros in particular can be difficult to understand because they are often nested, appended to, and defined conditionally (so that they take on different values depending on the target being compiled). MakeTool contains a browser to help developers interpret makefiles by expanding rules and macros. Note that the makefile browser shows rules and macros but does *not* provide the means to edit them.

Browser Window

Open the Browser window by clicking on the Browser button in the MakeTool base window. The window is shown in Figure 3.24.

Rules and Macros. The Makefile Browser displays all the rules and macros in the makefile in a single list. Rules and macros are defined as follows:

- **Rule** — a makefile *rule* is defined as a target, its dependencies, and the method used to build the target from the dependencies. Typically, a rule is a command line in a makefile that invokes a compiler or linker.
- **Macro** — a makefile *macro* is a variable that is used in dependency lists and rules. Macros are used in makefiles to increase their flexibility and maintainability.

Chapter 3. The SPARCworks Programming Environment

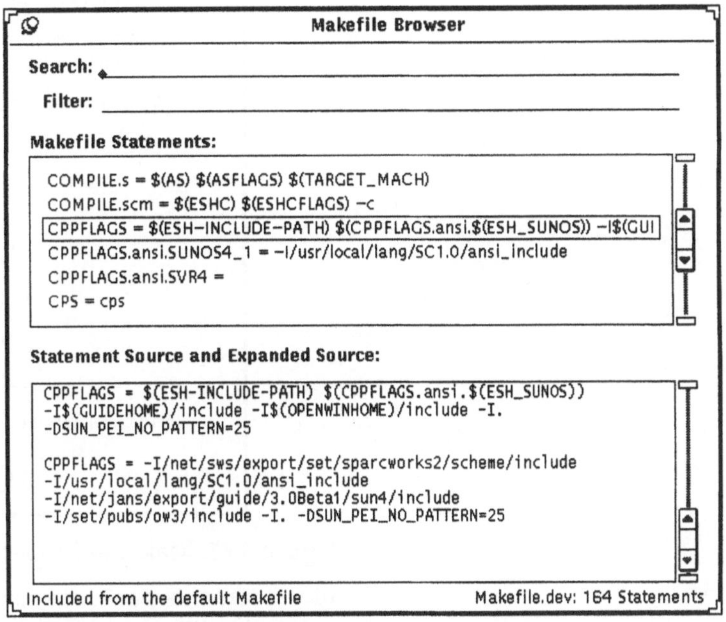

```
  ⚲                    Makefile Browser
  Search: ◆_____
  Filter: _____
  Makefile Statements:
  ┌──────────────────────────────────────────────────────────┐ ▤
  │ COMPILE.s = $(AS) $(ASFLAGS) $(TARGET_MACH)                │
  │ COMPILE.scm = $(ESHC) $(ESHCFLAGS) −c                      │ ▲
  │ ┌────────────────────────────────────────────────────────┐│
  │ │CPPFLAGS = $(ESH−INCLUDE−PATH) $(CPPFLAGS.ansi.$(ESH_SUNOS)) −I$(GUI││
  │ └────────────────────────────────────────────────────────┘│
  │ CPPFLAGS.ansi.SUNOS4_1 = −I/usr/local/lang/SC1.O/ansi_include││ ▼
  │ CPPFLAGS.ansi.SVR4 =                                       │
  │ CPS = cps                                                  │
  └──────────────────────────────────────────────────────────┘

  Statement Source and Expanded Source:
  ┌──────────────────────────────────────────────────────────┐ ▤
  │ CPPFLAGS = $(ESH-INCLUDE-PATH) $(CPPFLAGS.ansi.$(ESH_SUNOS))│
  │ -I$(GUIDEHOME)/include -I$(OPENWINHOME)/include -I.         │
  │ -DSUN_PEI_NO_PATTERN=25                                     │
  │                                                            │
  │ CPPFLAGS = -I/net/sws/export/set/sparcworks2/scheme/include │
  │ -I/usr/local/lang/SC1.O/ansi_include                       │
  │ -I/net/jans/export/guide/3.0Beta1/sun4/include             │
  │ -I/set/pubs/ow3/include -I. -DSUN_PEI_NO_PATTERN=25         │ ▲
  │                                                            │ ▼
  └──────────────────────────────────────────────────────────┘
  Included from the default Makefile           Makefile.dev: 164 Statements
```

Figure 3.24. Makefile Browser.

In makefiles, any line of the form STRING1 = string2 is a macro definition. STRING1 is the name of the macro, and string2 is the definition of the macro. Following such a definition, whenever make encounters the expression $(STRING1) in the makefile, it expands the string to the value string2.

Rules can be sorted into three categories for display purposes: special rules, implicit rules, and ordinary rules defined within the current makefile. Similarly, macros can be sorted into two categories: conditional macros and all others.

You can narrow the range of statements displayed in the Browser by setting filters in a Properties window (Figure 3.25). The filters allow only certain statements to be shown — only rules used to make the current target, for example — so that confusing, extraneous statements are hidden from view. Within each category of rule or macro, the Browser sorts statements into the following types:

- Special rules first, then regular rules, then implicit rules
- All macros that are *not* conditional macros first, followed by conditional macros.

Viewing Statement Sources and Expansions

As shown in Figure 3.24, each statement is displayed on a single line in the Makefile Statements pane. Below the Make-

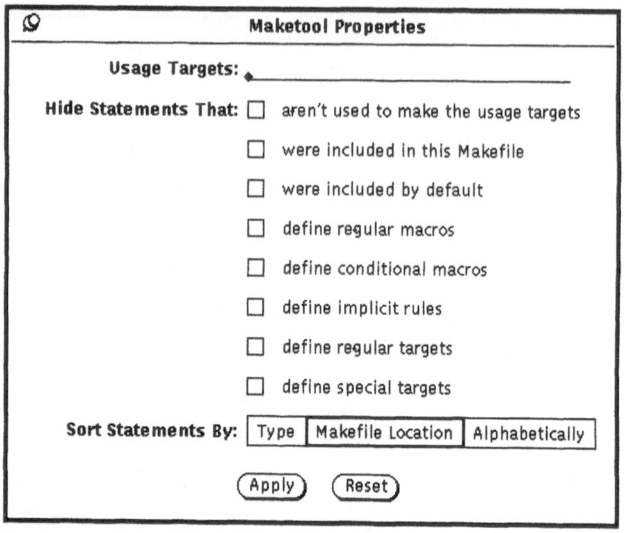

Figure 3.25. Makefile Properties window.

file Statements pane, the complete source of a selected statement (its literal representation in the makefile) and its expanded version are shown in a separate pane.

Statement Sources.   Seeing the source of a statement is useful when the entire rule or macro is too long to be shown on a single line; the display of source wraps the line so that all of it is visible.

Statement Expansions.   To expand a statement, MakeTool replaces all macro expressions of the form $ (NAME)$ with their values. Because many macros are made up of other macros, determining their expanded values from source statements can be difficult for a user without the aid of MakeTool Browser.

Searching for Text

The Browser window provides a text entry field for entering search strings. In Figure 3.26, a user has typed the word "Sun" into the search text entry field. The first line that contains the word is automatically selected in the Makefile Statements pane. To select other lines that contain "Sun," the user would press the down-arrow key. The search *wraps* through the makefile, so repeated pressing of the down-arrow key would eventually bring the user back to the first line that contains "Sun."

Filtering Statements

The Browser window also provides a text entry field for entering filter characters. When text is entered in the Filter field, only statements that contain the text are displayed.

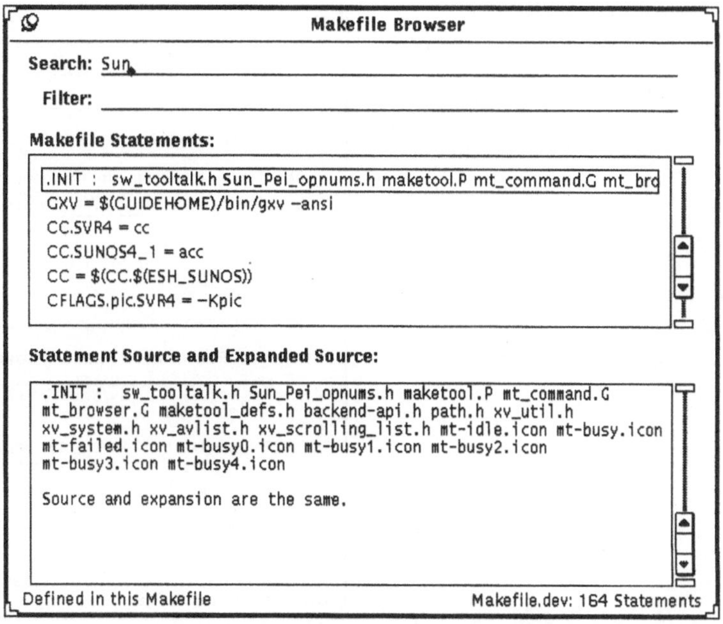

```
 ⊘                        Makefile Browser
Search: Sun
Filter:
Makefile Statements:
┌────────────────────────────────────────────────────────────────┐
│ .INIT : sw_tooltalk.h Sun_Pei_opnums.h maketool.P mt_command.G mt_br│
│ GXV = $(GUIDEHOME)/bin/gxv -ansi                                   │▲
│ CC.SVR4 = cc                                                       │
│ CC.SUNOS4_1 = acc                                                  │█
│ CC = $(CC.$(ESH_SUNOS))                                            │▼
│ CFLAGS.pic.SVR4 = -Kpic                                            │
└────────────────────────────────────────────────────────────────┘

Statement Source and Expanded Source:
┌────────────────────────────────────────────────────────────────┐
│ .INIT : sw_tooltalk.h Sun_Pei_opnums.h maketool.P mt_command.G    │
│ mt_browser.G maketool_defs.h backend-api.h path.h xv_util.h       │
│ xv_system.h xv_avlist.h xv_scrolling_list.h mt-idle.icon mt-busy.icon│
│ mt-failed.icon mt-busy0.icon mt-busy1.icon mt-busy2.icon          │
│ mt-busy3.icon mt-busy4.icon                                       │
│                                                                   │█
│ Source and expansion are the same.                                │▼
│                                                                   │
└────────────────────────────────────────────────────────────────┘
Defined in this Makefile                      Makefile.dev: 164 Statements
```

Figure 3.26. Browser window with "Sun" search string.

Figure 3.27 shows a Browser window in which the user has set a filter for the string "Pei" and combined it with a search for the word "Sun." The Makefile Statements pane shows only statements that contain the string "Pei." From those statements, the Browser searches for statements that contain the word "Sun."

Starting MakeTool from Other SPARCworks Tools

Users often initiate program builds with make from other SPARCworks tools such as Debugger and SourceBrowser. These tools give users the option of initiating the build directly or by calling on MakeTool as the make interface. When other SPARCworks tools activate MakeTool, they pass it the following information to use during the build:

- Name of the makefile to use
- Name of the working directory
- Shell environment variables in force, and their values.

When MakeTool receives the information, it reacts as follows:

- Starts a temporary subshell in which to run make
- Loads the specified makefile
- Changes to the working directory in the subshell
- Sets the necessary environment variables in the subshell
- Issues the make command in the subshell.

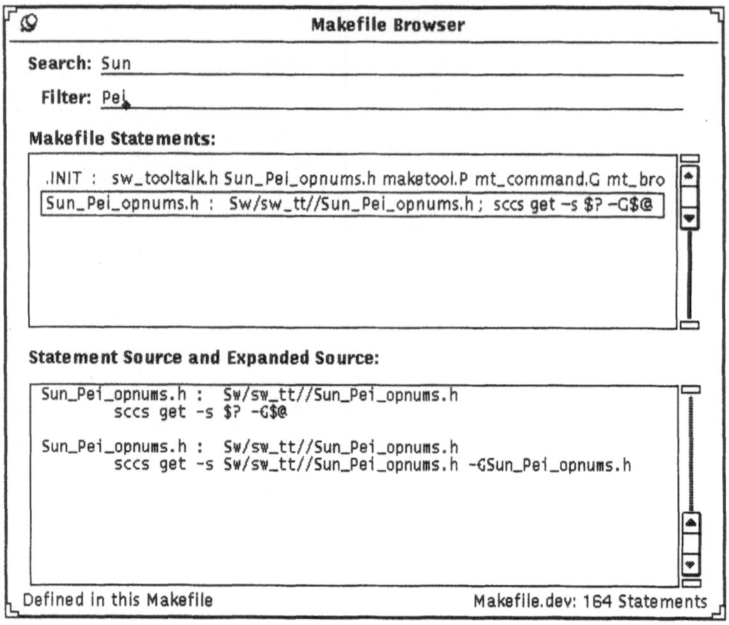

```
┌─────────────────────────────────────────────────────────────────────┐
│ ◎                        Makefile Browser                             │
├─────────────────────────────────────────────────────────────────────┤
│  Search: Sun                                                          │
│  Filter: Pe̶                                                           │
│  Makefile Statements:                                                 │
│  ┌──────────────────────────────────────────────────────────────┐ ▲ │
│  │ .INIT :  sw_tooltalk.h Sun_Pei_opnums.h maketool.P mt_command.G mt_bro│ ▒ │
│  │ Sun_Pei_opnums.h :  Sw/sw_tt//Sun_Pei_opnums.h ; sccs get −s $? −G$@ │ ▼ │
│  │                                                              │   │ │
│  │                                                              │   │ │
│  │                                                              │   │ │
│  │                                                              │   │ │
│  └──────────────────────────────────────────────────────────────┘   │
│                                                                       │
│  Statement Source and Expanded Source:                                │
│  ┌──────────────────────────────────────────────────────────────┐ ▲ │
│  │ Sun_Pei_opnums.h :  Sw/sw_tt//Sun_Pei_opnums.h                │   │ │
│  │        sccs get −s $? −G$@                                     │   │ │
│  │                                                                │   │ │
│  │ Sun_Pei_opnums.h :  Sw/sw_tt//Sun_Pei_opnums.h                │   │ │
│  │        sccs get −s Sw/sw_tt//Sun_Pei_opnums.h −GSun_Pei_opnums.h│ ▒ │
│  │                                                                │   │ │
│  │                                                                │ ▼ │
│  └──────────────────────────────────────────────────────────────┘   │
├─────────────────────────────────────────────────────────────────────┤
│  Defined in this Makefile                        Makefile.dev: 164 Statements│
└─────────────────────────────────────────────────────────────────────┘
```

Figure 3.27. Browser window with "Sun" search string and "Pei" filter.

This scheme allows users to use MakeTool easily during debugging sessions when, for example, the load library path (LD_LIBRARY_PATH environment variable) has been set to a nonstandard directory.

3.9 Conclusion

SPARCworks tools, with their high performance and full feature set, enhance the already rich SunOS software development environment. Together, SPARCworks tools provide the following advantages:

- The consistent look and feel provided by the standard OPEN LOOK interface shortens learning time for new users.
- Visual and functional compatibility with DeskSet™ tools such as File Manager and Text Edit give SPARCworks tools added value in the Sun development environment.
- SPARCworks Manager provides a uniform way to integrate new tools into the SPARCworks toolset and coordinate them with the standard SPARCworks tools.

- For simultaneous static and dynamic program analysis, SourceBrowser and Debugger form a powerful combination.
- The concise graphical presentation of data provided by SourceBrowser and Analyzer quickly clarifies program structure and uncovers performance bottlenecks.
- The process of building programs and maintaining makefiles is assisted by MakeTool, a graphical interface for the popular `make` utility.
- Differences between source files can be found easily and a merged version of two source files can be created quickly with FileMerge.

Integrating Development Tools with SPARCworks

4.1 SPARCworks Tool Integration

The SPARCworks toolset is a suite of tools for software application developers. As mentioned earlier, Release 2.0 of SPARCworks consists of six standard development tools:

- SPARCworks Manager
- Debugger
- SourceBrowser
- FileMerge
- MakeTool
- Analyzer

SPARCworks Manager is a unifying graphical desktop tool for managing SPARCworks programming tools. SPARCworks Manager is a visual organizer that provides easy accessibility for starting and quitting tools. SPARCworks Manager also provides software *session* control and the means to customize the environment in which the tools operate.

In addition to the six standard tools supplied by Sun, it is possible for you as a third party developer to integrate your software development tools into SPARCworks. With Release 2.0 of SPARCworks, two types of integration are possible:

- A tool may be integrated so that its execution and operation environment are controlled by the SPARCworks Manager.

- A tool may be integrated so that it can obtain realtime program analysis data from the Sun debugger (dbx).

SPARCworks Manager

There are many advantages to integrating your tool with SPARCworks Manager.

- Your tool appears on the same graphical "palette" as the standard Sun programming tools.
- SPARCworks Manager provides an easy-to-use, unified means to execute programs and control the programming environment. All tools (both yours and Sun's) are executed and managed through a single graphical interface. Integrating your tool with SPARCworks Manager provides your users with:

  ° Drag-and-drop execution for all integrated tools.

  ° The ability to group development activities into logical SPARCworks Manager *sessions*. Multiple sessions can execute simultaneously, each within its own environment.

  ° The ability to organize and maximize screen real estate visually. Groups of programming tasks can be closed to a single icon, and SPARCworks Manager sessions can be *completely* hidden from view.

  ° A centralized facility through which environment variables and the working directory can be simultaneously set for all development tools.

dbx

The Sun debugger—dbx—is a powerful tool for doing static and dynamic analysis of program execution. During program execution, dbx obtains detailed information about a program's behavior. In SPARCworks 2.0, dbx broadcasts this information via the Sun ToolTalk™ service. This is the method that dbx uses to provide information to its graphical interface program—SPARCworks Debugger.

By integrating your application, it is possible for your application to receive the same detailed information as the SPARCworks Debugger.

The ToolTalk Service

SPARCworks Manager session control and dbx interaction is accomplished through use of the Sun ToolTalk service. The ToolTalk service is a network-spanning, interapplication communication service that allows applications to communicate with other autonomous applications. Special SPARC-works protocols have been designed from the larger ToolTalk service to provide the means for SPARCworks Manager and dbx to communicate with and transfer data to your tool.

Organization

The remainder of this section is divided into three sections:

- An overview of the SPARCworks Manager.
- An overview of the ToolTalk service and its general use in tool integration.
- A description of the special ToolTalk protocols designed for SPARCworks Manager and dbx.

4.2
SPARCworks
Manager

The SPARCworks Manager is a visual organizer that unifies the SPARCworks toolset by allowing applications to be executed and managed through a single graphical interface. SPARCworks Manager provides software session control plus the flexibility of customizing tools and the SPARCworks Manager. Your tool integrated with SPARCworks can take advantage of the utilities provided by SPARCworks Manager.

This section first describes the SPARCworks tools whose icons appear by default on SPARCworks Manager, then describes the features of SPARCworks Manager itself.

SPARCworks Toolset

SPARCworks 2.0 Toolset consists of six standard tools:

- SPARCworks Manager
- Debugger
- SourceBrowser
- FileMerge
- Maketool
- Analyzer

Debugger

Debugger is a sophisticated window-based tool that interfaces with dbx. It helps in debugging programs and significantly reduces time in the debug-edit-compile cycle. Debugger offers a program editing facility so the user need not change tools continuously.

The user-configurable graphical interface provides visual feedback and mouse control for most debugging operations. It also offers OPEN LOOK® drag and drop support for integration with other desktop applications.

SourceBrowser

SourceBrowser is an interactive window-based tool for analyzing source code. This tool enables you to find all occurrences of an identifier, string, or regular expression in source code with ease. SourceBrowser maintains a list of all queries, making it easy to return to a previous query to compare results. In addition, SourceBrowser offers powerful features for customization of browsing. For example, users can restrict queries to search for symbols based on how they are used in the source.

The SourceBrowser consists of four windows:

- The *Code Browser* enables you to analyze, query and edit your source code.
- The *Class Browser* enables you to browse through C++ source code libraries quickly and easily. You can view the base and defined classes, their data members and member functions, as well as class-defined interfaces and relationships.
- The *Call Grapher* enables you to inspect graphically the interrelationships of the functions in your program.
- The *Class Grapher* enables you to visualize the classes in C++ programs.

SourceBrowser is integrated with Debugger and SCCS.

FileMerge

FileMerge aids in comparing files and merging their differences. It displays two files side-by-side in read-only text comparison windows. Beneath the comparison windows is an editing subwindow that contains a merged version of the two files. The merged version contains selected lines from either, or both files. A user can edit this version to produce a final merged version of the two original files.

MakeTool

MakeTool is the OPEN LOOK interface to make, the SunOS™ utility that oversees program building and ensures that programs are built from the newest sources. In addition, MakeTool contains a browser that helps with interpretation of makefiles by expanding macros and rules.

Analyzer

The Analyzer is part of a set of performance analysis tools that software application developers can use for measuring, recording, understanding, and improving the performance of an application program. The Analyzer provides an easy-to-use graphical user interface for specifying and displaying data collected on a target application. The Analyzer can be used by all software developers, regardless of whether performance tuning is their main responsibility.

Data collection for performance analysis is initiated through the Collector pop-up window in the Debugger.

SPARCworks Manager and Tools Activation

Users start SPARCworks Manager by typing `sparcworks` at the command line.

Using SPARCworks Manager, programmers can start all SPARCworks tools for a particular project from one SPARCworks Manager. Doing so unifies control of opening, closing, hiding, and showing tools during a programming session. More than one SPARCworks Manager can be active at one time. Tools can be started in two ways:

- With the OPEN LOOK Drag-and-Drop utility – using the mouse to move the cursor on top of the tool icon, holding down the SELECT mouse button and dragging the selected icon onto the desktop. When the mouse button is released, the tool opens, ready for use, at the spot where the icon was dragged.
- Double Click – moving the cursor to the icon of the appropriate tool and clicking twice on the selected icon.
- Users quit SPARCworks Manager through the standard OPEN LOOK window menu. If a tool is active when SPARCworks Manager is quit, then SPARCworks Manager requests verification before quitting that tool.

SPARCworks Manager Display Formats

SPARCworks Manager buttons, menus, and pop-up windows in standard OPEN LOOK format implement SPARCworks Manager functionality.

Two formats are offered for displaying SPARCworks Manager:

- SPARCworks Manager – (shown below in the default format) displays OPEN LOOK standard control buttons along with SPARCworks tool icons.

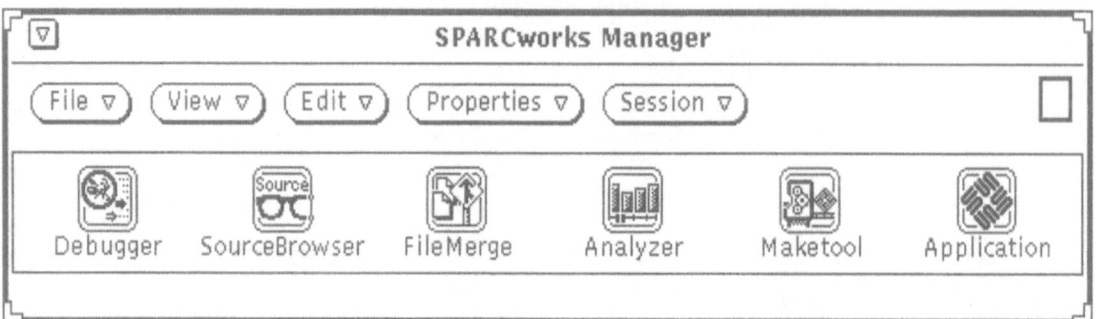

- Tool Palette – (shown below) provides concise, condensed organization and display of SPARCworks tool icons only. The Tool Palette allows easy access to SPARCworks tools while conserving desktop space. The Tool Palette can also be reshaped to a vertical format.

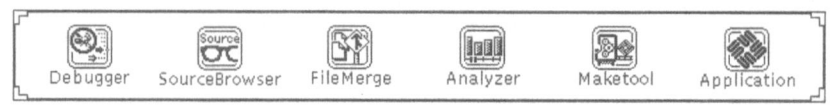

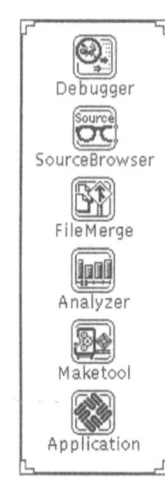

SPARCworks Manager Buttons, Menus, and Popup Windows

The function buttons at the top of the default SPARCworks Manager window summon menus by which users:

- Save customizations
- Display a log window
- Change the default SPARCworks Manager window
- Delete or duplicate tools
- Set tool or SPARCworks Manager properties
- Manage tools during a programming session.

File Button

The File button saves configurations for the SPARC-works Manager and individual tools. The pull-down menu displays the following options:

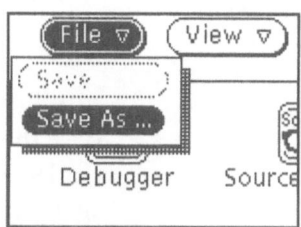

Save

Stores customizations under the current file name.

Save As

Displays a worksheet for modifying the path and file name before the customizations are saved.

View Button

The View button provides a SPARCworks Manager option that summons a log window for tool startup processes. The pull-down menu displays the following options:

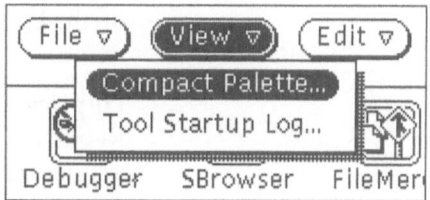

Compact Palette

Changes the default SPARCworks Manager format to the compact palette format, which displays only the icons of the tools.

Tool Startup Log

Pops up a tool startup Log window. The Log window displays a list of activated tool processes.

Once the Log Window is displayed, users can see startup messages for the tools they have launched. In the example below, the startup messages for FileMerge are displayed in the Log Window after the FileMerge icon was selectedEdit Button

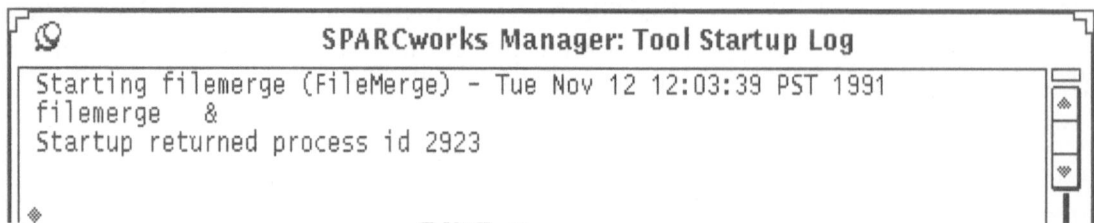

```
⌀          SPARCworks Manager: Tool Startup Log
Starting filemerge (FileMerge) - Tue Nov 12 12:03:39 PST 1991
filemerge    &
Startup returned process id 2923
```

Edit Button.

With the Edit button, users delete and duplicate SPARC-works tools or align their icons on the SPARCworks Manager display.   The pull-down menu displays the following options:

Delete Tool

Deletes a selected tool. Up to ten deleted tools are listed on the Edit button menu and can be restored through that menu.

Duplicate Tool

Replicates a selected tool. The duplicated tool has all the properties and functionality of the original with the exception of a unique label. The properties of a duplicated tool can be modified through the Properties button.

Snap Icons to Grid

Automatically realigns icons to an invisible grid at the top of the window. The option is particularly helpful when a significant number of tool icons are displayed on a SPARCworks Manager or after a user rearranges the icons on a SPARCworks Manager.

Properties Button   Users can change the start-up properties of SPARCworks tools and other tools on the SPARCworks Manager palette, customizing them to personal specifications. Once a tool is customized, the customizations can be saved for future use. Advanced customization techniques even allow users to set parameters for starting up non-window-based tools, such as vi.

The pull-down menu displays the following options:Se

Selected Tool

Displays a property sheet for the selected tool, from which users customize the tool, its label, and theSPARCworks Manager icon.

Here is an example of the property sheet for customizing a tool.

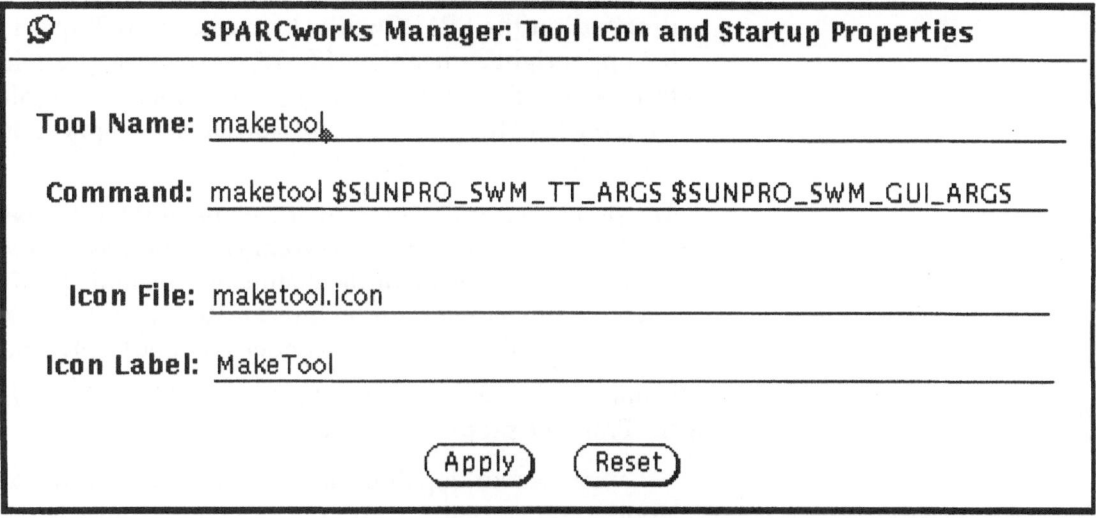

The following environment variables are specific to SPARCworks Manager and may appear on the command line of the Tool Property sheet.

$SUNPRO_SWM_TT_ARGS
Special command line argument that all SPARCworks tools use so that SPARCworks Manager session commands are recognized. This variable is set by the SPARC-

works Manager. Applications that support the SPARC-works session management protocol should specify this variable as the first command line argument.

`$SUNPRO_SWM_GUI_ARGS`
Command line arguments that specify the initial position of windows when drag and drop is used. If double click is used to open a window, this value is set to zero.

$SUNPRO_SWM_APP_DIR
Directory path that is set when a pathname or a FileManager icon is dropped on the SPARCworks Manager Drop Target in the upper right corner of the SPARCworks Manager control panel. The current working directory is changed to the directory component of the pathname and the `SUNPRO_SWM_APP_DIR` environment variable is updated.

$SUNPRO_SWM_APP_FILE
Path that is set when a pathname or FileManager icon is dropped on the SPARCworks Manager Drop Target in the upper right corner of the SPARCworks Manager control panel. The `SUN_SWM_APP_FILE` is set to the file component of the path. The tool icon labeled Application starts `$SUNPRO_SWM_APP_FILE`.

The properties are indexed by the name of the tool. Beneath the Tool Name entry is the command line executed to start the tool. You can edit the command line and specify different commands for a tool, thus creating a customized version of a tool that can be saved under a unique label name.

All Tools Displays a property sheet for SPARCworks Manager. From the property sheet, users can:

- Change the working directory for starting SPARCworks tools
- Change environment variables and then alter the value displayed for the variable in the right column.

Here is an example of the SPARCworks Manager property sheet.

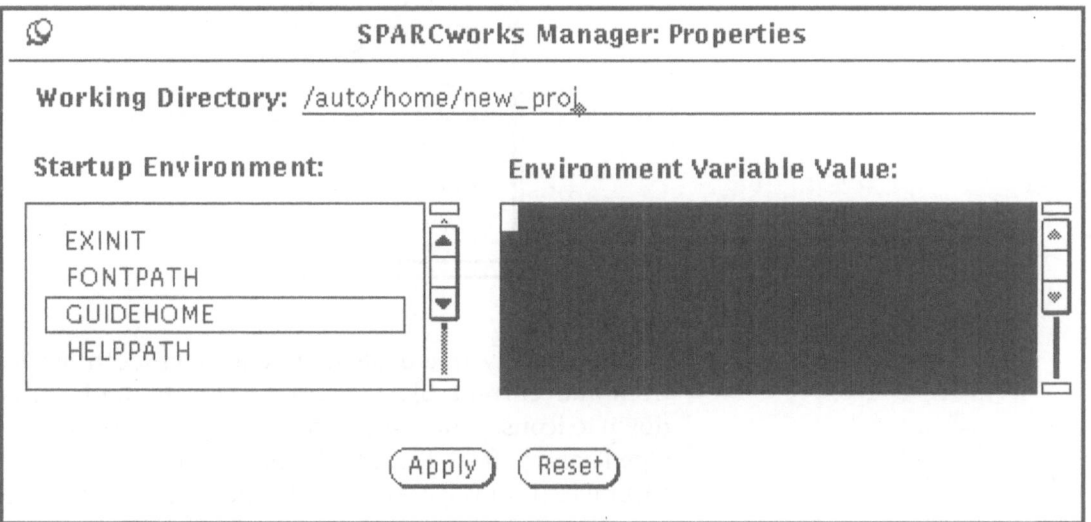

Version   Displays the current SPARCworks Manager version number in the status area at the bottom of the SPARCworks Manager window.

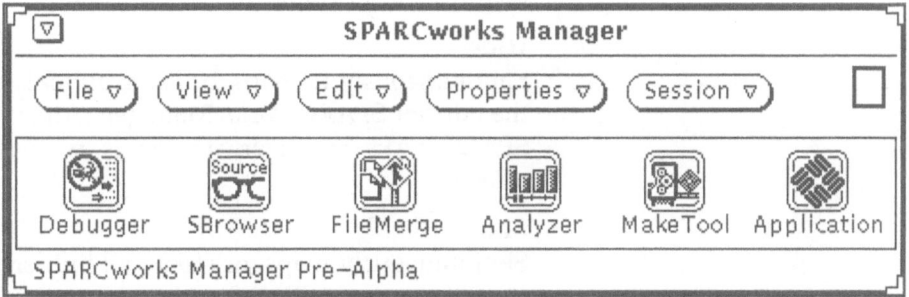

Figure 4.1. Version windowl.

Session Button.   The Session button provides the functionality for monitoring a programming session. The menu options make it easy to work with several window-based tools at a time by opening, closing, hiding, or showing all the tools associated with a SPARCworks Manager. The button options are particularly helpful to a user working with multiple instances of SPARCworks Manager at one time.

    The pull-down menu of the Session button displays the following options:

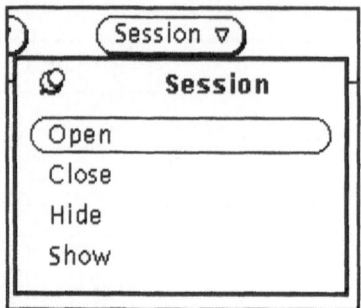

Open

Simultaneously opens all tools that have been started from the current SPARCworks Manager and closed down to icons. If no tools have been closed to icons, then Open has no effect. Figure 4.2 illustrates the display after several tool icons were opened by means of the Open option.

Close

Closes all tools that have been opened from the current SPARCworks Manager. The open tools close down to icons. In the example below, the tools that were open in the previous example are closed to icons.

Hide

Simultaneously unmaps, or *hides*, all tools opened from the current SPARCworks Manager. All evidence of the SPARCworks Manager session is removed from the screen.

Show

Simultaneously maps, or *shows*, all hidden tools started from the current SPARCworks Manager. *Showing* tools reverses the effect of *hiding* tools.

Drop Target

The Drop Target provides drag and drop capabilities for starting non-SPARCworks tools. To start a non-SPARCworks tool with the Drop Target, you can:

- Cut the pathname of the application from a Command tool or Shell tool window and drop it onto the Drop Target.
- Drag a FileManager icon and drop it onto the Drop Target.

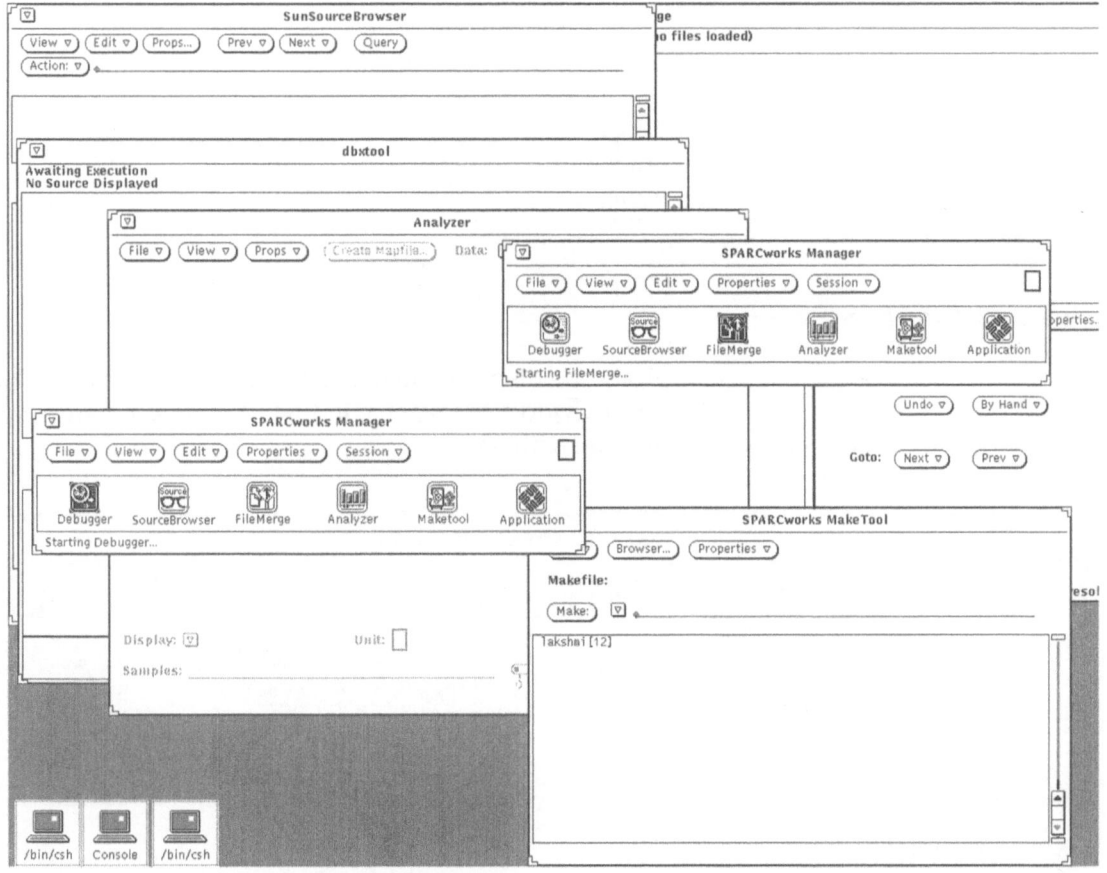

Figure 4.2. Multiple SPARCworks managers and multiple open tools.

> **Note –** User-defined *Application* tools may not support the
> SPARCworks ToolTalk protocol and therefore operate dif-
> ferently under SPARCworks Manager than SPARCworks
> tools. The main difference will be that the Session options
> will not be supported.

The Drop Target is located in the upper right corner of the
SPARCworks Manager control area as shown in Figure 4.3
below. When you drag a FileManager icon or path name on
top of the Drop Target, it becomes shaded.

Once you drop a path name or FileManager icon onto the
Drop Target, the current working directory is changed to the
directory component of the pathname. The path name of the

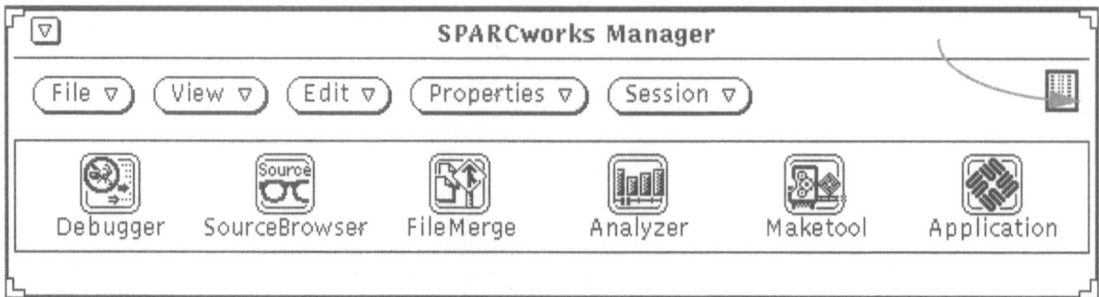

Figure 4.3. Drop target.

application is displayed in the message area at the bottom of the SPARCworks Manager window. Figure 4.4 shows the application path name display.

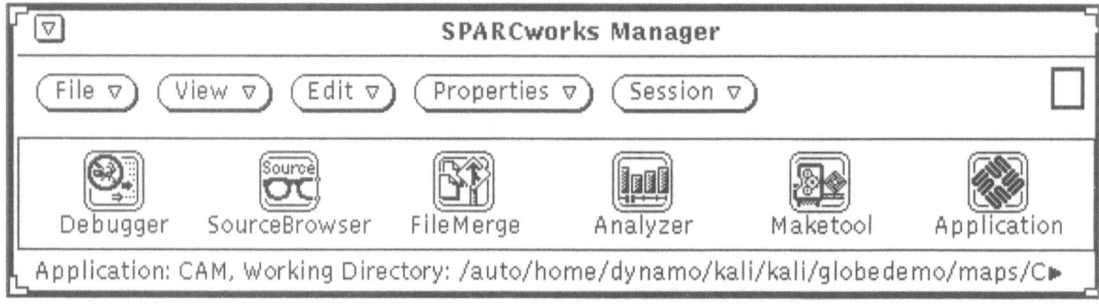

Figure 4.4. Drop target message display.

- To start the application that you dropped on the Drop Target, double click on the Application icon.

Note – Dropping a path name onto the Drop Target that is not the path of an application will results in an error message.

SPARCworks Manager Background Menu

The SPARCworks Manager background menu can be accessed at all times. The background menu offers the same options as the Session pull-down menu and the View pull-down menu combined.

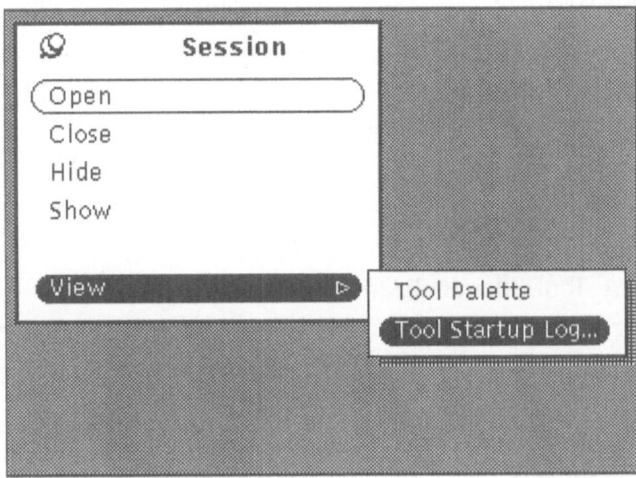

4.3
Integrating Development Tools with the ToolTalk Service[1]

This section describes how the *ToolTalk* service allows your application to communicate with other autonomous applications. Tutorial-style instructions for modifying your application to communicate via ToolTalk messages are given in the latter half of this section.

As mentioned earlier the ToolTalk service provides *multicast* messaging; that is, an application sends a message that is delivered by the ToolTalk service to multiple receivers. Multicast messaging, with the concept of one-to-many communications, falls between broadcast messaging (one-to-all) and point-to-point messaging (one-to-one). The ToolTalk service also provides point-to-point messaging between applications.

Recall that the ToolTalk service supports two types of messaging, *process-oriented* and *object-oriented* messaging. Process-oriented messages are addressed to other processes; object-oriented messages are addressed to objects managed by processes.

This section introduces you to multicast, process-oriented messaging and how to modify your application to send and receive these messages. For more information beyond what is given in this book on object-oriented messaging and the ToolTalk service in general, refer to *ToolTalk Programmer's Guide*.

1. This section is adapted from the SunSoft Deskset Integration Guide.

Preparing for Interaction with the ToolTalk Service

To prepare for interacting with the ToolTalk Service, you will:

- Open communication with the ToolTalk Service
- Obtain a file descriptor that will notify you when messages have arrived
- Setup to receive messages.

The functions used in these operations are listed in Table 4.1.

Table 4.1. ToolTalk initialization functions.

Function	Return Value Type	Description
tt_open	char*	Opens communication, sets default session to current user session, returns procid.
tt_fd	int	Obtains file descriptor.

Open Communication and Obtain File Descriptor

To initialize your process with the ToolTalk service and prepare it to receive messages, you must obtain a process identifier (procid) and a file descriptor (fd). The file descriptor informs your process when messages are delivered. tt_open() returns the procid for your process and sets this procid as the default procid.

tt_fd() returns a file descriptor. When a message arrives for the default procid in the default session, the file descriptor becomes active.

Here's sample code to initialize and register with the ToolTalk service.

```
/*
 * Initialize ToolTalk, using the initial default session, and
 * obtain the file descriptor that will become active whenever
 * ToolTalk has a message for this process.
 */

my_procid = tt_open();
ttfd = tt_fd();
```

Setting Up to Receive Messages

When a message has arrived for your application, the file descriptor becomes active. How you are alerted that the file descriptor is active will vary depending on how your application is structured.

XView™ Programs. A program that uses the XView notifier, through `XV_main_loop()` or `notify_start()`, can have a callback function invoked when the file descriptor becomes active. Invoke `notify_set_input_func()` with the handle for the message object as a parameter.

Here's how `ttsample1`, an XView program, is set up to receive messages.

```
ttfd = tt_fd();

/*
 * Arrange for XView to call receive_tt_message when the ToolTalk
 * file descriptor becomes active.
 */
notify_set_input_func(base_frame, receive_tt_message, ttfd);
```

X Window System Xt (Intrinsics) Programs. A Xt-based program uses `XtAddInput` to watch for arriving messages. **TNT Programs.** A TNT-based program uses `wire_Add-FileHandler` to watch for an active file descriptor. **Other Xlib Programs.** Programs structured around a `select(3)` system call use the file descriptor returned by `tt_fd()`. When the file descriptor becomes active, the select call will exit.

Using Message Patterns to Register Interest in Messages

After setting up to receive messages, you need to tell the ToolTalk service what types of messages you want to receive. To create and register message patterns that the ToolTalk service will use when determining message recipients, you:

- Obtain a message pattern handle
- Set and add pattern attributes
- Register the message pattern
- Unregister the message pattern when you no longer want to receive messages that match this pattern.

The functions used in these operations are listed in Table 4.2.

Table 4.2. Message pattern functions.

Function	Return Value Type	Description
`tt_pattern_create`	Tt_pattern	Obtains a handle to a message pattern.
`tt_pattern_`<*attri-bute*>`_set`	Tt_status	Sets the value for this pattern attribute.
`tt_pattern_`<*attri-bute*>`_add`	Tt_status	Adds values to this pattern attribute.
`tt_pattern_reg-ister`	Tt_status	Registers pattern with the ToolTalk service.
`tt_pattern_unreg-ister`	Tt_status	Unregisters pattern from the ToolTalk service.
`tt_pattern_destroy`	Tt_status	Destroys the message pattern.

Create a Message Pattern
To get a "handle" or "opaque pointer" to a new pattern object, use `tt_pattern_create()`. Use this handle on succeeding calls to reference the pattern.

Set and Add Pattern Attributes
To fill in pattern information, use the `tt_pattern_`<*attribute*>`_add()` or `tt_pattern_`<*attribute*>`_set()` calls for each attribute of the pattern. See Table 4.3 for pattern attributes relevant to process-oriented messages.

Table 4.3. Message pattern attributes.

Attribute	Values
arg	`char`
barg	`unsigned char`
iarg	`int`
address	`TT_PROCEDURE, TT_OBJECT, TT_HANDLER, TT_OTYPE`
category	`TT_OBSERVE` or `TT_HANDLE`
class	`TT_NOTICE, TT_REQUEST`
disposition	`TT_DISCARD, TT_QUEUE, TT_START`
file	`char *file`

Attribute	Values
op	`char *opname`
opnum	`int opnum`
scope	`TT_SESSION, TT_FILE, TT_FILE_IN_SESSION`
sender	`char *procid`
session	`char *sessid`
state	`TT_CREATED, TT_SENT, TT_HANDLED, TT_FAILED,` `TT_QUEUED, TT_REJECTED`

Note – You can supply multiple values for each attribute in the pattern except for category; the pattern attribute matches a message attribute if any of the values in the pattern match the value in the message.

The following pattern attributes must always be supplied:

- Category
- Scope

Registering a Message Pattern

When the pattern is complete, register it with `tt_pattern_register()`, and join the sessions or files you specified.

Here's sample code to create and register a pattern:

```
/*
 * Create and register a pattern so ToolTalk knows we are
 * interested in "ttsample1_value" messages within the session we
 * join.
 */

pat = tt_pattern_create();
tt_pattern_category_set(pat, TT_OBSERVE);
tt_pattern_scope_add(pat, TT_SESSION);
tt_pattern_op_add(pat, "ttsample1_value");
tt_pattern_register(pat);
```

Deleting Message Patterns

To stop receiving messages that match a message pattern, use `tt_pattern_unregister()` to unregister the pattern or `tt_pattern_destroy()` to unregister and then destroy the pattern object.

The ToolTalk service will automatically destroy message pattern objects when `tt_close()` is called.

Registering Interest in a Session or File

After registering message patterns, join a session and/or file to update the session and file attributes in your message pattern. If you specified a scope of `TT_SESSION` in your message pattern, you need to join the session to notify the ToolTalk service to add your sessid to the sessid attribute of the message pattern. This automatic update of message patterns by joining sessions or files saves the effort of registering a new pattern for each session or file your application is interested in.

To join or quit a session or file, use one of the functions listed in Table 4.4

Table 4.4. Registering interest functions.

Function	Return Value Type	Description
`tt_session_join`	Tt_status	Registers interest in the indicated user session.
`tt_session_quit`	Tt_status	Unregisters interest in the indicated user session.
`tt_file_join`	Tt_status	Registers interest in the indicated file.
`tt_file_quit`	Tt_status	Unregisters interest in the indicated file.

Session

Use `tt_session_join()` to register interest in messages that name a specific session monitored by the ToolTalk service. When you join, supply the sessid of the session you want to join. Joining a session automatically updates all of your session-scoped message patterns with the specified sessid.

Here's sample code for joining the default user session in which this program was started.

```
/*
 * Join the default session
 */

tt_session_join(tt_default_session());
```

Chapter 4. Integrating Development Tools with SPARCworks

When you no longer want to participate in the default session, inform the ToolTalk service with `tt_session_-quit()`. The sessid will be removed from your session-scoped message patterns.

File

To register your interest in messages about a particular file, call `tt_file_join()`. Joining a file automatically updates all of your file-scoped message patterns with the name of the file. The file name is added to a list; it does not replace existing file names.

When you're no longer interested in receiving messages that refer to the file, call `tt_file_quit()`. The file name will be removed from your file-scoped message patterns.

Sending Messages

To create, fill in, and send a message, use the functions listed in Table 4.5.

Table 4.5. Sending messages functions.

Function	Return Value Type	Description
`tt_pnotice_cre-ate`	Tt_message	Creates a procedure addressed notice and returns a handle to the message.
`tt_prequest_-create`	Tt_message	Creates a procedure addressed request and returns a handle to the message.
`tt_message_<attribute>_set`	Tt_status	Sets the value for a message attribute.
`tt_message_<attribute>_add`	Tt_status	Adds a value for a message attribute.
`tt_message_send`	Tt_status	Registers interest in the indicated file.
`tt_message_destroy`	Tt_status	Destroys a message that is no longer useful.

Create and Fill In Message

To get a "handle" or "opaque pointer" to a new message object for a procedural notice or request, use `tt_pno-tice_create()` or `tt_prequest_create()`. Use this handle on succeeding calls to refer to the message.

To fill in message information, use the `tt_message_<attribute>_set()` calls for the following attributes.

- Scope

  Fill in the scope of the message delivery. Potential recipients could be joined to

  ° TT_SESSION

  ° TT_FILE

  ° TT_BOTH

  ° TT_FILE_IN_SESSION

  Depending on the scope, the ToolTalk service will fill in the default session and/or file.

- Op

  Fill in the operation that describes the notice or request you are making. To determine the operation name, consult the message protocol definition.

  In addition to these required attributes, you can fill in other attributes, such as operation arguments.

Send the Message

To send a message, use `tt_message_send()`. If you no longer need the message (for example, you are not expecting a reply) destroy the message and free memory with `tt_message_destroy()`.

Here's the code for creating and sending a pnotice from the `ttsample1` program.

```
/*
 * Create and send a ToolTalk notice message
 * ttsample1_value(in int new_value)
 */

msg_out = tt_pnotice_create(TT_SESSION, "ttsample1_value");
tt_message_arg_add(msg_out, TT_IN, "integer", NULL);
tt_message_arg_ival_set(msg_out, 0, (int)xv_get(slider, PANEL_VALUE));
tt_message_send(msg_out);

/*
 * Since this message is a notice, we don't expect a reply, so
 * there's no reason to keep a handle for the message.
 */

tt_message_destroy(msg_out);
}
```

Table 4.6. Functions for receiving messages.

Function	Return Value Type	Description
`tt_message_receive`	Tt_message	Retrieves the currently available message.
`tt_mark`	mark	Marks storage for information you retrieve from a message.
`tt_release`		Frees storage used by the information retrieved from the message.
`tt_message_<attribute>`	(depends on attribute)	Obtains the value for a message attribute.
`tt_message_destroy`	Tt_status	Destroys a message that is no longer useful.

Receiving Messages

To retrieve a message, use the functions listed in Table 4.6.

When a message arrives for your process, the ToolTalk service-supplied file descriptor becomes active. When notified of the active state of the file descriptor, call `tt_message_receive()` to get a handle for a message object containing the incoming message.

When you use functions that return information such as the `tt_message_<attribute>()` calls, the ToolTalk service creates a copy of the information (the original copy is in the message structure in this case) and stores the copy in an allocation stack in the API library. The ToolTalk service actually returns a pointer to the copy to you. If you don't need the information returned by the function, use `tt_free()` to free the storage in the API stack.

The ToolTalk API also provides a more general mechanism, the `tt_mark()` and `tt_release()` functions, to mark and free information returned by a series of functions. The `tt_mark()` and `tt_release()` functions are typically used at the beginning and end of a routine where the information returned by the ToolTalk service is no longer interesting after the routine has ended.

Note – The API allocation stack should not be confused with your program's run-time stack. The ToolTalk service returns information from ToolTalk functions by providing pointers to the information in the API stack. The API stack will not discard information until you tell it to.

In the following example, ttsample1 calls tt_mark()
at the beginning of the routine that examines the information
in a message. The ToolTalk service returns a mark, an integer
that represents a location on the API stack. When the information examined in the routine is no longer needed and the
message has been destroyed, tt_release() is called with
the mark to free storage on the stack.

Use the tt_message_<*attribute*>() calls to examine the
attributes of the message to determine the action you should
take.

You can recognize replies to messages you sent by comparing the handles. This is why it is important not to destroy
a request after you send it. When you have finished examining a message you received, be sure to destroy the message
using tt_message_destroy() to free memory allocated
for the message.

Here's the code from ttsample1 for receiving a message.

```
/*
 * When a ToolTalk message is available, receive it; if it's a
 * ttsample1_value message, update the gauge with the new value.
 */
void
receive_tt_message()
{
Tt_message msg_in;
int mark;
int val_in;

msg_in = tt_message_receive();

/*
 * It's possible that the file descriptor would become active
 * even though ToolTalk doesn't really have a message for us.
 * The returned message handle is NULL in this case.
 */

if (msg_in == NULL) return;


/*
 * Get a storage mark so we can easily free all the data
 * ToolTalk returns to us.
 */
```

Chapter 4. Integrating Development Tools with SPARCworks

```
mark = tt_mark();

if (0==strcmp("ttsample1_value", tt_message_op(msg_in,0))) {
    tt_message_arg_ival(msg_in, 0, &val_in);
    xv_set(gauge, PANEL_VALUE, val_in, NULL);
}

tt_message_destroy(msg_in);
tt_release(mark);
return;
}
```

Stopping Interaction with the ToolTalk Service

Use `tt_close()` when you want to stop interacting with the ToolTalk service and other ToolTalk session participants. `tt_close()` closes the current default procid. Here's how the `ttsample1` program uses this call.

```
/*
 * Before leaving, allow ToolTalk to clean up.
 */
tt_close();

exit(0);
}
```

4.4 SPARCworks Manager and dbx Protocols

This section describes the ToolTalk service messages that are used to connect individual tools that are part of the SPARC-works 2.0 programming environment.

Messages Description Syntax

The ToolTalk service messages that are used are described below. (Note that a BNF-like syntax is used for clarity; standard Sun font conventions are used thereafter.)

message::='('Tt_message <attribute>* [<args>] ')'

attribute ::= '(' <field_name> <value> ')'

args ::= '(' Tt_args <arg>+ ')'

arg ::= '(' <direction> [<type>] <value> ')'

direction ::= TT_IN | TT_OUT | TT_INOUT

type ::= string | int

Values in upper-case are ToolTalk enumeration constants. Those in lower-case are variable names (except for the type names "string" and "int"). The second level of nesting is required because arguments do not have separate field names, and position in the sequence is significant. This is also required because of the distinction between <direction> and **<field_name>**.

In addition to the above, two additional notations are defined:

1. Optional arguments are enclosed in square brackets ([]), and are always preceded by an int argument that indicates whether the optional argument is present in the message.

2. Variable length lists are indicated by bracketing ("{ }*") groups of arguments that may be repeated. These lists are preceded by an int argument that tells the number of repetitions.

SPARCworks Session Protocol

SPARCworks 2.0 tools are started and controlled in two ways, either:

- Directly by the user, or
- By the SPARCworks Manager.

SPARCworks Manager

In Release 2.0 of SPARCworks, tools can be started and manipulated by means of the SPARCworks Manager. When the SPARCworks Manager is used to start your tool, the SPARCworks Manager and your tool must exchange information about each other in order to subsequently communicate properly using the ToolTalk service. SPARCworks Manager must know your tool's procid. Your tool must know:

- The SPARCworks Manager's procid
- Its own unique ID key
- The SPARCworks session number.

When the SPARCworks Manager itself is started it sets the value of the environment variable SW_TT_STARTUP_PRO-CID to the value of its own procid.

1. When SPARCworks Manager launches your tool it passes it a unique ID string (*key*) as the argument to the -swtm option.

2. Your tool receives the *key* and sends a ToolTalk startup message back to the originating SPARCworks Manag-

er. The message contains the *key* and the tool's own procid. It determines the SPARCworks Manager's procid by reading the `SW_TT_STARTUP_PROCID` shell environment variable.

(**Tt_message** (**Tt_class**TT_REQUEST) (**Tt_op**
"PEI_STARTED")
(**Tt_address** TT_HANDLER) (**Tt_handler** *procid*)
(**Tt_args** (TT_IN *key*) (TT_OUT *sw_session*)))

3. The SPARCworks Manager replies to the startup message and supplies your tool with the SPARCworks session number (*sw_session*).

A tool that has been started by the SPARCworks Manager may, in turn, start additional tools; the automatic pass-down of the environment variable will connect them with a SPARCworks Manager.

Note – The `-swtm` argument is not required for proper operation, but is provided so that SPARCworks Manager can track the tool it starts.

Alternatively, a tool may acquire more control over tools it starts by changing the environment variable and receiving the `PEI_STARTED` message itself.

A set of messages control SPARCworks sessions. The first is a simple ping:

(**Tt_message** (**Tt_class** TT_REQUEST) (**Tt_op** "PEI_NOP")
(**Tt_args** (TT_IN *sw_session*)))

The remaining messages allow coordinated control of a collection of tools.

These are commands are sent by SPARCworks Manager to the tools running in the SPARCworks session:

(**Tt_message** (**Tt_class** TT_NOTICE) (**Tt_op** "hide")
(**Tt_args** (TT_IN *sw_session*)))

  ° Hide the tool's window.

(**Tt_message** (**Tt_class** TT_NOTICE) (**Tt_op** "expose")
(**Tt_args** (TT_IN *sw_session*)))

  ° Expose the tool's window (if it is hidden).

(**Tt_message** (**Tt_class** TT_NOTICE) (**Tt_op** "PEI_OPEN")
(**Tt_args** (TT_IN *sw_session*)))

  ° Open the tool's window.

(Tt_message (Tt_class TT_NOTICE) **(Tt_op** "PEI_-CLOSE")
(Tt_args (TT_IN *sw_session*))

° Close the tool's window to its icon.

(Tt_message (Tt_class TT_NOTICE) **(Tt_op** "quit")
(Tt_args (TT_IN *sw_session*))

° Quit the tool.

When a tool is about to exit, it informs SPARCworks Manager by means of:

(Tt_message (Tt_class TT_NOTICE) **(Tt_op** "departed")
(Tt_args (TT_IN *sw_session*))

Debugger Protocol

SPARCworks Debugger   The ptype of the SPARCworks Debugger is Sun_Microsystems_DUI. No static declaration is required for SPARCworks Manager interaction (tools register *sw_session* specific dynamic patterns).

Underlying Debugger   The SPARCworks Debugger starts dbx directly inside the command window so it can properly handle user TTY I/O both to and from the program being debugged. The Debugger supplies an option and argument: -T *procid*, where *procid* is the ToolTalk service procid of the Debugger. dbx then uses the PEI_STARTED request defined above to synchronize with the particular Debugger that started it and to obtain the SPARCworks session ID to insert in all subsequent messages.

Commands.   All commands are sent to dbx via the pseudo-teletype connected to dbx standard input; dbx writes its normal output to standard out, which is connected to the command sub-window of the Debugger.

Notifications.   When dbx is running under the SPARCworks Debugger, it supplies additional information to the Debugger via ToolTalk service messages. The messages have the form:

(Tt_message (Tt_class TT_NOTICE) **(Tt_op** "DBX_PIPE")
(Tt_args (TT_IN *sw_session*) ...))

with the next argument being the message type code and the remainder depending on the type. The Debugger identifies the notification coming from the particular dbx it started based on the sender procid obtained from the `PEI_STARTED` request.

The first message sent by `dbx` identifies the version of the message protocol being used.

(`TT_IN I_VERSION`) (`TT_IN` *version*)

The list of ToolTalk messages used to broadcast debugger events include:

(`TT_IN I_NEWINITDONE`)
(`TT_IN` *current_dir*) (`TT_IN` *program*)
(`TT_IN` *cursource*) (`TT_IN` *curfunc*) (`TT_IN` *cursrcline*)
(`TT_IN` *brksource*) (`TT_IN` *brkfunc*) (`TT_IN` *cur.brkline*)
- ° `dbx` is ready for user commands.

(`TT_IN I_RESUME`) (`TT_IN` *command_name*)

- ° Program execution is about to resume.

(`TT_IN I_BRKSET`) (`TT_IN` *file*) (`TT_IN` *lineno*)

- ° A breakpoint was set at *lineno* in *file*.

(`TT_IN I_BRKDEL`) (`TT_IN` *file*) (`TT_IN` *lineno*)
- ° A breakpoint at *lineno* in *file* was deleted.

(`TT_IN I_STOPPED`)
(`TT_IN` *cursource*) (`TT_IN` *curfunc*) (`TT_IN` *cursrcline*)
(`TT_IN` *brksource*) (`TT_IN` *cur.brkfunc*) (`TT_IN` *cur.brkline*)
- ° Program execution has been stopped (includes stop location).

(`TT_IN I_DISPLAY`) (`TT_IN` *file*)
- ° File *file* that contains display information has been updated.

(`TT_IN I_CALLSTACK`) (`TT_IN` *cursource*) (`TT_IN` *lineno*)
- ° *lineno* in *cursource* is an address in the call stack.

(`TT_IN I_TRACE`) (`TT_IN` *cursource*) (`TT_IN` *curfunc*)
(`TT_IN` *cursrcline*)
- ° Program execution was traced at *cursrcline* in *curfunc* in *cursource*.

(`TT_IN I_KILL`)
- ° The program being debugged was killed.

(`TT_IN I_REINIT`)
- ° The debugging environment was initialized.

(TT_IN I_QUIT) (TT_IN *status*)
  ◦ The debugging session was quit.

Another group of messages are used to change the debugger display:

(TT_IN I_PRINTLINES) (TT_IN *cursource*) (TT_IN l1)
(TT_IN l2)
  ◦ Display source code fragments.

(TT_IN I_CHDIR) (TT_IN *directory*)
  ◦ Change the working directory.

(TT_IN I_USE) (TT_IN *path_ct*) {(TT_IN *path*)}*)
  ◦ Set the source file search path.

(TT_IN I_EMPHASIZE) (TT_IN *cursource*) (TT_IN *lineno*)
  ◦ Highlight a line of source code.

(TT_IN I_FONT) (TT_IN *file*)
  ◦ Set the display font.

(TT_IN I_BOTMARGIN) (TT_IN *n*)
  ◦ Set the bottom margin of the source display.

(TT_IN I_CMDLINES) (TT_IN *n*)
  ◦ Set the number of display lines in the command pane.

(TT_IN I_DISPLINES) (TT_IN *n*)
  ◦ Set the number of display lines in the data display window.

(TT_IN I_TOPMARGIN) (TT_IN *n*)
  ◦ Set the top margin of the source display.

(TT_IN I_WIDTH) (TT_IN *n*)
  ◦ Set the width of the tool window.

(TT_IN I_TOOLENV)
  ◦ Set debugger environment attributes.

(TT_IN I_MENU) (TT_IN *seltype*) (TT_IN *string*)
  ◦ Define the debugger menu items.

(TT_IN I_BUTTON) (TT_IN *seltype*) (TT_IN *string*)
  ◦ Define the debugger command buttons.

(TT_IN I_UMENU) (TT_IN *string*)
  ◦ Undefine the debugger menu items.

(TT_IN I_UNBUTTON) (TT_IN *string*)
  ◦ Undefine the debugger command buttons.

Chapter 4. Integrating Development Tools with SPARCworks

Devguide — The OpenWindows G.U.I. Builder

5.1
Introduction

This section describes SunSoft™'s OpenWindows™ Developer's Guide (Devguide), comparing it to similar products. Devguide can help you solve some of your user interface programming problems, and help you easily port applications running on other hardware platforms to SPARC platforms. You will also gain an understanding of how a User Interface Builder compares to a User Interface Management System (UIMS) and a User Interface Prototyper.

What is Devguide? Devguide is a user interface builder that enables a developer to graphically and interactively design an OPEN LOOK interface for an application.

The ideal application is separated into two independent parts: application-specific code, and a user interface that shows the capabilities and status of that application to the user.

Using Devguide, you can design and lay out the user interface part of your application on the screen, test it and modify it as many times as you like, then save a description of this interface in one or more files. Figure 5.1 shows the Devguide base window.

Devguide provides facilities for automatically generating SunSoft window system toolkit C, C++, or PostScript code from the interface description files. In the 1.1 release, Dev–

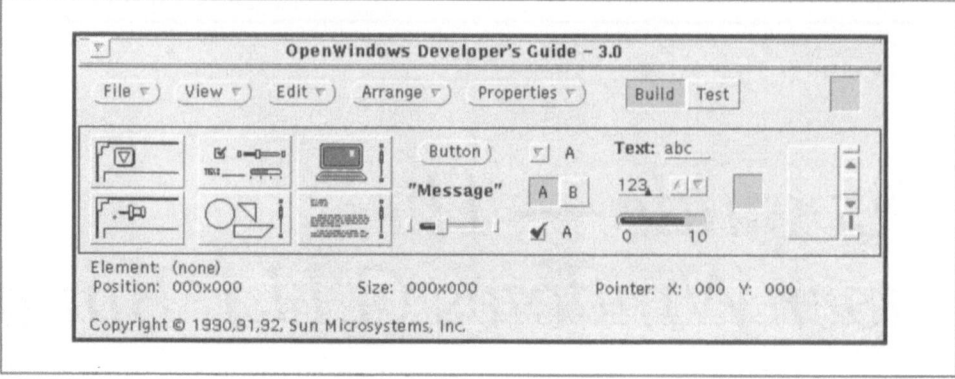

Figure 5.1. Devguide base window.

guide includes code generators for the XView toolkit (GXV and GXV++). In the 3.0 release, Devguide includes code generators for XView (GXV, GXV++), The NeWS® Toolkit (GNT), and OPEN LOOK Intrinsics Toolkit (OLIT). You can also generate ANSI C for XView using a command line option to GXV.

Developers can design an interface without writing any code. However, someone has to write the actual application (graphics previewer, electronic mail reader, for example) and has to connect the application to the user interface.

As an analogy, picture your graphical user interface (GUI) as the control console of a car. The application is the chassis, wheels, brakes, transmission, and engine, or other working parts of the car. Think of Devguide as the tool you can use to generate the speedometer, odometer, tachometer, steering wheel, or other control and status elements for the console. Devguide in this example would save the car manufacturer's engineers from inventing the design for each instrument, requiring a lot of time and resources.

To carry the analogy further, GXV (or GNT or GOLIT) is the agent that specifies how the controls work. The engineers just have to go in and physically hook up the mechanical parts to the control console (connect the application to the interface). The application is fully built when the controls are hooked up so that the controls affect the working parts and the instruments provide live readings of status. After the user interface and application are connected, you can run the application (read and send electronic mail, for example); or, back to the car analogy, you can start the car and all the working parts and instruments function as you expect.

5.2
Overview

Figure 5.2 shows how Devguide relates to the underlying applications and SunOS software.

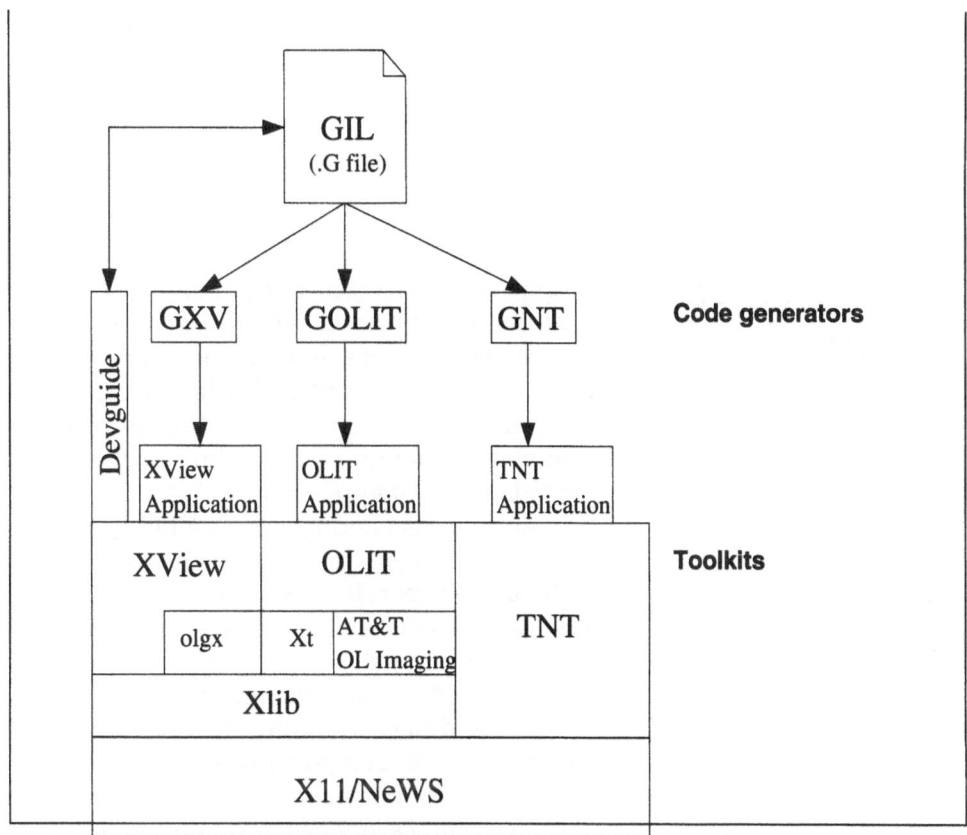

Figure 5.2. Devguide, code generators, toolkits and underlying software.

When you instruct Devguide to save the user interface you've created, it saves it in a file or files ending in .G (such as speedometer.G, oilgauge.G, steeringwheel.G, and so forth). These .G files (or GIL files, for Guide Interface Language) can be read in again to Devguide and modified, if desired, as many times as necessary.

When you are satisfied with the interface you've designed, save the interface files, then run a code generator program to produce window system toolkit C, C++, or PostScript code. The currently available code generators are GXV, GXV++, GNT, and GOLIT. Choose the option to produce C or C++ code for XView, PostScript, C, or C++ code for the NeWS Toolkit, or C code for the OPEN LOOK Intrinsics toolkit.

The window system toolkits are implemented using the OPEN LOOK graphics libraries or the AT&T OPEN LOOK imaging routines with Xt intrinsics on top of Xlib. X11/NeWS™ incorporates the X Window System from the Massachusetts Institute of Technology and the Network extensible Window System, an innovative PostScript language development environment.

5.3
What does Devguide do for You?

Using Devguide to generate user interface code, you can:

Speed Up Program Development

Using Devguide to generate or modify a user interface saves time and effort since it's not necessary to hand-code all the tedious elements of a user interface. The interface design can also proceed concurrently with the application development. Devguide can also generate the "boiler plate" interface objects and concentrate on the usability of the interface and presentation of their application.

You can select and position OPEN LOOK user interface objects such as windows, control items, gauges, and menus right on the screen. It's as easy as dragging an object from the Devguide palette and dropping it onto the workspace.

Once positioned, you can move or resize objects, remove them, add others, and change the design. You can take advantage of design freedom, knowing that the interface will be OPEN LOOK-compliant when finished.

Templates for frequently used windows and menus are included with Devguide to save development time and promote a standard look and feel among all applications.

Quickly Port Your Existing Application to OPEN LOOK

Porting your application to OPEN LOOK using Devguide typically takes from a few hours to a few weeks, depending on the complexity of the application.

In the absence of a user interface builder like Devguide, generating the code for the user interface part of the application is extremely tedious and time-consuming. Think of trying to describe a drawing in terms of coordinates and lines instead of simply being able to draw it directly on the screen. All the user interface elements would have to be laboriously and repetitively programmed, compiled, and tested. This could take months.

Devguide handles the chores of building the user interface portion of your application. Using Devguide, you select user interface objects such as canvases (drawing surfaces) and control panels (with buttons, choices, sliders, gauges, menus, and so on) and place the objects directly on your prototype application.

Devguide helps you specify exactly how your application appears to the user — and, you can test it before generating any code. Select control items and view menu layout, changing them around until you are satisfied. To test the behavior of the user interface before generating the code for it, Devguide provides a test mode. In test mode, buttons can be pressed, settings can be selected, and the interface behaves exactly as it will when later attached to the actual application.

When satisfied with the user interface, you save its *description* in a Devguide interface file, the GIL file. The GIL file is independent of the particular toolkit you use for the interface to your application. You can use one of several conversion programs to convert the GIL language into toolkit code for the chosen toolkit.

You are now ready to generate toolkit code by running one of the code generator programs available with Devguide: GXV, GXV++, GNT, or GOLIT. GXV stands for Guide-to-XView, and generates files to be used with the XView toolkit (including C++ code if you use GXV++). GNT and GOLIT create a similar number of files specific to The NeWS Toolkit (PostScript) and the OPEN LOOK Intrinsics Toolkit. In Figure 5.3, you see a diagram of the process of generating code for The NeWS Toolkit. This process also applies to the other code generators.]

Once you generate toolkit code, you probably want to tweak it. You can easily modify the user interface, rerun the code generator and then retest, perhaps repeating the cycle several times.

You can modify the *interface-name_stubs.c* file (later referred to as *_stubs.c* file) to fill in the substance of any callback routines generated when the interface was specified. It is *not* a good idea, however, to modify the Devguide-generated *interface-name_ui.c* file. If you do, and later want to use Devguide again to modify the interface, your manual changes will not get saved. It is best to keep the interface creation code separate and untouched from the interface callback code, which is in the *_stubs.c* file.

Each code generator produces its own set of files to include interface and application code. As an example, GXV produces the following files:

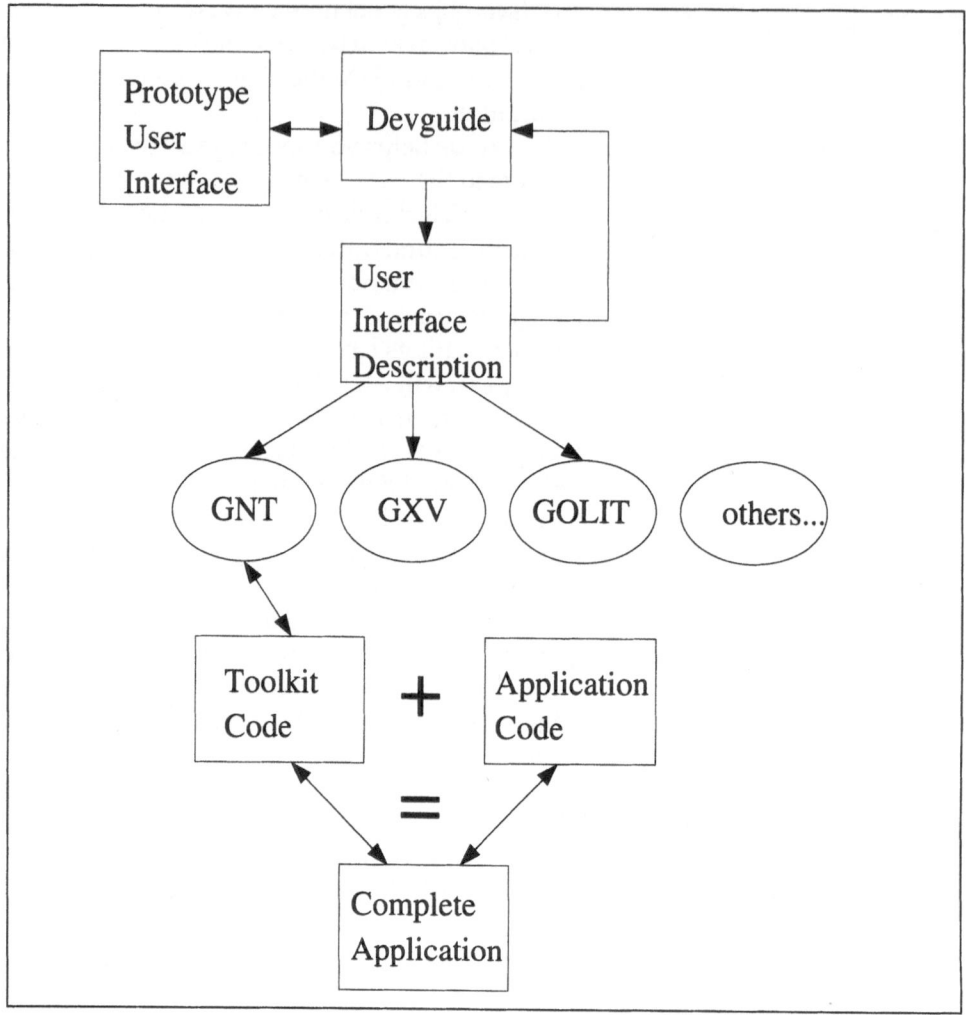

Figure 5.3. Generating code for the NeWS toolkit (TNT).

- *interface-name_ui*.c. Contains the interface creation routines for all the elements.
- *interface-name_ui*.h. Contains structure declarations.
- *interface-name_stubs*.c. Contains the "main" function and any callback routines associated with interface operation.
- *interface-name*.info. Contains any help text specified for any of the interface elements.
- Makefile. Generated if it does not already exist.

For Devguide 1.1, GXV and GXV++ are the only code generators available. Once you've compiled your interface and generated toolkit code, you can do one of two things:

1. Rename your "stubs" file (ends in `_stubs.c`) and edit the renamed version to insert your application code, then compile and run your application, or:

2. Add your application code to the original `_stubs.c` file produced by GXV, compile and run your application, then edit your interface using Devguide. When you save the new version, you get a new `.G` file.

If you are running Devguide 1.1, run `gxv_merge` on the new `.G`, which creates new interface code and merges that with your previously added application code.

In Devguide 3.0, `gxv_merge` is built into GXV, so it is not necessary to run it separately, as described in the previous paragraph.

Note – You may also have to edit your `Makefile`, set environment variables, and take care of anything else needed to combine the application and the user interface.

Quickly Design and Test a User Interface

Devguide offers enhanced alignment features to quickly lay out and modify portions of a user interface. You can select objects to be aligned horizontally, vertically, or to a grid. You can also specify the distribution for those objects. They can be distributed evenly in the horizontal or vertical space or laid out with a specific number of pixels between them.

Devguide's grouping feature enables you to select objects and put them into a group. (A group is a collection of user interface objects that is treated as a single unit.) A group can be copied, moved, or deleted as a single entity. Objects included in a group maintain a physical relationship with other objects in that group. Therefore, when the group is moved, or if an object in the group changes size, the relative positioning of the individual objects remains the same. This is especially important for localizing applications when button sizes may change due to different font sizes or languages.

Generate Online Help

When you're creating elements of your user interface, you may want to write some explanatory help text. Devguide simplifies the process of creating help by providing a Help Editor window in which you can type the help text and specify which element to attach it to. The help text gets incorporated into the interface element's `.G` file when you save it.

When you run the code generator, Devguide creates the help files for you and puts the appropriate window system subroutine call or attribute value into your source code file.

In the 3.0 release, you can view the help text even before you save the interface. Put Devguide in test mode, move the mouse pointer over the element you are interested in, and push the Help key.

Easily Design or Modify User Interfaces

No programming is required to generate the user interface with Devguide. It can even be used by those without programming experience, such as interface or graphic designers. So, try out many different ideas: resize, move, and change the look and feel as much as you like.

Integrate With Other OPEN LOOK Tools

When you develop an application to be integrated with other OPEN LOOK tools, you can specify that the application respond to drag-and-drop events. Your application can then be used easily with File Manager because a user can drag a file from File Manager onto your application. If you do nothing in your application to support drag-and-drop, then nothing will happen. Devguide writes the drag-and-drop code into the event procedure in the `_stubs.c` file when you specify an event handler in the control area's property window.

Internationalize Your Application

First a little background on internationalization. Two issues quickly present themselves: one, the text of your application needs to get translated into other languages; two, depending on the language family (Indo-European or Asian, for example) and the font, the characters you want to display may require varying amounts of space—in memory (multiple bytes) and on your screen. The default size of user interface objects is partially determined by the font of the characters displayed within them.

You must add two mechanisms to an application for it to be truly internationalized:

- A way to translate text strings from a text database.
- A way for the interface to be laid out correctly in the new language.

Translation

The developer inserts function calls into the application source code wherever strings are used. These calls will be used to look up the strings in other languages, or "locales." Once the internationalization "hooks" are in the source code, you run a utility against the source to produce a specially-formatted ASCII file. This ASCII file contains the original text strings and placeholders for their translations. Someone (usually someone other than the developer) translates the strings into the local language, then, using another utility, creates a binary version (the text database, or text domain) from the previously-mentioned ASCII file.

Size and Position of Elements

There are two mechanisms for positioning objects. The most general method is to use relative layout or "grouping," in which object positions are based on other objects. See the *Quickly design and test a user interface* section, given earlier for a discussion of Devguide's grouping feature. Grouping facilitates the use of multiple fonts and sizes.

Another method for positioning objects is available if you choose to explicitly position and size the objects making up your interface. This method uses an X Windows-style resource database. The application retrieves the size and position information of the objects making up the application's interface from the resource database.

If you use a relative layout scheme in which objects are positioned relative to other objects you shouldn't need to use the size and position database. If you explicitly specify x,y coordinates for your interface objects, you will need to use the size and position database.

The code generator produces function calls and attributes for the interface that allow an application to access the locale-specific databases. The code generator can also generate the X resource database (containing size and position information) for the developer, if desired.

If you do not use the grouping feature of Devguide, after the strings have been translated, you run a utility called `gmomerge` to merge the translated text back into an existing English `.G` file. This merged `.G` file can be read into Devguide (displayed in the new language) and the interface can be laid out accordingly. Once the new interface is laid out properly, it can be written out as a new `.G` file. This new file now contains the translated strings as well as the size and position information. This `.G` file is used to build the size and position database for a specified locale so applications can be shipped in local languages. Only one binary is needed; locale-specific databases are shipped for strings and, possibly, size and position information.

Manage a Large User Interface Development Project

Devguide enables you to store the windows of your user interface in separate interface files (.G files). This convention makes editing interface files simpler. If you want to edit or add an object in only one window, then you have to edit only one file.

Devguide also enables you to define a project in which you incorporate separate interface (.G) files into one large interface. The Project Organizer Window presents a visual representation of a project's contents (.G files). You can add, modify, or delete .G files from the project as needed.

When you run the code generators for the project interface, you will generate several _stubs.c files, one for each of the interface files. The one Makefile that is produced will incorporate all the .G files of a project.

Modifications to include application-specific code should only be incorporated into the _stubs.c files. Changes made in the _stubs.c files will be maintained and updated if you modify the user interface and rerun the code generators.

Browse the Interface

Devguide also offers an interface browser that provides a hierarchical graphical representation of the user interface. Used in conjunction with the new Project Organizer, the interface browser enables you to view all or portions of the user interface. The interface browser is updated dynamically as you add to or modify the user interface.

The interface browser also provides another quick means to modify portions of the user interface. For example, a developer can copy a control panel with all its control objects from one window to another, rather than copying the objects individually.

Utilize Code Generator Options

Devguide provides the option to use one of three toolkit code generators. The GXV and GXV++ code generators output C and C++ code for the XView toolkit. The GOLIT code generator outputs C code for the OLIT toolkit. The GNT code generator outputs C, C++, and PostScript code for the NeWS toolkit. For an in-depth discussion of toolkit options, see *Choosing a Code Generator*, below.

There are also language code generators offered by SunSoft language products and by third party vendors.

The Devguide .G file stores the interface design following the GIL format. This format is documented in the User Manual. Following this format, developers could write their own language or toolkit code generator.

Connect Actions Between Interface Objects

In Devguide 3.0, you can connect an event generated on one element to an action occurring on another using the Connections window on the Properties menu. You can specify an element to be the source of the event and an element to be the target (the source and target elements may be the same), then specify the event you want to trigger the action and the action to occur. Devguide generates the toolkit code to connect the event and the action.

A common example is to connect the pressing of a button to the appearance of a popup window.

What Doesn't Devguide Do for You?

Devguide doesn't write your application for you — that is, it won't generate a text editor or spreadsheet application. Devguide also does not link your application with the user interface. You insert the application code into the `_stubs.c` file, generated by one of Devguide's companion code generators.

5.4 Choosing a Code Generator

Devguide 3.0 has code generator support for all the OPEN LOOK toolkits provided by OpenWindows V3. Before designing your user interface, you should select the toolkit you will eventually use: choose Devguide from the Devguide Properties menu and use the Toolkit pulldown menu to choose a toolkit.

The XView code generators, GXV and GXV++, have been enhanced to take advantage of the new features of the XView environment, such as internationalization. In addition, there are two new code generators, GOLIT for the OPEN LOOK Intrinsics Toolkit (OLIT), and GNT for the NeWS Toolkit (TNT).

Each code generator has been uniquely designed to take advantage of the strengths of its toolkit, and to address the needs of the developers using it. Hence the output of each code generator can best support its specific toolkit.

Read this section to understand the design goal of each of the code generators and the issues to consider when using them.

GXV, GXV++

The Devguide GXV code generator produces C code and the GXV++ code generator produces C++ compliant C code for the XView toolkit. The generated code is much like code a programmer would write, therefore it is very readable. It is not "machine generated," or in a proprietary format that is difficult to decode and understand.

The created files contain user interface code as well as some application-specific code, such as the code found in the _stubs.c file which contains the XView main loop with the stub call back procedures. Developers should only need to modify the _stubs.c file to add their own application-specific code. This file is maintained and updated whenever the developer modifies the user interface and regenerates the code.

A code generator that generates real toolkit code for the application has both advantages and disadvantages. One of the advantages is that it generates real code that can be easily read, modified, and maintained. In fact, developers who are unfamiliar with the XView environment can actually use the generated code to learn about XView programming.

The disadvantage is that the code generator can generate voluminous amounts of code. For example, GXV generates both executable code and resource data that grows in proportion to the complexity of the user interface implementation. In an application that contains a large or intricate user interface, the ui.c file can contain thousands of lines of code. This code, which is frequently only executed once during the user interface initialization, takes a long time to compile and creates a very large executable file. In addition, the user interface is not easily separated from the application, so dynamic modifications cannot be made to the user interface.

Both GXV and GXV++ support the internationalization (I18N) features of the XView environment, producing code that allows the resulting application binary to be localized. Two flags enable this feature:

-g

causes dgettext wrappers to be placed around all strings associated with the interface, allowing easy extraction of the text by the xgettext utility. xgettext produces a portable object file (.po file) that can be localized, compiled into a text database, and supplied at runtime. The localized database string values will override the string values in the binary code, presenting the user with a localized version of the product.

-r

Devguide, by default, uses an absolute layout scheme for all user interface objects. This layout scheme can cause problems when the localized strings are not the same length as the original text strings (for example, buttons can overlap). The developer can use Devguide to relayout the user interface, using the new localized text strings, and then set the -r flag to invoke the XView XV_USE_DB wrapper around object attributes associated with object size and positioning. This wrapper causes the application to check the resource database file for object size and position information when the localized application is run.

Note – Devguide provides a group layout feature that eliminates the need to use the -r flag. Group layout allows for relative layout at runtime. The group layout is the preferred and recommended method to use for applications that will be localized.

GOLIT

The Devguide GOLIT code generator for the OLIT toolkit provides an OLIT programmer with a fast and efficient method to implement a user interface. GOLIT generates "C" data structures, which define the user interface widget hierarchy and their associated resources. This user interface is highly efficient, compact, and consistent—that is, a widget descriptor takes only 44 bytes plus the resources, create proc, and callbacks (per widget instance), regardless of the user interface object. GOLIT does not produce a lot of "one-time" code (initialization functions). An example of this would be a call such as XtCreateManagedWidget(). Instead, a small runtime component enumerates and instantiates this widget hierarchy when the application is initialized, thereby reducing the amount of executable code.

The advantages of using GOLIT:

- The executable code size does not vary with the complexity of the user interface.
- The description of a particular user interface object (called a widget) is highly efficient relative to the equivalent hand-written C code.
- The concise API to libgolit provides the developer with a set of library functions that are easy to understand and use. These functions allow the programmer greater flexibility in the manipulation and control of the instantiation of the user interface objects within the hierarchy.
- A clear separation between the user interface and application code.
- New customized "group widget." This widget was created to support   Devguide's sophisticated relative lay-

out mechanism. The group widget is subclassed off of the OLIT Manager widget and resides in the `libgolit` runtime library.

- Create procs—these are used to instantiate objects from their descriptors. A few examples of when you would use them are:

  ° to provide additional resources at widget creation

  ° to get a widget ID

  ° to do a `SetValues()` on a widget just after creation

  ° to access an internal widget

  ° to support glyphs for user interface objects.

An example of an internal widget is: attaching menu items (such as `OblongButtons`) to a `MenuButton` widget. Specify a create proc for the `MenuButton` widget and in the create proc after instantiating the `MenuButton` widget, retrieve the `MenuPane` widget with a call to `GetValues()` and then attach menu items with the `MenuPane` widget as the parent.

Use create procs the same way that you use any other callback. Create procs are not meant to be called from the application code.

- The source for `libgolit` is available.
- Internationalization support in OLIT and GOLIT is 8-bit clean and supports use of the Compose key.

GNT

The Devguide GNT code generator for the TNT toolkit follows the model of the GXV code generator for the XView environment in that it generates toolkit code. The TNT and NeWS environment have a fairly steep initial learning curve. Once that learning curve is topped, the benefits of the environment can be fully utilized. GNT assists in completing that learning curve. It not only generates the user interface code, it also provides assistance to the developer learning the TNT and NeWS environments by providing example code.

GNT opens the door to TNT and provides enhancements to the toolkit (for example, internationalization support and linking of controls).

The GNT design allows for the following advantages and disadvantages:

- Flexibility in the client-server split. Callbacks can be defined as either client side or server (PostScript only).

- Incremental downloading of windows to the server. Using Devguide's project organization, GNT only downloads interface files that contain open windows. When a new window is requested, GNT checks to see if the interface has been downloaded, and, if required, downloads the interface (including all internationalization).
- Subclassing of OPEN LOOK objects. For example, to replace a menu with a pie-shaped menu, turn on subclassing, define the pie-shaped menu subclass, and GNT automatically utilizes the new subclass.
- Minimizes the modifications that have to be made when the interface changes. The user interface consists of three separate files, of which only one is changed when the interface is modified. The other two files define subclassing and initialization routines and therefore do not need to be changed.
- Control areas in "border bags" allow text or graphics panes to resize both vertically and horizontally.
- Computes the layout of control objects so that the objects can move logically upon resize of the window. This scheme also allows string substitution for easy internationalization and localization.

For more technical information on each of the code generators please refer to the *OpenWindows Developer's Guide 3.0 User's Guide* and the programmer's guide for each of the toolkit code generators included with the software.

5.5 Common Problems and Recommended Solutions

The following are common questions that arise for Devguide 3.0:

1. How do I attach a popup window to a button?
    You may want to press a button in one window and have a popup window appear on the screen. You can use Devguide to create both the button and the popup window by dragging and dropping the elements on the interface.

    To create the attachment, select the meta key in conjunction with the left mouse button and visually link (you will see a cord and electrical plug on the screen) the button with the popup window. The Devguide action-event Connections window appears, where you can link the notify action performed on the button to the show action performed on the popup. The link is effective in test mode, so selecting the button will display the popup. When you run a code generator, it will generate the toolkit code that links the objects and actions.

2. How do I build a menu?
    To create a menu, choose Menus from the Devguide Properties menu. This brings up the Menus property window. Press the Create button to create and name the menu. You can rename the menu by typing in the Object Name field. Choose the Insert button once for each menu item you want. Each item is called Item until you edit the Label field.

    Using the Connections window (choose Connections from the Devguide Properties menu), you can create callbacks for the menu and menu items by specifying the actions and events you want to attach to the menu or menu items.

3. How do I change the fonts in my application built by Devguide?
    The OPEN LOOK specification restricts the way you can use fonts. All items in a single control area have to use the same font. Items in a menu or scrolling list can be in different fonts. For scrolling lists you need to set the font on every item in the list when you insert it:

```
Xv_font          font;


font = (Xv_font) xv_find(control_area, FONT
        FONT_FAMILY,      FONT_FAMILY_COUR,
        FONT_STYLE,       FONT_STYLE_NORMAL,
        FONT_SIZE,        ...
        NULL);


xv_set(list,
        PANEL_LIST_INSERT, row,
        PANEL_LIST_STRING, row, "String here",
        PANEL_LIST_FONT,   row, font,
```

Chapter 5. Devguide — The OpenWindows G.U.I. Builder

For more information on fonts, see Chapter 16 of the *XView Programming Manual* written by Dan Heller and published by O'Reilly & Associates, Inc.

4. How do I group and anchor objects?
   For example, you might have a set of three buttons that you want to be equally spaced apart in a horizontal row. First, create the three buttons. Next, select all three buttons. Choose Group from Devguide's Arrange menu. Next, choose Groups from Devguide's Properties window to bring up the Groups property window. Specify the row layout option, the centered horizontal option, and you'll notice that a 10-pixel separation is the default spacing. Then select Apply. The group you create lays out the buttons according to the rules you specify. The first button is kept in its current position, the second is placed 10 pixels to the right of the first, vertically centered, and so on.

   As another example, consider the Apply and Reset buttons that appear at the bottom of most OPEN LOOK property windows. Use the anchoring facility to center these buttons as they should appear. Create a group consisting of the two buttons. Choose the South point of the group's bounding box as the reference point. (A group's bounding box includes nine compass points. South is the group's bottom center point.) Choose the South point on the panel as the anchor point. Choose the control area as the anchor object.

   A good example of using groups to support dynamic resize behavior is the file chooser, also available in `libguidexv`.

5. How do I gray out items in a menu?
   One way is to set up a notify handler for that menu or menu item. Inside that, have a condition in the `MENU_DISPLAY` case that sets the item active or inactive as appropriate for the current state; for example, the Copy menu item on the Edit menu, as shown below:

```
/*
 * Menu handler for 'edit_menu (Copy)'.
 */
Menu_item
copy_menu_handler(item, op)
        Menu_item         item;
        Menu_generate     op;
{

        switch (op) {
        case MENU_DISPLAY:
                /* Find out if anything is selected... */
                if (items_selected)
                    xv_set(item, MENU_INACTIVE, FALSE, NULL);
                else
                    xv_set(item, MENU_INACTIVE, TRUE, NULL);
                break;
        case MENU_NOTIFY:
                copy_selected_items();
                break;
```

6. How do I include my own objects (such as a triangular-shaped button) in my application? (Devguide doesn't provide the object, yet my users expect the object.)

Except for putting a glyph inside the existing OPEN LOOK button that XView implements, this is not yet possible.

5.6
Similar Products

A user interface builder is sometimes grouped logically with user interface management systems (UIMS's) and user interface prototypers. Each of these user interface programs provides unique features, however, that meet different people's needs.

What is a User Interface Builder?

A user interface builder enables developers to lay out graphically the design of a user interface. It also generates the window system toolkit or language code that defines the interface.

A developer designs the user interface on a computer screen by selecting user interface elements from a palette and moving them to desired locations on the prototype application. The elements can be sized, positioned, colored, and laid out exactly to the designer's liking.

A user interface builder sometimes enables a developer to define specific relationships of objects to objects, or objects to actions (such as using a button to bring up a popup window). A user interface builder does more than just define the look; it can define relationships between elements.

When the design is finished, the user saves a description of the interface elements and invokes a program to generate code for the desired window system toolkit.

The developer then has to "fill in the blanks," specifying how the application interacts with the user interface by writing the necessary code.

Besides Devguide, some examples of user interface builders are ExoCODE™ from Expert Object Corporation, Builder Xcessory™ from ICS, Xbuild™ from Nixdorf, and UIMX™ from Visual Edge Software.

What is a User Interface Management System (UIMS)?

A UIMS is a system for designing user interfaces that abstracts the user interface design from an application, then provides a dialog mechanism (often a separate language) for linking the user interface with the application. A UIMS typically includes a user interface builder as part of the product. In other words, a UIMS is a superset of a user interface builder.

With a UIMS, a designer separately specifies what a user interface looks like, how the user interacts with the elements it contains, how the elements interact with each other, and how the user interface and the application communicate.

The primary advantage to using a UIMS is to keep the application and user interface separate from one another. Also, you could make changes to the user interface without having to recompile the underlying application.

A couple of other advantages of a UIMS are the ability to internationalize your user interface and to create a user-customizable user interface.

Some examples of UIMSs are TeleUSE from TeleSoft, and Interviews from Stanford University.

What is a User Interface Prototyper?

A user interface prototyper is a tool for mocking up the screen appearance of an application. You can quickly and easily build user interface elements on the screen, adjusting properties such as their location, size, and color. The major feature of a prototyper is the ease with which you can play with, test, and change the objects in the interface.

Some prototypers generate only pseudo-code and some produce real, compilable code. If you use a prototyper that generates pseudo-code, you'll know exactly what you want your interface to look like, but you'll have to start from scratch to produce the actual, executable code for it. In contrast, Devguide produces real application toolkit code.

5.7 Conclusion

Devguide is a useful tool for laying out user interface elements and for generating source code for these elements. Devguide shortens software development time, enables quick porting of applications from other hardware platforms, and facilitates the creation of quality user interfaces. Devguide eases the tasks of internationalizing and localizing applications by automating string translation and configuration, and by enabling the designer to group objects and lay them out relative to one another.

Integrating Applications on the Sun Desktop

6.1 Introduction

Desktop integration is the name given to a suite of technologies that allow seamless cooperation and interoperability between applications on the desktop. Desktop integration allows the following:

- Users can select data from one application, and drop it into a different application without regard to format.
- A data object on the desktop can be dragged to the Print Tool where it will be printed in the appropriate format.
- A user can attach an icon representing a desktop publishing file to a mail message. The message receiver could then open the document into the desktop publishing application by simply double-clicking the icon.
- Groupware. Applications can be developed that allow several people to work simultaneously on a document or program while the system automatically performs the various housekeeping chores such as updating files on the fly and informing other users of file changes.

Desktop integration lets applications share information and processes with other applications. This sharing results in a higher degree of communication, cooperation, and software productivity.

The guide is written for independent software vendors who have previous window programming experience, and who wish to integrate their applications with other applications on the SunSoft desktop. This guide presents an overview of desktop integration and its constituent technologies, selections and drag and drop, the Classing Engine, and ToolTalk services.

6.1.1
UNIX Evolution

OpenWindows desktop integration represents an evolutionary step in the growth and maturation of the UNIX® operating system. Although UNIX itself is an extremely powerful operating system, its command line interface is nonintuitive, cryptic, and difficult for most users to master. In recent years the UNIX command line interface has been supplanted by windowing systems interfaces such as the OPEN LOOK^{TM} graphical user interface, which provides a simpler and more intuitive way to control the system. By the end of 1990, there were more than 1000 OPEN LOOK applications programs offered by over 100 vendors.

Software Evolution

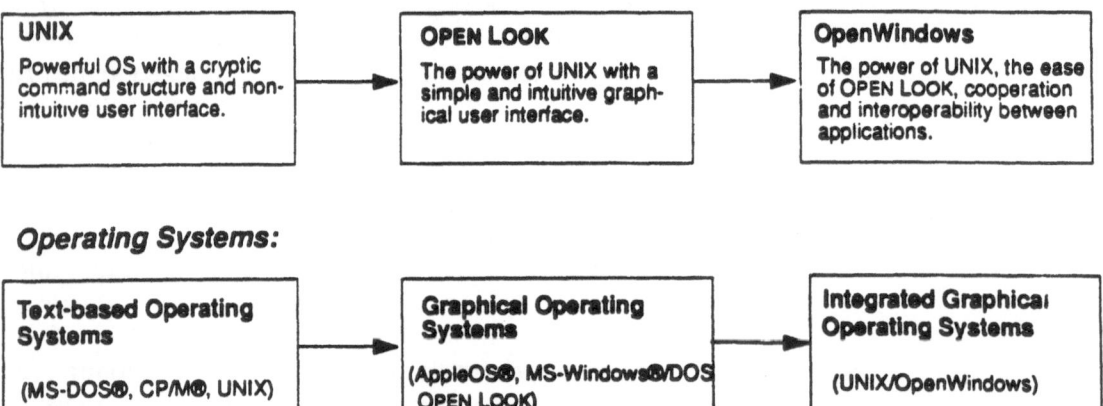

UNIX:

UNIX	OPEN LOOK	OpenWindows
Powerful OS with a cryptic command structure and non-intuitive user interface.	The power of UNIX with a simple and intuitive graphical user interface.	The power of UNIX, the ease of OPEN LOOK, cooperation and interoperability between applications.

Operating Systems:

Text-based Operating Systems	Graphical Operating Systems	Integrated Graphical Operating Systems
(MS-DOS®, CP/M®, UNIX)	(AppleOS®, MS-Windows®/DOS OPEN LOOK)	(UNIX/OpenWindows)

Chapter 6. Integrating Applications on the Sun Desktop

Although OPEN LOOK greatly increases the usability of UNIX, there are some limitations to the graphical interface: pathnames and other elements of command line UNIX still need to be manually specified on occasion. Furthermore, data exchange is severely limited by incompatible file formats, and cannot always be performed on files, folders, or other large units of data.

6.1.2 SunSoft's Desktop Integration Technologies

To move from the existing windowed user interface to a fully integrated desktop, the following enhancements are needed:

- A mechanism to provide a user-directed flow of information from one application to another. (Selections and drag and drop)
- A method for applications to determine the identity and operating characteristics of objects on the desktop. (Classing Engine)
- A mechanism for passing messages and commands between applications. (ToolTalk service)

These enhancements are the sum of three distinct technologies: selections and drag and drop, the Classing Engine, and the ToolTalk service. Together these OpenWindows technologies provide the desktop with a powerful cohesiveness and data interchangeability between applications.

Selections and Drag and Drop

These technologies allow users to exchange data between or within applications with a mouse. The user need not be concerned with the subtleties of moving data between applications, such as the data's format, or whether data translation is required. All of this is handled by the drag and drop API. Selections are covered in Section 6.2. Drag and drop is discussed in Section 6.3.

Application

Drag and drop can move data within an application. For example, a user can rearrange a text file by selecting text, dragging the text to a new position, and dropping (inserting) the text at that position.

Drag and drop can also move data between applications. An example of this would be copying data from Mail Tool and dropping it into a desktop publisher. Another example is copying an appointment from a mail message and dropping it onto Calendar Manager where it is properly entered.

| Implementation | Selections and drag and drop provide a communications link between an *owner* client (the client that owns the data) and a *requestor* client (the client that receives the data). All data transferred through selections and drag and drop is transferred through the X-server. Each toolkit (XView/OLIT/TNT) provides a selections and drag and drop API. Though the APIs for each toolkit are somewhat different, selection between the toolkits is seamless and invisible. |

Classing Engine

The Classing Engine identifies the characteristics, or *attributes*, of desktop objects. In other words, the Classing Engine stores attributes such as print method, icons, and file opening commands of desktop objects.

If an application is to interoperate with other objects, the application must be able to identify those objects and determine their various operation characteristics. That is, if the object is another application, can they intercommunicate? If the object is a file, can the application read it? Every object on the desktop must be readily identifiable-is it an ASCII file, a SunSoft DeskSet tool, a spreadsheet program, a spreadsheet data file, etc. The Classing engine provides a database for storing this information, and an API to access the information. Applications query the Classing Engine database to determine an object's type and the attributes associated with that object. The Classing Engine is discussed in Section 6.4.

| Application | File Manager, a DeskSet application shipped with OpenWindows, provides the best example of using the Classing Engine. File Manager graphically displays a UNIX file system as a set of folders (directories) and documents (files). Users can move, copy, and rearrange files by dragging and dropping file icons into directory icons. Files may be deleted by dropping icons into the waste basket icon. File Manager also uses information in the Classing Engine to allow users to double click on a file icon and open the file with its associated application. For example, double clicking on a spreadsheet data file icon opens the file into the spreadsheet program. Double clicking a desktop publishing file opens the file into the correct desktop publishing application. Using print instructions from the Classing Engine, File Manager also allows users to print a data file by dragging and dropping it on the Print Tool. |

Another feature of File Manager is that different file types are represented by different icons. Thus, one application's file will have one type of icon, and another application will have a different icon. again, the Classing Engine provides File Manager with the icon display information.

ToolTalk Service

As explained earlier in this book, the ToolTalk service is used by independent applications to communicate with each other without having direct knowledge of each other. Applications communicate by creating and sending ToolTalk messages. The ToolTalk service receives these messages, determines the recipients, and then delivers the messages to the appropriate applications.

To use ToolTalk on your application, you must first specify an existing message protocol. A message protocol is a set of ToolTalk messages that describe operations that applications agree to perform. By adopting a message protocol, applications can thus speak the same ToolTalk language. The message protocol specification includes the set of messages, as well as how applications will behave when they receive the messages. Refer to the first part of this book for further details on ToolTalk. Refer to Appendix D, "DeskSet Defined ToolTalk Messages," for a discussion on the DeskSet message protocol.

Application Example

In computer-aided software environments (CASE), the ToolTalk service provides a way to connect and coordinate individual programs in a programming environment. For this scenario, a tool manager, graphical debugger, call grapher, editor, and source browser are all tools used in this ToolTalk-based developer's environment. These tools have been modified to use the ToolTalk service and implement the messages shown in Table 6.1.1.

Table 6.1.1. CASE message protocol.

Message	Description
Started	Informs tool manager that this tool is started.
Stopped	Informs tool manager that this tool is stopped.
Launch	Requests a certain tool to start.
Quit	Requests a certain tool to stop.
Display	Requests that a tool that can edit a file load the file and scroll the file to a particular line number.
CallGraphFunction	Requests that a tool that can graph calls display the graph for this function in this file that is part of this program.

Message	Description
GetSelection	Requests that the tool with the current selection return the file name and line number.

To determine what's causing a particular error message, a programmer starts the tool manager, a program used to co-ordinate the development tools in the environment. From the tool manager, the programmer double-clicks on the source browser and graphical debugger icons to start them. The tool manager sends a Launch message to each tool and as they start, they send a Started message to the tool manager with initialization information.

The programmer loads a source code file in the source browser and finds out where the error message is located in the source code. After selecting the text of the error message, the programmer moves to graphical debugger and selects a "Set BreakPoint" menu item. The debugger sends a GetSelection message to the tools currently running in the environment (in this case, just the source browser.) The source browser returns the file name and line number and the debugger loads the file, moves to the line number, and sets the breakpoint.

The programmer then runs the program and locates the call that results in the error message. A feature of the debugger is the menu item, "Show Call Graph". After this menu item is selected, the debugger send a `CallGraphFunction` message. ToolTalk starts up the installed call grapher if one isn't already running and delivers the message.

The call grapher loads the call graph for the specified file and scrolls to the specified function. The programmer sees a sibling function that looks suspicious that's called just before the function producing the error. The programmer double-clicks on the sibling function and the call grapher sends a Display message.

The ToolTalk service starts an editor and delivers the Display message. The editor loads the file and scrolls to the specified line number where the engineer discovers an error. After fixing the error, the programmer needs to stop work and using the tool manager, asks that all tools be shut down. The tool manager sends Quit messages to all tools that are currently running. The tools clean up, send a reply to the Quit message, and exit.

Chapter 6. Integrating Applications on the Sun Desktop

6.1.3
ISV Registration

Maximum desktop integration requires public notice of application data types, naming conventions, custom icon design and ToolTalk message protocols. By making this information public, ISVs can be sure that their applications and data files are recognized by other applications. SunSoft provides a vehicle for making this information public through the Vendor Data Type Registration program. Independent software vendors can register the data type information for their applications with SunSoft. This information will be made available to other ISVs through the SunSoft SUCCESS database, an on-line electronic support service for software developers. Refer to Appendix C, "Vendor Data Type Registration," for details.

6.2
Selections

Selections are a mechanism for moving data between or within on-screen applications. Drag and drop, and the CUT, COPY, and PASTE command keys are two examples of how selections are used. The term *selection* refers to the way the user highlights an object, such as a block of text, a file icon, or a window, for moving or copying.

Selections are often used to move text. For instance, suppose you want to move a sentence from one location to another location.

1. Make the selection. Use the mouse to place the insert point at the start of the sentence and momentarily press the SELECT mouse button. Move the pointer to the end of the sentence and press the ADJUST mouse button; the *selection* will be highlighted in reverse video.[1]

2. Store the selection. Press the CUT key on the keyboard to temporarily store the selection in the clipboard.

3. Insert the data. Use the mouse to place the insert point at the desired location. Insert the text by pressing the PASTE key.

Selections provide a communications link between a *holder* client (the client which owns the data) and a *requestor* client (the client that receives the data). All data transferred through selections is transferred through the X-server. Each toolkit (XView/OLIT/TNT) provides a selections API. Although the API for each toolkit are somewhat different, selections between the toolkits are seamless and invisible.

---

1. Another selection method is to place the insert point at the beginning of the sentence, press the SELECT mouse button and hold it down as you "wipe" across the text to the end of the sentence, then release the button.

User interface conventions for selections are outlined in the *OPEN LOOK GUI Functional Specification*. For further selections programming instructions, refer to the *XView Programming Manual* and *XView Reference Manual* from O'Reilly and Associates, *The NeWS Toolkit 3.0 Reference Manual* from SunSoft, and *The X Window System Programming and Applications with Xt, OPEN LOOK Edition* from Prentice Hall. These documents are provided with the OpenWindows Version 3 Release.

XView and OLIT selection examples are at `$OPENWIN-HOME/share/src/dig_samples/olit_sel.c` and `xview_sel.c`.

6.2.1
Selections Outline

Selections provide a well-defined method of implementing the COPY and PASTE keys. The following outline describes the generic steps for implementing the COPY and PASTE with any of the OpenWindows toolkits.

Selections communicate between an owner client and a requestor client. The *owner* client has the data representing the value of the selection. The *requestor* client desires the value that the selection provides. Selection code is required for both the owner and requestor clients. Refer to the Inter-Client Communications Conventions Manual (ICCCM) for a detailed discussion of the selections protocol.

Selection Owner

1. Mark Selection

   Visual feedback of the selected object should be provided to the user. For example, the selection can be shown by displaying the selected text in reverse video.

2. Make Selection

   When the user presses the COPY key, create a selection holder and set the other attributes required by the application.

   Note that a conversion procedure must be written to handle conversion requests from the selection requestor. The request for text is handled automatically.

3. Associate Data

   Associate selection (highlighted text) with the owner client. If the selection is currently owned, the owner receives an event and is expected to do the following:

- Convert the contents of the selection to the requested data type
- Place this data in the named property on the named window
- Send the requestor an event to let it know the property is available.

Selection Requestor

1. PASTE Event

The event handler must detect the PASTE event, so that the PASTE operation (selection request) can be initiated.

2. Request Data

Request data from the owner client. Post a request to get data from the selection owner. The owner has the data representing the value of its selection, and the requestor client wishing to obtain the value of a selection provides:

- The name of the selection
- The name of a property
- A window
- An atom representing the data type required.

6.2.2 Implementing Selections with DeskSet

Call the SunSoft Catalyst Information Center (see Appendix C, "Vendor Data Type Registration,") for information on the selection protocol for DeskSet. Note, however, that ICCCM currently does not specify the protocol supported by Desk-Set. The current DeskSet selection protocol may change to comply with future ICCCM specifications.

6.3
Drag and Drop

Drag and drop is an implementation of selections which allows users to select a data object (text block, graphic, audio object, file icon, etc.) with the mouse, drag it across the screen, and drop it into another application for usage. For example, a text file icon can be selected, dragged to the Print Tool, and dropped, where it is printed. Another example would be dropping a spreadsheet data file onto a spreadsheet application icon where it will be loaded and displayed on the screen. Note that drag and drop differs from the CUT, COPY, and PASTE command keys in that it is not limited to moving only text blocks, but can move complete data objects.

Applications that implement drag and drop can exchange data with other applications. Drag and drop, like selections, has a different API for the XView, TNT, and OLIT toolkits. Once implemented in a client, however, drag and drop works invisibly and seamlessly among all three toolkits.

This chapter discusses the following:

- Drag and drop user interface
- The steps required to implement drag and drop in one of the three toolkits
- A detailed example of drag and drop as implemented in the XView environment.

For further drag and drop programming instructions, refer to the *XView Programming Manual* and *XView Reference Manual* from O'Reilly and Associates, *The NeWS Toolkit 3.0 Reference Manual* from SunSoft, and *The X Window System Programming and Applications with Xt, OPEN LOOK Edition* from Prentice Hall. These documents are provided with the OpenWindows Version 3 Release.

6.3.1
Drag and Drop
User Interface

To implement drag and drop, you must understand the drag and drop user interface. This section briefly describes this interface for purposes of terminology. Refer to Appendix A, "Drag and Drop User Interface Specification" for descriptions of:

- the kinds of objects that can be dragged
- the meanings of dropping objects on specific locations (such as on a window header, on a pane in a window, or on a drag and drop target)
- the differences between dragging with and without the DUPLICATE modifier key held down
- the visual feedback associated with the stages of drag and drop operation
- how the process of data translation appears to users
- how users can cancel drag operations in progress, and undo completed drag operations
- how error messages are presented to users.

Overview

Drag and drop allows users to transfer data objects using the mouse among or within applications. A drag and drop action consists of a *source* (object to be transferred), and a *destination* (the place where the source will be dropped). Before an object can be dragged or dropped, it must be *selected*. There are two types of objects that can be selected: a *data span* or glyph. A data span is a segment of on-screen data. It can be a segment of text, digitized audio, video, and so forth. A glyph is an on-screen representation of some object, such as a file, application, or directory.

A data span can be selected in three ways: the wipe method, the select-adjust method, and the multi-click method. With the wipe method you place the pointer at the beginning of the data span, press the SELECT button, drag the mouse to the end of the selection, and release the mouse. In the select-adjust method, you place the pointer at the beginning of the selection and click the SELECT button to select the starting point. Then you move the pointer to the end of the desired span and click the ADJUST button on the mouse to make the selection. With the multi-click method you rapidly press the SELECT button to select increasingly larger segments of the segment. For example, two rapid clicks selects a word, three a line, and four a paragraph. A selected data span is displayed in reverse video.

Glyphs are selected by simply clicking the SELECT button on the glyph. To select additional glyphs, click ADJUST on additional glyphs.

Initiating the Drag

Drag and drop can be initiated as either a *cut-and-paste* or a *copy-and-paste* operation. In a cut-and-paste operation. the original object is deleted after it is dropped. In a copy-and-paste operation, the original object remains after the object is dropped on a destination--the original object is not deleted.

Visual Feedback

Drag and drop requires visual feedback to inform the user of the status of the drag. At a minimum, once an object is selected, the pointer should change appearance and a representation of the object should follow the pointer as the mouse is moved. In addition, the pointer should indicate the receptivity of potential drop sites. The drag and drop specification includes details about changes in pointer appearance and other visual feedback associated with drag operations.

The Drop

The final action in the drag and drop gesture is to drag the selection over the destination object and release the SELECT mouse button. The destination is determined by the position of the pointer's hot spot at the time the user releases the SELECT button.

Applications supporting drops other than a simple cut or copy sometimes require a specific drop site, referred to as a *drag and drop target*. A drag and drop target is a graphical element located in the control area of an open window. In addition to serving as the destination in drag and drop operations, drag and drop targets sometimes contain a glyph which can be used as the source in a drag and drop operation.

6.3.2 Implementing Drag and Drop

The following sections summarize the toolkit independent processes required for sourcing drags and receiving drops.

Sourcing a Drag

To adapt an application to source a drag, the following steps are required:

1. Define a drag and drop object and associate a drag pointer with it. The window manager will use the drag pointer to provide visual feedback to the user when the object is selected.

2. Associate a selection with your drag and drop object that will contain the data you want to make available to the target.

3. Provide an event callback procedure for your drag and drop object that will detect when it has been dragged. Set the actual data in the data object for the source to retrieve, and wait for a source response or error condition.

Depending on the application, you may also want to perform the following:

4. Define a section conversion procedure for your own data types.

5. Provide the data through an alternate transport mechanism (ATM), such as sockets or the ToolTalk service.

Receiving a Drop

To adapt your application to receive drops, the following steps are required:

1. Define a drop site and associate an event procedure with it.

2. (Optional) Provide an image for drop site previewing which will provide visual feedback when the pointer is over the drop site.

3. In your event callback procedure, determine the event type and obtain data from the source selection.

Depending on the application, you may also need to do the following:

4. Provide drop site feedback when pointer enters and leaves the drop site.

5. Use and alternate transport method (ATM) such as sockets or the ToolTalk service to transfer data if your application design requires it.

6.3.3
Drag and Drop Programming Example: XView Toolkit

This program, $OPENWINHOME/share/src/dig_samples/sview_dnd.c, illustrates the use of drag and drop using the XView toolkit. When the program is executed, it opens a text window with a drag and drop target. Users may drag any text file from the file manager and drop it on the windows drop site. The text will be displayed in the text pane and the filename path will appear in the window header. The file can also be imported by entering the filename in the window header.

The document can be exported by dragging the drag and drop target to another window. A portion of the text can be moved by selecting the desired text and dropping it at a specific insert point. An OLIT example can be found at `$OPEN-WINHOME/share/src/dig_samples/olit_dnd.c`.

Overview of the Functions

main()	Calls DnD_init() and create_user_interface
create_user_interface()	Creates the frame and text window
DnD_init()	Crates drop site & drag object
drop_proc()	Event callback procedure; the event procedure for the drop
get_primary_selection()	Called from drop_proc(); gets the data from the source.
load_file_proc()	Event callback procedure; callback that displays the file name on the panel.

Opening Declarations

The program begins with a comment giving the correct compile command. The compiler includes directives, and the global object definitions. Note that the header file `dragdrop.h` is only distributed with OpenWindows Version 3.

Four data types are defined:

Frame	Pointer to opaque structure defining the frame
Panel	Pointer to opaque structure defining the panel
Textsw	Pointer to opaque structure defining the text subwindow
Panel_item	Pointer to opaque structure defining a panel item (the load_file prompt)

A structure with two members (atom and *name) is declared to store three server atoms. It is initialized with zeros at this time. Actual server atom values will be loaded during the initialization (in the `DnD_init()` function called later). Note that the structure does not have a formal name declared. A formal structure name is not required when a structure is declared if the storage is allocated at the same time.

```
/*
 * dnd_dig_sample.c
 * compile: cc -I$OPENWINHOME/include dig_dnd_sample.c -lxview -lolgx -lX11
 */

#include <xview/xview.h>
#include <xview/panel.h>
#include <xview/text sw.h>
#include <xview/dragdrop.h>
#include <xview/xv_xrect.h>

                                        /*Global Object definitions */

Frame           frame;
Panel           panel;
Textsw          textsw;
Panel_item      load_file;

#define FILE_NAME_ATOM               0
#define _SUN_AVAILABLE_TYPES_ATOM    1
#define XA_STRING_ATOM               2
#define TOTAL_ATOMS                  3

struct
{
      Atom    atom;
      char    *name;
} atom_list[TOTAL_ATOMS] =
{
      {0,     "FILE_NAME"},
      {0,     "_SUN_AVAILABLE_TYPES"},
      {0,     "XA_STRING"}, };

Drag_drop       drag_object;                 /* The drag object */
```

Chapter 6. Integrating Applications on the Sun Desktop

Function: Main()

The program's main function is straightforward. Two functions without return values, create_user_interface() and DnD_init(), are declared. The xv_init() procedure establishes connections with the X server, initializes the Notifier, reads the ~/.Xdefaults database and reads any passed arguments.

The program then calls the two functions: create_user_interface() creates the frame, the panel, and the text sub window; DnD_init() creates the drop site and the drag object.

Finally, xv_main_loop() is executed, telling the Notifier to start dispatching events.

```
main (argc, argv)
int argc; char *argv[];
{
    Xv_Server server;

    void create_user_interface(), Dnd_init() ;
    server = xv_init (XV_INIT_ARGC_PTR_ARGV, &argc, argv, NULL) ;
    create_user_interface() ;
    Dnd_init (server) ; xv_main_loop (frame) ;
}
```

Function: create_user_interface()

The create_user_interface() function, called from main(), uses the xv_create() procedure call to create the frame, the panel, the panel text (the file name prompt), and the text subwindow where the file is displayed. Notice that the xv_create() procedure with the load_file handle that creates the "Filename:" prompt also registers the load_file_proc() function with the Notifier.

```
/* create_user_interface: Create the user interface components. */
void
create_user_interface()
{
      Panel_setting load_file_proc() ;
      frame = xv_create (NULL, FRAME,
                    XV_LABEL,                  "Drag-n-Drop Demo",
                    XV_WIDTH,                  600,
                    XV_HEIGHT,                 300,
                    FRAME_SHOW__FOOTER,        TRUE,
                    NULL) ;

      panel = xv_create (frame, PANEL,
                    XV_X,                      0,
                    XV_Y,                      0,
                    XV_WIDTH,                  WIN_EXTEND_TO_EDGE,
                    XV_HEIGHT,                 50,
                    NULL) ;

      load_file = xv_create (panel, PANEL_TEXT,
                    PANEL_VALUE_DISPLAY_LENGTH,   45,
                    PANEL_VALUE_STORED_LENGHT,    80,
                    PANEL_LABEL_STRING,           "Filename:",
                    PANEL_LAYOUT,                 PANEL_HORIZONTAL
                    PANEL_READ_ONLY,              FALSE,
                    PANEL_NOTIFY_PROC,            load_file_proc,
                    NULL) ;

      textsw = xv_create (frame, TEXTSW,
                    WIN_BELOW,                 panel,
                    XV__WIDTH,                 WIN_EXTEND_TO_EDGE,
                    XV_HEIGHT,                 WIN_EXTEND_TO_EDGE,
                    NULL) ;
      }
```

Function: Dnd_init()   The Dnd_init() function creates the drag and drop target as well as the drag and drop target "busy" glyph. The for loop gets the three server atoms and loads them into the structure (which was declared in the global object definitions at the beginning of the program). Note that the last xv_create() procedure registers the drop_proc() function with the Notifier.

Chapter 6. Integrating Applications on the Sun Desktop

```
/*  DnD_init: Create a drop site, and a drag object.  */

void
DnD_init (server)
Xv_Server server;
{
      Xv_drop_site drop_site;
      Xv_opaque drop_glyph;
      Xv_opaque busy_glyph;

      static unsigned short drop_icon [] = {
#include "drop_site.icon"
      };
      static unsigned short busy_icon [] = {
#include "busy_site.icon"
      };

      int i;

      for (i = 0; i < TOTAL_ATOMS; i++)
      {
            atom_list [i].atom = xv_get (server,
                        SERVER_ATOM,
                        atom_list [i].name);
      }

atom_list [XA_STRING_ATOM] .atom = XA_STRING;

drag_object = xv_create (panel, DRAGDROP, NULL);

drop_glyph = xv_create (XV_NULL, SERVER_IMAGE,
            SERVER_IMAGE_BITS             drop_icon,
            SERVER_IMAGE_DEPTH,           1,
            XV_WIDTH,                     32,
            XV_HEIGHT,                    32,
            NULL);

busy_glyph = xv_create (XV_NULL, SERVER_IMAGE,
            SERVER_IMAGE_BITS,            busy_icon,
            SERVER_IMAGE_DEPTH,           1,
            XV_WIDTH,                     32,
            XV_HEIGHT,                    32,
            NULL) ;

xv_create (panel, PANEL_DROP_TARGET,
            PANEL_DROP_DND,               drag_object,
            PANEL_DROP_GLYPH,             drop_glyph,
            PANEL_DROP_BUSY_GLYPH,        busy_glyph,
            PANEL_NOTIFY_PROC,            drop_proc,
            PANEL_DROP_FULL,              TRUE,
            NULL);
}
```

Function: drop_proc()   The `drop_proc()` routine is the event callback procedure
that initiates the drag and drop operation. If the operation is
a drag, the case statement handles it either as a move or a
copy. If the operation is a drag from the drag and drop target,
the third case statement (`LOC_DRAG`) is used. This code determines whether the filename or the data string is passed.

This first `xv_create()` associates the selection targets
with a corresponding selection atom. The second `xv_cre-
ate()` will determine if a filename is being passed, and the
third, if the text string is to be passed. In addition, the message "Start dragging" is printed in the lower left of the frame.
Notice that the argument lists of `xv_create()` and `xv_
set()` are variable length and must be terminated with
NULL statements.

The `create_user_interface()` function, described
earlier, registers `drop_proc()` with the Notifier.

```
/* drop_proc: Set up the drag operation and handle the drop. */

void
drop_proc(item, value, event)
Xv_opaque    item;
unsigned int value;
Event        *event;
{
        long                  length;
        int                   format;
        char                  *sel_string;
        Selection_requestor   sel_req;
        char                  *buff;
        int                   txt_len;
        Atom                  list[4];

        static void           get_primary_selection();

        sel_req = xv_get (item, PANEL_DROP_SEL_REQ);

        printf("sel_req = %X/n", sel_req);
        switch(event_action(event))
        {
        case  ACTION_DRAG_MOVE:            /* they are moving the object */
                printf("drag move\n");
                get_primary_selection (sel_req);
                break;

        case ACTION_DRAG_COPY:             /* they are copying the object */
                printf("drag copy\n");
                get_primary_selection (sel_req);
                break;
        case LOC_DRAG:
                list [0] = atom_list [_SUN_AVAILABLE_TIMES_ATOM].atom;
                list [1] = atom_list [FILE_NAME_ATOM].atom;
                list [2] = atom_list [XA_STRING_ATOM].atom;
                list [3] = NULL;
```

```
        xv_create (drag_object, SELECTION_ITEM,
                SEL_DATA,                   list,
                SEL_FORMAT,                 32,
                SEL_LENGTH,                 4,
                SEL_TYPE,         atom_list[_SUN_AVAILABLE_TYPES_ATO M].atom,
                SEL_OWN,                    TRUE,
                NULL);

        string = (char *) xv_get (load_file, PANEL_VALUE);

        xv_create (drag_object, SELECTION_ITEM,
                SEL_DATA,                   string,
                SEL_FORMAT,                 8,
                SEL_LENGTH,                 strlen (string),
                SEL_TYPE,                   atom_list[FILE_NAME_ATOM].atom,
                SEL_OWN                     TRUE,
                NULL);

        txt_len = xv_get (textsw, TESTSW_LENGTH) + 1;
        string = (char *) calloc (txt_len, 1);
        xv_get (textsw,
                TEXTSW_CONTENTS, 0, string, txt_len);

        xv_create(drag_object, SELECTION_ITEM,
                SEL_DATA,                   string,
                SEL_FORMAT,                 8,
                SEL_LENGTH,                 strlen (string),
                SEL_TYPE,                   atom_list[XA_STRING_ATOM].atom,
                SEL_OWN                     TRUE,
                NULL);

        xv_set (frame,
                FRAME_LET_FOOTER, "Start dragging",
                NULL);
                printf("Start dragging\n");
                break;
        default:
                printf ("unknown event %d\n", event_action (event));
        }
}
```

Function: get_primary_selection()

The get_primary_selection() function is called from either the move or copy switch statements of the drop_proc() callback function. This function will get data from the source in the format mutually agreed upon. The first xv_ get() function determines from the passed atom the selection datatype. If the selection is a filename, the text string is retrieved from the file and placed in the text subwindow. If the selection is a text string, the last xv_get() function retrieves the string and places it in the text subwindow.

```
void
get_primary_selection (sel_req)
Selection_requestor sel_req;
{
        long            length;
        int             format char *sel_string;
        char            *sel_string;
        char            *string;
        Atom            *list;
        int             i;

        list =NULL;
    xv_set (sel_req, SEL_TYPE, atom_list[_SUN_AVAILABLE_TYPES_ATOM].atom, 0);
        list = (Atom *) xv_get(sel_req, SEL_DATA, &length, &format);
        if (length == SEL_ERROR)
        {
                printf ("*** Unable to get target list .\n");
        }
        else
        {
                printf ("length = %d format = %d\n", length, format);
                while (*list)
                {
                        printf ("list = %X\n", list);
                        for (i = 0; i < TOTAL_ATOMS; i++)
                        {
                                if (*list == atom_list [i] .atom)
                                {
                                        printf ("supports %d %s\n", i,
                                        atom_list [i] .name);
                                        break;
                                }
                        }
                        list++;
```

```
xv_set(sel_req, SEL_TYPE, atom_list[FILE_NAME_ATOM].atom, 0);
      string = (char *) xv_get (sel_req, SEL_DATA, &length, &format);
      if (length != SEL_ERROR)
      {
            printf ("length = %d format = %d\n", length, format);

            /* Create a NULL-terminated version of 'string' */

            sel_string = (char*) calloc (1, length + 1);
            strncpy (sel_string, string, length);
            xv_set (load_file, PANEL_VALUE, string, NULL);
            xv_set (textsw,
                    TEXTSW_FILE, string,
                    NULL);
            return;
      }
      else
      }
            printf ("*** Unable to get FILE_NAME_ATOM selection. \n");
      }
      xv set(sel_req, SEL_TYPE, atom_list [XA_STRING_ATOM] .atom, 0);
      string = (char *) xv_get (sel_req, SEL_DATA, & length, &format);
      if (length != SEL_ERROR)
      {
            printf("length = %d format = %d\n", length, format);

             /* Create a NULL-terminated version of 'string' */

            sel_string = (char *) calloc (1, length + 1);
            strncpy (sel_string, string, length);

            textsw _reset (textsw, 0, 0);
            textsw_insert (textsw, string, length);
      }
      else
      {
            printf ("*** Unable to get XA_STRING_ATOM selection. \n";
      }
}
```

Function: load_file_ proc()

The function load_file_proc() is the event callback procedure that loads the selected file into the text subwindow when the user enters a valid file name followed by a RETURN.

```
/* Notify callback function for 'filename'. This routine loads the
 * named file into the textpane. */

Panel_setting
load_file_proc (item, event)
      Panel_item      item;
      Event           *event;
{
      char *value = (char *) xv_get (item, PANEL_VALUE);

      fprintf(stderr, "DnD_demo: load_file: value: %s\n", value);

      xv_set(textsw,
              TEXTSW_FILE, value,
              NULL);

      return panel_text_notify (item, event);
}
```

6.3.4 Data Type Registration

If a receiving application is to receive a droop from a source application, the source application must sent the data in a format readable by the receiving application.[1] For example, if Text Editor wishes to drop data into Mail Tool, Text Editor must be able to convert the data to a format which Mail Tool can read. Conversely, if Mail Tool wishes to drop data into Text Editor, Mail Tool must be able to convert the data to a format text Editor can read.

Although the source application is responsible for converting data to a format readable by the receiving application, it also behooves the receiving application to be able to receive data in some of the more common data formats like ASCII, Sun raster imaging, or PostScript page description language.

Programmatically, drag and drop handshaking works as follows:

- data is selected from the source application
- data is sent (dropped) on the receiving application
- receiving application requests a list of the data formats in which the source application can send the drop
- source application replies with a list of data formats

1. In this discussion we use data format and data type interchangeably.

- receiving application tells the source application in which format it would like the data sent
- data is transferred.

A source application must have data conversion routines for each application to which it wishes to drop data. Creating conversion routines consists of finding out the data format of the desired drop applications, and writing conversion routines specifically for those formats.[1] Again, if you wish your application to be able to receive drops from other applications, ensure that your application can receive data in some of the more common data formats.

SunSoft has undertaken a data type registration program to help standardize the data format names by which applications request data formats from each other. SunSoft encourages all companies that wish to share their data with other applications to register data format names for their application's data. This name will be used by other applications to reference desired data formats. Refer to Appendix C, "Vendor Data Type Registration" for more information on data type registration.

A central repository for data format names as well as additional format information will be available on SUCCESSsm, the SunSoft on-line electronic support service for Sun's software developers.

6.3.5 Implementing Drag and Drop with DeskSet

Call the Sunsoft Catalyst Information Center (Appendix C, "Vendor Data Type Registration") for information on the selection, and drag and drop protocol for DeskSet. Note, however, that ICCCM currently does not specify the protocol supported by DeskSet. The current DeskSet protocol may change to comply with future ICCCM specifications.

---

1. Refer to the receiving application's manuals or call the company that produces the receiving application for details of the data format.

6.4
Classing
Engine

The Classing Engine (CE) identifies the characteristics, or *attributes*, of files. The CE specifies attributes such as print method, icons, and opening commands for specific *file types*. File type is defined by a file's format (e.g., ASCII, PostScript, and Sun raster files), its parent application (FrameMaker® and Lotus 1-2-3® data files) or the application executable itself (File Manager, Mail Tool, or Wingz® executable file).

The CE consists of two parts: a database which stores file type names and attributes, and a collection of routines which query the database. Some of the more common file attributes are:

- A content string, or filename pattern to identify the file type
- Directory location of a file type icon
- Foreground and background colors of a file type icon
- Print command of a file type, if applicable
- Edit, display, or open command of a file.

Other attributes, such as data exchange filters, text compression procedures, and ToolTalk attributes can be associated with a file type as well—the CE is completely extensible. In addition, it is also possible to add custom databases for other data objects to the CE.

The CE acts as a central repository for all file types and their attributes. The CE also provides applications with a set of routines for determining a file's type and retrieving its attributes.

This chapter describes the CE technology and how one program, File Manager (a graphical file and directory tool shipped with OpenWindows) uses it. The CE can be used similarly in any desktop application.

Note – The CE is currently used by both the File Manager and the ToolTalk services. This chapter only discusses the CE as it relates to the technology used in File Manager. Refer to ToolTalk documentation for details on ToolTalk usage.

6.4.1
File Type
Registration

Before an application can access a file's attributes, the file and its attributes must be in the CE database. This requires that the file's originators, typically the vendor whose application created the file, incorporate the file's type and its attributes into the CE database. File types can be incorporated into the CE database in the following ways:

1. Software vendors may register file types and their attributes with SunSoft through the Vendor Data Type Registration program. The new file types will be incorporated into the CE database and distributed in subsequent CE releases. Refer to Appendix C, "Vendor Data Type Registration," for detailed registration instructions.

2. Software vendors may use the CE utilities in their software installation process to update their user's CE databases with new file type information. Thus, a vendor's application can, as part of the installation process, enter its file types and attributes into the CE database.

3. Users can use CE utilities or Binder, a DeskSet application, to enter new file type information into the CE database.

6.4.2 Classing Engine Usage

File Manager, displayed in Figure 6.4.1, provides an example of how the CE can be used. File Manager is a DeskSet application that graphically displays a UNIX file system. Users may move, copy and delete files by dragging and dropping file icons onto directory icons, or onto a wastebasket icon. In addition, File Manager allows users to double-click on a data file icon to open the file in its parent application (file opening commands are stored in the CE database). For example, double-clicking in a spreadsheet data file could start the spreadsheet application program and open the data file. Double-clicking on an ASCII file will open the file with the Text Editor. File Manager also lets users print a data file by simply dropping the file's icon on the Print Tool.

Another feature of the File Manager is that different file types are represented by different icons. Thus, one application's files will have one icon, and the files of another application will have a different icon. Unique icons allow users to identify a file without opening it. File Manager retrieves the icon location from the CE. Refer to the *OpenWindows Version 3 DeskSet Reference Manual* for details on how to use File Manager.

6.4.3 Adding and Changing CE File Types and Attributes

Adding or changing file types and attributes in the CE consists of changing the CKE database to reflect these new filetypes and attributes. Before discussing how to do this, it is necessary to discuss the structure of the CE database.

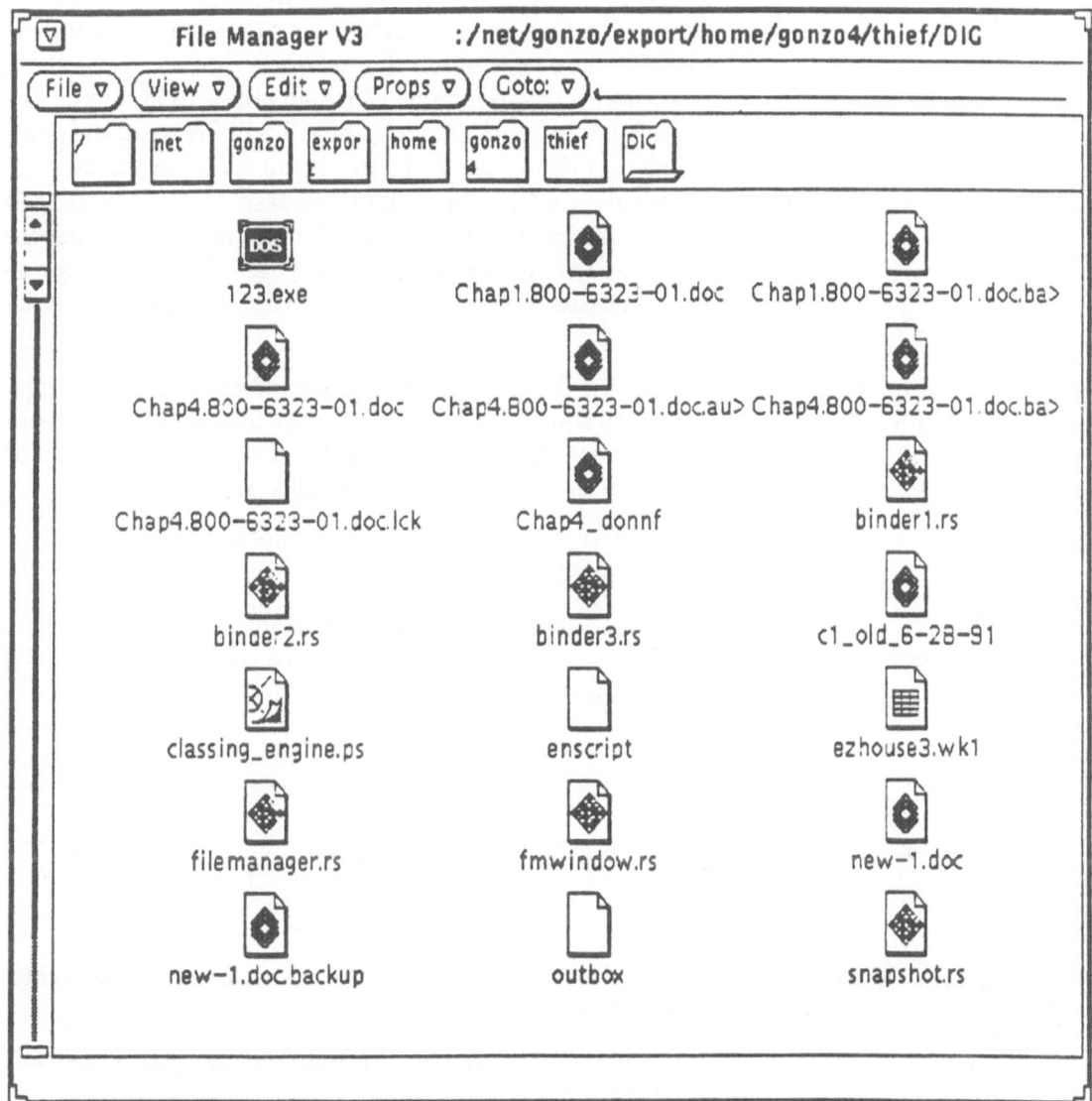

Figure6.4.1. File manager.

Classing Engine Database

The CE database contains file type names, identification patterns, and attributes, The CE database is one logical database that is the composite of three physical databases called the *user, system,* and *network* databases. Multiple databases allow users to personalize their environment while still having access to global data.

The user database is unique to each user and resides in the user's directory structure, the system portion is common to all users on that specific machine, and the network portion is available to everyone on the network. The CE treats these three portions as overlays. When an application queries the CE database for information, the CE will first read the entry in the user database. If an entry is not found in the user database, the CE tries the system database, and finally the network database. This assures that any CE database information network information is used. The following discussion treats the three databases as a single aggregate database.

Default Location of Classing Engine Databases

Each of the three Classing Engine databases has a default location, as shown in Table 6.4.1. These files are in a non-readable format. To convert these files into an ASCII-readable format, use the `ce_db_build` utility as follows:

```
ce_db_build <user | system | network> -to_ascii
<file name>
```

Table 6.4.1. Default Classing engine database locations.

database	default location
user	~/.cetables/cetables
system	/etc/cetables/cetables
network	$OPENWINHOME/lib/cetables/ cetables

Namespace Tables

Each CE database file consists of two *namespace tables*, which are data base of file entries:

- A *files namespace table*, containing file type names and identifiers
- A *types namespace table*, which stores file type attributes.

Both of these namespace tables are resident in the same file. A third namespace table for ToolTalk services is also in this file, but is not included in this discussion. To view the namespace tables use the `ce_db_build` command described in the previous section.

Each namespace table has an accompanying *namespace manager*, a collection of routines used to query that namespace table. Future releases of the CE will permit ISVs

File Type Identification

to define unique namespace tables and write custom namespace manager libraries.

Before an application can use a file's attributes, the application must identify, or *derive*, the file type. In other words, it must determine whether a file is an ASCII file, Mail Tool executable file, PostScript file, and so forth. Two methods are used to determine file types: type-by-*pattern* or type-by-*content*.

Typing by pattern involves matching the filename with a filename pattern. For example, all files whose names end in .c are C source files, all files that end in .exe are DOS executable files, and all files that end in .ps are PostScript files.

Typing by *content* involves matching the contents of a file to a pre-defined string or number. For example, files that have the string WNGZWZSS as their first characters are Wingz worksheet files. Files that contain <Framemaker as its first characters are FrameMaker files. This is similar to the procedure that is used by the standard UNIX file command which uses the /etc/magic file.

Files Namespace Table

The files namespace table contains entries which are used to derive file types. A excerpt of a files namespace table is shown below.

```
NS_NAME =Files                                        # Beginning of Files namespace table
NS_ATTR= ((NS_MANAGER, junk, <$CEPATH/fns_mgr.so>))# The Files namespace manager
 NS_ENTRIES=(
( . . .
      (FNS_TYPE, refto-Types, <filemgr-prog>)         # File type = File Manager
      (FNS_FILENAME, str, <filemgr>)                  # File pattern = filemgr
) ( . . .
      (FNS_TYPE, refto-Types, <mailtool-prog>)        # File type = Mailtool program
   (FNS FILENAME, str, <mailtool>)                    # File pattern = mailtool
  ) ( . . .
      (FNS_TYPE, refto-Types, <lotus-spreadsheet>)# File type = lotus spreadsheet
      (FNS_FILENAME, str, <*.wk?>)                    # File pattern = *.wk?
) ( . . .
      (FNS_TYPE, refto-Types, <msdos-executable>      # File type = MS DOS Application
      (FNS_FILENAME, str, <*.exe>)                    # File pattern = *.exe
) ( . . .
      (FNS_TYPE, refto-Types, <c-file>)               # File type = C source file
      (FNS_FILENAME, str, <*.c>)                      # File pattern = *.c
) ( . . .
      (FNS_TYPE, refto-Types, <sun-raster)            # File type = Sun Raster
      (FNS_MAGIC_OFFSET,str,<0>)                      # Offset = 0 bytes
      (FNS_MAGIC_MATCH,str,<0x4d4d002a>               # Content Pattern = 0x4d4d002a
      (FNS_MAGIC_TYPE,str,<long>)                     # Content Type = long int
) ( . . .
      (FNS_TYPE,refto-Types,<framemaker-document>)# File type = Framemaker Document
      (FNS_MAGIC_OFFSET,str,<0>)                      # Offset = 0 bytes
      (FNS_MAGIC_MATCH,str,<<MakerFile>)              # Content Pattern = <Makefile
      (FNS_MAGIC_TYPE,str,<string>)                   # Content Type = string
) ( . . .
      (FNS_TYPE,refto_Types,<sunwrite-document>)      # File Types =SunWrite Document
      (FNS_MAGIC_OFFSET,str,<3>)                      # Offset = 3 bytes
      (FNS_MAGIC_MATCH,str,<pgscriptver>)             # Content pattern = pgscriptver
      (FNS_MAGIC_TYPE,str,<string>)                   # Content Type = String
) ( . . .
      (FNS_TYPE,refto-Types,<postscript-file>)        # File type = Postscript file
      (FNS_FILENAME,str,<*.ps>)                       # File pattern = *.ps
) (
      (FNS_TYPE,refto-Types,<postscript-file>)        # File type = Postscript file
      (FNS_MAGIC_OFFSET,str,<0>                       # Offset = 0 bytes
      (FNS_MAGIC_MATCH,str,<%!>)                       # Content Pattern = %!
      (FNS_MAGIC_TYPE,str,<string>)                   # Content Type = String
) ( . . .
```

Entries in the files namespace table consist of the following arguments:

`FNS_TYPE`, or *file type name*, is the name (identifier) assigned to a file type. In the following example, the file type name for the File Manager program is `filemgr-prog`. The file type name for Lotus 1-2-3 R spreadsheet files is `lotus-spreadsheet`.

`FNS_FILENAME` is the file name pattern which identifies a file's type. The file name pattern is used to match a file name to its type. For example, a file ending with `.c` is a C Source file. A file ending with `.exe` is a DOS executable file.

If a file type is derived with the type-by-content method, the file type entry requires these arguments:

`FNS_MAGIC_MATCH` or *magic match*, is a string contained on all files of the type specified by `FNS_TYPE`. Thus, all Frame-Maker document files contain the string `<MakerFile`. All PostScript files contain the string %!.

`FNS_MAGIC_TYPE` specifies the data type of the magic match. In the example, all type-by-content entries match with strings, except for sun-raster files which use a long integer.

`FNS_MAGIC_OFFSET` specifies the number of bytes preceding the magic match. As shown in the following example, `<MakerFile` starts at the first byte in a FrameMaker document file `pgscriptver` starts after the third byte in a Sun-Write document file.

If both a file name pattern and a magic match are defined like as shown in the PostScript example, a file must pass both tests before it is typed.

Types Namespace Table

The types namespace table contains the attribute values of the file types. Once a file type is derived, the CE can retrieve the files attributes from the types namespace table. An excerpt of a types namespace table is shown below.

```
NS_NAME=Types                                         # The namespace named "Types"
NS_ATTR= ((NS_MANAGER,string, <$CEPATH/tns_mgr.so>))# The Types namespace manager
NS_ENTRIES= (...
     (TYPE_NAME,type-id,<filemgr-prog>)
     (TYPE_ICON,icon-file,<$OPEONWINHOME/include/images/filemgr.icon>)
     (TYPE_BGCOLOR,color,<79 241 255>)
     (TYPE_PRINT,string,<lpr -Plp>)
  )( . . .
     (TYPE_NAME, type-id,<lotus-spreadsheet>)
     (TYPE_OPEN,call,<dos -c 123>)
     (TYPE_ICON,icon-file,<$OPENWINHOME/include/images/spreadsheet.icon>)
     (TYPE_ICON_MASK,icon-file,<$OPENWINHOME/include/images/doc.mask.icon>)
     (TYPE_BGCOLOR,color,<255 225 255>)
     (TYPE_TEMPLATE,string,<lotus%t.wks>)
  )( . . .
     (TYPE_NAME,type-id,<compress>)
     (TYPE_OPEN,call,<uncompress>)
     (TYPE_ENCODE_PROG,call,<compress>)
     (TYPE_ENCODE_ARGS,string,<-c>)
     (TYPE_DECODE_PROG,call,<uncompress>)
     (TYPE_DECODE ARGS,string,<-c>)
     (TYPE_ICON,icon_file,<$OPENWINHOME/include/images/compress.icon>)
     (TYPE_ICON_MASK,icon-file,<$OPENWINHOME/incluke/images/doc.mask.icon>)
     (TYPE_BGCOLOR,color,<255 0 0>)
     (TYPE_FILE_TEMPLATE,string,<data%t.Z>)
  )( . . .
     (TYPE_NAME,type-id,<default-app>)
     (TYPE_ICON,icon-file,<$OPENWINHOME/include/images/application.icon>)
     (TYPE_FGCOLOR,color,<0 0 0>)
     (TYPE_BGCOLOR,color,<183 229 193>)
  )(
     (TYPE_NAME,type-id,<default-doc>)
     (TYPE_OPEN,call,<textedit>)
     (TYPE_OPEN_TT,tt,<textedit>)
     (TYPE_PRINT,string,<cat $FILE | mp -lo | lpr -h>)
     (TYPE_ICON,icon-file,<$OPENWINHOME/include/images/doc.mask.icon>)
     (TYPE_FGCOLOR,color,<0 0 0>)
     (TYPE_BGCOLOR,color,<183 193 229>)
  )( . . .
```

Entries in the type namespace table consist of the following arguments:

TYPE_NAME is the name of the file type. TYPE_NAME matches FNS_TYPE in the files namespace table.

TYPE_ICON is the file containing the icon representation of the file type.

`TYPE_ICON_MASK` is the file containing the icon representation of file when it is selected.

`TYPE_BGCOLOR` specifies the background color of the file icon. Values are in red-green-blue (RGB) values ranging from 0 (lighter) to 255 (darker).

`TYPE_FGCOLOR` specifies the foreground color of the file icon in RGB values.

`TYPE_OPEN` specifies the command to open the file. (For File Manager this is triggered by a double mouse-click.)

`TYPE_PRINT` gives the print command for the file.

`TYPE_FILE_TEMPLATE` specifies a unique filename generated and used by the application as a filename identifier.

`TYPE_OPEN_TT` is the ToolTalk identifier used when starting applications.

The attribute entry for `compress` demonstrates CE extensibility. In addition to the standard attributes, `compress` file types have four additional attributes: `TYPE_ENCODE_PROG`, `TYPE_ENCODE_ARGS`, `TYPE_DECODE_PROG`, and `TYPE_DECODE_ARGS`. A program designer has added these attributes to compress file types in order to provide automatic file compression/decompression. For example, these attributes can be used to link large files to a mail message. Instead of pasting the file into the message, the file could be automatically (using the UNIX compress command) when the file glyph is selected and dropped on the mail tool. The compressed file appears as a file glyph. After the message is sent, the file is automatically decompressed when the file glyph is selected.

The last two entries of the code segment, `default-app` and `default-doc`, demonstrate two other interesting features. Each represents the attributes of undefined data and application files. If a file does not have a definition in the files namespace, it is given a set of generic attributes depending on whether it is an application or document.

Adding a New File Type

The basic steps for adding a new file type to the CE database are as follows:

1. Create an ASCII description file for the new file entry. Either extract the ASCII description file for the entire CE database using `ce_db_build` (the man page is in

the back of this chapter), or create a new ASCII description file for the new file type entry. The process for creating a single entry ASCII description file is described in the section that follows.

2. Add a file type name and file type pattern to the files namespace table in the ASCII description file. You only need to add the file type pattern if the file type is derived using the type-by-pattern method. If the file is derived using the type-by-content method, add a magic match, magic match data type, and an offset.

3. After a new file type has been added to the files namespace table, add its attributes to the types namespace table.

4. Once the attributes are added, you can overwrite the old CE database file with the one you just created using the `ce_db_build` command. Use this command only if you are replacing the entire CE database file. If you created an ASCII description file for a subset of the entire CE database (this procedure is described in the next section), merge the file into the current CE database with the `ce_db_merge` command (the man page for this command is in the back of this chapter).

Adding a New File Type to the Classing Engine— Example

This section shows a step-by-step example of adding a new file type to the CE.

1. Define the file type name, its unique file name pattern or content string, and its attributes. For this example we'll use a hypothetical program called `Peakstool` that works on files of a type called `twin-peaks-type`:

```
Object Name = twin-peaks-type
Content Pattern = Good Coffee!
Offset = 0
Content Type = string
Open Command (program note) = peakstool
Icon Location= $OPENWINHOME/include/images/
laura.icon
Icon Mask Location = $OPENWINHOME/include/
images/laura.mask.icon
Foreground Color = r=91, g= 229, b= 229
File Pattern = *.pks
```

Only file type name and either a file content pattern (with offset and type) or file pattern are necessary to add a valid entry in the CE database. All other parameters are optional.

2. Create a CE database definition file in ASCII and give it a name. The file illustrated in Figure 6.4.2, newtype.ascii, corresponds to our twin-peaks file. Note that the attributes go in the types namespace table, and the file/content patterns go in the files namespace table.

```
# newtype.ascii: A sample ASCII CE database description file
{
 NS_NAME=Types
 NS_ATTR= ((NS_MANAGER,string, <$CEPATH/tns_mgr.so>))
 NS_ENTRIES= (
             (
             (TYPE_NAME,type-id,<twin-peaks-type>)
             (TYPE_OPEN,call,<peakstool>)
             (TYPE_ICON,icon-file,<$OPENWINHOME/include/images/laura.icon>)
             (TYPE_ICON_MASK,icon-file,<$OPENWINHOME/include/images/laura.mask.icon>)
             (TYPE_FGCOLOR,color,<91 229 229>)
             (TYPE_BGCOLOR,color,<91 126 229>)
             (TYPE_FILE_TEMPLATE,string,<peaks.%t>)
             )
                )
)
# Tell CE how to match files of your type. If the file begins with Good_coffee!,
# it's of type twin-peaks-type. The string begins at offset 0 in the file.
{
NS_NAME=Files
NS_ATTR=((NS_MANAGER,junk,<$CEPATH/fns_mgr.so>))
NS_ENTRIES=(
                (
                (FNS_TYPE,refto-Types,<twin-peaks-type>)
                (FNS_MAGIC_OFFSET,str,<0>)
                (FNS_MAGIC_MATCH,str,<Good-coffee!>)
                (FNS_MAGIC_TYPE,str,<string>)
                )
                )
}
```

Figure 6.4.2. A sample ASCII Classing Engine database description file.

3. After creating the ACII description file, execute the ce_db_merge command to add the new file type to one of the three CE databases. The *network* database is used in this example, with an ASCII description file called newtype.ascii.

```
% ce_db_merge newwork -from_asscii newtype.ascii
```

4. Note that you can also use `cd_db_build` to add a new file type. Refer to the man page for details.

Syntax of ASCII Database Description File

The grammar that describes the Database Description File is given here in Backus-Naur Form (BNF):

```
database         ::= name_space
                   | database name_space
name_space       ::= { name ns_attrs entries }
name             ::= NS_NAME = variable
ns_attrs         ::= NS_ARRT = (av_list)
av_list          ::= av
                   | av_list av
av               ::= (av_name, av_type, av_val)
entries          ::= NS_ENTRIES = (entry_info_list)
entry_info_list  ::= entry_ent
                   | entry_info_list entry_ent
entry_ent        ::= ( av_list )
av_name          ::= variable
av_type          ::= variable
variable         ::= Id
av_val           ::= av_token
```

The terminals are:
```
Id               = a-z, A-Z, 0-9, _, -.
NS_NAME, NS_ATTR, NS_ENTRIES,
"{", "}", "(", ")", ",", "=", Id, and av_token.
```

`av_token` can come in two forms:

- It can begin with a "<" and end with a ">" and can have any ASCII character (except a ">") within it.
- It can begin with one or more digits (which represent a number *n*), followed by zero or more spaces, followed by a "<", followed by any *n* characters closed off by a ">". This is the escape mechanism to allow for arbitrary byte string attributes that could have ">" characters within them.

Binder

Attributes can be added or changed by editing the types namespace file, or by using Binder shown in Figure 6.4.3. Binder is a DeskSet tool which provides an interactive display of the CE database (refer to the *OpenWindows DeskSet Reference Guide* for operating instructions). With Binder, an advanced user can bind together a file type, its application, a print method, and an icon by setting the desired attributes.

The Binder is also helpful in understanding the Classing Engine, since it interacts directly with the CE database. When you open the Binder, you are given a selection of file types shown in icon form. These correspond to the file types contained in the files namespace table. Once you select a file type, you can view the attributes in either the *icon properties sheet* or *files property sheet*. Binder allows you to change attributes or create new file types interactively.

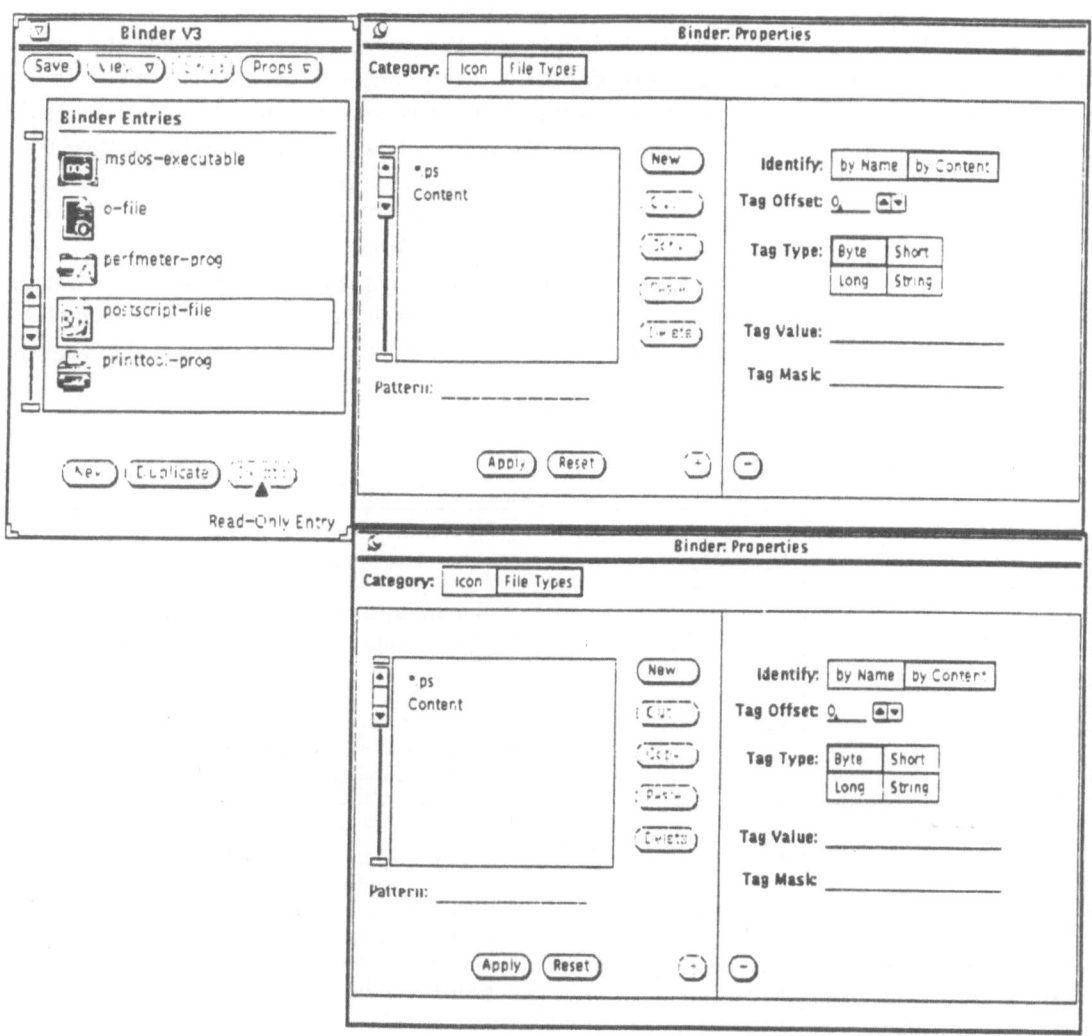

Figure 6.4.3. Binder—Icon and file types property sheet.

6.4.4
Accessing the Classing Engine Database

Example program— Querying the Classing Engine Database

Access to the CE database is provided by the namespace manager, a collection of routines used to query the CE database and perform other database chores. These routines are described in The Classing Engine API on page ??. It may, however, be helpful first to see two simple programs which use the CE.

The program illustrated below, $OPENWINHOME/share/ src/dig_samples/ce_simple.c, shows how the CE database is queried. When compiled and executed, the program prompts the user to enter the name of an object (a filename). When a filename is entered, the program accesses the CE database then displays the file type and the location of its icon file on the screen. The user types "quit" to exit the program. This program must be executed on a SPARCstation running OpenWindows Version 3.

The program is divided into code segments with a detailed explanation of how each code segment works. Table 6.4.2 shows the variable definitions for the sample program.

Table 6.4.2. Variable definitions for `dig_ce_sample.c`.

Tyep	Variable	Comment
`CE_NAMESPACE`	`f_name_space` `t_name_space`	file namespace table handle types namespace table handle
`CE_ENTRY`	`ftype_ent` `ttype_end`	filenamespace table entry handle types namespace table entry handle
`CE_ATTRIBUTE`	`fns_type` `tns_icon` `fns_attr` `tns_attr`	file type icon filename file namespace tbl: file type attr. handle types namespace tbl: icon attr. handle
`int`	`argcount` `fd;`	`ce_get_entry arg` counter file descriptor for file to be typed
`char`	`filename[81]` `buf[256]`	buffer for file name buffer for contents of file
`int`	`bufsize` `status`	return values

Preliminary Setup

This first segment includes a short program description and the compile statement. Loading the program requires the Classing Engine and dynamic linking libraries. The include files and variable definitions are:

<stdio.h>	For standard io to get input and output
<desktop/ce.h>	Needed for the Classing Engine variables
<desktop/ce_err.h>	Error return codes from Classing Engine (not used in this program, except for ce_begin).

```
/* ce_simple.c - Simple Classing Engine Example that types a
 * file and determines its icon.
 *
 * cc -g -o ce_sample -i$OPENWINHOME/include -L$OPEONWINHOME/lib
 * ce_simple.c -lce -ldl
 */

#include <stdio.h>
#include <desktop/ce.h>
#include <desktop/ce_err.h>

/* variable definitions */
CE_NAMESPACE    f_name_space, t_name_space;
CE_ENTRY        ftype_ent, ttype_ent;
CE_ATTRIBUTE    fns_type, tns_econ, fns_arrt, tns_attr;
int             argcount;
```

Open the CE Database

After declaring the global variables, the program declares the variable definitions for the file to be typed: the file descriptor (fd), the file name (sufficiently long to include any likely path name), and a 256-byte buffer to hold the first characters of the file.

The CE is initialized by ce_begin() using the mandatory NULL argument (see the API section for details). The call returns zero is successful; otherwise, it returns a positive integer representing an error code, which is printed to standard error, after which the program exits.

```
main (argc, argv)
int argc;
char *argv[];
{
        int fd;
        char filename[81];
        char buf[256];
        int bufsize, status;

        /* Initialize the Classing Engine. */

        status = ce_begin ( NULL );
        if ( status ) {
            fprintf (stderr, "Error Initializing Classing Engine
                    Database - Error no: %d.\n", status );
            exit ( 0 );}
```

Setting the Namespace Pointers

The code segment below sets up the pointers in anticipation of reading the namespace entries for both the files and the types namespaces.

`ce_get_namespace_id("Files")` returns a handle to the files namespace table in f_name_space. If the either the file namespace table is not found, or the file namespace manager is not found, the call returns NULL and the program exits.

A similar `ce_get_namespace_id()` call and error routine is used for the types namespace table. These calls only need to be done once.

```
/* Read in Namespace Entries. */
f_name_space = ce_get_namespace_id( "Files" );
if ( !f_name_space ) {
   fprintf( stderr, "Cannot find File Namespace\n" );
   ce_end();
   exit(0);
}

t_name_space = ce_get_namespace_id( "Types" );
if ( !t_name_space ) {
   fprintf( stderr, "Cannot find Types namespace\n" );
   ce_end();
   exit(0);
}
```

Retrieve Desired Attribute IDs

`ce_get_attribute_id(f_name_space, "FNS_TYPE")` returns a handle to the file type attribute in the files namespace table and assigns it to the object ID `fns_attr`. Similarly, the second `ce_get_attribute_id()` returns a handle to the icon filename attribute in the types namespace table and assigns it toe the object ID `tns_attr`

```
/* Get the attribute ID's that we're interested in
 */

   fns_attr = ce_get_attribute_id ( f_name_space, "FNS_TYPE" );

   if (!fns_attr){
      fprintf (stderr, "Cannot find FNS_ATTR IN files\n");
      ce_end();
      exit(0);
   }

   tns_attr = ce_get_attribute_id (t_name_space, "TYPE_ICON");

   if (!tns_arrt) {
      fprintf (stderr, "Cannot find TYPE_ICON in Types\n");
      ce_end();
      exit(0);
   }
```

Loop to Read File Names

The next segment starts the loop to read in file names and derive their types. A while loop prompts the user for the name of the file that will be tested in the CE. If the user types "quit" the loop is exited (break) and CE database is closed (shown in next segment).

The second if statement attempts to open the file. If the file is found, but cannot be opened, an error message is printed and the loop starts again.

If the open is successful, an attempt is made to read the beginning of the file into the 256-byte buffer (to be used later by the CE). If the file is empty is actually a directory, an error message is printed and the loop starts again.

```
/* Start loop to read in filenames */

   while (1) {
      fprintf(stdout, "Filename: ");
      gets(filename);
      if ((strcmp(filename, "quit")) == 0)
         break;

      if ((fd = open (filename, 0)) == -1) {
      fprintf(stderr, "Cannot open: %s\n", filename);
      continue;
      }

      bufsize = read (fd, buf, size of (buf));
      if (bufsize <= 0) {
         fprintf(stderr, "Empty file or Directory: %s\n",
                  filename);
         close (fd);
         continue;
      }
```

Get Entry in the Files Namespace

This next code segment searches through the files namespace table for the file name and/or file content obtained in the previous segment. If a match is found, the file type is returned.

The program calls ce_get_entry() to search the files namespace table and return the handle for the matching files namespace table entry. ce_get_entry() requires the files namespace ID (f_name_space), the number of arguments used to match entries in the files namespace table (3), and the three arguments themselves (the file name entered by the user, the buffer that contains the contents of the previous read, and the length of the buffer).

ce_get_entry() returns a handle for the files namespace table entry that matches the filename pattern, contents of the file, or both if both are present. The handle to the entry is assigned to ftype_ent. If no entry is found in the files namespace table, a NULL is returned, and the while loop resumes.

The program then gets the requested attribute value (file type) by calling ce_get_attribute(). ce_get_attribute() requires the files namespace handle (f_name_space), the handle to the entry (ftype_ent), and the file type attribute handle (`fns_attr`). After the attribute value is obtained the value is printed.

```
/* Get a matching entry in the files namespace */
   argcount = 3;
   ftype_ent = ce_get_entry (f_name_space, argcount,
                          filename, buf. bufsize);
   if ( !ftype_ent ) {
      fprintf (stder, "No match in Files Namespace\n" );
      continue;
   }

   fns_type=ce_get_attribute (f_name_space,ftype_ent,fns_attr);
   if (!fns_type) {
      fprintf(stderr,"No FNS_TYPE for entry in Files
                        Namespace\n");
      continue;
}
else{o
      fprint(stdout, "FNS_TYPE = %s\n", fns_type);
```

Get Entry in the Types Namespace

The final segment of this program retrieves the icon information from the types namespace table. Use `ce_get_entry()` to retrieve a handle for the desired entry. `ce_get_entry()` is passed the types namespace handle (`t_name_space`), the number of arguments used to match entries in the types namespace table (1), and the argument itself (`fns_type`). If a matching entry is not found, an error message is printed and the while loop is resumed. If a correct entry is found, the program calls `ce_get_attribute()` with `t_name_space` (types namespace), the handle to the entry (`ttype_ent`), and the icon handle (`tns_attr`) to return the icon filename.

Finally, the icon name (path and name) is printed, the Classing Engine is closed, and the program exits normally.

```
/* Get a matching entry in the types namespace found from
 * getting type from the files namespace and find icon
 */
argcount = 1;
ttype_ent = ce_get_entry ( t_name_space, argcount,
                     fns_type );

 if ( !ttype_ent ) {
    fprintf( stderr, "No match in Types namespace\n" );
    continue;
 }
    tns_icon = ce_get_attribute (t_name_space, ttype_ent,
        tns_attr);

 if (!fns_icon) {
    fprintf(stderr,"No TYPE_ICON in Types Namespace\n");
    continue;
 }
 else
    fprintf(stdout, "TYPE_ICON = %s\n", tns_icon);
 }
}
    cd_end ( );
    exit (0);
}
```

Example Program— CE Mapping Functions

This program, $OPENWINHOME/share/src/dig_sam-ples/ce_map1.c, demonstrates the use of the CE mapping functions. Refer to the API section that follows for further details.

```
/* dig_ce_mapl.c - Classing Engine example that print all the types
 * in the Files and Types namespaces.
 *
 * cc -g -o dig_ce_mapl -I$OPENWINHOME/include -L$OPENWINHOME/lib
 * dig_ce_.mapl.c -lce -ldl   */

#include <stdio.h>
#include <desktop/ce.h>
#include <desktop/ce_eer.h>

/* variable definitions */
CE_NAMESPACE f_name_space, t_name_space;
CE_ENTRY     ttype_ent;
CE_ATTRIBUTE fns_attr, fns_type;

main (argc, argv)
int argc;
char *argv[]
{
      int   status;
      void *map_func(), *type_map_func();

/* Initialize the Classing Engine. */

      status = ce_begin( NULL );
      if ( status ) {
            fprintf( stderr, "Error Initializing Classing Engine
                     Database - Error no: %d.\n", status );
            exit( 0 );
      }

/* Get Files and Type Entries. */

      f_name_space = ce_get_namespace_id( "Files" );
      if ( !f_name_space ){
            fprintf( stderr, "Cannot find File Namespace\n" );
            exit( 0 );
      }
}
```

```
        t_name_space = ce_get_namespace_id( "Types" );
        if ( !t_name_space ) {
                fprint( stderr, "Cannot find Type Namespace\n" );
                exit ( 0 );
        }

        /* Get the FNS_TYPE attribute ID */
        fns_attr = ce_get_attribute_id (f_name_space, "FNS_TYPE");

        if (!fns_attr) {
                fprintf (stderr, "No FNS-TYPE in Files Namespace\n");
                ce_end();
                exit (0);
        }

        /* ce_map_through_entries() passes each entry handle and
         * namespace handle to the map_func()
         */
        ce_map_through_entries (f_name_space, map_func, NULL);
        ce_end();
        exit (0);
}
/* Function to handle each entry as it is passed from the mapping
 * function */
void
*map_func (fns_handle, ent_handle)
CE_NAMESPACE fns_handle;
CE_ENTRY ent_handle;
{
        int argcount = 1;

        /* Get File type value (FNS_TYPE) and print out */
        fns_type = ce_get_attribute (f_name_space, ent_handle,
                                        fns_attr);
        if (!fns_type)
                return (NULL);
        else
```

```
        /* Get matching entry in the Type namespace */
        ttype_ent = ce_get_entry (t_name_space, argcount, fns_type);
        if (!ttype_ent){
                fprintf (stderr, "No match in Type namespace\n");
                return (NULL);
        }

        /* Map through all the attributes of the entry and send to
         * type_map_func()
         */
        ce_map_through_attrs (t_name_space, ttype_ent, type_map_func,
                               NULL);
        fprintf (stdout, "\n");
        return (NULL);
}
/*
 * Function to print all the Type attributes associated with the File
 *type
 */
void
*type_map_func (tattr_handle, tattr_value, args)
CE_ATTRIBUTE tattr_handle;
char  *tattr_value;
void  *args;
{
        char *attr_value;

        attr_name = ce_get_attribute_name (tattr_handle);

        if (attr_name)
                fprintf (stdout, "%s = %s\n", attr_name, tattr_value);

        return (NULL);
}
```

6.4.5
The Classing
Engine API

The CE API can be called from C,C++, or ANSI C programs. All CE calls have names that begin with ce_, with each session begun with a ce_begin() and ending with ce_end().

The arguments manipulated by the API are either Classing Engine object handles or client-decipherable argument values and return values. Classing Engine object handles are of type CE_NAMESPACE, CE_ENTRY, CE_ATTRIBUTE and are returned when a client successfully accesses a namespace, an entry, or an attribute. Client-decipherable argument values and return values are expected to be of type void*, if they are pointers, or of type int.

Mapping Functions

The `ce_map_through_*` functions loop through namespace, entry, and attribute lists, applying a client-supplied function to each member of a list. The previous example shows how the mapping functions work in detail.

Error Reporting

`ce_begin` returns 0 if it succeeds, otherwise it returns an error number. All Classing Engine `ce_get_*` calls return NULL is they fail, otherwise they return a valid handle or return value.

The `ce_map_through_*` calls map through namespaces, entries, or attributes and terminate if they encounter a non-null return value from the map function, and return the non-null value. If the map function returns null in every instance, the `ce_map_through_*` function returns null.

Location of Namespace Managers

Every namespace manager library file should be named as the `NS_MANAGER` namespace attribute. This should be a full pathname with both environment variables and the 'arch' command allowed.

If a namespace manager library name is preceded by a `$CEPATH`, the search rules implied by `$CEPATH` will be used to search for the namespace manager library.

6.4.6 Reading from the Classing Engine Database

Initializing the Classing Engine

```
int
ce_begin(void * args);
```

Reads in the CE database and makes CE internal structures suitable for subsequent CE API calls (except for another `ce_begin()`). Subsequent calls to `ce_begin()` will re-read the CE databases. `args`, which is reserved for future use, must be NULL.

This call returns 0 if sucessful. Otherwise, the return codes from this call have the following meanings:

`CE_ERROR_READING_DB`

This message indicates that an unrecoverable error occurred while reading a CE database. Note that the non-existence of a particular CE database file is not considered an error.

Determining if the Classing Engine Databases Changed

```
int
ce_db_changed();
```

Returns 0 if CE databases have not been changed since the last call to `ce_begin()`. It will return 1 if the databases have been changed.

Closing the Classing Engine

```
int
ce_end();
```

Frees all resources being used by the CE. All CE returned handles and values are invalid after this call. `ce_end()` returns 0 in all cases.

Determining Which Databases are Available

```
int
ce_get_dbs(
        int *num_db,
        char ***db_names
        char ***db_pathnames);
```

Returns a count of the databases in `*num_db`. The names of the databases read in is returned in `db_names`. The pathnames of the databases is returned in `db_pathnames`. There are three possible database names:

user   the user-level database
system   the system-level database
network   the network level database.

Returns database names and pathnames even if there was no database at a particular pathname. Thus, it provides the caller information about where the CE databases would be even if one or more CE databases do not exist.

Accessing a Namespace

```
CE_NAMESPACE
        ce_get_namespace_id(
        char *namespace_name);
```

Returns a handle to a namespace. The namespace handle can be used in all subsequent calls to the CE in this process. This call returns NULL if the namespace was not found.

This call also returns NULL if the namespace manager for the given namespace was not found.

Accessing an Entry in a Namespace Table

```
CE_ENTRY
        ce_get_entry(
        CE_NAMESPACE namespace,
        int argcount,
        void *arg1,
        void *arg2,...,
        void *argN);
```

Searches through a specified namespace table and returns an entry that contains a matching argument. This call requires a handle to a namespace, the number of arguments used to match entries, and the arguments themselves.

Getting an Attribute Handle

```
CE_ATTRIBUTE
        ce_get_attribute_id(
        CE_NAMESPACE namespace,
        char *attr_name);
```

Retrieves a handle to an attribute type within a namespace table. All attributes with the same name within a namespace, can be retrieved using the same attribute handle. This handle is retrieved with this call.

For example, all attributes named ICON will have the same attribute handle within a single namespace. This call returns NULL if the named attribute was not found in this namespace.

Getting an Attribute

```
char
*ce_get_attribute(
        CE_NAMESPACE namespace,
        CE_ENTRY entry,
        CE_ATTRIBUTE attribute);
```

Retrieves the value of an individual attribute. This call returns NULL if the attribute could not be found in this entry. It requires a handle for the namespace table (`ce_get_namespace_id()`), entry (`ce_get_entry()`), and attribute (`ce_get_attribute_id()`)

Getting the Size of an Attribute

```
int
ce_get_attribute_size(
        CE_NAMESPACE namespace,
        CE_ENTRY entry,
        CE_ATTRIBUTE attribute);
```

Returns the size (in bytes) of an attribute value. Returns 0 if the attribute was not found in this entry.

Getting an Attribute's Type String

```
char
*ce_get_attribute_type(
        CE_NAMESPACE namespace,
        CE_ENTRY, entry
        CE_ATTRIBUTE attribute);
```

Returns the character string denoting the type of an attribute. Attribute types are not enforced nor understood by the CE. Returns NULL if the attribute was not found in this entry.

Getting a Namespace Entry

```
CE_ENTRY
        ce_get_ns_entry(
        CE_NAMESPACE namespace);
```

Returns the namespace entry handle for the specified namespace. Namespaces can have attributes of their own; for example, a range of bytes to read for magic number information in the case of files. Namespace attributes are stored in a namespace entry. This call returns a handle to a namespace's entry. All calls that apply to entries can be made using the returned entry handle. Returns NULL if the namespace entry was not found.

Mapping Through Namespaces

```
void
*ce_map_through_namespaces(
        void *(*map_func)(),
        void *args);
```

Maps through all installed namespaces, calls `map_func()` for each namespace, and passes each namespace handle as the first argument to `map_func()` and any other args as subsequent arguments. `map_func()` is a user-defined function. args are optional additional arguments for `map_func()`. If no arguments are to be passed, use NULL.

The map will be stopped either when there are no more namespaces or when `map_func` returns a non_null value, which will be returned to the caller.

Mapping Through Entries

```
void
*ce_map_through_entries(
        CE_NAMESPACE namespace,
        void *(map_func)(),
        void *args),
```

Maps through all the entries in a namespace, calls `map_func()` for each entry, and passes the namespace handle as the first argument to `map_func()`, entry handle as the second argument, and any other `map_func()` args as subsequent arguments. `map_func()` is a user-defined function. args are optional additional arguments for `map_func`. If no arguments are to be passed, use NULL.

The map will be stopped either when there are no more entries or when `map_func` returns a non_null value, which will be returned to the caller.

Mapping Through Attributes

```
void
*ce_map_through_attrs(
        CE_NAMESPACE namespace,
        CE_ENTRY entry,
        void *(*map_func)(),
        void *args);
```

Maps through all the attributes in an entry, calls `map_func()` for each attribute, and passes the attribute handle as the first argument to `map_func()`, each attribute value as the second argument, and args as the subsequent arguments to `map_func`. `map_func()` is a user-defined function. args are optional additional arguments for `map_func`. If no arguments are to be passed, use NULL.

The function will be stopped either when there are no more attributes or when `map_func` returns a non-null value, which will be returned to the caller.

Mapping Through the Attributes of a Namespace

```
void
*ce_map_through_ns_attrs(
        CE_NAMESPACE namespace,
        void *(*map_func)(),
        void *args);
```

Maps through all the attributes of a namespace, calls `map_func()` for each attribute, and passes each attribute handle as the first argument to `map_func()`, each attribute value as the second argument, and `args` as subsequent arguments. `map_func()` is a user-defined function. `args` are optional additional arguments for `map_func`. If no arguments are to be passed, use NULL.

The map will be stopped either when there are no more attributes or when `map_func` returns a non-null value, which will be returned to the caller.

Getting the Name of a Namespace

```
char
*ce_get_namespace_name (CE_NAMESPACE
namespace);
```

We envision some namespace mapping functions requiring to know the name of a namespace, given a namespace handle. This function will return a namespace name, when passed a namespace handle.

Getting the Name of an Attribute

```
char
*ce_get_attribute_name(CE_ATTRIBUTE
attribute);
```

We envision some attribute mapping functions requiring to know the name of an attribute when passed a handle to it. This function will return an attribute name, when passed an attribute handle.

Determining Which Database Contains an Entry

```
int
ce_get_entry_db_info(
        CE_NAMESPACE namespace,
        CE_ENTRY entry,
        char **name_ptr,
        char **path_ptr);
```

Returns the name of the database (either user, system, or network) in which an entry is stored. The name is returned in `*name_ptr` and the pathname of the database in `*path_ptr`. This call returns 0 if it is successful, otherwise it returns `CE_ERR_WRONG_ARGUMENTS`.

Classing Engine Utility Programs

Sun provides two utilities that enable reading and writing the Classing Engine database files to and from an ASCII form, to allow developers to view the database. The `man` pages for these utilities follows on the next pages.

`ce_data_build`

The build utility, `ce_db_build`, will generate a readable ASCII file from the CE database, if given the `-from_ascii` argument. The user must also indicate the desired database (user, system, or network) and the filename where the file should be written. This allows a developer to print and peruse a hard copy of the database for familiarization or troubleshooting.

Caution – The `ce_db_build` utility will overwrite an existing CE database if given the `-from_ascii` argument. This will overwrite the existing CE database and replace it with the information from an ASCII file.

An optional argument, `-db_file` *filename*, can be given to generate a CE database file without disturbing the existing CE database files.

`cd_db_merge`

The merge utility, `ce_db_merge`, permits the merging of an ASCII database description file with an existing CE database file. This utility permits the merging of custom CE entries to the database.

NAME	ce_db_build—build an entire CE database
SYNOPSIS	`ce_db_build user|system|network -from_ascii|-to_ascii filename \ [-db_file db-filename]`
DESCRIPTION	**cd_db_build** reads from/writes to the Classing Engine databases and an ASCII description file.
	**user	system	network** indicates which CE database is to be used, either the user, the system, or the network database.
	-from_ascii *filename* indicates that the user wishes to write to the stated CE database from the ASCII file *filename*. The entire CE database will be re-written. This is an all-or-nothing update of the CE database; that is, effectively the old database is erased and a new one is created based solely on the contents of the ASCII file.
	-to_ascii *filename* indicates that the file named *filename* should be written with the ASCII description of the stated CE database. This ASCII description may then be modified and supplied as input to an invocation of **ce_db_build** with the **-from_ascii** argument.
OPTIONS	**-db_file** should be used in the case that a particular database is to be read from/written to using *db-filename* as the pathname of the CE database, instead of the default database files noted below.
FILES	The Classing Engine uses the following default database files: user ~/.cetables/cetables system /etc/cetables/cetables network $OPENWINHOME/lib/cetables/cetables

EXAMPLE	Create and ASCII definition file `newdef` from the existing **user** CE database.
	    `ce_db_build user -to_ascii newdef`
	Create the user CE database from file `new_db`.
	    `ce_db_build user -from_ascii new_db`

NAME	ce_db_merge—merge a Classing Engine ASCII database description file into the CE database
SYNOPSIS	**ce_db_merge user | system | network -from_ascii** `filename`\[**-db_ file** `db-filename`]
DESCRIPTION	**ce_db_merge** will attempt to merge namespace and entry definitions from an ASCII description file into an existing CE database. It will overwrite namespace attributes; that is, namespace attributes from the ASCII file will replace existing namespace attributes.

user \| system \| network indicates whether the user wants to update the user, the system, or the network CE database.

-from_ascii *filename* indicates that the user wishes to write the stated CE database from the ASCII file *filename*. The named CE database will be updated based on the ASCII description file. Any existing entries that also exist in the ASCII description file will be updated. Any new ASCII descriptors will be entered in the database.

OPTIONS	**-db_file** should be used in the case that a particular CE database is to be written to, using *db-filename* as the pathname of the CE database, instead of the default database files noted below.
FILES	The Classing Engine uses the following default database files:

database:	default location:
user	`~/.cetables/cetables`
system	`/etc/cetables/cetables`
network	`$OPENWINHOME/lib/cetables/cetables`

EXAMPLES	Merge an ASCII definition file newdef into the existing user CE database.

```
ce_db_merge user -from_ascii newdef
```
Merge the ASCII file newdef into the Classing Engine system database at /foo/bar/sysfile.
```
cd_db_merge system -from_ascii newdef -db_file
/foo/bar/sysfile
```

6.A
Drag and Drop
User Interface
Specification

6.A.1
Introduction

Drag and drop is a convenient, powerful, general purpose accelerator for transferring data within and between applications. This specification establishes conventions for the user interface of the drag and drop mechanism. It is intended to guide the implementation of drag and drop for OpenWindows Version 3, and to guide application developers toward consistent uses of the technique. It does not describe implementation details of the drag and drop mechanism, nor does it describe the API.

This document includes descriptions of:

- the kinds of objects that can be dragged
- the meanings of dropping objects on specific locations (such as on a window header, on a pane in a window, or on a drag and drop target)
- the differences between dragging with and without the DUPLICATE modifier key held down
- the visual feedback associated with the stages of a drag and drop operation
- how the process of data translation appears to users
- how users can cancel drag operations in progress, and undo completed drag operations.
- how error messages are presented to users.

Classic Examples

Drag and drop is a technique for manipulating data and applications by directly manipulating graphical objects on the display screen. It has become a standard accelerator on the SunSoft desktop for transferring data between applications and for moving data around within an application. A classic example of the use of drag and drop is to move documents around in the directory hierarchy. For example, in File Manager you can move a document into a folder by dragging a document glyph and dropping it on a folder glyph. Technically speaking, the document is the *source object*, and the folder is the *destination object*. First you press and hold the SELECT mouse button while the pointer is on the document you want to move (the source) and then you drag it onto the folder glyph (the destination) and release the mouse button.

In addition to dragging the documents between folders in File Manager, you can also drag documents from a File Manager folder into the wastebasket to delete them, or onto Print Tool to print them. See Figure 6.A.1. Whereas moving documents among folders in File Manager or from a folder to the wastebasket involves only one application (File Manager), dragging documents to the Print Tool involves the transfer of data between two applications, File Manager and Print Tool. In other words, in the latter case the *source application* and the *destination application* are different, whereas in the former cases they are the same.

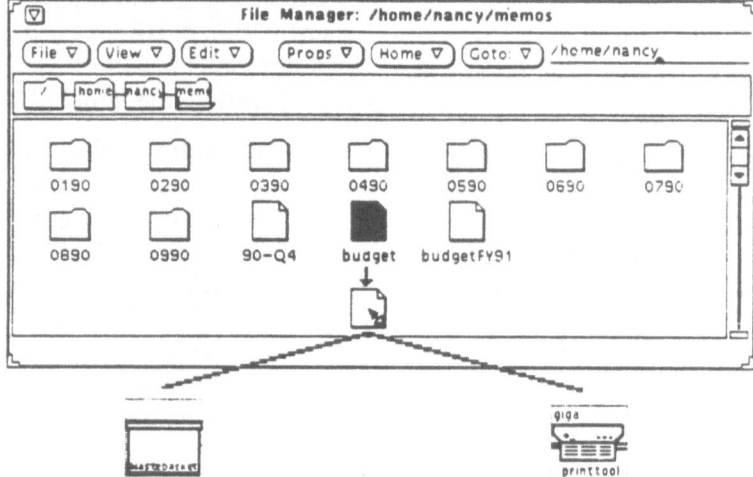

Figure 6.1. Dragging File Manager documents..

Drag and Drop as Cut and Paste

Another classic use of drag and drop is as an alternative to the Cut and Paste commands. For example, Text Editor allows you to move selected text from one document to another either by using the Cut and Paste commands, or by using drag and drop. To use drag and drop, you follow these steps. Before you begin, you need to have the two documents loaded into Text Editor, and visible in two windows. Then you select the part of the first document that you want to move. Next you press the SELECT mouse button on the selection, and drag it to the location where you want to insert it in the other document. Releasing the mouse button completes the drag and drop operation. See Figure 6.A.2.

Figure 6.2. Dragging text between textedit documents.

Although drag and drop is often used as an alternative to Cut and Paste, as described above, the two techniques have subtly different effects. First, whereas the Paste command inserts the source object at the caret in the destination document (replacing the selection if there is one), drag and drop inserts it at the hot spot of the pointer. Second, drag and drop does not involve the clipboard, whereas the commands Cut and Paste do. Third, after a drag and drop operation the newly inserted text is selected, whereas after a Paste it is not selected.

To Cut or to Copy?

In the example above, drag and drop was used as an alternative to Cut and Paste. However, if the user had held down the DUPLICATE modifier key[1] during the drag operation, the source would have been copied. As a result, the drag and drop operation would be analogous to Copy and Paste rather than Cut and Paste.

Where We Are Headed

As these examples indicate, the drag and drop technique is used in a variety of different ways by OPEN LOOK applications. It has proven to be a convenient, powerful, general purpose accelerator for transferring data within and across applications. To exploit the paradigm to its fullest, we need conventions for its use so that applications will use it in similar ways, and consequently, users will know what to expect of it. Conventions are necessary for everything from the meaning of dropping onto an iconified application base window (a *miniwindow*), to the feedback that appears when the user attempts a drop in an inappropriate place.

The following sections of this Appendix describe the details of the user interface for drag and drop. They include a formal definition of drag and drop, and a description of the kinds of operations that applications may use drag and drop for. They also specify the meaning of dragging with and without the DUPLICATE modifier key held down, and the meanings of dropping on specific types of destination objects. Finally, they specify the visual feedback associated with the stages of the drag and drop operation, and describe how a variety of special conditions should be handled.

6.A.2
Formal Definition

Technically speaking, drag and drop is a gestural technique for manipulating objects,[2] with the following characteristics:

- The source is indicated by initiation of the drag operation on an object that typically has been selected, or that will become selected as the drag operation begins.
- The drag operation is initiated by pressing and holding down a mouse button while dragging the mouse. Dragging the mouse involves moving it by five pixels or more.[3]

1. The DUPLICATE modifier key is the CTRL key by default.
2. The term *object* is used in the loose, generic sense in this document.
3. Users should be able to adjust the drag threshold through a workspace property.

- Following initiation of the drag operation, a drag mode persists in which the user indicates a continuous path from the source to the destination.
- The drag operation terminates when the user releases the mouse button.
- The destination is indicated by the pointer position at the end of the drag operation. More specifically, the destination is indicated by the location of the pointer's hot spot when the user releases the mouse button.

On the SunSoft desktop, drag and drop is defined as an *accelerator*-anything that you can do using drag and drop you should also be able to do in another way, often by selecting commands from menus.

6.A.3 The Source

Any object that is selectable can potentially be dragged, excluding, of course, selections in most controls (such as exclusive and non-exclusive settings and menus). Typically, the source is a data object, such as a document or a text selection, or a container of data objects, such as a folder.

When the source object is a text selection, a data object, or a container of data objects, the source is the primary selection. After the drag operation has completed, the new object at the destination location is the primary selection. for example, if you drag a text selection from one window to another, after the drag operation the text that has been inserted at the destination location is selected.

Multiple Source Objects

You can drag many different source objects in a single drag operation, provided that you can create a selection that includes all the objects. When the primary selection includes objects in a window, this naturally restricts you to dragging objects only from a single window, since the primary selection cannot span windows.

If the source objects have a natural logical ordering in the source application, the drag operation should preserve the ordering. For example, if the source objects are document glyphs that are displayed in the source application organized by filename, the drag operation should order them alphabetically by filename. However, the destination application should not presume that the source objects it receives are ordered in any way.

Windows as Source Objects

Open windows and iconified windows (that is, miniwindows) also may be source objects in drag and drop operations; however, these drag and drop operations are atypical in several regards.

First, when you drag a window it does not become selected. Because the window is not selected, you can drag it without losing the current primary selection. So, for example, you can make a selection in a window; then drag the window to reposition it; and your selection in the window will still be there.[1]

Second, you can't duplicate a window by holding down the DUPLICATE key when starting a drag operation. Whenever you drag an open window or a mini-window, the effect of the drag action is to move the window, not to clone it.

Third, when you are dragging an open window or mini-window, the only place you can drop it is onto the workspace. In other words, when a mini-window or an open window is the source, the only *legal* destination is the workspace. of course, you can drop one window onto another, because our workspace supports overlapping window placement.[2] However, even in this case the destination is the workspace. That is, the overlaid window is not the destination, the workspace is.

Fourth, when you drag an open window or a mini-window, the mouse pointer does not change into one of the pointers that are typically used for drag and drop operations (see Figure 6.A.6 on page 374). We have chosen to use the normal pointer because users are unlikely to view dragging open windows and mini-windows as drag and drop operations. and due to all of the restrictions on dragging open windows and mini-windows, we want to encourage users not to view dragging a window as a drag and drop operation.

6.A.4
The Destination

The destination of a drag operation is determined by the location of the pointer's hot spot at the time the user releases the mouse button. If the source object is a data object or a collection of data objects, the destination may be a workspace; a mini-window; or a location in an open window, such

1. In the future we may identify other cases where it is useful to be able to drag an object without selecting it. However, presently only open windows and mini-windows can be dragged without being selected.
2. There is one exception to this. You cannot drop a mini-window onto an open window. More specifically, you cannot terminate a drop when the source is a mini-window and the hot spot of the pointer is within the border of an open window. If you attempt such a drop, a Notice will be presented which will tell you the drop operation is not allowed, and the drop will be terminated.

as a data pane, a text field, or a *drag and drop target*. Drag and drop targets are a new type of graphical element, whose purpose is to support drag and drop operations. They are described in a following section of this document. If the source object is a mini-window or an open window, the only allowed destination is the workspace.

The legal source and destination combinations are shown in Table 6.A.1.

Table 6.A.1. Legal combinations of sources and destinations.

Source	Data Object/ Container	Destination Mini-Window	Open Window	Workspace
Data Object/Container	Yes	Yes	Yes	Yes
Mini-Window	No	No	No	Yes
Open Window	No	No	No	Yes

The Drop Method

The primary purpose of the *drop method* is to specify the processing that the source object undergoes at the destination. That is, the drop method determines the *effect* of the drag and drop operation on the destination. The application that owns the graphical element underneath the pointer at the time of a drop (the *destination application*) identifies the *drop method*. The destination may use different drop methods depending on what type of object the source is and depending on where the user dropped the source object.

To ensure conformity among applications and to make it easy for users to guess what the results of a drag operation will be, we have established guidelines for the drop methods that applications may use with different parts of the workspace. These guidelines specify which standard elements of the workspace can be used as destinations, and they describe appropriate types of drop methods.

Dropping onto Specific Locations

Text Fields and Text Panes

When you drop a source object onto a single-line text field, multi-line text field, or text pane, the source object should be inserted into the destination text at the position of the pointer's hot spot. If the source object is a text selection, then the text selection is inserted, whereas if the source object is a named object (such as a document), the name of the source object is inserted.

Naturally, source objects that are neither named objects nor text selections cannot be dropped onto text fields.

Non-Text Panes

As is the case with text panes, when the user drops a source object onto a non-text pane, the source is inserted onto the destination object. However, whereas in a text pane the source is always inserted at the pointer's hot spot, in a non-text pane the destination application has several options to choose from. The destination application may choose either to insert the source object at the pointer's hot spot, or to:

- insert the source object at a location that depends solely on characteristics of the source object

Calendar Manager processes mail messages dropped on it in this fashion. If you drop a mail message onto an open Calendar Manager window, and the mail message contains a correctly formatted appointment, Calendar Manager will insert the message into the calendar at the appropriate date and time.

- place all source objects at single location in the destination pane

For example, imagine a graphical cartridge tape manager that has a data pane that displays glyphs for the files on the tape. Imagine that you can drag a document from File Manager onto the Tape manager pane to add the document to the tape. Because tapes are sequential media, regardless of where you drop the document in the pane, the document file is added to the end of the tape.

- apply processing specific to the glyph the source object was dropped onto.

For example, File Manager's Path Pane and Folder Pane behave this way. If you drop a document onto a folder in either pane, the document moves into the folder you dropped it on. In contrast, if you drop a document onto the background of the Folder Pane, the document is moved into the directory displayed in the pane.

Scrolling Lists

A scrolling list may accept a source object and insert it as a new entry in the list. The destination application may insert the source into the list either:

- at a location that depends on the pointer's hot spot[1]

1. By default, when an object is dropped on a list item, the source object is inserted above the item it was dropped onl

- at a location that depends on characteristics of the source object

For example, in an alphabetical list the source object could be inserted alphabetically by name (or by content if the source object is a text selection).

- at a single fixed location

For example, when you drop a document onto the Print Tool scrolling list, the document is inserted at the end of the queue.

Scrolling lists that allow users to drop items into the list, and/or to drag items already in the list, should have a small icon to the left of each item in the list.

Mini-Windows

When you drop a source object on an iconified application base window (a mini-window), the result of the drop should match the results of a drop method that the open base window supports. If the base window supports more than one drop method, the mini-window should use the drop method that is most closely associated with the base window as a whole. For example, if the application supports a *load* drop method, that drop method should be supported by the mini-window.

Naturally, a mini-window cannot use a drop method that inserts the source object into a data pane at the pointer's hot spot (since the pointer's hot spot is over the mini-window, not over a data pane). For example, a drop onto the Text Editor mini-window *cannot* correspond to a drop onto the Text Editor base window's text pane, because the results of a drop onto the text pane depend on the precise location of the pointer's hot spot in the text pane.[1]

Applications should follow these guidelines in choosing a drop method for a mini-window:

- If the associated open window uses only one drop method, and the drop method does not insert the source object at the pointer's hot spot, then that drop method should also be used for the mini-window.
- If the associated open window supports more than one drop method that does not involve an insertion at the pointer's hot spot, then the miniwindow should use the

1. We do not allow the use of the caret as a substitute for the pointer hot spot.

drop method that is most closely associated with the base window as a whole.

- If the associated open window has a drop method which loads the source object into the application (replacing the data there) that drop method should be used for the mini-window.
- If the associated open window allows drops onto its header, dropping onto the header should have the same effect as dropping onto the mini-window.

Window Backgrounds

Applications may not allow objects to be dropped the backgrounds of open windows, except, in some cases, onto the window header.[1] In addition to the header, the background of a window includes:

- the footer
- areas to the left and right of data panes, excluding areas immediately adjacent to scrollbar drag boxes and cables
- the backgrounds of control areas.

When an application wants to provide a drop method that there is no obvious receptacle (i.e., destination object) for, the application should use a drag and drop target in a control area. For example, when an application supports a *load* drop method, a drag and drop target should be provided for it. Applications that don't have control areas may use their window headers instead of drag and drop targets.

The Workspace

Dropping an object onto the workspace should not cause the object to transform, such as becoming a mini-window for a running application (which is what File Manager does).

In the future, it may be possible to drop data objects onto the workspace and have them appear to rest on the workspace. However, because there is presently no mechanism in place for displaying data objects on the workspace, this guideline represents a long-term objective. It is included here as a hint to applications about how we intend to use the workspace in the future. Also, it is intended to preclude ap-

1. Drops onto the background are not allowed for two reasons. First, a background should be a neutral zone, which means that it should not have magical properties, such as the ability to accept dropped objects. Second, if a background had a drop method and elements on it had other drop methods, it could be difficult for users to predict the effects of a drop. In cases where a destination doesn't have a clear boundary, as a text field doesn't, it would be hard to know where one destination object ends and the other begins.

plications from using drops onto the workspace for other purposes.

Drag and Drop Targets

If an application wants to support a drop method and there is no obvious destination receptacle for the drag and drop operation, it should use a drag and drop target. Such obvious receptacles include text panes, single-line text fields, glyphs displayed in non-text panes, and scrolling lists, among others.

What Drag and Drop Targets Are. A drag and drop target is a rectangular graphical element, typically located in a control area, whose primary purpose is to serve as a destination for drag and drop operations. See Figure 6.A.3.

Figure 6.A.3. A drag and drop target.

A typical use of a drag and drop target is as a receptacle for dropping an object to be loaded into the destination application. Imagine an editor window that has a drag and drop target in its control area. Imagine further that the data pane is displaying The_Simpsons, the file currently loaded in the editor. Imagine that this editor window supports two types of drag and drop operations, one which uses the text pane as a destination, and one which uses the drag and drop target. If you drag a document—call it Bart—from File Manager and drop it onto the text pane, Bart will be inserted into The_Simpsons at the location where you dropped it. If instead of dropping Bart onto the text pane, you had dropped it on the drag and drop target, Bart would replace The_Simpsons as the document presently loaded. If you had unsaved edits in The_Simpsons, the editor would present a Notice window asking whether you want to save them before closing The_ Simpsons.

As a secondary feature, some drag and drop targets contain images which can themselves be dragged. That is, the images can be source objects in drag operations. Consider again the Text Editor example above. Imagine that the drag and drop target contains a glyph which can serve as a source object that represents the document presently loaded. For example, if Bart is currently loaded, you can drag the Bart image out of the drag and drop target and onto the Print Tool to print Bart. This action prints the version of Bart which currently appears in the window (which may contain unsaved edits), and does not unload Bart from the Text Editor. See Figure 6.A.4.

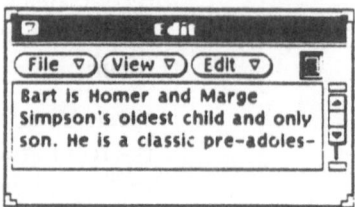

Figure 6.A.4. An editor window with a drag and drop target.

Windows are not required to include a drag and drop target. When an explicit drag and drop target is used, there should typically be only one per window or, at most, one per control area. Multiple drag and drop targets should be used only when the control areas in which they appear have explicit borders separating one panel from another. The drag and drop target always applies to the entire window or control area in which it appears. In particular, drag and drop targets should not be used to load data into single-line text fields or other individual controls, since these objects can accept drops directly when appropriate and do not require explicit targets of their own.

An explicit drag and drop target may, however, be included as an alternative to the *primary* drop site in a window or control area—provided there is a clear primary drop site that applies to the window or control area as a whole. In such cases, the explicit target will indicate to the user that drops are permitted when the presence of a drop site might not be sufficiently obvious based on the appearance of the drop site itself. An application whose primary drop site is a scrolling list, for example, might choose to provide a drop target to indicate that drops are permitted. In such cases, dropping on the drag and drop target should have the same effect as dropping on the primary drop site. Because it will typically be smaller and thus more difficult for the user to hit, the alternative drop site should only be added if the primary drop site will not be apparent to the user.

Introducing a drag and drop target to an existing application should not cause larger, more accessible drop sites to ignore drop requests. For example, many read-only data viewing applications permit users to drop files onto their data panes for immediate display. This method should continue to be supported for backward compatibility with established conventions even after a drag and drop target is added, because it is easier for the user to point at the data pane than at at the drag and drop target. In addition, drops over read-only data panes do not create any ambiguity over whether the data being dropped should replace, or be inserted into, the current data.

Visual Appearance of a Drag and Drop Target. As Figure 6.A.3. shows, a drag and drop target appears to be a box whose open top is flush with the screen. The *sunken* appearance signifies that the object is a receptacle. Drag and drop targets have two standard sizes (see Drag and Drop Target Engineering Specification, Section 6.A.15). The smaller standard size allows the drag and drop target to be added to the control area that typically appears at the top of an OPEN LOOK base window without increasing the normal height of the control area. Drag and drop targets should use the smaller standard size whenever the control area contains only one row of buttons. The larger standard size provides a target that is somewhat easier to drop on and that is also large enough to permit the display of an application-specified image inside the target's frame. The larger standard size should be used whenever there is sufficient room in the control area containing the drag and drop target. Drag and drop targets can be created in arbitrary sizes if necessary, but the two standard sizes should be used whenever possible, since the size and proportions of the target are important means of identification.

Like other standard OPEN LOOK controls, drag and drop targets should appear only in control areas; they should never appear in data panes. The drag and drop target is typically located in the upper right-hand corner of the control area. When it is located in a control area above a data pane, the drag and drop target should be right-aligned with the right edge of the data pane. If the drag and drop target has a textual label, the label should appear to the left of the drag and drop target in the standard bold font and be followed by a colon. The bottom of the drag and drop target should be positioned slightly below the baseline of the text.

When a window containing a drag and drop target is resizable, the target should be positioned relative to the top and right-hand edges of the window or control area. The drag and drop target should remain in the same relative position whenever the window is resized to ensure its continuous visibility when the size of the window is reduced. If the application permits its window to be resized such that the drag and drop target would extend into the space occupied by another control, the drag and drop target should appear to overlap the other control.

Drag and Drop target Content Images. In their normal states, some drag and drop targets are empty, whereas others contain object images. A drag and drop target is ordinarily empty if it doesn't allow objects to be dragged out of it. These *empty* drag and drop targets contain an image only while they're processing dropped objects. This image has a grayed-out, or *busy* appearance. Refer to the center figure in Figure 6.A.5. Once the drop has finished being processed, the object image and the busy feedback vanish and the drag and drop target is empty again.

In contrast, is a drag and drop target allows an object to be dragged out of it, there is an object image inside the drag and drop target at all times that dragging-out is possible. For example, in the editor example described above, the drag and drop target always contains an object image, except when there is no document presently loaded in the window. The default content image is a series of horizontal lines spaced evenly across the receptacle. Applications may choose to provide other, customized images. The object image is overlaid with the standard OPEN LOOK *busy* feedback while a drop is being processed. After the drop completes, the object image resumes its normal appearance. Refer to the right figure in Figure 6.A.5. When a drag and drop target is inactive, the borders of the box as well as its content and label should be dimmed.

Figure 6.A.5. Drop targets: empty, busy, and containing an image.

Applications may occasionally need to display an object that can serve as the source for a drag operation, but which nevertheless cannot serve as a legal drop site. The standard, "sunken" drag and drop target should not be used in these cases. The recommended solution is to display a glyph that represents the data and serves as a source for drag operations. This *drag source image* should appear in one of the standard sizes defined for use with the drag and drop target and should be positioned according to the same set of rules. The drag source image should be surrounded by a one-pixel border line that matches the interior dimensions (i.e., the "sunken" rectangle inside the bevel) of an appropriately sized drag and drop target. In color implementations, the border should be a standard "chiseled" line comparable to the border of a control area.

Drag and drop targets (and drag sources) appearing in the smaller standard size should normally use the default content image (see Figure 6.A.5) because the available imaging area is not large enough to make distinctions between images representing different data types practical. If an application-specified content image is required, or if space for a larger target is already available, the drag and drop target should use the larger standard size, which is designed to accommodate a standard (32 x 32) File Manager document glyph for the data in the window. If the content image is used to represent a specific type of data object, it should use the same image that appears in the File Manager for data objects of that type. (The application should query the classing engine for the appropriate glyph rather than using a hard-coded image, since users can change the glyph assigned to a particular type of data object at any time.)

6.A.5
To Copy or Not
to Copy?

Drag and drop operations *transfer* an object. Transferring an object may mean relocating a document in the file system; loading a document into an editor; printing a document; inserting a text selection into a document; or any number of other actions determined by the characteristics of the source object, the nature of the destination application, and where in the destination application the source object is dropped.

You can use drag operations simply to transfer a source object, or to duplicate the source object and transfer the duplicate. To support these two forms of drag and drop, there are two types of drag operations which differ in whether the user holds down a modifier key while initiating the drag. The standard form of drag and drop is the unmodified form, where the user does not hold down a modifier key. In this section this form is referred to as *unmodified-drag*. The second form involves holding down the DUPLICATE modifier while initiating the drag operation, and is referred to as DU-PLICATE-*drag*. Whereas DUPLICATE-drag always copies the source object, an unmodified-drag may or may not, depending on what is most intuitive in the current context.[1]

Unmodified Drag

Because users are most likely to learn the unmodified form of drag and drop first, and to use it when they are exploring new drag and drop actions, it has been designed to do the most obvious thing in a given situation. That is, it either does or does not duplicate the source object depending on what the source object is and what the destination is doing with it.

Typically, when a drag operation is relocating data, the source object is not duplicated. For example, when you drag a document from one folder to another in File manager, it is clear that you meant to reorganize your directories, and the document is not duplicated. Similarly, when you drag a document from a folder onto the wastebasket, it is clear that you meant to relocate the document to the wastebasket, and in this case as well the document is not duplicated. Similarly, when a drag operation loads data into an application, it does not duplicate the data.[2]

By contrast, in many cases when a drag operation carries data from one application to another, the data are transformed, and the user would typically prefer that the operation not affect the original source object. For example, when you drag a document form the File manager onto the Print Tool, the data are transformed into a hardcopy document, and you are not likely to want to lose the original document. As another example, consider dragging a message from Mail Tool onto calendar Manager. This action transforms the mail message into a scheduled appointment, assuming the mail message is formatted correctly. In this case as well, it is not clear that a user would be happy to lose the original mail message.

1. Another type of drag operation may be added in the future to support link creation.
2. In fact a copy of the source object is loaded. However, from the user's perspective he or she is operating on the original object, since the original source object's name appears in the destination application header, and by default changes will ultimately be committed to the original object.

Chapter 6. Integrating Applications on the Sun Desktop

Note that both the source and destination applications play a role in determining whether or not an unmodified drag operates on a duplicate of the source object. The impact of the drag operation on the original source object in the source application depends on where the user drops it. For example, imagine that you drag a document from a File Manager folder. The source may or may not eventually be removed from the folder, depending on whether you drop the document on Print Tool, or on the wastebasket, or onto a *load* drag and drop target in Text Editor. When a drop has been completed, the destination application advises the source application as to whether the source object should be removed from its original location.[1]

Naturally, the successful completion of the drop is a necessary condition for removing the source. That is, any time that a drag and drop operation does not complete successfully, the source will not be removed.

6.A.6
Loading Data

In many cases, using drag and drop to load a file into a destination application is identical, in effect, to loading the file via more conventional means (such as by choosing "Open" from the application's File menu). Specifically:

- If there are any unsaved modifications to the currently-loaded file, a Notice window is presented that gives the user the opportunity to save the changes.
- The currently-loaded file is closed and the new file is loaded.
- The newly-loaded file's name and path are displayed in the window header following the application name.
- After the user modifies the newly-loaded file, he or she can save the changes back to the original file, typically using "Save" in the File menu.

In other cases, a load resulting from a drag and drop operation may differ in one or more regards from loading a file via more conventional means. First, occasionally, such as when the file is dragged from a File Manager running on a remote machine with an inaccessible file system, only the filename (not the path) is accessible. In such cases the window

---

1. Generally, the destination application should recommend that the source be removed only when it is clear that the user intended to relocate the source object. The original source object should be left behind whenever it is not intuitively obvious that the user would expect the operation to remove the source.

header should display the filename and the name of the application the file came from. Specifically, the window header should display:

Current Application—Filename From *Source Application*

For example, if you were to drag a file called Lisa from a File Manager running on a remote machine to a Text Edit application window running on the local machine, the window header should display:

Text Edit—Lisa From File Manager

Second, occasionally it may not be possible to save the modified document back to the original file. For example, if you had dragged the file from a File manager running on a remote system, and the remote file Manager application then died, you could not save the file back. In cases such as this the "Save" item in the File menu should be inactive (i.e., grayed out). Users presumably will still be able to use the "Save As" command to save the file to the local file system. They may also be able to restart the remote file Manager and drag the file into it.

Third, unlike the more conventional methods of loading files, when you are loading a file via drag and drop you have the option to duplicate the original source file, and then load the duplicate. If you press the DUPLICATE key and then perform a drag operation whose drop method is a load, the source object is duplicated in the source application and then the copy is loaded into the destination application. Ordinarily, if the original source object was named "Bart", the duplicate is called "copy_of_Bart". However, if the original source object name begins with "copy_of_", or if there is already a file named "copy_of_Bart" in the current directory, then the duplicated name begins with the string "copy2_of_", and so forth.

6.A.7 Data Format Conversion

Frequently the source object is in a data format that differs from the destination's data format. For example, imagine that you drag some text from Text Editor into a painting application's window and drop it onto the painting canvas. Whereas Text Editor stores data in ASCII format, the painting application might store it in Postscript format. In order for the painting application to insert the source object into its document, the source must be converted from ASCII to Postscript.

Ideally, when a drop entails data format conversion, the conversion should occur transparently. That is, the user shouldn't even need to know it happened. However, in some cases the destination application may not be able to decide how to handle the source data format. In those cases, the destination application should let the user choose among alternative formats listed in a Notice window.

6.A.8
Handling Multiple Source Objects

Typically, when the destination receives multiple source objects during a single drag and drop operation, it should treat them as independent drag and drop events. However, they may be treated as a single, atomic event in cases where:

- undesirable results would be obtained if all the source objects were not successfully processed by the destination; and
- the destination can reverse the effects of any processing already completed at the time that a failure occurs.

When the destination application treats multiple source objects as independent drag and drop events, it should present a Notice window for each source object that is not successfully processed. The user may terminate processing of all the source objects by pressing the STOP key (once).

6.A.9
Visual Feedback
While Dragging

When you begin a drag and drop operation, the pointer changes shape and an image of the source object is attached to the pointer to provide feedback that a drag and drop operation has begun. As you drag the pointer over different graphical objects, it changes shape to indicate whether a drop is allowed. In addition, the prospective destination object. For example, a folder might open to show that it can accept the source object.

The visual appearance of the pointer, and the visual image of the source object that the pointer drags along, differ depending on whether the source object is a text selection or not. The two sets of visuals are described in the following sections.

While Dragging Data Objects and Containers

When you begin dragging a data object or a container of data objects, the pointer changes to either the *move* pointer or the *copy* pointer (see Figure 6.A.6). It changes to the *move* pointer if you initiated an unmodified-drag, and to the *copy* pointer if you initiated a DUPLICATE-drag.

Figure 6.A.6. Normal pointer, move pointer, and copy pointer.

In addition to changing the shape of the pointer, the source application should attach to the pointer a graphic image to represent the source object. See Figure 6.A.7. The source object image should be a relatively compact representation of the source that fits around the pointer. If the source object itself is a small graphical object, the shape of the image that is dragged should be the same as the shape of the original source object. If the source object has no obvious visual representation or is too large to be previewed in its entirety during the drag operation, an image that is roughly the size of a File manager glyph should be designed to represent the source object.

Figure 6.A.7. Move and copy pointers with source images.

The source image should be transparent, and should not have much internal detail, so that users can see through the source image to the object underneath the pointer's hot spot. The *move* or *copy* pointer should be placed on the source image in a way that: (a) the hot spot of the pointer is as near as possible to the middle of the source image; and (b) the "tail" of the pointer is not obscured by the outline of the source image. When a user drags multiple source objects at once, a representation of the collection of source objects should surround the pointer.

Feedback About Prospective Destinations. Whenever possible, when you drag the pointer over a graphical object on the screen during the drag operation, the *drop allowed* or the *drop not allowed* symbol should be added to the pointer. See image being dragged, an area equal to the size of the symbol should be cleared in the center of the source image before the *drop allowed* or *drop not allowed* symbol is added. The object under the pointer may also change its appearance to indicate that it can accept the source object.

Chapter 6. Integrating Applications on the Sun Desktop

Figure 6.A.8. Drop allowed and drop not allowed pointers.

In some cases applications may not be able to predict with certainty whether a drop on the destination object will succeed or not. However, applications should try to be as accurate as possible. So long as the feedback is typically accurate, and errors seem like reasonable errors, users will forgive occasional misinformation.

With respect to the *drop allowed* and *drop not allowed* pointers, three areas of the screen are considered *neutral*: the workspace itself, window and control area backgrounds in general, and the background of the data pane (if any) from which the drag operation was initiated (all areas of the data pane except those explicit graphical objects that are either legal or illegal destinations for a drop are considered part of its background). With one exception, the pointer image always changes to the *move* or *copy* pointer while it is over these areas. The exception to the rule is: If an application supports drag and drop actions within a single window, but not between windows, then the pointer should change to the *drop not allowed* shape as soon as the pointer leaves the source window.

While Dragging a Text Selection

When you begin dragging a text selection, the pointer image changes immediately to the *text move* or *text copy* pointer, depending on whether you are holding down the DUPLICATE key. See Figure 6.A.9. These pointers include a rectangular area containing at least the first three characters of the text selection as a "preview" of the data being dragged. If the selection contains more characters than will fit within the rectangle, a dimmed Move arrow follows the characters in the rectangle.

Figure 6.A.9. Text Move and Text Copy Pointers.

The *text move* and *text copy* pointers in Figure 6.A.9 are *neutral* pointers. In other words, they are pointers that appear whenever the pointer's hot spot is not over graphical objects that are either legal or illegal destinations for the drop.

Figure 6.A.10. Text insert drop allowed pointers.

These pointer shapes appear while the pointer is over the workspace, over the backgrounds of windows or control areas, or over objects that don't subscribe to the drag and drop protocol.[1]

When the pointer's hot spot is over a text data pane or a text field, its image changes to one of the *text insert drop allowed* pointers shown in Figure 6.A.10. Specifically, the arrow changes to look like a cross-hair. To facilitate the accurate insertion of the data being dragged into the existing text, the interior of the cross-hair itself must be transparent. Ideally, the cross-hair pointer should be used only when the pointer is over a drop site whose semantics call for insertion of the data being dragged into the data at the drop site. Note that the change to the *text insert drop allowed* pointer should take place immediately when dragging a text selection in a data pane (unless it is read only), since the text can be dropped anywhere within the same pane.

When the pointer is over a drag and drop target (or any other drop site where the drop semantics indicate a replacement of the current data), the pointer should change to one of the *text replace drop allowed* images shown in Figure 6.A.11. Specifically, the arrow in the pointer should change to a bull's-eye that is the same as the *drop allowed* feedback used elsewhere. If an implementation is unable to support different pointer images over explicit drag and drop targets and implicit drop sites (data panes or individual controls), then the *text insert drop allowed* (cross-hair) pointer should be used to provide drop allowed feedback over all legal drop sites

1. These pointers are also used over graphical objects that *do* subscribe to the protocol, but for some reason cannot provide feedback about whether a drop is allowed.

Chapter 6. Integrating Applications on the Sun Desktop

(including drag and drop targets) while the text is being dragged.

Figure 6.A.11. Text replace drop allowed pointers.

When the pointer is over a graphical object that cannot accept the text selection as a drop, the pointer changes to one of the *text drop not allowed* pointer. See Figure 6.A.12. Specifically, the arrow changes to look like the *drop not allowed* symbol shown in Figure 6.A.8 on page 375.

Figure 6.A.12. Text drop not allowed pointers.

While Dragging Selected Data other than Text

When dragging a selection containing non-text data that does not itself represent an object or a container, the pointer changes to the *selection move* or *selection copy* pointer, depending on whether you are holding down the DUPLICATE key. See Figure 6.A.13. These pointers are analogous to the *text move* and *text copy* pointers shown in Figure 6.A.9 on page 375, but they do not include any "preview" of the data being dragged (that is, there is no indication of the actual contents of the selection). The source application may choose to include an optional glyph within the rectangular area of the pointer to indicate the type of data being dragged (see Figure 6.A.13) but, by default, the rectangle is empty.

As in the case of text selection, the implementation should allow for the use of both *selection insert drop allowed* and *selection replace drop allowed* pointers (See Figure 6.A.13) when it can make the appropriate distinctions between drop sites with insert semantics and those with replace semantics. If the implementation cannot support different pointer images over drag and drop targets and implicit drop sites (data panes or individual controls), then the *selection insert drop allowed* (cross-hair) pointer should be used to provide drop allowed feedback over all legal drop sites (including drag and drop targets).

When dragging selections in data planes containing *sequential* data types (that is, types such as audio that are characterized by a one-dimensional array in which new data displaces existing data at a specific insert point), the pointer image should change immediately to the *selection insert drop allowed* pointer, since an insert point must be specified even in the source data pane.

When dragging selections within data planes containing *non-sequential* data types (that is, types such as structured graphics, in which data can be moved to arbitrary spatial locations and can overlap any data that is already displayed in those locations), the pointer image should change immediately to the *move* or *copy* pointer. However, the pointer image should not display the *drop allowed* or *drop not allowed* symbol while over the original data pane, since any point in the source data pane while over the original data pane, since any point in the source data pane constitutes a legal drop site. In addition to changing the pointer's shape, the source application should attach a graphical image—as similar as possible to the size and shape of the actual selected data—that provides a WYSIWYG preview of the effect of a drop. If the pointer and image being dragged are moved out of the source data pane, the appropriate *selection drop allowed* pointer should be displayed whenever the hot spot is over any legal drop spot, including other compatible data panes or the original source data pane.

When the pointer is over a graphical object that cannot accept the data being dragged, the pointer image changes to one of the *selection drop not allowed* pointers. See Figure A.13. As in the case of text drags, the arrow changes to look like the *drop not allowed* symbol shown in Figure 6.A.8.

Figure 6.A.13. Drop feedback pointers for non-text selections.

During the Drop

The destination assumes a *busy* appearance while processing a drop. Once the operation is complete, the destination resumes its normal appearance. If the application can process the drop in the time it would take to post and clear the busy appearance change, then the application may choose not to post the busy appearance.

6.A.10
Input Focus Management

When you drag an object between windows, the input focus moves to the destination window. Within the destination window, the input focus moves to the element the object was dropped on, assuming it is an element that ordinarily receives the input focus. For example, if you drop a text selection into a text pane, the text pane receives the input focus. If the destination element cannot receive the input focus (as, for example, drag and drop targets can't), the input focus goes to the element in the window that ordinarily receives it when the window receives the input focus.

When you drag an object from one location to another within the same window, the input focus moves to the destination element, assuming it is capable of receiving the input focus. If the destination element cannot receive the input focus, the input focus remains at the source location.

6.A.11
Error Handling

The best user interfaces are designed for error, and drag and drop is no exception. Errors inevitably occur as a result of user mistakes and as a result of system errors. Drag operations may fail for any of the following reasons:

- The user dropped the source object over a destination that does not subscribe to the drag and drop protocol.
- The source object is of a type the destination cannot accept.

Although the visual feedback on the pointer is designed to minimize this sort of problem, the feedback is not infallible. And, of course, we can't count on users' actions conforming to the recommendations of the feedback, in any case.

- For some reason the drop operation was aborted.

A drop might be aborted either because of a failure of the transport mechanism used by drag and drop; or because of complications the destination application encounters while processing the drop (such as running out of space in the file system); or for other reasons.

When a drag operation fails, either, but not both, the source application or the destination application presents a Notice window telling the user what has happened. During the drag before the source application has established communication with the destination, the source is responsible for all Notice windows. After communication with the destination has been established, the destination assumes responsibility for Notice windows. The application that does not present the Notice window may choose to display an error message in its base window footer.

In cases of intra-application drags, the application may present a message in a window footer rather than in a Notice window. In either case, the message should explain why the drop failed, and provide constructive guidance to the user about how to avoid failure in the future (if possible).

6.A.12
Undoing the Effects of Drag and Drop

You can undo the effects of a drag operation by using an Undo menu item or command button, or the Undo function key, in both the source and destination applications (assuming the operation is undo-able).[1] An Undo action in the source application undoes the effect of the drag operation on the source; whereas an Undo action in the destination application undoes the effect there.

6.A.13
Canceling a Drag Operation in Progress

If you decide to cancel a drag operation while you still have the mouse button held down, you can press the STOP key and then release the mouse button.

6.A.14
Deviations from the OPEN LOOK Style Guide[1]

For the most part, the guidelines in this document extend the guidelines in the *OPEN LOOK Style Guide*. However, a few of the guidelines described in this document differ from those of the style guide. Applications designed to run on Sun workstations should follow the guidelines described here rather those in the style guide.[2]

A summary of the discrepancies follows:

- Differences between unmodified-drag and DUPLI-CATE-drag

According to the style guide, whenever a user initiates a drag operation without holding down the DUPLICATE key (i.e., CNTRL), the drag operation should be interpreted as a request to relocate the source object. In other words, unmodified-drags should always be interpreted as requests to move the source object from its original location to the destination. In cases where such actions would result in unexpected loss of data, the destination application may refuse to receive data

1. The Undo function key operates on the window with the keyboard input focus.
2. Sun Microsystems, Inc. (1990) OPENLOOK Graphical User Interface Application Style Guidelines. Reading MA: Addison-Wesley Publishing Company, Inc.

transferred by unmodified-drag operations. The destination application should present a Notice window to allow users either to cancel the drag operation or to change it to a duplicate operation.

The guidelines described in this document allow applications to interpret unmodified-drag operations as identical to DUPLICATE-drag operations to prevent unanticipated loss of data.

Refer the style guide and to the section called "To cut or to Copy" in Section 6.A.1 of this document.

- Dropping one mini-window onto another

The style guide recommends that applications allow users to drop mini-windows onto one another, which should transfer or copy data from the source application to the destination application.

This document states that when one mini-window is dropped onto another it is as if they are resting on top of one another on the workspace. That is, when you drop one mini-window onto another, the destination application is not overlaid mini-window, it is the application that owns the workspace (i.e., the window manager).

Refer to the style guide and to Section 6.A.3 of this document.

- Dropping objects onto window backgrounds

The style guide says that a user may drop a source object onto the background of a base window, resulting in loading the source into the window (replacing the previous content).

This document specifies that applications should use drag and drop targets in their control areas for this purpose. If an application doesn't have a control area, and, consequently, doesn't have a place to put drag and drop target, it may allow drops onto its window header.[1]

Refer to the style guide and to the section called "Drag and Drop Targets" in Section 6.A.4 of this document.

---

1. Applications that convert from the old policy to the new one should provide constructive guidance in error messages to help users with the transition. Specifically, if a user drops onto the window background, the application should present an explanatory error message that describes that the drag and drop target (or window header) should be used in place of the window background.

6.A.15
Drag and Drop Target Engineering Specification

Two standard sizes are defined for the drag and drop target. The smaller size (see Figure 6.A.14) is used in the control area above an OPEN LOOK base window when that control area contains only one row of buttons. The larger standard size (see Figure 6.A.15) is designed to display a standard File Manager document glyph within its borders. Its dimensions are the same for all scaling factors because the same set of File Manager glyphs is used in all cases.

Applications can specify the position of the drag and drop target as well as its width and height. The standard "3D" border must always be used, since this is the only aspect of the target itself that directly identifies the drag and drop target as an explicit drop site.

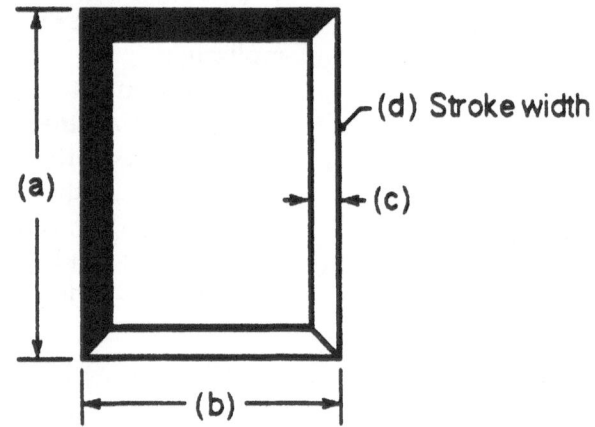

Figure 6.A.14. Small drag and drop target.

Table 6.1.2. Dimensions for small drag and drop target (in points).

	10 pt	12 pt	14 pt	19pt
(a)	19.0	21.0	23.0	30.0
(b)	14.0	15.5	17.0	22.0
(c)	2.6	3.0	3.4	4.4
(d)	0.8	1.0	1.2	1.6

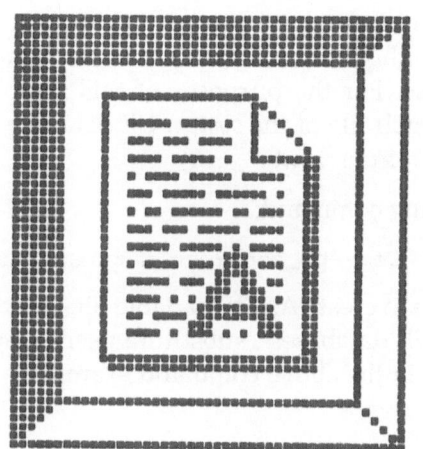

Figure 6.A.15. Large drag and drop target.

Table 6.1.3. Dimensions for large drag and drop target (in pixels)

	All
(a)	50
(b)	45
(c)	6
(d)	1

6.B
Examining a
Classing
Engine
Database

You may use the `ce_db_build` utility program to create an ASCII Classing Engine database file that you may either print out or examine using any ASCII editor. Perform the following steps to create the readable CE database file:

1. Determine which CE database you wish to transcribe. You may select either the *user*, the *system*, or the *network* CE database. For the purposes of this sample, let's create an ASCII file of the *system* CE database in a file called `ce.system.txt`.

2. Issue the following command:

    ```
    ce_db_build system -to_ascii ce.database.txt
    ```

3. If you would like to create ASCII readable files for the *user* or *network* FE databases , substitute user or network for system in the above command example.

6.C
Vendor Data Type Registration

If you want your application to be able to exchange data with other applications on the OpenWindows Desktop, you will need to make your application's file format, process types, object types, and file attributes public. SunSoft facilitates the desemination of this information through its Vendor Data Type Registration program.

Registration is required for the three technologies discussed in this guide: drag and drop, Classing Engine, and ToolTalk. As data type information is gathered, it will be publicly available through the SUCCESS database, SunSoft's on-line electronic support service for software developers.

Call the number below to receive your Vendor Registration Packet. The packet will contain detailed information on the program, as well as the forms you need to register you data types.

SunSoft Catalyst Information Center phone number: 1-800-227-9227

The remainder of this appendix discusses the technical issues of why data types must be registered.

6.C.1
Drag and Drop Data Types

If a receiving application is to receive a drop from a source application, the source application must send the data in a format readable by the receiving application. For example, if Text Editor wishes to drop data into Mail Tool, Text Editor must be able to convert the data to a format which Mail Tool can read. Conversely, if Mail Tool wishes to drop data into Text Editor, Mail Tool must be able to convert the data to a format Text Editor can read. Although the source application is responsible for converting data to a format readable by the receiving application, it behooves the receiving application to be able to receive data in some of the more common data formats such as ASCII, Sun raster imaging format, or PostScript page description language.

Programmatically, drag and drop handshaking works as follows: (1) data is selected from the source application; (2) data is dropped on the receiving application; (3) the receiving application requests a list of the data formats in which the source application can send the drop; (4) the source application replies with a list of data formats; (5) the receiving application tells the source application which format it would like the data sent; (6) data is transferred.

The SunSoft data type registration program helps standardize the data format names by which applications request data formats from each other. All companies that wish to share their data with other applications are encouraged to register data format names for their application's data files. This name will be used by other applications to reference desired data formats.

A central repository for data format names, as well as additional format information, will be available on SUCCESS, the SunSoft on-line electronic support service for software developers.

6.C.2
Classing Engine File Types and Attributes
File Type Identifiers

As described in Section 15, "Classing Engine," File Manager and other applications identify a file's type with a unique identifier. Once the file is typed, the file's attributes can be determined.

The file type identifier is used to derive a file's type. File type identifiers can be associated with a filename pattern (such as *.ps or *.wk), a unique string value within the file, or both. If the type-by-pattern method is used, you will need to register a file pattern. If the type-by-content method is used, you will need to register a content pattern, byte offset, and content data type (short, long, string). Two file type registration examples are shown below.

1. Content Value = SSQLReport; Offset =0; Type = string

This file type can be identified by the string "SSQLReport" starting at byte zero.

2. Content Value = 0x4d4d002a; Offset = 10; Type = long

This file can be identified by the longword value 0x4d4d002a starting at offset 10 (decimal) in the file.

It is important that your file identifier be unique. The best identifier is a string that identifies your company, the application, and the file type.

File Type Attributes

File type attributes are used to specify the correct method to open or read the file, print the file, and the display icon. The current Classing Engine database attributes are shown below. Refer to Section 15, "Classing Engine," for more information on these attributes.

Table C.1. Classing engine database attributes.

Attribute	Description
TYPE_NAME	File type name.
TYPE_OPEN	String used to open the file.
TYPE_PRINT	String used to print the file.
TYPE_ICON	icon file $OPENWINHOME/include/images/compress.icon
TYPE_ICON_MASK	icon file, <$OPENWINHOME/include/images/doc.mask.icon
TYPE_FGCOLOR	Icon foreground color.
TYPE_BGCOLOR	Icon background color.
TYPE_OPEN_TT	ToolTalk identifier used when starting applications.
TYPE_FILE_TEMPLATE	Unique filename generated and used by the application as a filename.

File Type and Attribute Reference

If you want to peruse a file of previously registered file types, you may view the Classing Engine database by using the program map1.c in the Classing Engine chapter, or use the ce_db_build utility to create an ASCII description file.

6.C.3 ToolTalk Type Information

ToolTalk messages can be addressed to specific application, a type of application, a specific object, or a type of object. To send messages addressed to types of applications or objects, you must know the application's process type or object type. It is the name of an application's process types and object types that need to be registered. For more information on process and object types, see the *ToolTalk Programmer's Guide*.

To provide process type and/or object type information to the ToolTalk service you must supply static type information at installation time by compiling your type file (which puts your type information into the Classing Engine database) and register your process type with the Tooltalk service. When you register your `ptype` with the ToolTalk service, it will read the type information from the Classing engine database. If you use `otypes`, you need to also create a `ptype` for your application.

Process Type

To send messages to a particular type of application, an application needs to know the process type (`ptype`) of the receiving application(s). The `ptype` is identified by the process type identifier (`ptid`). A `ptid` must be unique for every installation. This identifier cannot be changed at installation time, so it is important that a unique name be chosen. Ideally you will use a name that includes the trademarked name of your product or company, such as `Sun_EditDemo`. Also, use upper-case letters to help make your `ptid` unique. The `ptid` cannot exceed 32 characters, and should not be one of the reserved identifiers (`start`, `queue`, `file`, `session`, `observe`, `handle`, `ptype`, `otype`, `per_file`, `per_session`, and `opnum`).

Object Type

To send messages to a particular type of object, an application needs to know the object type (`otype`). The otype is identified by the object type identifier (`otid`). An `otid` must be unique for every installation. This identifier cannot be changed at installation time, so it is important that a unique name be chosen. It is recommended that the name begin with the `ptid` of the tool that implements the `otype`; e.g., `Sun_EditDemo_object`. The `otid` is limited to 64 characters, and should not be one of the reserved identifiers (`start`, `queue`, `file`, `session`, `observe`, `handle`, `ptype`, `otype`, `per_file`, `per_session`, and `opnum`).

Ptype and Otype Reference

If you want to peruse a file of previously registered ptypes and otypes, you may view the Classing engine database by using `ce_db_build` utility to create an ASCII file.

6.D
DeskSet
Defined
ToolTalk
Messages

6.D.1
Sender to Handler Messages

This appendix lists the initial set of ToolTalk messages that many DeskSet applications support. Each individual application is responsible for handling these messages. Note that some applications may determine that more specialized messages are required for their interaction and add these to the list of messages that they can handle. For further information, refer to the *ToolTalk Programmer's Guide*.

The majority of the messages are ones that are sent form a sending process to a handling process. A launch message must be sent first to start the handling application. After this, messages may be sent in any order. Typically, one application would *launch* another, send the appropriate data using the dispatch_data message, send the move message to position the handler's base frame at a desired location and finally send an expose message to force the handler to appear.

The messages are:

```
launch(
      string display
      string locale)
```

Start the handling application. The first argument is the display on which the application should be started. This should be the same display on which the sending application is running. The second argument indicates which language should be used to display text.

```
status(string status_string)
```

Sends any status information that the sending process feels the handling process should know about. The handling process will determine what to do with this status. An example of the status a sending process might send would be the name of the sending application, which the handling process could then display in its footer to let the user know which application controls it at the moment.

```
dispatch_data(string sel_name)
```

Sender wants to send data to the handler. The `sel_name` is the selection name used for the data transfer. The handler may then access this selection and retrieve the data.

```
move(int xpos,
     int ypos,
     int width,
     int height,
     int placement)
```

The sending process would like the handling process to move its (the handling processes) base frame to a new position. Arguments are the sender's frame location (x and y coordinates), sender's frame size (height and width) and a hint as to where the handler should position itself (one of the following values `DS_POPUP_LEFT`, `DS_POPUP_RIGHT`, `DS_POPUP_ABOVE`, `DS_POPUP_BELOW`, `DS_POPUP_LOR`, `DS_POPUP_AOB`).

```
quit()
```

The sending process would like the handling process to exit.

```
hide()
```

The sending process would like the handling process' window to disappear, but not exit.

```
expose()
```

The sending process would like the handling process' window to appear.

```
retrieve_data(in string sel_name)
```

The sending process would like the handling process to send back any data that it has manipulated. The argument is the selection name used for the data transfer.

6.D.2
Handler to Sender Messages

Currently, there is only one message that a handling process initiates. In this case , the sending processes must be able to handle this message when it is received.

```
departing()
```

The handling process tells the sending process that it is going to exit.

6.E
ToolTalk
Example
Program

6.E.1
treceive.c

This appendix presents two code examples (tteceive.c and ttsend.c) and a header file (ttdig.h) which illustrate the use of ToolTalk service.

```c
/*
 * ttreceive - show receiving tooltalk message based on pattern.
 *
 * This simple example program is the counterpart to ttsend. It registers
 * a pattern which describes the message it is interested in, and then
 * waits for them.
 */

#include <xview/xview.h>
#include <xview/panel.h>
#include <xview/tt_c.h>

#include "ttdig.h"

Frame base_frame;
Panel_item controls;
Panel_item gauge;

char *my_procid;

void receive_tt_message();
void create_ui_components();
void
main(argc, argv)
int argc;
char **argv;
{
    int ttfd;
    Tt_pattern pat;

    /* Initialize XView. */
    xv_init(XV_INIT_ARGC_PTR_ARGV, &argc, argv, 0);
```

```
/* Tell XView to call my receive procedure when there are messages. */
notify_set_input_func(base_frame,
                      (Notify_func)receive_tt_message, ttfd);
/*
 * Create and register the pattern we are interested in.  We are
 * registering as an observer; all observers will receive a message
 * destined for them (try a few ttreceives).  If we had registered
 * as a TT_HANDLE, we would be the one to handle the message.
 */
pat = tt_pattern_create();
tt_pattern_category_set(pat, TT_OBSERVE);
tt_pattern_scope_add(pat, TT_SESSION);
tt_pattern_op_add(pat, RECEIVE_PATTERN);
tt_pattern_register(pat);

/* Join the default session to get messages. */
tt_session_join(tt_default_session());
xv_main_loop(base_frame);

/* Clean up ToolTalk on exit. */
tt_close();
exit(0);
}

/*
 * receive_tt_message is the procedure that gets called by the XView
 * notifier when my tooltalk file descriptor becomes active with a message.
 */
void
receive_tt_message()
{
  Tt_message msg_in;
  int mark;
  int val_in;

  /*
   * Pull in my message handle.  If it is null, we became active even
   * though there wasn't a real message for us.
   */
  msg_in = tt_message_receive();
  if (msg_in == NULL) return;
```

Chapter 6. Integrating Applications on the Sun Desktop

```
    /*
     * Get a storage mark so we can free storage that tt obtains for
     * our message contents.
     */
    mark = tt_mark();

    /* If the message pattern matches our interest, fetch the value.  */
    if (0==strcmp(RECEIVE_PATTERN, tt_message_op(msg_in)))  {
      tt_message_arg_ival(msg_in, 0, &val_in);
      xv_set(gauge, PANEL_VALUE, val_in, NULL);
    }

    tt_message_destroy(msg_in);
    tt_release(mark);
    return;
}


/*
 * create_ui_componentsis the procedure called to set up the panel.
 */
void
create_ui_components()
{
  base_frame = xv_create(NULL, FRAME,
                    XV_LABEL, "TT Receiver Example",
                    FRAME_SHOW_RESIZE_CORNER, FALSE,
                    NULL);
  controls = xv_create(base_frame, PANEL,
                    WIN_BORDER, FALSE,
                    NULL);
  gauge = xv_create(controls, PANEL_GAUGE,
                    PANEL_LABEL_STRING, "Received:",
                    PANEL_MIN_VALUE, RECEIVE_MIN,
                    PANEL_MAX_VALUE, RECEIVE_MAX,
                      PANEL_SHOW_RANGE, FALSE,
                      NULL);
  window_fit(controls);
  window_fit(base_frame);
}
```

6.E.2
tsend.c

```c
/*
 * ttsend - Demonstrate sending a message with a particular pattern.
 *
 * This simple program is the counterpart to ttreceive.  It sends
 * a message with a particular pattern that all receivers that are
 * listening will receive.
 *
 */

#include <xview/xview.h>
#include <xview/panel.h>
#include <xview/tt_c.h>

#include "ttdig.h"

Frame base_frame
Panel_item controls;
Panel_item slider;

char *my_procid;

void  broadcast_value();
void  create_ui_components();

void
main(argc, argv)
int argc;
char **argv;
{

  /* Initialize XView and Tooltalk; enter XView main loop.  */
  xv_init(XV_INIT_ARGC_PTR_ARGV, &argc, argv, 0);
  create_ui_components();
  my_procid = tt_open();
  xv_main_loop(base_frame);
  /* Clean up ToolTalk on exit.  */
  tt_close();
  exit(0);
}
```

```
/*
 * broadcast_value is the procedure that gets called when you
 * release the slider.  It gets the current slider
 * Value and broadcasts it with ToolTalk.
 */
void
broadcast_value(item, value, event)
Panel_item item;
int value;
Event *event;
{
  Tt_message msg_out;
  /* Create and send ToolTalk msg.  */
  msg_out = tt_pnotice_create(TT_SESSION, RECEIVE_PATTERN);
  tt_message_arg_add(msg_out, TT_IN, "integer", NULL);
  tt_message_arg_ival_set(msg_out, 0, value);
  tt_message_send(msg_out);

  /* Destroy the handle since we don't expect a reply.  */
  tt_message_destroy(msg_out);
}


/*
 * create_ui_components is the procedure called to set up the panel.
 */
void
create_ui_components()
{
  base_frame = xv_create NULL, FRAME,
                     XV_LABEL, "TT Send Example",
                     FRAME_SHOW_RESIZE_CORNER, FALSE
                     NULL);
  controls = xv_create(base_frame, PANEL,
                     WIN_BORDER, FALSE,
                     NULL);
  slider = xv_create(controls, PANEL_SLIDER,
                     PANEL_LABEL_STRING, "Send:",
                     PANEL_SLIDER_END_BOXES, FALSE,
PANEL_SHOW_RANGE, FALSE,
                     PANEL_SHOW_VALUE, FALSE,
                     PANEL_MIN_VALUE, RECEIVE_MIN,
                     PANEL_MAX_VALUE, RECEIVE_MAX,
                     PANEL_TICKS, 0,
                     PANEL_NOTIFY_PROC, broadcast_value,
                     NULL);
                        window_fit(controls);
  window_fit(base_frame);
}
```

6.E.3
tdig.h

```
/*
 * RECEIVE_PATTERN is the message identifier for our tooltalk messages.
 * It is prefixed with Sun_ as a simple mechanism to avoid namespace
 * conflicts with other apps in the default session.
 */
#define RECEIVE_PATTERN "Sun_ttexample_pattern"

/*
 * RECEIVE_MIN  and _MAX is our slider/gauge range.
 */
#define RECEIVE_MIN 0
#define RECEIVE_MAX 100
```